JOHN HOLLANDER received his B.A. and M.A. from Columbia University and his Ph.D. from Indiana University. He taught at Connecticut College from 1957 to 1959 and at Yale from 1959 to 1966, and since 1966 has been Professor of English at Hunter College. Mr. Hollander is also known as a poet and has published numerous books of poetry.

As from the Pow'r of Sacred Lays
   The Spheres began to move,
And sung the great Creator's Praise
   To all the bless'd above;
So, when the last and dreadful Hour
This crumbling Pageant shall devour,
The TRUMPET shall be heard on high,
The dead shall live, the living die,
And MUSICK shall untune the Sky.

     —JOHN DRYDEN, *A Song for
     St. Cecilia's Day* (1687)

THE

ᘳNTUNING OF

THE SKY

IDEAS OF MUSIC

IN ENGLISH POETRY

1500-1700

BY JOHN HOLLANDER

The Norton Library NEW YORK
W · W · NORTON & COMPANY · INC ·

For My Parents

PUBLISHED SIMULTANEOUSLY IN CANADA
BY GEORGE J. MCLEOD LIMITED, TORONTO

W. W. Norton & Company, Inc. also publishes *The Norton
Anthology of English Literature,* edited by M. H. Abrams et al;
The Norton Anthology of Poetry, edited by Arthur M. Eastman
et al; *World Masterpieces,* edited by Maynard Mack et al; *The
Norton Reader,* edited by Arthur M. Eastman et al; *The Norton
Facsimile of the First Folio of Shakespeare,* prepared by Charlton
Hinman; and the *Norton Critical Editions.*

First published in the Norton Library 1970
by arrangement with Princeton University Press

SBN 393 00551 8

PRINTED IN THE UNITED STATES OF AMERICA

2 3 4 5 6 7 8 9 0

PREFACE TO THE 1970 EDITION

THE appearance of this study in the Norton Library will make more easily available a book published nearly a decade ago. But because of the limitations of the offset reproduction process, it is in no way a new edition. I should have liked to be able to make some substantial revisions had it been so, both in response to points raised in generous reviews by Paul Henry Lang, George Steiner, and John Stevens, and because further study has convinced me that in a few instances my scope was unduly narrow.

Had I been able to rewrite parts of this book, I should have expanded the introduction slightly, making less hesitant the structuralist approach at the beginning, and using more sophisticated linguistic models than the example from phonemics available to me at the time. Then, too, I would have wanted to make use of some of the scholarship mentioned in the original preface as having appeared too late for consideration, as well as even more recent work. The past ten years have seen the publication, in book form, of Leo Spitzer's work on world harmony and Thomas Wythorne's journals; studies by Gretchen L. Finney and on musical thought in classical antiquity by Edward A. Lippman; Stephen Orgel's fine book on the Jonsonian masque; the assemblage of pictorial and textual documentation of musical images by Kathi Meyer-Baer, and the sophisticated discussions of the iconology of musical instruments by Emanuel Winternitz. It has been during this same decade that medieval, Renaissance, and Baroque music has become increasingly familiar to general audiences, through high standards of public performance and a large recorded repertory; it might now be possible, in several places in the present volume, to assume a broader knowledge of the music of the period on the part of the reader, and to be able to go into some technical matters more deeply, than I could originally do.

Most pressing, however, seem the demands of a number of texts which now appear to me to have been neglected in the original study, through ignorance, injudicious cutting, or misplaced attention. Bacon's remarks on music and sound, for example, get no notice, and in general, the use of musical sound as an epitome of the sense of hearing is ignored. I would like, following a suggestion of Frank Kermode, to have gone more deeply into Cowley. I should have liked to discuss the treatment of *auditus* in Chapman's *Ovid's Banquet of Sence*, and its counterpart in Marino's *l'Adone*. The whole theme of the natural music of the *locus omoenus* in pastoral tradition and its later consequences are largely ignored here, and perhaps rightly so; but their absence weakens my discussion of the music in Spenser's Bower of Bliss, which I now see as central to the whole later development of musical imagery (I have since written more on this). I should also have wanted to discuss at length certain passages in *Paradise Lost*, Books IV and XI, and to deal, in *l'Allegro* and *Il Penseroso*, with the relation between sound and light in both poems. I hope to deal with all of this in a book in progress on the poetic treatment of sound.

I want to thank Douglas Bush and Thurston Dart for catching me out in some small errors that I was able to correct in the second hardcover printing from which this edition has been reproduced, and Candace Watt for bringing it about.

New York, August 1970

PREFACE

THE following study concerns certain beliefs about music rather than music itself; moreover, it is less about those beliefs alone than about the English poetry of the sixteenth and seventeenth centuries which expressed and employed them. With the death of the Ancient World and the emergence in the West of utterly distinct notions of music and poetry, the former of these became a possible subject for treatment by the latter. In the course of the scrutiny which that treatment came to entail, poetry, alternately staring and gazing at her musical sister, came to see in that visage more and more of herself; and if, in time, she began to judge what she saw more severely, it was only as a result of her growing suspicion of certain of her own features and charms.

It is not surprising, then, to discover that the subject of an investigation of musical subjects and images in the richest period of English poetic development and change must come down to literary history itself, after all. In the very relationship between subject and image may be seen some of the bases of poetic growth and variation during the epoch known casually as the English Renaissance. It is particularly in this connection that beliefs of any sort—religious, political, metaphysical, or what we would call today esthetic—enter into the continuous dialectic of style, or manner, and purpose that has produced the materials of the class of utterances called literature. As elements of belief become widely received, they tend to crystallize into images. Through repeated use, the nonliteralness of such figures or images tends to wear off, and they remain as clichés of thought, habitual responses to intellectual stimuli. Similarly, what can serve in one phase of the history of a literature as a subject for exposition can become a stock image or allusion in a succeeding one.

In the treatment of music by Renaissance English poets there is a constant interplay of ideology and fact, of beliefs accumulated through intellectual habit and those thrust upon the consciousness by experience of a more direct kind. The very notion of music is so broad and deep in the sixteenth and seventeenth centuries, fed by startling developments in the history of the art itself and at the same time inundated by floods of authoritative doctrine on the subject of music, that it is fair to say that in these musical beliefs most others lay implicit. The roles of cosmology, metaphysics, "natural philosophy," psychology, ethics, and politics, to name a few bodies of speculation, are of the greatest importance in the interpretation of music's nature and effects during the Middle Ages and Renaissance. During the period covered by this study, fundamental changes in the parts played by these areas of knowledge in that interpretation may be observed. They parallel changes in both musical and poetic practice that occur in significant conjunction and mutual dependency with them. By and large, these changes might be described as substituting for previous ideologies of musical effect others which sought more to accommodate actuality—a kind of de-mythologizing of musical esthetics. It is the course of this de-mythologizing, and the simultaneous course of literary history, that are plotted in the following pages. I hope that, if following these charts will take the reader over familiar territory, he may thereby be allowed to observe some well-known contours from a new perspective, and perhaps to catch an occasional fresh prospect.

I regret that I was unable to make more extensive use of two excellent studies which appeared too late for me to do more than skim. Nan Cooke Carpenter's *Music in the Medieval and Renaissance Universities* (Norman, Oklahoma, 1958) and Frank Ll. Harrison's *Music in Medieval Britain* (London, 1958) should otherwise have merited more frequent citation in these pages. I was most sorry in not having been able to consult John Stevens' *Music and Poetry in the Early Tudor Court*, the long-awaited publication of which has just been announced at the time of writing this preface.

I am indebted to many people for much assistance. To

Professor Roy W. Battenhouse I am obligated for his patience and attention throughout the course of the writing of this project, in an earlier form an Indiana University doctoral dissertation. Professors Rudolph B. Gottfried and Willi Apel saved me from many blunders through their careful reading of my manuscript. The musicological knowledge, both speculative and practical, of Professor John Ward and of Mr. Thurston Dart, of Jesus College, Cambridge, constantly steered my historical vagrancies back onto course in frequent and generously extended discussion. To Professors James W. Halporn, Frederick W. Sternfeld, Willis Doney, Erwin Panofsky, Rudolf Wittkower, Millard Meiss, Marshall Cohen, Moses Hadas, and William Nelson I am grateful for many sorts of advice. Miss Patricia Egan allowed me to consult her collection of photographs of paintings with musical subjects. My father-in-law, Arthur Loesser, discussed many of my ideas with me at some length. Professor Northrop Frye gave me the benefit of his knowledge and insight in making some valuable suggestions. My friends James Zito, Stephen Orgel, and Donald Friedman, read and encouraged my work at various points. The staffs of Houghton Library at Harvard, of the Palmer Library at Connecticut College, and of the Yale University Library all gave me considerable help. A three-year term as Junior Fellow in the Society of Fellows at Harvard made it possible for unhurried research to come to eventual fruition in this book. My wife's enthusiasm and forbearance in assisting me at every stage of the writing of it have been beyond all value.

Parts of this study originally appeared, in considerably different form, in *Sound and Poetry*, ed. Northrop Frye (The English Institute Essays, 1956) and in the *Journal of Aesthetics and Art Criticism*, and I acknowledge permission to incorporate them herein. I am also grateful to Alfred A. Knopf, Inc. for permission to quote from Wallace Stevens' *Collected Poems* and from Joseph Kerman's *Opera as Drama*.

ILLUSTRATIONS

Following page 242

CONTENTS

[1]

CHAPTER I · INTRODUCTORY

Ut Musica Poesis

THE similarities between music and poetry remain interesting to us despite the fact that the two have become utterly different as human enterprises. Notwithstanding the closeness of the social roles played by the poet and the composer in contemporary life (and even their identification with the painter, in later Romantic conceptions of the artist as hero), practitioners of the two arts are less able to understand each other's work, and even less acceptable to each other as audiences, than ever before. *Expertise* in one practice seems today to rule out knowledge of even the fundamentals of the other. Art song and opera continue to exist, and in the sung text the two are still brought together. But the present age is an eclectic one, and the pursuit of novelty as an end in itself always renders uneasy the entrenchment of styles.

In other periods, consistently operating conventions in either art could absorb divergent traditions in the other: the German Romantic lyric could supply texts for *lieder* by many widely differing composers throughout the nineteenth century. Conversely, the style of the later seventeenth-century English solo song could set with equal alacrity the words of Shakespeare and Nahum Tate. When no received conventions can govern either music or poetry for more than a decade or in more than one cultural milieu, however, richness and a kind of chaos rule together. The question of what particular composer could most effectively set to music the works of a particular poet can become, as it has not been before, a significant one. And yet the commitment of the two arts to each other continues to be reasserted, and attempts to understand each in terms of the other continue to be made. Most of us would tend to admit today the triviality of Sidney Lanier's well-known linking of music and poetry (in what he seems to feel was a taxonomic discovery) as "the two species of the genus art of sound."[1] But loath to offer as succinct a statement of our own in its stead, we would be even less inclined to confess that our inability to do so was a function of some categorical difference between the two arts.

Today we are closer to one kind of understanding of the common ground of music and poetry than has been hitherto possible. Purely formalistic analysis, cleansed on the one hand of the incipient platonism and, on the other, of the polemical intentions that have traditionally encumbered stylistic studies, has been gradually increasing its scope. The abstract theory of communication may be able to provide a basis even more general than Lanier's (but potentially far more fruitful) for treating in one frame all languages and other systems of non-linguistic signals, both visual and aural. As our knowledge of the nature and uses of language and of the structure of musical configurations increases, the materials that ultimately comprise both music and poetic language may become more and more susceptible of identification in terms of the mathematical concept of information. The common treatment of the two arts as intricate structures of coded systems may soon be possible, despite the extremely questionable merits of certain recent attempts to deal in such a manner with music alone.[2]

Any epistemological similarities between poetry and music, after all, would appear to be accessible to a more general study of sound and meaning. Both arts have a stylistic history, and musical conventions, like literary ones, are proliferated under particular cultural conditions. Furthermore, just as poetic tra-

[1] Sidney Lanier, *The Science of English Verse*, ed. Paull F. Baum (Baltimore, 1945), p. 39.

[2] See, for example, Richard C. Pinkerton, "Information Theory and Melody," *Scientific American*, 194 (February 1956), pp. 77-86, for a recent popular exposition. An excellent corrective to the weaknesses of this kind of approach may be found in George P. Springer, "Language and Music: Some Parallels and Divergencies," in *For Roman Jakobson: Essays on the Occasion of his Sixtieth Birthday*, ed. Morris Halle *et al.* (The Hague, 1956), pp. 504-513. Also see Leonard B. Meyer, "Meaning in Music and Information Theory," *Journal of Aesthetics and Art Criticism*, xv (1957), pp. 412-424.

ditions have always been in some ways contingent upon the nature of the particular languages in which the poetry is written, so musical styles may be said to depend upon what might be called "tonal languages." Particular societies and cultural epochs cultivate basic repertories of distinctive sound patterns, distinctive with respect not only to the selected pitch intervals but to rhythmical considerations and to more sweeping categories of monody or polyphony, instrumental usage, and habits of performance as well. Now we have gradually come to understand that spoken languages are based on just such repertories of distinctions between sounds. In learning his native tongue in childhood, a person starts out by actually performing certain very arbitrary legislations over the nature of sound. An American may listen to a speaker of Arabic and come to the conclusion that he is clearing his throat, while the speaker of Arabic may have been uttering a speech-sound as significant for him as any normal consonant is for English-speakers. Even more important would be the fact that what the American would have heard as one throat-clearing sound would be for the speaker of Arabic the result of making a distinction between two speech-sounds, a distinction as crucial in Arabic as the one between the initial sounds of "kill" and "hill" in English. No matter how well the American might be able, in later life, *to learn to reproduce* these phonemes of Arabic, the distinction between them will be one that he can seldom grasp with the same unconscious sureness with which he holds fast to the phonemic distinctions of his native tongue.

It is in a similar way that the postulations of the tonal language of our society are made for us at a relatively early period in our experience. It will always require conscious work for a contemporary Western listener, even a musically sophisticated one, to react naturally to music written in a rational system based on microtones, or intervals less than the diatonic semitone to which he is accustomed. And while he may eventually *learn to treat such music* as having musical propriety, he will never react to it with quite the same immediacy as a native listener, for whom the musical system was coextensive with the whole domain of properly musical sounds. It is because of the firmness with which we all make these arbitrary discriminations with respect to the distribution of sound that many varieties of both primitive Western and Oriental music, all based on a pentatonic system, would sound identical to modern cultivated listeners. Actually, a listener native to one of these foreign musical languages might argue for the existence of vast differences between his own and the others, between melodies that we ourselves (by the very act of calling them all "pentatonic") would casually lump together as those playable on the black keys of a piano. The point is that we would require the prior experience of a piano (or at least of the tonal system that determines its construction) in order to make such classifications. We are acting in the same manner as that proverbial linguistic absolutist, the English tourist, who pronounces every foreign language in such a way as to make its native speakers struggle to communicate to him that they do not understand English. In describing musical systems in terms of concepts upon which our own music rests, as well as in writing what modern linguists like to call "pre-phonemic" grammars of non-Indo-European languages, we take the tremendous epistemological risk of treating our own purely habitual methods of segmenting the continuum of audible sound as if they produced universal, necessary, a priori distinctions.

Both tonal and spoken languages, then, seem to possess a common basis in what I shall call "phonic norms," in the sets of parochial discriminations about the structure and significance of sound to which any speaker of a language and any member of a community with any musical habits at all is committed almost from birth. Poetry and musical compositions (in the more familiar sense of the term) are both specially planned, carefully constructed, and, in some sense, ceremonially motivated utterances in their respective types of language. In many important ways they are both dependent upon tonal and spoken linguistic resources, and thus, ultimately, upon collectivized habits of dealing with sound. It is only at this level, I feel, that Lanier's characterization of poetry and music becomes acceptable.

But with the exception of oral, pre-literary poetry, added complications to the consideration of poetry as sound arise in the existence and use of written languages. If a poem is to be treated as a highly complex utterance in a spoken language, its written form becomes a simple coding of it, word by word, onto a page. The poem will thus be defined in terms of patterns of sound classes. But starting as early as the first Latin use of Greek meters, literary analysis has been confronted with poems whose written versions, or codings, contain significant individual and conventional elements which do not appear in the original, or aural, versions, and vice versa. To state that both music and poetry are composed of sound, without specifying the degree to which this is true, therefore, becomes misleadingly inadequate. The difficulties of such a reduction have resulted not only in categorical esthetic confusions, but in those which produced the unnecessary conflicts among traditional European prosodic theories since Hellenistic times. The *locus classicus* of these confusions for our literary history occurred in the equation of what was actually a musical system (Greek meter) to a more graphic prosodic one (Latin quantitative scansion). It seems to be generally true that borrowed foreign literary conventions, as well as revivals and adaptations of past traditions, invade the linguistic structure of poetry at the written level. Any thorough formalistic analysis of the structure of poetry, and of its relation to the language in which it is written, must deal with the written language as a system in itself, as well as with the spoken one.[3]

The major difficulty that confronts modern comparisons of poetry and music, however, resides in the problem of "meaning." By "the music of poetry" we generally refer to all of

[3] The matter of this and the following three paragraphs is treated at greater length in my article on "The Music of Poetry," *Journal of Aesthetics and Art Criticism*, XV (1956), pp. 232-244.

the non-semantic properties of the language of a poem. We tend to include not only the poem's rationalized prosody and its sound on actually being read (which would not commonly be said to carry "meanings") but certain characteristics of its imagery and syntax as well. Throughout literary history, the "musical" elements of language have been assigned various purposes, from those of adornment, by Neoclassicism, to those of intrinsic irrational necessity, by the *symbolistes*. No matter what our view, or that of a poet whose work we are attempting to analyze, might be on this score, we would probably agree that because of this "musical" quality the language of a poem would affect us as readers in ways in which the words of a telegram would not. From a purely formalistic point of view, the "music of poetry" would be confined to patterns of linguistic redundancy, of those elements which, the poem being treated as a coded message, would be beside the point. But in any rational attempt to distinguish poetry from other utterances, it is precisely these elements which become of greatest concern.

It is also generally agreed that the materials of musical languages do not carry "meanings" either; in fact, the phrase "music of poetry" would generally be defended as useful because of the apparent similarity between the ways that music affects us and the manner in which formal, non-semantic poetic elements contribute to our experience of poetry. There are good overall reasons for likening the significance of music to the significance of literary form. Particularly in the case of poetry, the functional relationship of form to content continues to pose the most demanding critical questions. It was the strategy of the Russian Formalist critics to question the utility of any distinctions traditionally drawn between form and content, their skepticism being based on a realization of the inadequacy of previous relegations of "meaning" to content, and of some other shadowy notion of import to form.[4] Previ-

[4] See Victor Erlich, *Russian Formalism* (The Hague, 1955), pp. 145-163, 182-198.

ous literary epochs, of course, had cast form in different roles. Neoclassicism, for example, held elegant adornment to be a necessary complement of material or factual substance, but the relationship between form and content, as between embellishment and instructive import in any art, was not usually seen as an organic one. "Judgment," asserted Hobbes, "begets the strength and structure, and fancy begets the ornaments of a poem."[5] "The sound must seem an echo to the sense,"[6] said Pope, but it remained for him an echo to be awaited almost out of good manners alone. Expression remained for him "the dress of thought." And although different occasions required different costumes proper to them, Neoclassicism followed the analogy through in a rigorous way to maintain the senselessness of form, which could no more be said to be meaningful than could clothing, doffed and donned at will, be said to have a life of its own.[7]

It has been common in literary studies, following T. S. Eliot, to bemoan the "dissociation of sensibility" of Neoclassicism, the separation of thought and feeling forced by rationalism upon the views of what is held to be a too-willing later seventeenth century. In some ways, the division between content and form remains to this day an analogue of this supposed bifurcation of thought and feeling. The problem of meaning is very much in evidence here, for while appeal to history can usually settle disputes over the reading of particular words, no such methods of agreement are obtainable on the question of the significance of form, of the "musical" elements of verse, or, indeed, of music itself. Recent attempts to deal with this problem on the part of modern textual critics have not met with success. In attempting to banish a reified "emotion" from

[5] Thomas Hobbes, *The Answer to the Preface to "Gondibert"* (1650), in *English Works*, ed. Sir William Molesworth (London, 1839), IV, 449.

[6] *Essay on Criticism*, II, 165.

[7] Locke also figuratively connected fancy and clothing, speaking of the former as a courtly fop, superfluous and seductive. See the *Essay Concerning Human Understanding*, III, x, No. 34. Also see Samuel Johnson's *Life of Cowley*, in *Lives of the English Poets* (Everyman Edition), I, 39.

the language of poetry, they have in general only pushed its ghost back into another linguistic closet. In employing the rather vague concept of the "reinforcement" of meaning by the "music" of a poem, the New Criticism has in general tended to fall back on the impressionism that it so neatly did away with in regard to questions of imagery and rhetorical structure. The result is that modern poetic theory is still left with the notion that the relationships between language and music, prose and poetry, meaning and feeling, even content and form, are somehow parallel.

It would perhaps require a study of the psychology and esthetics of music similar in methods and approach to those of modern linguistics in order more fully to understand some of these relationships.[8] Musical habits, like those of speech, are held in common by members of cultural and social groups who always tend to feel that their habits are, in some mysterious way, universal.

It has been the great accomplishment of modern linguistics to chart the boundaries of speech habits and to unveil the extremely primitive levels at which they create barriers between the linguistic experience of groups and individuals. It is also generally understood that what the linguist Benjamin Lee Whorf called the "segmentation of nature"[9] that the structure of particular languages entails, the fundamental abstractions forced on a speaker of any language are mirrored in the "routines of sensation" of sound shared by cultural groups. The applicability of these notions to music has been understood, on the whole, only by musicologists who have worked with "primitive" music, and with the music of non-Indo-European cultures.[10] For even the most basic concepts

---

[8] Leonard B. Meyer, in *Emotion and Meaning in Music* (Chicago, 1956), proceeds somewhat along these lines, particularly in pp. 1-82, where he reviews very cogently past analyses of the nature of musical experience. He then proceeds to construct a new, quasi-linguistic model.

[9] Benjamin Lee Whorf, "Science and Linguistics," in *Language, Thought and Reality*, ed. John B. Carroll (New York, 1956), pp. 207-219.

[10] See Bruno Nettl, *Music in Primitive Culture* (Cambridge, Mass., 1956), pp. 2-44; also, David P. McAllester, *Enemy Way Music: A Study of Social*

of Western musical theory, such as diatonic harmony, are rooted in the styles and practices they were developed to describe. It would thus appear that only in terms of a rigorous study of how musical experience accumulates, conducted with the neutral commitment of the ethno-musicologist and based perhaps on linguistic models, could a long tradition of half-understood observation of the power of music be explained. The idea that prior musical experience affects the way in which one hears musical sounds is, of course, not a new one. But previous expressions of it seldom came to the immediate point. Hobbes remarked on the general importance of memory for the operation of fancy, for example,[11] and John Stuart Mill came one step closer in characterizing the effects of music upon him as "winding up to a high pitch those feelings of an elevated kind which are already in the character."[12] But a final analysis of meaning in music need not resort to discussion of feelings any more than a grammar need do so.

Sidney Lanier declared at the end of *The Science of English Verse* that "music is *not* a species of language, but language is a species of music."[13] Despite the elaborate but misleading system he had just constructed for analyzing the "music" of prosody, one feels that he meant by this that the power of poetic language to move its readers partakes, after all, of some of the same mystery as the affective force of music. With this remark, Lanier joins the party of Verlaine in abandoning both poetry and music to the shadow of the Irrational, for "*De la musique avant toute chose*" is but an exhortation to divide sound from sense and to choose the sound.

The temptation to regard the effects of music on a hearer as Irrational, and the workings of those effects as Mystery, is a deeply rooted one. The history of the abandonment of the

and Esthetic Values as Seen in Navaho Music, Papers of the Peabody Museum of American Archaeology and Ethnology, Harvard University, Vol. XLI, No. 3 (Cambridge, Mass., 1954), pp. 3-6, 63-88.

[11] *Op.cit.*, p. 449.

[12] John Stuart Mill, *Autobiography* (New York, 1924), p. 101.

[13] Page 340.

imagination of Western man to that temptation is long and complex. This book is concerned with certain phases of that history, notably at a time when it was the province of poetry to figure forth what we should today characterize as irrational in the most concrete terms. When, toward the end of that time, Leibniz in a famous remark referred to music as a kind of "occult arithmetic,"[14] he merely meant that a hearer's perception of the mathematically analyzable relations in musical arrangements of varying pitches, durations, timbres, even of the compositions of tones themselves, are, by the hearer, unconsciously tabulated. This notion is well on the way to a modern view of music's operations upon the listener that would reinterpret the Mystery in terms of the normally obscure workings of the Unconscious, and of the most deeply ingrained habits.

In an age of empiricism, a systematic account of the workings of language and music must needs comply with the demands usually made on all accounts of behavioral processes. For poetry to concern itself with music is no more or less necessarily fanciful a pursuit than for poetry to consider anything else. The following pages will largely concern an epoch in which poetry felt itself to have a privileged position with respect to the interpretation of the workings of music and of musical language. It was the epoch immediately preceding that which saw the origins of our own kinds of empirical

---

[14] "*J'ay montré ailleurs que la perception confuse de l'agrement ou des agremens qui se trouve dans les consonances ou dissonances consiste dans un Arithmetique occulte. L'âme compte des battemens se recontrent regulierment à des intervalles courts, elle y trouve du plaisir. Ainsi elle fait ses comptes sans le savoir. C'est ainsi qu'elle fait encore une infinité d'autres petites operations très justes, quoyqu'elles ne soyent point volontaires ny commes que par l'effet notable ou elles aboutissent enfin, en nous donnant un sentiment clair mais confus, parceque ses sources n'y sont point apperçues.*" Gottfried Wilhelm Leibniz, "Remarks on an extract from Bayle's dictionary" (1703). In *Philosophischen Schriften*, ed. Gerhardt (Berlin, 1880), IV, 550-551. See also Leibniz' *Philosophical Papers and Letters*, tr. and ed. Leroy E. Loemken (Chicago, 1956), II, 795-796; also Gerhardt's edition, VI, 598ff. The interesting distinction invoked between *ratio* and *auditus* by the eighteenth-century writer on music, J. D. Heinichen, is also relevant here. See his *Der Generalbass in der Composition* (Dresden, 1728), pp. 2-5.

accounts, and of the view of the nature of Reality that came to demand them.

Music as Myth and Poetic Subject

If modern beliefs about music and poetry tend to bring the two practices together in theory, history itself provides a tradition of both actual and theoretical unifications of the two long-since-divorced arts. Like the folk balladeer's identification of the notions of "song" and "story," the Greek word *mousike* designated neither a linguistic nor a tonal art but the craft of composing *song*, considered as a unified entity. It is extremely difficult for a modern reader to grasp the significance of this combined concept of music-poetry, although all of Western literary history has conspired to make him accept a metaphorical identification of the two. When he hears of a Classic poet being referred to as a "singer," or his poems as "songs," *carmina*, or whatever, he unconsciously accepts a figurative equation of the same sort, for him, as would be exemplified in Mrs. Sigourney's epithet of "The Sweet Singer of Hartford." But the actual practices of Greek music and poetry would belie the necessity for a figurative interpretation.

The history of Occidental lyric, narrative, and dramatic poetry proceeds along a course mapped by the ever-widening gulf between the crafts of tone and word. Nevertheless, the unification of the two in Antiquity hangs on as a kind of literary racial memory, and many beliefs about music were perpetrated and retained by the strong will and imperfect memory of a completely autotelic literature, independent of any necessary musical association. It was the Renaissance that uncovered and revivified many of these dormant and moribund memories; in an attempt to justify poetic and musical practices, long since become utterly separate concerns, against the measure of the past, a broad and ambitious program was established whose aim was to return both arts to their Classical, original (almost, as it came to be felt, pre-lapsarian) union.

And while much argument and disagreement marked all united consideration of how the aims of this program might be accomplished, the intent was always to regain the perfect condition of the arts in Antiquity.

That perfect state had always been known to the post-Classic world through the great musical fables of Orpheus and his ability to animate lifeless and motionless objects; of Amphion and the power of his lyre playing which caused the walls of Thebes to form themselves of strewn and scattered stones, flying through the air into place at the irresistible bidding of his music; of Arion and his power to charm a wild dolphin into carrying him to safety on his back; of the beautiful and dangerous song of the Sirens, and many more. The fact that Orpheus and the others were also considered to be poets in Classical literature added to the newly discovered musical and poetic discussions of Plato, Aristotle, pseudo-Plutarch, and other writers, created for the Renaissance an Olympian image of a musico-poetic golden age. But other notions about music, in particular, complicated the picture. For the development of musical practices in the Medieval world had been accompanied by the transmission and ramification of a whole body of musical theory of a kind that would hardly be classed as such today. Not only were certain confused and garbled shreds of Greek musical theory and accounts of practice handed down by successions of commentators and writers on many subjects. Growths and changes of various phases in the historical development of vocal and instrumental music, both sacred and secular, were recorded in successive layers of addition to the stock of musical theory extant at any one time. The result was, on the one hand, a great hodgepodge of basic harmonic and rhythmic theory, particular stylistic prescriptions, descriptions of Ancient and contemporary musical practice, etc.; and on the other, scraps of a larger philosophy of music, accounting for its fabled effects in the Classic myths, detailing the place of musical phenomena in the general scheme of nature, and locating the role of musical practices in the ethical and theological processes of a Christian world-view. Since the transmission of speculative material of any kind depended for so many centuries upon the use and citation of prior authority, often reaching back to an age in which technical terms of many sorts had different meanings, it is easy to understand how the Medieval legacy of musical knowledge and thought could involve the most concrete of practical considerations mingled together with the wildest and most general of abstractions.

For beliefs about music, even more than those about poetry, had engendered in the Ancient world a wealth of abstract speculation. From politics, ethics, psychology (in the Aristotelian sense), even into the realms of cosmology, musical notions and ideas received the continual attention of speculative writers. For many philosophers, music was more than a ritualized cultural practice which was to be considered in the same way as were many other human activities. The study of music, rather, would lead to the understanding of some of the most fundamental principles of the structure of the whole universe; because of the way in which the intervals between musical tones in customary use submitted to the most primitive as well as the most sophisticated types of mathematical analysis, music was thought to be the mysterious source of certain abstract relationships. Because some general mathematical discoveries of Pythagoras resulted from experiments with a vibrating string and an investigation of the relationship between the length of that string and the pitch of the tone produced by plucking it, the establishment of certain branches of musical study as the adjunct of those of mathematics became secured. Finally, the attempts of Classic philosophers to account for music's fabled effects upon a hearer, having to contend as they did with these philosophers' own observations of the actual musical practices of their own age, led to three main branches of musical speculation in the Ancient world.

These branches comprised the mathematical study of tonal intervals and sequences (together with corollary considerations of the application of these mathematical studies to other ordered systems), the psychological study of the effects of music upon listeners through an analysis of the various tonal combinations and styles and types of composition and performance then in use, and, finally, the overall place of music in society, given an understanding of its nature and the reasons for its effects. But the very concepts and terms in which these branches of musical speculation were carried on depended not only upon an understanding of the peculiarly close relationship of music to poetry, or verbal to tonal patterns in the Greek world, but of the practices of the purely tonal art as well. From the phonic norms of the tonal system, through the harmonic systems employed, the compositions wrought from these systems, the methods and styles of vocal and instrumental sound production, to the occasions upon which certain patterns rather than certain other ones were regularly used, the whole of Greek musical practice lay continually behind all theoretical discussions. Any future age, inheriting in written form any sizable body of discussion on the subject of Classic music, would have needed those musical customs, preserved in the practice of some groups at least, in order to understand them.

But this is just what did not happen. The history of Western music may be considered as the gradual characteristic movement of "rational" music (that is, the music which was at any time notated, preserved, and theorized about, rather than the folk-music, never notated or transmitted in a kind of "oral" tradition) away from monody and toward polyphony. The development in the ninth and tenth centuries of the *organum* in the chant of the Church was just the beginning of a series of steps which would lead the music of subsequent ages so far away from the practices of Classical Antiquity that it would soon become impossible for those ages to understand the theoretical and speculative writings that were handed down to them from the Ancient world. There consequently developed a huge rift between the musical theory of successive epochs in the history of Western music and the inherited notions and formulations about music that had descended from Classical times. Musical terms had changed their meanings utterly, and practices, both sacred and secular, were complex and varied in ways that no Ancient theory could comprehend. On the other hand, the little general speculation about music's nature and effects that did filter down through late Roman writers became incorporated into a growing and deepening Christian world picture. Again, the gap between the practical musician's concerns and the speculative writer's interest in giving an account of music's real or fancied nature grew wider in itself because of this.

The poetry of the Renaissance all over Europe was always in some measure concerned with itself. Not that it carved out an area of what we might call esthetics in which to operate; but, rather, the literature of the revival of Classical learning and the substitution of historical for ecclesiastical authority was beginning to usurp, even in its lyric, narrative, and dramatic forms, some of the domains that had formerly been reserved for authoritative systematic speculation. The struggle of Renaissance thinkers to adapt traditional and newly discovered Classical authorities to the facts and practices of their own languages and habits is reflected in the poetry of the sixteenth and seventeenth centuries. The subject of music is no exception to this general condition, and one finds poets as well as speculative prose writers attempting to contend with the conflict of mode and tradition in contemplating the music-poetry of Antiquity through the inconsistently distorting glass of the conventions of the tonal and verbal arts of their own day. Both in the treatment of music as a formal subject for poetry, and in the incidental use of allusions to musical explanations, mythologies, or even actualities, the verse of the period called the Renaissance (in Northern Europe) demonstrates the changing attitudes and beliefs toward Ancient and contemporary music of a rapidly changing overall world-view.

Perhaps at no other time was music a more fruitful subject for poetic treatment. An age that was consciously attempting to reunite, however factitiously, the divorced arts in both its vocal music and its lyric poetry was better able than many since to try to break down the metaphorical character of the use of "song" for a written inscription that was hardly ever intended even to be read aloud. And while the history of English music is a rather retarded one, compared with that of the music of France, Italy, and, later, Germany, the Elizabethan and Jacobean worlds afforded musical speculation as prominent a place as they did its secular and sacred practice.

The early seventeenth century saw the beginnings of vast changes in world perspectives. One of these changes affected what up until then had been considered an adequate account of the world or of any part of it; a final and most crucial chapter in what Max Weber has called the *"Entzauberung der Welt,"*[15] the de-mythologizing of the world, had opened with the dawn of empirical science as a model for explanation or account of any phenomenon. All human activity was eventually to come under the scrutiny of an examination that could no longer accept a beautifully ordered plan as belonging to an edifice that had grown, through eons of changing architectures, to resemble no conceivable blueprint. At a time when, in Italy and France, musical conventions, forms, and fundamental principles of composition and performance were undergoing a transformation from the musical epoch called *Renaissance* to that called the *Baroque*, general speculative demands for an explanation of the new and old musical phenomena, as well as of all the mythology and lore that had accumulated for about fifteen centuries, were changing too.

The period in the history of English poetry and music reaching from the beginning of the sixteenth century until about 1700, then, may be shown to contain this period of change in the practice and philosophy of music, and to reflect that change in the poetic representation of musical subjects.

[15] See Max Weber, *Die Protestantische Ethik und der Geist des Kapitalismus, Gesammelte Aufsätze zur Religionssoziologie* (Tübingen, 1947), I, 94-95.

In the following pages the poetry of that period will be studied in this regard. After some preliminary discussion of the musical thought, or rather, as I have chosen to call it, the musical ideology, of the poet *qua* writer and thinker, and of the non-musical and non-musicianly writer in general, the successive stages in the de-mythologizing of poetry's view of music will be opened up. From the canonical Medieval Christian view that all actual human music bears a definite relation to the eternal, abstract (and inaudible) "music" of universal order, to the completely de-Christianized, use of such notions in late seventeenth-century poetry as decorative metaphor and mere turns of wit, a gradual process of disconnection between abstract musical mythology and concrete practical considerations of actual vocal and instrumental music occurs.

To suggest this process of rationalization, of an *Entzauberung der musikalischen Welt*, I have employed a reference to a line from a poem of John Dryden that will be considered as a kind of *terminus ad quem* of the process. When he concluded his "Song for St. Cecilia's Day" of 1687 with "And MUSICK shall untune the Sky," Dryden was referring to the Final Trump of the Last Judgment. But in the course of the following discussion, I have allowed "the untuning of the sky" to stand for the gradual process of change reflected in the poetry therein studied. I shall attempt to draw connections between the various stages of this process and the successive changes in the practice and theory of poetry, as they seem relevant, along the way. And I shall try to show how the poetry of the period under consideration employs the musical ideologies of the climates of opinion that surround their composition much as it employs political or religious ideologies, and how the vigorous reinterpretation of received ideas and the personal quality of this reinterpretation always marks the major poet from the minor one, the founder and adapter of conventions from the mere user of them.

CHAPTER II · "FROM HEAV'NLY HARMONY"

From Harmony, from heav'nly Harmony
This universal Frame began;
When Nature underneath a heap
Of jarring Atomes lay,
And cou'd not heave her Head,
The tuneful Voice was heard from high,
Arise, ye more than dead.
Then cold and hot and moist and dry
In order to their Stations leap
And MUSICK'S *pow'r obey.*

Music Speculative and Practical

"AS for the division," wrote Thomas Morley in the last decade of the sixteenth century, "music is either speculative or practical. Speculative is that kind of music which, by mathematical helps, seeketh the causes, properties and natures of sounds, by themselves and compared with others, proceeding no further, but content with the only contemplation of the art. Practical is that which teacheth all that may be known in songs, either for the understanding of other men's, or making of one's own. . . ."[1] There is perhaps an echo of dispraise shown here by Morley, a most enterprising practical musician, for studies involving "the only contemplation of the art." But in his *Plain and Easy Introduction to Practical Music*, published in 1597, Morley could well choose to enforce such a distinction. His own century had inherited a rich tradition of discourse about music, both

[1] Thomas Morley, *A Plain and Easy Introduction to Practical Music*, ed. R. A. Harman (New York, 1953), p. 101.

speculative and practical, from the Middle Ages. It had produced a body of practical theory occasioned by particular
problems arising from contemporary musical questions and
usages. Both of these and the growing Renaissance interest
in the musical speculation and practices of Antiquity combined
in a tradition of encyclopedic musical learning.

Such a monumental work was Gioseffe Zarlino's *Istituzione
harmoniche*, published in 1558, which devoted as much attention to such matters as classical myths of the power of music,
general speculations of the nature of mathematical proportion,
correspondences obtaining among tonal configurations, the
elements and the humors, etc., as it did to the exigencies of
contrapuntal writing. The production of such compendia of
lore, natural science, esthetics, and principles of craftsman-
ship was continued through the seventeenth century, as evidenced by the treatises of Robert Fludd, Mersenne, Prae-
torius, and Athanasius Kircher. Even before 1600, however,
music as a subject for systematic writing embraced many
different categories of thought and experience. At a time when
musical practice had varied forms, each playing its respective
social role and each generating its particular stylistic conventions, a simple description of "practical music" would be
complex enough. But to this has to be added the strange body
of theory and doctrine, mathematical, cosmological, prosodical,
mythological, ethical, and pseudo-physiological that had accumulated during the Middle Ages. The Renaissance, with
its increasing requirements by both amateur and professional
musicians for practical investigation, was unable to dispense
with such an accumulation of authority on the subject of
music's *raison d'être*.

In order fully to understand the widening gap between
speculative and practical music and the kinds of discourse
expended upon them during the first fifteen centuries of the
Christian era, we must first turn to the peculiar transitional
period at the end of the Classic world. The musical practices
and conventions about which Athenian and Alexandrian phi-

losophers had theorized had already started to change, but those theoretical writings themselves had been transmitted, if only at third or fourth hand. Throughout this study it will be generally observed that the practical music, the conventions of tonal structure and texture, compositional pattern, manner and social function of performance, etc., of one generation or culture becomes the speculative music of its historical heirs. The division between the theoretical and practical portions of the science of music is first drawn up by Aristides Quintilianus in his treatise on music of the first or second century A.D. But the subsequent legacy of this distinction, as well as his tripartite division of a subset of the theoretical portion into "harmonics," "rhythmics," and "metrics," was a confused one. Medieval authors, writing on a music fundamentally different in almost every respect from that of even late Classical times, employed these distinctions and terms in a way that can only, once their original meanings are understood, be termed metaphorical.

For example, Cassiodorus, in the sixth century, defines music itself as being composed of harmonics, rhythmics, and metrics,[2] while his predecessors had so designated only one sub-branch of the study. Even more confusing is the fact that such a tripartite division makes a great deal of sense if the music-poetry of the Greek world is being considered: there the quantities of the syllables of the lines of poetry, the very prosodic feet themselves, constitute the metrical and rhythmic notation of the music. Greek music was notated by pitch signs alone. It was the sound patternings of the text which provided the other two necessary elements to the notation of a musical line: the duration of the tones at each pitch, and the rhythmic groupings of these durations. Information about these was provided by the foot-structure of the verse, and probably by the ictus-pattern, respectively.[3] And while there eventually

[2] Cassiodorus, *Institutiones*, v. See Oliver Strunk, ed., *Source Readings in Music History* (New York, 1950), pp. 87-92, for translation of and comment on this section, "*De Musica*."

[3] See Curt Sachs, *The Rise of Music in the Ancient World* (New York,

arose a school of musical theorists interested in the independence of melody from the text which it set (a notion frowned on by both Plato and Aristotle), who wanted to add rhythmical signs of their own to the pitch-signals, the incorporation of what we would call prosody or metrics into musical theory, even at the most practical level, was ordinarily inevitable. But when text and melody became fundamentally separated in the Middle Ages (or perhaps we might even say in Roman times), a division of music into harmonics, rhythmics, and metrics could be considered only an academic and highly artificial one. The names of the categories themselves would have to be reattached to other meanings.

Thus do we find it possible for St. Augustine's *De Musica* to devote all but its metaphysical and psychological portions to what we would consider purely matters of poetic prosody; and, in general, we find that all kinds of similar confusions in the use of ideas and terms from the musical theory of the past become extremely common during the Middle Ages. For Cassiodorus' treatise on music in his *Institutiones* was assiduously imitated and even copied by Isidore of Seville in his *Etymologarium* in the following century; and Isidore himself was copied by many Medieval encyclopedists whenever they came to consider the nature of music in their studies of the *proprietatibus rerum*.

Medieval writers were forced to make some kind of order out of the blend of Classical mythology, Pythagorean and Neoplatonist theologizing about number and harmony in the abstract and in its relation to music, Greek metrics, discussions of the mathematical interpretation by certain Ancient writers of the divisions of the Greek scales, and many other topics, which faced them as the legitimate concern of musical theory. I refer to Medieval writers, that is, whose concerns were not specifically those of practical music. It should be made very clear at this point that a tradition of discourse, concerned with

1943), pp. 259-265; also, the same author's *Rhythm and Tempo* (New York, 1953), pp. 115-146.

the purely technical problems confronting the composer of
music in all the successive stylistic epochs of the Middle Ages,
continued to be largely unhampered by all the speculation for
some time. From the first treatises (in the ninth and tenth
centuries) on the parallel *organum* which gave birth to Western polyphony, through the exceedingly practical, hardheaded
writings of some English and French theorists of the twelfth
and thirteenth centuries, down to the stylistic and notational
revolution of the so-called *ars nova* of the fourteenth, a pragmatic strain of what I shall call practical theory perpetuated
itself. Amidst a host of divisions à la Cassiodorus of the nature
of music into three parts of various sorts, the thirteenth-
century writer Johannes de Grocheo could simply divide music
into three types of his own: *musica vulgaris* (popular monody,
instrumental or vocal); *musica mensurabilis* (the measured,
notated polyphonic music of courtly and literary society); and
musica ecclesiastica (the liturgical music of the Church, comprising both monody and cultivated polyphony.[4] Grocheo is
unique in rejecting unequivocally the whole burden of *musica
speculativa* that most theorists inherited, and in voicing in no
uncertain terms his suspicions about the truth of many de-
voutly held musical myths. His general purpose is to record
and discuss the practical music of the start of the fourteenth
century, which he does more than adequately.[5]

But the primary division of music into parts for the Middle
Ages, the one that remained canonical even well into the
sixteenth century, was the tripartite arrangement of Boethius.
His *De Institutione Musica* remained an unquestioned authority on the music of Antiquity and on music in general for a

[4] Johannes de Grocheo, *Theoria.* See Johannes Wolf, *"Die Musiklehre
des Johannes de Grocheo,"* Sammelbande der Internationalen Musikgesellschaft, I (1899), pp. 65-130.

[5] Other pragmatic distinctions, such as that drawn by Regino of Pruem
between *musica artificialis* and *musica naturalis*, often cut across the specu-
lative-practical distinction. For an excellent discussion of classifications of
this sort, see Eric Werner and Isaiah Sonne, "The Philosophy and Theory of
Music in Judaeo-Arabic Literature," *Hebrew Union College Annual*, XVII
(1942-1943), pp. 253-272.

thousand years after its composition in the early sixth century. According to his scheme, the three branches of music (and Boethius made no distinction between practical and speculative) were *musica mundana, musica humana,* and *musica instrumentalis.* By *musica mundana* Boethius meant the harmony of the universe, including the cosmological order of elements, astral bodies, and seasons whose typical model, as we shall see shortly, was, for the Ancient and Medieval worlds, the music of the spheres. By human music he denoted "that which unites the incorporeal activity of the reason with the body . . . a certain mutual adaptation and as it were a tempering of high and low sounds into a single consonance."[6] This paralleled the cosmic music in causing "a blending of the body's elements"; the most significant term in Boethius' whole discussion of *musica humana* is the notion of "temperament," which was made to apply almost from the beginning of its linguistic history both to the tuning of strings and to the tempering of various parts of the human soul, thoughts, feelings, the relation of the soul to the body, etc.[7]

Boethius' third category, *musica instrumentalis,* involves simply what we would call music itself; but Boethius makes it clear that a true musician is not merely a practical singer, instrumentalist, or maker of songs. He must be one who "on reflection has taken to himself the science of singing, not by the servitude of work, but by the rule of contemplation."[8] Thus Boethius guards against an implicit fragmentation of music into the speculative lore of his first two categories, and the practical considerations of his final one. These first two

---

[6] Boethius, *De Institutione Musica,* I, 2, tr. O. Strunk, in *Source Readings in Music History,* p. 85. It must be remembered that the *musica instrumentalis* of Boethius, for us the most "real," is for Boethius and his followers merely "actual," and hence, "unreal"—merely an imitation of *musica mundana.*

[7] The history of this idea of "temperament," as well as of many other musico-psychological terms, is traced through many examples of its use in Leo Spitzer, "Classical and Christian Ideas of World Harmony," *Traditio,* III (1945), pp. 307-340.

[8] Boethius, I, 33, in Strunk, p. 86.

categories, of course, designate what is in our sense not music at all but part of a more general philosophical scheme, figuratively ascribing an order to nature. The notions of the harmony of the universe and the tempering of warring elements in the human organism are both metaphors that come from important areas of Greek thought.

Behind even Boethius' division, however, lies the complex and imposing body of both speculative and practical theory of the Classical world. In the previous chapter it was suggested that a convenient division of this body would separate three areas of speculation.[9] A brief consideration of these, taken one at a time, may make clear some matters to be discussed further on.

Harmony

The Greek word *harmonia*, meaning originally a fitting or joining together of discrete and disparate entities, had a musical meaning that differs so subtly from the modern musical use of the word "harmony" that many translations of Classical texts, overlooking the difference, give the derived word for the original. To any reader with a knowledge of music and its history, however, such a translation is not only wrong but fundamentally misleading. In the first place, our whole modern sense of "harmony" and "harmonious" is conditioned by our experience of polyphonic music, so that "harmony" cannot help but suggest *the ordering of simultaneously sounding musical tones*, taken together as a "package" or *gestalt*. In the abstract sense, "harmonious" tends to carry over this suggestion of a chord, and events to which it is applied are so designated because they consist of discrete and dissimilar sub-entities which lose their individuality to the degree of being perfectly blended into a whole.

Greek musical theory devoted little discussion to what we would call today "harmonics." The Greek *harmoniai* were scales, or melodic schemata; in general, *harmonia* is to be

[9] See above, pp. 15-18.

thought of as referring to *melody* rather than to vertical tonal aggregates. In the still more extended senses of the Platonic metaphors of the ordering of the cosmos and of the soul of man, the notion of a harmonious blending of opposite qualities is extremely easy for the modern reader (and has been for readers, actually, since about the tenth century) to misinterpret: a musical chord can be thought of as "blending" and marrying dissimilar or even contrary elements. The notion is rather like that of *e pluribus unum*. But even a little exploration of extant musical and metamusical theory (for we should so distinguish between the writings of Aristoxenus, Aristides Quintilianus, pseudo-Plutarch, Ptolemy, etc. on the one hand, and the philosophical speculations of Plato in the *Republic*, *Laws*, and *Timaeus*, for example, or Aristotle in the *Politics*, on the other) will lead us to avoid such an error.

For the Greek notion of "harmony" we should rather seek to understand an idea of relative proportion, of an order that consists in the ratios of quantities to each other, rather than of a notion of blending that depends on the *simultaneous* effects of separate or even warring elements. It is almost as if our modern architectural term "scale" (referring to the *relative* sizes of portions of buildings) were to be interpreted as having derived from a purely musical sense. The disposition of musical intervals (considered merely as distances between successive scalar steps and leaps, rather than between simultaneously sounding tones) in terms of ordered ratios would then be seen as applicable to architecture, or even to all smoothly functioning systems: "scale" would mean "proportion" and "just disposition of the relative role of parts in a whole." This would be close to the Greek notion of *harmonia*.[10]

An understanding of this notion will explain clearly the combined interests of the Pythagoreans in music and mathe-

---

[10] See R. G. Collingwood, *The Idea of Nature* (Oxford, 1945), pp. 49-55, esp. p. 52 n; also, Robert S. Brumbaugh, *Plato's Mathematical Imagination* (Bloomington, Indiana, 1954), pp. 85-87. Of general relevance to this discussion is the exposition of Greek musical thought in Julius Portnoy, *The Philosopher and Music* (New York, 1954), pp. 4-44.

matics in forming the basis of their cosmology. The Pythagorean experiments with the monochord showed that the intervals of the diatonic scales could all be produced, with reference to a given fundamental pitch, by successively dividing a string of given length and observing the tone produced upon plucking the divided string. Certain intervals, such as the octave, fourth and fifth, were shown to result from dividing the string in the most "perfect" ratios, such as ½, ⅔, etc., where the numerators and denominators of the fractions consisted of the smallest possible integers. Since these intervals *happened to play significant roles in the tonal systems of Greek music as it was already developing*, it was concluded that these "consonant" intervals were most pleasing to the ear because they were most "harmonious" or perfect, mathematically speaking. With reference to the idea of harmony as proportion outlined above, we might say that these intervals could be comprehended in terms of the simplest basic ratios, and therefore were most harmonious in the sense of being most perfectly rationalizable in terms of a system of such ratios. These intervals, to pursue our modern analogy, had the clearest and best "scale" with respect to their fundamental pitch.

The Pythagorean notion of the perfect consonances and their necessarily beautiful effects upon a hearer is an important one in Western history. Up through the Renaissance and even later, the harmony of the parts of the cosmos, on the one hand, and of the parts of the human psyche, on the other, were seen as the basic elements of the same universal order. In the Ptolemaic astronomy, for example, the universal proportions could be seen as realized in the ratios to each other of the diameters of the heavenly spheres. In terms of this "harmony," the old myth of the music of the spheres as representing the sounds of heavenly perfection could be reinterpreted as a metaphysical notion, characterizing not only the order of the universe but the relation of human lives to this cosmological order.

The music of the spheres becomes such a central image in

Christian musical thought that we may usefully turn to it for a moment. In the *Republic*, Book x, Socrates' relation of the myth of Er includes a mention of this Pythagorean myth; it describes the heavenly spheres bearing "on the upper surface of each" a siren, "who goes round with them, hymning a single tone or note. The eight together form one harmony; . . ."[11] It is not, of course, that we are to think of *a chord of eight tones* here; rather, the "harmony" is an ordered intervallic relationship among all of these tones, more in the manner of the intervals obtainable by step or skip in a scale. The singing siren that produces the tone on each sphere, of course, becomes beautifully adaptable, eventually, to membership in a Christian angelic choir. But the more common version of the myth, such as is put down elaborately by Aristotle in *De Caelo*,[12] maintained that it was the rubbing against each other of the supposedly hard, glassy celestial spheres that produced the sound. In answer to the objection that no mortal had ever heard that music, it was often retorted that the constant droning of that noise deadened the ears of earthly inhabitants by custom alone, and that because it was so constant, it was inaudible.

The form in which the myth of the music of the spheres is handed down to the Middle Ages, however, may be seen in its treatment by Cicero in the *Somnium Scipionis* and in the somewhat Neoplatonized commentary upon the latter by the fourth-century writer Macrobius. The passage from Cicero describing the heavenly music revealed in Scipio's dream might be considered the *locus classicus* of the heavenly music motif:

"What is this large and agreeable sound that fills my ears?"

"That is produced," he replied, "by the onward rush and motion of the spheres themselves; the intervals between them, though unequal, being exactly arranged in a fixed proportion,

[11] Plato, *Republic*, 617a-617b, tr. Jowett.
[12] Aristotle, *De Caelo*, II, ix. This should be consulted for its excellent exposition of the doctrine, as well as for its refutation of it.

by an agreeable blending of high and low tones various harmonies are produced; for such mighty motions cannot be carried on so swiftly in silence; and Nature has provided that one extreme shall produce low tones while the other gives forth high. Therefore this uppermost sphere of heaven, which bears the stars, as it revolves more rapidly, produces a high, shrill tone, whereas the lowest revolving sphere, that of the moon, gives forth the lowest tone; for the earthly sphere, the ninth, remains ever motionless and stationary in its position in the centre of the universe. But the other eight spheres, two of which move with the same velocity, produce seven different sounds—a number which is the key of almost everything. Learned men, by imitating this harmony on stringed instruments and in song, have gained for themselves a return to this region. . . ."[13]

It might be added that Cicero's seven tones constituted the seven discrete pitches of a *harmonia* or scale. The significance of the fact that stringed instruments specifically are mentioned here will be treated later. We might observe here that it is Macrobius' comment on this last sentence that lays the groundwork for eventual Renaissance expositions of the ethical character of man's relationship to the music of the spheres: "Every soul in the world is allured by musical sounds so that not only those who are more refined in their habits, but all the barbarous peoples as well, have adopted songs by which they are inflamed with courage or wooed to pleasure; for the soul carries with it into the body a memory of the music which it knew in the sky, and is so captivated by its charm that there is no breast so cruel or savage as not to be gripped by the spell of such an appeal."[14] Thus microcosmic man, imitating in his *musica instrumentalis* or practical music the ideal order of the *harmonia mundi*, can regain in some small way the *musica*

[13] Cicero, *De Re Publica*, VI, 8, tr. C. W. Keyes (Loeb Edition), pp. 271-273.

[14] Macrobius, *Commentary on the Dream of Scipio*, tr. W. H. Stahl (New York, 1952), p. 195.

humana, the ordering of his being, that characterizes the music of the spheres and the prior good state of his soul.

The abstract harmony or proportioned order of the universe that was figured forth in a *musical* order (and we must recognize the metaphorical nature of such a notion, almost from the beginning), was itself applicable to the individual human soul, as well as to the *anima mundi*. The notion of the soul as a *harmonia* or proportionate distribution of unlike parts accommodated itself equally well to the musical metaphor and to the same kind of interpretation of it as was given in the myth of heavenly music. Treatments of the harmony of the soul as a "blending" of opposites must, again, be understood not as the kind of blending of tonal elements into a chord, but rather as a division of a whole into parts in the ratio of two to three, three to four, etc. Boethius' *musica humana* is the result of the common utilization of the idea of harmony in connection with ethics and psychology.[15] Like the music of the spheres, the music of the individual soul (and the music of the harmonious *polis*, for that matter) was to undergo a kind of conceptual dislocation with the development of polyphonic music in the later Middle Ages: the concept of *harmony* as chordal blending would also color the interpretations of Classical psychology by later Medieval and Humanist writers.

Ethos

The link between the music of universal order and the music of human composure lies in the identity of the kind of order imposed in both cases. In a more literally musical sense, the actual effects of musical sounds upon a listener were also elaborated by Greek theory. Now, it is not the Western Classical world alone whose musical systems embody the notion of modal *ethos*. Aside from Judaeo-Arabic modal systems, and

---

[15] Aristotle, *De Anima*, 407b-408a, calls the soul a "kind of harmony" because a harmony is a *krasis kai synthesis*, a "blending and combination" of opposites. The harmonious structure of the World Soul and of the human soul is elaborated in Plato's *Timaeus*.

the Hindu *ragas*, which bear close affinities with Greek music, amazingly intricate sets of correspondences were maintained in ancient Chinese music between pitches, mystical numbers, physical elements, directions, seasons, constellations, divinational trigrams, and hexagrams, etc.[16] But the Greek theory of the character of each of the various musical scales, and of the effects of these inherent characters upon any listener, remained always within the realm of the theory of practical music. As such, it became the interest of all manner of writers dealing with the most concrete musical subjects, and even of those who would tend not to be concerned with Pythagorean and Neoplatonist ideas of world harmony.

Literary history has preserved some familiarity with the names of the Greek scales, such as the Dorian, Lydian, Phrygian, Mixolydian, etc., and of the various moral characteristics conventionally associated with them. These characteristics are perhaps best known through the discussion in Plato's *Republic* of what scales (or keys)[17] ought to be allowed in the Just City. It was specifically in connection with melodies (and hence with scales or melodic species) that the various shades of psychic tension or laxity represented by the different sorts of *ethos* were supposed to operate; the precise explanation for the power of music to produce these effects in its melodic patterns, however, was usually rather obscure. It was felt that, to use a modern analogue, the "sad" and "joyful" characteristics of major and minor keys resided, somehow, in the tonal configurations themselves. One has only to imagine an elaborate set of keys, each with as firmly established a character as

---

[16] See Kazu Nakaseko, "Symbolism in Ancient Chinese Music Theory," *Journal of Musical Theory*, I (1957), pp. 147-180. Also see Curt Sachs, *The Rise of Music in the Ancient World*, pp. 105-113, 172-183.

[17] In this brief discussion, I have not differentiated between the *harmoniai* and the *tonoi* or transposing scales. For a clear exposition of the structure of the Greek modal system, see Sachs, *The Rise of Music in the Ancient World*, pp. 216-238. Gustave Reese, *Music in the Middle Ages* (New York, 1940), pp. 11-44, also provides an excellent discussion of this and other such questions; considerably dated is the treatment of Henry S. Macran in his edition of *The Harmonics of Aristoxenus* (Oxford, 1902), pp. 1-85.

those of major and minor scales in Romantic music, in order to understand the complete certainty of Ancient writers with respect to the modal *ethea*.

The reason for the association of an attitude with a musical pattern, however, would seem to be no great mystery. Let us examine for a moment the Dorian scale, whose character was "manly" or "calm and grave" or sometimes "warlike, but not frenzied." Musically speaking, the so-called Dorian tetrachord upon which the scale is based was an historically important one and retained in Attic times in a chauvinistically tinged name. It lay at the center of the fully developed greater perfect system, and its specific tonal center coincided with that of the system itself (in it, the thetic and dynamic *mese* were identical). We may also assume that the texts sung to it, and the ceremonies and occasions upon which it was employed, all contributed to its ethical aura. To pursue a modern analogy, we might propound a fictional situation for nineteenth-century America in which all music was extremely formalized and regimented. Let us assume that only a few keys are in use, namely, C major, F major, and B-flat minor. Let us also imagine that all musical compositions were of one of three types: either military marches and patriotic songs accompanied by brass bands; or homely, sentimental songs to be accompanied by a guitar, banjo, or some other plucked string; or thick, impassioned string quartets without texts at all, originally composed and usually played by foreign musicians with unpronounceable names. If these three sorts of composition were to be invariably written in C major, F major, and B-flat minor respectively, some sense of character might easily arise for these keys. The first, or "American," key would have the advantages of "simplicity and straightforwardness" (we must put aside here the problem of transposing brasses), in having no sharps or flats in its signature, and in being somehow appropriate for patriotic activities and sentiments. The second key would be "milder, higher and thinner" than the first, and its *ethos* (might it be called the "home" or "mountain" mode?)

would be more "warm," "relaxed," and "fond." The third key, on the other hand, would be "wild and irrational," having a key signature cluttered with flats, no text upon which to depend for ethical clarification, a generally suspicious foreign air, etc. (it might be called the "barbarous" mode). If this situation sounds strained and caricatured, it is really only a dramatically illuminated representation of the Dorian, Lydian, and Phrygian scales of the Greeks.[18]

Central to the notion of *ethos*, however, and as can be seen in the last key in our fictitious model, is the whole problem of text and melody. There was, by and large, a suspicious attitude toward textless, purely instrumental music on the part of Greek thinkers. While it was granted that *ethos* was a property of scales and melodies written in those scales (and not of the consonances, nor of the texts accompanying the melodies),[19] it was nevertheless made quite clear that *rational* music needed the infusion of the tone by the word for its effects. Aristotle may be attempting to gloss over the need for a text here in his distinction in *De Anima* between two sorts of tone-producing vibrating air-columns: those possessing souls (such as human windpipes), and those without (such as wind instruments, etc.).[20] But it was primarily language that was of importance in this connection (Aristotle's "rational" sound-producers, having souls, could also produce speech). One of the fundamental reasons for the disapproval of the music of the *aulos* or oboe involved the fact that the performer thereon cannot sing while he is playing, as in the case of the lyre, *kithara*, or other stringed instrument.

It is instrumental music, devoid of words, that is the model of "pure" music for the nineteenth- and twentieth-century listener, but it is only since the Renaissance that instruments

[18] For other discussions of the troublesome problem of *ethos*, see Reese, *op.cit.*, pp. 44-50; also, Sachs, *The Rise of Music*, pp. 248-252.

[19] The pseudo-Aristotelian *Problems*, XIX, 27, treats of this in some detail. Also see Egon Wellesz, *A History of Byzantine Music and Hymnography* (Oxford, 1949), pp. 44-52.

[20] *De Anima*, 407b-408a.

have developed anything like their modern roles. In Classical antiquity, the task of the instrument was to accompany by doubling (or at best, heterophonically embroidering upon) the vocal line.[21] Distinctions between winds and strings were made by philosophers on many bases, however, of which the ability to frame a singer's text was only one. The myth of Marsyas tells how the goddess Athena picked up an *aulos*, blew upon it, happened to catch sight of the dreadful grimace into which the exigencies of the embouchure had twisted her face, and cast the instrument aside as being unfit for dignified use. Marsyas, who picked it up, was later flayed by Apollo, lord of the lyre, for his insolence and disobedience. The legend of Midas and his unwise choice of the Panic wind music over the sublime Apollonian string-produced sounds is a similar case in point. In general, the wind was deemed inferior to the string because of difficulties that attended its proper tuning (boring properly placed stopping holes in a conically pierced wind is always difficult). The well-tuned string was not only the Pythagorean model of the harmoniously proportioned sound producer, but the problems occasioned by various tunings of the lyre formed the basis of the whole rationalized musical system in Attic times and after, and of the notational conventions as well.

The polarity of string and wind, then, bore a long tradition of association with the antitheses of reason and uncontrolled passion.[22] Textless music, itself associated with wind instruments rather than with strings, constantly risked disapproval from technical and philosophical writers, and in general it was song that remained the pure type or model "music" in Classical times. We must thus remember that, all theoretical disquisitions to the contrary, the whole notion of musical effect is intimately involved with the notion of the sense of a text,

[21] See Sachs, *The Rise of Music*, pp. 256-258.
[22] See Kathleen Schlesinger, *The Greek Aulos* (London, 1939), pp. 57-62. For a suggestion about the role of the *aulos* in the development of *ethos*, see pp. 135-137. Aristotle, *Politics*, 1342b, remarks on the close connection between that instrument and the Phrygian tonality.

and, ultimately, of the meaning of words. There is thus no modern post-Romantic problem, in the case of Classical music, of the substitution of musical "meaning" for that of language, and no concomitant mystique about the "musical" power of "poetic language." The one notable exception to this may have been the widespread ancient belief in the curative powers of music, where only the soothing, healing effects of certain modes (often the lower pitched, "relaxed" scales were thus employed), completely independent of any sung text, were held to have therapeutic value.[23] But this belief in music's healing powers remains, on the whole, a distinct body of doctrine during the Classical period, and becomes associated with a general ideology of music and the human soul only in the Christian Middle Ages, when the ancient myths are accommodated to such Biblical events as David's soothing of Saul's madness, and when therapy can be considered, figuratively, as salvation.

Paideia

A third distinct branch of Greek musical speculation, and a most important one for the history of the later perpetuation of musical mythology, is the one which concerns the role of music in education. There are elaborate discussions of this question in Plato's *Republic* and in Book VIII of Aristotle's *Politics*; in the latter, music is spoken of as possessing the differing functions of education, intellectual enjoyment and general amusement, and finally, purification (*katharsis*).[24] Aristotle is in general more permissive about musical forms and types than is Plato, who sought to legislate the role of music in the State because of its exemplary and persuasive powers. Music for Plato, aside from its engagement of Pythagorean harmonies uniting world and individual souls, is a

---

[23] An excellent and compendious discussion of this is to be found in Bruno Meinecke, "Music and Medicine in Classical Antiquity," in *Music and Medicine*, ed. Dorothy M. Schullian and Max Schoen (New York, 1948), pp. 47-95.

[24] Aristotle, *Politics*, 1339b-1342b.

model discipline for study, as well as a useful and necessary one. Socrates' reason for banishing all but the Dorian and Phrygian tonalities from his City (the latter being retained as a warlike and military key, rather than, as Aristotle corrects him, more properly a frenzied one) ultimately depends on a notion that connects changes and degenerations of musical styles with the decay of the State itself. Myths such as that concerning the punishment of the Spartan musician and lyric poet Terpander for his addition of extra strings to the prescribed four of the traditional lyre are stories, really, of more general rebellion.

We might observe a general tendency in Western history in which ignorance of the musical practices of a past age leads to the enrichment rather than the impoverishment of the *musica speculativa* of a later one. It is certainly true that Renaissance writers, knowing next to nothing of Classical practical music, and confronting the discussions of music in education so common in ancient writers, seized upon judgments and directives from Plato and Aristotle and ruthlessly applied them, out of any proper context, to problems of musical controversy of their own age. Plato's prohibition of certain keys often gave a *carte blanche*, for example, to the complete denigration of music in any form, just as his remarks on the necessity of a musical education were employed to bolster the defenses of music against just such attackers. It is only in more considered treatments of music by Renaissance educationists and courtesy writers that we find any attempt to evaluate the relative natures of music's social and intellectual significance in both ancient and contemporary worlds.

The Survival of Classic Doctrine

The transmission of scraps of ancient musical theory by Boethius, Cassiodorus, Isidore of Seville, and other writers provided the Medieval world with the basis for a rapidly proliferating body of *musica speculativa*. Radical changes in

actual musical practice during the first millennium of the
Christian era began to lay the groundwork for the eventual
development of the full-blown polyphony that would come
to characterize Western music. Concepts and terms that had
been retained since the late Classical period either acquired
confusing new meanings or lapsed into misunderstood use.
The names of the Greek *harmoniai*, for example, became
transferred to the tones or "modes" of Gregorian chant in such
a confusing way that Renaissance and post-Renaissance musicians would call "Phrygian" the scale produced by running
from *E* to *e* on the diatonic keyboard, for example, while it
was that same scale which designated the Dorian tonality for
the Greeks. The "rhythmic modes" of twelfth-century polyphony took their names from the feet of Classical metrics
(iambic, trochaic, dactylic, etc.). Most important of all, the
consonant intervals of Greek harmonic theory were gradually
reinterpreted in terms of the simultaneously sounded, chordal
intervals of a polyphonic harmonic system. The very word
"harmony" began to change its meaning, and although the
change was an extremely subtle one, it allowed for great
changes in the notion of *harmonia mundi*, for example. It is,
I think, safe to suggest that writers of the twelfth century
and thereafter, confronting the image of the music of the
spheres, would "hear" it as actual polyphony. As contrapuntal
styles grow more complex and characteristic, even a particular
set of musical conventions may have been called to mind.
Surely a "harmony of the spheres," with each angel-mounted
sphere producing its own part in a heavenly consort, becomes
more plausible, even to the untrained musical experience, with
vocal polyphony as a model for all music.

An amusing instance, actually, of an overly literal interpretation of the avowedly metaphorical music of the spheres is a
rather well-known one of Johannes Kepler, in the early seventeenth century. The notion of an actually audible music, so
roundly pooh-poohed by Aristotle, continued to survive in a
figurative role, whether as an inaudible, ideal harmony (in

the most general sense), or as an ancient error, committed not in total darkness.[25] Even figuratively considered, it was a notion supportable by the scheme of Ptolemaic cosmology. But with the rise of the new astronomy of Copernicus, Galileo, and Kepler, the very notion of a set of geocentric spheres, bearing along with them the heavenly bodies and all participating in one vast, harmonious dance, vanished once and for all. Yet the old myth and, particularly, the literally musical interpretation of the idea of abstract harmony, remained extremely strong. Thus Kepler, in his *Harmonices Mundi*, published in Linz in 1619, concluded his extremely Pythagorean discussion of mathematics and world order (including the geometric "harmonies" of the regular polygons and solids, the psychology and metaphysics of acoustical harmony, etc.) with a remarkable version of the old story.

After having completely dismissed not only the actuality of the heavenly spheres but the very circularity of the planetary orbits (his great contributions to astronomy lay in this latter demonstration), Kepler nevertheless went on to prove that there was a harmony to the cosmos. If the Ptolemaic system's demise no longer allowed the tones generated by the planets to be attributed to the ratios of the diameters of their orbits (these having been shown by Kepler to be elliptical), God had nevertheless seen fit, Kepler insisted, to arrange for a heavenly music, inaudible though it might be. Therefore, he argued, if one plots an average angular velocity for each planet, and then works out ratios of these to each other, one can discover that each planet does indeed produce music. Far from being simply a tone, as in the older theory, Kepler's heavenly bodies each produced a little melodic fragment. And,

[25] See the first part of the article by Eric Werner and Isaiah Sonne, "The Philosophy and Theory of Music in Judaeo-Arabic Literature," *Hebrew Union College Annual*, XVI (1941), pp. 288-292. For the survival of the notion in the sixteenth century, see, for example, Montaigne's "Of Custome" in Florio's translation of the *Essayes* (1603), I, 22, in the reprint of the Tudor Translations (London, 1908), I, 114. Also, Barnabe Googe's translation of Palingenius' *The Zodiacke of Life* (1576), pp. 212-213.

finally, he argued that there was no real harmony without an agreement between differing parts; he arranged to show that these fragments could be woven together in six-part modal counterpoint (Venus proved a disrupting influence and a dissonant one, when employed in the same texture as the earth). His comments indicate how completely he accepted the notion that the sixteenth-century polyphonic style of his younger days *was* harmony, pure and simple:

"Accordingly the movements of the heavens are nothing except a certain everlasting polyphony (intelligible, not audible) with dissonant tunings, like certain syncopations or cadences (wherewith men imitate these natural dissonances), which tends towards fixed and prescribed clauses—the single clauses having six terms (like voices)—and which marks out and distinguishes the immensity of time with those notes. Hence it is no longer a surprise that man, the ape of his Creator, should finally have discovered the art of singing polyphonically (per concentum), which was unknown to the ancients, namely in order that he might play the everlastingness of all created time in some short part of an hour by means of an artistic concord of many voices and that he might to some extent taste the satisfaction of God the Workman with his own works, in that very sweet source of delight elicited from this music which imitates God."[26]

The *polyphonic interpretation* of the idea of abstract harmony, then, survived long after the original musical notion of proportion had been lost. It was probably only in the rediscovery of the proportions which generated the primary consonances by Renaissance architects that the notion of strictly proportional harmony maintained itself. The musical consonances, interpreted in the old Pythagorean way as intervals produced by stopping the monochord, played an important role in sixteenth-century architectural theory and practice, as

[26] Johannes Kepler, *Harmonices Mundi*, v, vii, tr. Charles Glenn Wallis, in *Great Books of the Western World* (Chicago, 1952), XVI, 1048. See E. A. Burtt, *The Metaphysical Foundations of Modern Science* (New York, 1954), pp. 52-71.

Rudolf Wittkower has so elegantly demonstrated.[27] But throughout the Middle Ages, speculative writers on all manner of subjects, and particularly theologians, could employ the figurative notion of *harmonia mundi*, embellishing the abstract idea with all sorts of literally musical correspondences, drawn either from the bits of Classical theory transmitted by Boethius or from the musical theory of their own day. This tradition extends even into the late Renaissance, when Classical models for speculation on many subjects were utterly commonplace and even outmoded.

Thus, while John Scotus Erigena can propound a complicated theological dialectic of harmony and discord, at times reversing the natural abstract significance of the musical notions,[28] Jean Bodin in the late sixteenth century can discuss at great length the harmonic proportions that govern the good commonwealth, reinforcing his conclusions about the harmonious music of monarchy with comparisons of classes and levels of society to musical parts in a polyphonic texture.[29] But despite the wide range of musical speculation in the Medieval period, despite the survival in many weird and adapted forms of elements of the musical theories of Antiquity, it was only in the fifteenth century that the scattered and usually separated parts of *musica speculativa* began to come together in one more or less organic body of theory. It seems to have been Marsilio Ficino who for the first time brought together cosmological harmonic theories, Greek doctrines of *ethos*, later Neoplatonist psychology and metaphysics,

[27] Rudolf Wittkower, *Architectural Principles in the Age of Humanism*, second edition (London, 1952), pp. 103-135. Otto von Simson, in *The Gothic Cathedral* (New York, 1956), xx n., 21-58 and *passim*, attempts to demonstrate the prior use of the musical consonances in Medieval architectural proportions.

[28] See J. Handschin, "Die Musikanschauang des Johan Scotus Erigena," *Deutsche Vierteljahrsschrift fur Literaturwissenschaft und Geistesgeschichte*, v (1927), II, 316-341.

[29] Jean Bodin, *The Six Bookes of a Commonweale*, tr. Richard Knolles (London, 1606), pp. 454-457. Marin Mersenne in *Harmonie Universelle* (Paris, 1636), III, viii, Prop. x, expounds this musical theory of the state at greater length, developing latent implications in some of Bodin's remarks.

and conclusions drawn not only from some knowledge of Classic music from ancient writers but from contemporary practical music as well. He was the first of a succession of comprehensive, almost encyclopedic musical theorists, such as Gioseffe Zarlino and Marin Mersenne (in the following century), to try to present as complete and fully rationalized as possible an account of the power of music to affect a listener. It is perhaps the unification of theories of *ethos* and of cosmological harmony, the comprehensive treatment of the connection between Boethius' *musica mundana* and *musica humana*, that, as one commentator has suggested,[30] is the most significant accomplishment of Ficino's comments on musical subjects. It is surely true that in such a combined view we can see an *account*, an *explanation* in the empirical sense, in its germinal form; even though the account given by Ficino is necessarily a metaphysical one, it is nevertheless cognizant of acoustical and musical fact, and aims at consistency and completeness.

It was with the revival of Classical learning that a fully developed musical ideology finally emerged. The use of musical concepts and figures derived therefrom in the Christian Middle Ages had by and large operated in brilliant flashes. A numerological symbol, a particular interpretation of harmonic unity, a sustained conceit here and there, illuminated points of metaphysical and cosmological doctrine. It is not surprising that the use of such figures flourished among mystical writers, in particular. Traditional word-plays helped to sustain and proliferate such images: a pun on *chorda* ("string") and *cor, cordis* ("heart"), possibly first introduced by Cassiodorus, became so deeply imbedded in habitual thinking that the very origins of the word "concord" (in the latter, rather than in the former of the pair of words) often even today are mistaken for being musical.[31]

But Renaissance thinkers united many themes: cosmology,

[30] See D. P. Walker, "Ficino's *Spiritus* and Music," *Annales Musicologiques*, I (1953), pp. 131-150.

[31] See Leo Spitzer, "Classical and Christian Ideas of World Harmony," *Traditio*, II (1944), 435-445.

physiology (correspondences between elements, humors, and musical modes were revived and made much of, as were those between the systole and diastole of the human heartbeat and the alternation of upbeat and downbeat in musical and prosodic rhythm), lore concerning the fabled effects of ancient music and myths of its heroes, old doctrines of music's powers of physical and psychic therapy, physical fact (the phenomenon of sympathetic vibration in two perfectly attuned strings became a commonplace image for the resonances of spiritual sympathy), and whatever could be accommodated of the practical music of the contemporary scene. Musical theorists in the proper sense employed this body of *musica speculativa* for polemical or laudatory purposes more than in technical exposition. But as a subject of human knowledge, embraced by both Classic and Christian world views, the musical ideology of the Humanist epoch was as current among non-musical thinkers and writers as among technical theorists.

To accommodate the myths and abstract schemes of *musica speculativa* to what was often the inflexible reality of practice, Renaissance musicians sought consciously to revolutionize that practice so as to make it conform more with Neoclassical ideals. But it is important to remember that much of the material of speculative music was actually much more *literary* than musical even throughout the Middle Ages; and this body of literary material created all the more conceptual and semantic confusion as it was more strongly believed.

The Musical Instrument in Image and Practice

Perhaps in no area of musical concern does the literary ideal confront the hard actuality of practice as in the case of instruments. Especially during the Renaissance, when instrumental music *per se* was beginning to emerge from its subservient role as a substitute or doubling voice in vocal polyphony, attempts to accommodate received doctrine concerning the use and nature of musical instruments to the instruments actually known and used in the music of the sixteenth century were widespread. Metaphors from Christian theologians, Classical attitudes toward the wind and stringed instruments, emblematic uses of musical instruments in the graphic arts—all put on contemporary dress; and musical instruments of the Renaissance become figuratively associated with those of Biblical times or Greek Antiquity.

By the simplest metonymy, a musical instrument can be made to stand for the music itself which is produced upon it, and we have already remarked that the wind and string instruments came to represent for Greek writers two different musical traditions. Such strict figurative uses of the different species of instruments were by no means invariable, however. It was by and large most common to allow the strings to represent abstract "harmony" and "order" by typifying musical harmoniousness and ordered tuning. Thus the Platonic notion of the World-Soul (as well as the individual psyche) considered as a tuning, or *harmonia*, finds figurative expression in the image of the World-Lyre, or the stringed instrument of the human soul. One seldom sees, during the Medieval or Renaissance periods, any such figure employing a wind or percussive instrument (the eventual metaphorical treatment of the organ becomes an exception, particularly in the seventeenth century). But, on the other hand, it is frequent to discover Roman or Medieval poets using the instruments' names indiscriminately;[32] and it is only in certain contexts that particular instruments retain or develop symbolic values.

The use of musical instruments for poetic imagery thus has a long history, and popular figurative associations of certain instruments with others, with certain musical styles, activities, states of feeling, and abstract notions tend to reinforce the

---

[32] See, for example, Horace, *Carmina* I, 12 *"Quem virum aut heroa lyra vel acri tibia sumis celebrare, Clio?"* but see also Epodes, 9, ll. 1-6, where there may be some irony expressed in the *"sonante mixtum tibiis carmen lyra, hac Dorium, illis Barbarum"*: the modes of peace and war, friend and enemy combine uneasily, even after a great victory.

effectiveness of instrumental metaphors in sixteenth-century verse and prose alike. The translation of Classical instruments and theories about them into strictly contemporary terms was a convention of Renaissance thought; and while one could only condemn any nineteenth- or twentieth-century translator who rendered "lute" for the Greek *kithara* or *lyra* (alas, a distressingly common practice, apparently based on the notion that any obsolete instrument is the equivalent of any other), one would have to treat the matter very differently in the case of an earlier translation. The "lute-harp-lyre" constellation, uniting the contemporary string instrument with those of David and Orpheus, for example, represents no capricious substitution of one term for another. Rather, it depends upon a consistent habit of figurative association of the instruments and what they stand for.

For example, we might turn for a moment to a popular sixteenth-century version of an ancient author's discussion of the Greek wind-string dichotomy, included in the biography of a popular historical figure. Thomas North's translation of Plutarch (1579) renders a particular passage from the life of Alcibiades as follows: "Afterwards when he was put to schoole to learne, . . . he disdained to learne to playe of the flute or recorder: saying, that it was no gentlemanly qualitie. For, sayed he, to playe on the vyoll with a sticke, doth not alter mans favour, nor disgraceth any gentleman: but otherwise, to playe on the flute, his countenaunce altereth and chaungeth so ofte, that his familliar friends can scant knowe him. Moreover, the harpe or vyoll doth not let him that playeth on them, from speaking, or singing as he playeth: where he that playeth on the flute, holdeth his mouth so harde to it, that it taketh not only his wordes from him, but his voyce."[33] Here, *lyra* ("lyre") is rendered as "vyoll" (and

<hr>

[33] Plutarch, "Life of Alcibiades," from *Lives, Englished by Thomas North* (1579), reprinted in the Tudor Translations (London, 1895), VIII, 91-92. Plutarch goes on to blame on Alcibiades' objections "partely in sporte, and partely in good earnest," the fact that "teaching to playe of the flute

plektron as "stick"); on another occasion, "harpe" is used. The almost universal translation "flute" for the oboe-like *aulos* is of less interest or significance. What is important is that in this passage, representing a typical storehouse of general learned knowledge of an element of ancient musical doctrine, the contemporization of the instrumental terms is almost automatic. Most often, the sixteenth-century translated version of the lyre or *kithara* (the smaller and larger forms of what is essentially the same instrument) will be the lute, the most important stringed instrument of the Renaissance. The lute was originally an Arabic importation into Europe; the fifteenth century saw its development along more characteristically Western lines and the eventual emergence of a standard tuning and stringing. In the following century, the lute's importance can be partially measured by the fact that it alone (aside from the keyboard instruments) possessed a unique kind of notational system (the various tablatures), while other instruments were simply employed at will to play any unspecified vocal parts that might fall within their ranges.

The significance of the lute as a Renaissance lyre, as opposed to the use of the harp in the same function, is an interesting question of iconography whose solution must depend upon further researches. In general, it might be remarked that the respective Biblical and Classical associations of the two instruments seem to be preserved quite clearly in sixteenth-century translation and graphic representation. A metonymic use of the lute (for the lyre) to represent poetry as well as music is a familiar one; occasionally a harp will be used in a similar context to refer to a religious muse.[34] In England, in particular, there were specific regional associations for the bardic harp, which by the sixteenth century had already undergone considerable decline as a courtly and folk instrument. It was acknowledged to be an instrument common to Scotland,

---

was put out of the number of honest and liberall exercises, and the flute it selfe was thought a vile instrument, and of no reputation" (p. 92).

[34] See below, Chapter III, pp. 140-141.

Ireland, and Wales;[35] in the latter case, along with the *crwth* or *crowd*, it was occasionally mentioned in poetry in order to evoke the venerable Welsh origins of the paternal side of the Tudor line.[36]

A most instructive case of the figurative use of lute and harp in sixteenth-century popular imagery involves one more link in the speculative chain connecting *musica mundana* and *musica humana*. An intermediary stage between microcosm and macrocosm, between men, each "a little world, made cunningly" and the widest universe of which they could conceive, was that of the body politic. The political aspects of Renaissance musical speculation involved certain elements of ancient political thought. Among these were the State treated as a harmonious organism (as we saw above in the case of Jean Bodin), music itself, in a political context, treated as if it were political or social ideology to be carefully controlled (as in Plato's ideal city), or else a crucial discipline in the training of citizens (Aristotle). But it is more than just a conventional symbolic reference to abstract harmony that is intended by the political use of the lute as a sixteenth-century image. An important source of both visual and poetic imagery is the first of the Renaissance emblem books, Andrea Alciati's *Emblemata* (first published 1531); it includes in all of its editions the picture of a lute, represented in an engraving as lying on a bed or couch (in later editions, with an open book of lute-music beside it). The emblem's motto proclaims it to be a figure of Alliance (*Foedera*), and an additional caption classifies the whole emblem under "*Fides,*" "trust." The Latin verses below the *impresa* are inscribed to the Duke of Tuscany, who, it is hoped, will unite all of Italy. In them, the lute is referred to as a "*cythara,*" and the Duke is begged to accept

[35] See John Selden's gloss on Michael Drayton, *Poly-Olbion*, in *Works*, ed. J. W. Hebel (Oxford, 1933), IV, 121. The whole description of the musical contention between England and Wales is of great interest, particularly for its lists of instruments and for its comparison of instrumental techniques to modes of versification. See *Works*, IV, 78.

[36] See Spenser, "Epithalamion," ll. 129-147, and below, Chapter III, note 93.

it as a gift when "*nova cum sociis foedera inire paras*" ("ready to enter into a new treaty with his allies"). It continues:

> *Difficile est, nisi docto homini, tot tendere chordas,*
> *Unaque; si fuerit non bene tenta fides,*
> *Ruptave (quod facile est) perit omnis gratia conchae.*
> *Illeque praecellens cantus, ineptus erit.*[37]

(It is difficult, except for a learned man, to attune so many strings; and if one string be not well tuned, or broken [which is easy,] all grace of the shell is destroyed, and that excellent music will be weak.)

The political parable here is obvious, and the implicit pun in the very notion of "concord" is somehow at work. Alciati's poem concludes with a repetition of a warning already made: "*At si aliquis desciscat (uti plerunque videmus) / In nihilum illa omnis solvitur harmonia*" ("But if anyone breaks away [as we often observe], all that harmony falls apart into nothing").

The emblem might well be taken for no more than a figurative treatment of *concord* in general (or more specifically, political treaties); but in the Hellenistic (?) *Hieroglyphics* of "Horapollo" (first published in 1505), the lyre is treated as the symbol of a political leader, a man who "binds together and unites his fellows," with the added explanation that "the lyre preserves the unity of its sounds."[38] While Alciati makes specific use of a polyphonically oriented notion of "harmony" or "concord" (a quasi-chordal "harmony" is produced by all the strings of the instrument, provided it is in tune), it seems clear that the older source employs a more extended metaphor which involves the rational and well-tuned associations of the lyre in antiquity. Alciati himself, incidentally, uses an implied pun on *fides* ("trust") and *fides* ("stringed instrument"), a connection retained in the emblem

---

[37] D. A. Alciati, *Emblemata* (Lyons, 1551), sig. A8v.
[38] *The Hieroglyphics of Horapollo*, tr. George Boas (New York, 1950), p. 111.

literature of the following centuries,[39] and which attains the currency, if not the importance, of the other pun expounded in such devices as *"Chorda trahit corda,"* and in the very notion of heart-strings.[40]

To complete the picture, it should be observed that Alciati's emblem book, which went through 175 editions between 1531 and 1750 (of which 125 were before 1600,[41] influenced directly and indirectly, many other such books in many other languages. In one of the most beautiful of the English emblem books, an interesting version of Alciati's conceit appears; Henry Peacham's *Minerva Brittana* (1612) contains a cut of an Irish harp, labelled in Latin "The Irish Republic to King James." Beneath it are the following lines:

> While I lay bathed in my native blood,
> And yielded nought save harsh & hellish soundes:
> And save from Heauen, I had no hope of good,
> Thou pittiedst (Dread Soveraigne) my woundes,
>   Repairdst my ruine, and with Ivorie key,
>   Didst tune my stringes, that slackt or broken lay.
>
> Now, since I breathed by the Royall hand,
> And found my concord, by so smooth a tuch,
> I giue the world abroade to vnderstand
> Ne'er was the musick of old Orpheus such,

---

[39] See for example Mario Praz, *Studies in Seventeenth Century Imagery* (London, 1939), I, 138; also. Joannes Michael van der Kelten's iconographical handbook, *Apelles Symbolicus* (Amsterdam, 1699), pp. 422-432, for a summary of emblems using stringed instruments; also, Henricus Oracus, *Viridarium Hieroglyphico-Morale* (Frankfort, 1619), sig. C4v; also Juan de Boria, *Emblemata Moralia* (Berlin, 1697), pp. 182-183. An amusing sentimental and trivialized version of Alciati's lute device may be seen in the anonymous *Emblems for the Improvement and Entertainment of Youth* (London, 1769), p. 11, where the lute lying on a book of music is called an emblem of "True Alliance; teaching us to make proper Associations with such as are agreable to our Humour, Ways and Manners; by whom we may profit, and receive Benefit."

[40] *Apelles Symbolicus*, p. 427.

[41] See the appendices to Henry Green, *Andrea Alciati and his Books of Emblems* (London, 1872).

> As that I make, by meane (Deare Lord) of thee,
> From discord drawne, to sweetest vnitie.[42]

Thus the instrument of state may be seen to take on a local character: the harp is at once the spirit of Ireland and the tuneable string instrument of Alciati and the ancient writers.

The correspondences and divergences between Classical and Renaissance instruments were amazingly fertile in the way of producing poetic and graphic imagery, but it must be remembered that such images depended for their effect upon a more general context of received ideas about music, both speculative and practical. Lately we have come to think of imagery as the most important element of the poetry of the sixteenth and seventeenth centuries; and literary criticism today, more than ever before, tends to trace the history of that poetry along lines of development of the increasing structural and functional complexity of its imagery. Even within the sixteenth century itself, a gradual change may be observed from the unadorned poetry of exposition (even in the case of lyrics), through the use of imagery to adorn statement, to the eventual usurpation of the role of exposition and statement by the imagery itself at the beginning of the following century. Musical ideas and images, then, may be seen to enter the corpus of narrative, reflective, lyric, and dramatic poetry in many ways; but whether as the subject of discourse, praise, blame, or explication, on the one hand, or as the material for amplifying imagery on the other, both speculative and practical music were

---

[42] Henry Peacham, *Minerva Brittana* (London, 1612), p. 45; also reproduced as Plate v in *The Mirrour of Maiestie*, ed. Henry Green and James Croston (London, 1870). The first stanza of the motto seems to show the influence of an emblem labelled *Industria Naturam Corrigit*, from Geoffrey Whitney's influential *A Choice of Emblemes* (Leyden, 1586), sig. M2v, which employs the image of repairing a broken lute. Also, cf. emblems 18 and 20 from *The Mirrour of Maiestie*, edition of 1618, sigs. F2 and F4. Aside from the actual iconography of instruments in graphic art, popular notions of musical lore were transmitted through encyclopedias and books of curiosities. A good example of this kind of material may be seen in the little maxims about music and the subsequent mythological and historical truisms found in Francis Meres' *Palladis Tamia* (London, 1598), sigs. Oo7v-Oo8v.

likely to be confused, compared, and contrasted against a constantly deepening background of received ideas about the nature and effects of musical sound.

A musical ideology, a set of almost automatic responses to questions about the ability of music to arouse feelings in a listener, seldom operates in a vacuum. In the foregoing remarks we have seen some of the ways in which the musical ideology of the Middle Ages and Renaissance was shaped by the operation of (practical) musical actualities upon historic speculative materials. But literary history constantly shows us how poetry always makes its own demands upon ideas and climates of thought. The following chapters, consequently, will attempt to follow the development of music's role in English poetry, both as subject matter and as image, with a view toward showing the changing nature of the relationship between poetry and doctrine in regard not only to the facts and mythology of music but with respect to some of the more general questions of metaphysics, cosmology, and psychology which the broad and rich area of speculative music so generously embraced.

CHAPTER III · "THE DIAPASON CLOSING FULL IN MAN": THE MUSICAL SUBJECT IN HUMANIST POETRY

From Harmony to Harmony
Through all the Compass of the Notes
it ran,
The Diapason closing full in Man.

Music as Subject: Toward Chaucer

THE distinction between speculative and practical music is an extremely important one for any consideration of the history of music as a subject matter for English poetry. In the first place, one must consider the fact that so little either of the standard encyclopedic treatment of *musica speculativa* or of "practical theory" (treatises on notation, rules of composition, etc., rather than compilations of philosophy and lore) appeared in the vernacular before the sixteenth century. Occasional translations of systematic treatments of music from an overall speculative point of view were usually like that contained in Trevisa's fourteenth-century Englishing of Bartholomaeus Anglicus' *De Proprietatibus Rerum*; this is little more than a few sections from Boethius and Isidore of Seville, and the treatment of musical instruments is only a guide to the Latin names for instruments of Antiquity, and has no bearing on the practical music of the thirteenth and fourteenth centuries.[1] The earliest English

---

[1] This translation was first printed by Wynken de Worde in 1496. Book XIX, Cap. 130ff., treats of music, starting out with the Boethian division, then the tripartite division into *Armonica*, *Rithmica*, and *Metrica* from Cassiodorus and Isidore, and from the latter remarks on the kinds of voices

works on what we would today call musical theory proper, notwithstanding the great contribution of English writers to Medieval musical theory in Latin, are three fifteenth-century treatises on the improvisation of the so-called *English discant*.[2] The vocabularies relating to contemporary practical music, on the one hand, and to the composite learning of *musica speculativa*, on the other, remained quite distinct. For a long time they lay as far apart as the gulf between Latin and English could keep them.

In the second place, the forms of vernacular poetry, up until the time of Chaucer, did not tend to adapt themselves to either speculative music, which would by and large have been treated as one of the liberal arts, or actual musical phenomena, more or less naturalistically represented. Lyric, narrative, and didactic verse, whether written on Continental models or evolving more indigenously, allowed for little exposition of an academic discipline whose discussion was confined to treatises written in the learned language. Narrative poetry in the tradition of metrical romance turned no attention to the careful description of contemporary courtly or peasant life, and topical verse was confined for the most part to vigorous political polemic. A technical musical vocabulary (or a literary one, for that matter) had been the legacy neither of Anglo-Saxon nor of Norman French. Aside from the liturgical singing, very little is known about the actual music heard

---

and instruments: *Tuba, Buccina, Tibia, Calamo, Cithara* (which is described as if it were a harp, contributing to the literary blurring of all stringed instruments), etc. The information contained therein could have been of no use with respect to practical music to an earnest user of the encyclopedia containing it from the thirteenth century down to the late sixteenth, when Stephen Batman revised it somewhat, although leaving the musical section unchanged save for an added defense of church music (*Batman Upon Bartholome*, London, 1582).

[2] See Sanford B. Meech, "Three Fifteenth-Century English Musical Treatises," *Speculum*, X (1935), pp. 235-269, where they are reprinted and commented upon. Parts of two other treatises are printed by Dr. Burney, *A General History of Music*, ed. Frank Mercer (New York, 1957), I, 692-697. Also see Manfred Bukofzer, *Geschichte des Englischen Diskants und des Fauxbourdons* (Strassburg, 1936), pp. 28-84, 132-160.

in England much before the thirteenth century.[3] But what little information there is remains, like the tantalizing descriptions of early secular and sacred polyphony in Giraldus Cambrensis' *Description of Wales* or of his praises of Irish instrumentalists in the *Topographica Hibernica*,[4] almost exclusively in Latin. Beowulf's recounting to Hygelac of his exploits at Heorot includes the famous mention of the singing at the banquet:

> hwīlum hildedēor   hearpan wynne,
> gomenwudu grētte,   hwīlum gyd āwraec
> sōð ond sārlic, . . .   (ll. 2107-2109)[5]

(sometimes a wild warrior would harp joy,
touch the glee-wood; sometimes would tell a
song true and sorrowful, . . .)

Any descriptions of the "*gyd*," however, are about the import of its text rather than an account of its musical setting. Aside from a number of verbs meaning "to sing," the names of the minstrel's or *scop's* harp, and the like, there are practically no abstract musical terms in the earliest English dialects that might possibly link together the singing of the liturgy and the popular and courtly vocal and instrumental music of the period before 1300.[6]

---

[3] Ernest Walker, *A History of Music in England*, third ed., rev. and enlarged by J. A. Westrup (Oxford, 1952), pp. 1-17.

[4] Giraldus Cambrensis, *Works*, ed. Brewer and Dimock, *Chronicles and Memorials of Gt. Britain and Ireland in the Middle Ages*, No. 21 (London, 1861-1891), V, 153-155; VI, 189-190.

[5] *Beowulf*, ed. F. Klaeber, third ed. (New York, 1950), p. 79.

[6] An eleventh-century glossary printed by R. P. Wulcker and Thomas Wright in their *Anglo-Saxon and Old English Vocabularies*, second ed. (London, 1884), p. 311, is of sufficient interest here to demand quoting in part: "*Fidis: streng; Cithara: hearpe; Citharista: hearpere; . . . Tuba: byma; Tibicen: pipere; Musa: pipe, odde hwistle; Fidicen: fidelere; . . . Cornu: horn; Fistula: hwistle; . . . Mimus, vel scurra: gligman . . . Saltator: hleapere.*" There are a few more names of instruments and their performers. Often the translation is simply a seeming cognate (*Fidicen, Fistula*); often it is quite arbitrary (the *Fides* group). One can see, in the rendering of *Mimus* as *gligman*, the eventual groundwork being laid for the association of all popular musicians with the targets of the worst patristic abuse. There

The earliest English poetry to concern itself with music in any sense, then, may in no way be said to possess a musical ideology at all; it does not, that is, treat of practical music from any particular speculative standpoint nor does it refer to music, in any kind of figurative way, as standing for any other kind of activity or experience. In any case, the distinction between speculative and practical music (itself the kind of systematic, theoretical division marked out by speculation rather than by musical practice) would tend to be maintained, for both the linguistic and literary reasons mentioned above, even without any formal acknowledgment of its existence by the poetry in question. In translations also there is a dearth of musical discussion. It is unfortunate that in Alfred's rendering of Boethius' *Consolatione*, the passage in Book II, Prose 1 that refers to gay and sad modes of music is completely avoided,[7] for a translation of it might throw some valuable light on the extent of a theoretical vocabulary in English at the time. The section of *The Phoenix* (probably ninth century) which is translated from a Latin original contains a relatively elaborate account of the sweetness of the song of that unique bird. The original text, attributed to Lactantius, compares (ll. 45-50) the Phoenix's wonderful warbling with the proper fabled sounds of nightingale and dying swan, on the one hand, and of the Cyllenian lyre and flute, on the other. The Old English version is no mere studious crib, however:

> *Biþ þaes hlēoðres swēg*
> *eallum songcraeftum   swētra and wlitigra*
> *and wynsumra   wrenca gewhylcum.*
> *Ne magon þām breahtme   bȳman nē hornas,*
> *nē hearþan hlyn,   nē haeleþa stefn*

are, of course, no technical terms here, relating to notation of plainsong, etc., nor is there anything connected with the general concerns of speculative music. This list seems to be merely a guide for the translation of Latin texts containing these names of instruments.

[7] The passage mentions Music, a handmaid of Rhetoric, who "*nunc leviores, nunc graviores, modos succinat.*" From *De Consolatione Philosophiae*, ed. H. F. Stewart (Loeb Edition, London, 1946), p. 174.

āenges on eorþan,   nē organan
sweghlēoþres geswin,   nē swanes feðre,
nē āenig þāra drēama   þe Dryhten gescōp
gumum tō glīwe   in þās gēomran woruld.

(ll. 131-139)[8]

(The sound of this song is sweeter and lovelier and
more joyful than any device whatsoever of artful
song. Neither trumpet nor horn may compare with
that call, nor notes of harp, nor singing of any man
on earth, nor sound of the singing of the *organum*,
nor [noise of the beating of] swan's feather, nor any
of the sounds created by the Lord to give men glee
in this miserable world.)

This passage might very well be said to represent the first
example of musical imagery proper in English poetry. Actually, the import of the passage is not that of the one in the
Latin *De Ave Phoenice*; the original is really much more
formulaic and represents merely an epitome of beautiful singing. The comparisons are all stock ones. Behind the Anglo-
Saxon version's praise, however, lies an implicit musical
doctrine which was to become widely circulated in the later
Middle Ages. The Phoenix-Christ is here treated as are other
musical birds (notably the nightingale): the singing is praised
because it is more *naturally* beautiful than any of the music
of human contrivance.[9] Thus here the instruments are mentioned first, followed by the artificial singing of men (I take
the sense of ll. 136-137 to be that the "*organan*" is not an
instrument, but the early parallel polyphony of the liturgy,
described in great detail in the *Musica Enchiriadis*, a late
ninth-century treatise).[10] Only at the very end of his list does

[8] *The Old English Elene, Phoenix and Physiologus*, ed. Albert S. Cook
(New Haven, 1919), p. 52.

[9] See below, Chapter IV, pp. 225-226; also, Chapter IV, notes 100-104.

[10] But see Cook's note, *op.cit.*, p. 110. No editor has yet suggested that
organan is anything but the instrument today known as "organ"; the reading
introduced above, however, has syntax as well as the logic of parallel reference to instruments and singing to recommend it.

the poet remember the examples of swan and nightingale in his Latin original, and even then he is unable, apparently, to bring himself to use the unfamiliar Classic myth of the swan song; instead he employs what appears to have been a poetic commonplace (as can be seen from a riddle about the swan in the *Exeter Book*) concerning the beautiful music of the swan's beating wings, breaking what is otherwise its total silence. The translator's list of instruments may very well have come from a less complete glossary of the type described above (note 6). What is important is that he adapted the original's terms of praise and cast them into the very stuff of his own kind of poetry: the appositive constructions stringing synonyms together, the whole sweep of the verse paragraph leading up to the gloomy Christian moral troped into the original, are the devices of an Anglo-Saxon poet.[11]

Lists of parallel examples, then, worked into an overall pattern contrasting vocal and instrumental music, and all going to show the superiority of the Phoenix's pure natural voice to that of any artificial "wrinkles" or devices of music, may be said to constitute a musical image not provided for in any way in the original Latin. Although the force of the native poetic conventions is unchallenged in the diction, vocabulary, and syntax of these lines, the point of the whole passage does not depend merely on the repetition and decorative accretion. There is a relatively abstract musical proposition being framed which embraces birds' singing, the sounds of ancient instruments that the poet had possibly never heard (*"Tuba,"* rendered *"byman"*), the sound of the harp that he both knew and felt to be poetically conventional as a reference, the probably purely formulaic sound of the swan's wings, and finally, the "newfangled" *organum.* They are all, at any rate, branches of a common, general music. Elsewhere we find many vivid descriptions of harp playing, such as in *The Fates of Men* and

[11] For some general remarks on the *Phoenix* and its relation to the Latin original, see Oliver Farrar Emerson, "Originality in Old English Poetry," *Review of English Studies,* II (1926), pp. 18-31; unfortunately, the lines under consideration are not dealt with there.

The Arts of Men (both in the *Exeter Book*), in which the rapidity of the movements of the harper's hand are brightly figured. The first of these contains an interesting passage with the injunction: *"laet an scralletan   sceacol se þe hleapeþ / naegl neomegende"*[12] (let shrill the leaping plectrum, the singing nail); this suggests either a Classical borrowing (lyres and citharas were so played) or the fact that some instrument other than the *"hearp"* is actually being described. But these descriptions are just like those of any other human activity. They cannot be said to represent either a concept of practical or speculative music in any general sense. The *Phoenix* passage seems to be a sole exception.

The earliest period of Middle English literature presents no startling contrasts with the immediately preceding centuries. Insofar as there is any *genre* description in the verse romances corresponding to the references to details of Old English court life, both observed and conventional, the situation is very much the same with respect to music: names of instruments will be mentioned[13] and the sounds of instruments and human and avian voices will be compared sometimes to the advantage of one, sometimes of the other. For example, the sweet voice of the more hedonistic of the two contenders in the famous *débat* of *The Owl and the Nightingale* is praised by being favorably compared with the sounds of instruments rather than by being said to surpass them. The nightingale's voice is such that

> Bet þuhte þe drem þat he were
> Of harpe & pipe þan he nere:
> Bet þuhte þat heo were ishote
> Of harpe & pipe þan of þrote.
>
> (ll. 21-24)[14]

---

[12] "The Fates of Men," ll. 83-84. Text from *The Exeter Book*, Part II, ed. W. S. Mackie, EETS 194 (London, 1934), p. 30.

[13] Marvin Alpheus Owings, *The Arts in the Middle English Romances* (New York, 1957), pp. 131-133, confines his remarks on music to the rather haphazard and not overly well-informed listing of a number of instruments that appear in the works covered by his study.

[14] *The Owl and the Nightingale*, ed. J. W. H. Atkins (Cambridge, 1922),

Here the "harpe and pipe" are almost formulaic, and no
material from the poet's experience or acquired knowledge of
music or its lore is brought to bear on elaborating the praise
of the bird's singing. An early fourteenth-century text that
one might expect more of in this same regard is that of the
romance of the minstrel *Sir Orfeo*; but here one musical term
(aside from the "melody" introduced in the last line) is
harped on again and again:

> Orfeo mest of ani þyng
> Loved the gle of harping;
> Siker was everi gode harpour
> Of him to have miche honour.
> Him-self he learned for-to harp
> & leyed þer-on his witter scharp;
> He lerned so, þer no-þing was
> A better harpour in no plas.
> In all þe world was no man bore
> þat ones Orfeo sat bifore
> (& he might of his harping here)
> But he schuld þenche þat he were
> In one of þe ioies of Paradis,
> Swiche melody in his harping is.
>
> (ll. 25-38)[15]

There is no transmission of the lore about Orpheus' power
over insensible things; Sir Orfeo is simply a well-born minstrel
of unusual gifts. The great gulf between the hero of this
romance and the Thracian musician can be seen in a later
version of that romance from Shetland, in which the hero
loses even that small connection with his supposed prototype
that the "similarity" between lyre and harp can afford. Here,
he is, quite properly, a Northern piper:

> Dan he took out his pipes to play
> Bit sair his hert wi dol and wae.

"J" text, p. 5. Also see later on, ll. 141-142, p. 15.
[15] *Sir Orfeo*, ed. J. A. Bliss (Oxford, 1954), pp. 4-5.

> And first he played da notes o noy
> An dan he played de notes o joy.
>
> An dan he played de god gabler reel
> Dat meicht ha made a sick hert hale.
>
> (st. 7, 8)[16]

But even here, the alteration of effect described in the difference between the "notes o noy" and "notes o joy" is a far cry from the kind of sparse, redundant description that the same scene receives in the earlier version.

Almost unique for its period is a poem directed to the subject of the study of the Guidonian notation for sacred polyphony, and the rigors thereof when contrasted with the lesser difficulties of popular secular singing. Dating from the early fourteenth century, this set of fifty-two lines in alliterative couplets[17] (the entire text is given in Appendix A) bewails the plight of one Walter who finds it hard to learn to sing at sight ("The song of the cesolfa. dos me syken sare, / And sitte stotiand on a song. a moneth and mare"). He is particularly plagued by the notation:

> Summe notes arn shorte. and somme a long noke,
> Somme kroken a-weyward. als a fleshoke.
> Qwan i kan mi lesson. mi meyster wil i gon,
> That heres me mi *rendre*. he wenes i have wel don:
> Qwat hast thu don, dawn Water. sin saterdai at non?
> Thu holdest nowt a note. by God! in riht ton.
>
> (ll. 11-16)

Walter runs to complain to William, who has been having his own troubles with learning to read liturgical music and who asks

---

[16] Quoted by Bliss, *op.cit.*, p. L, from F. J. Child, *English and Scottish Popular Ballads* (London, 1892), I, 217.

[17] From MS. Arundel. 292, f. 71v. Printed in *Reliquae Antiquae*, ed. Thomas Wright and J. O. Halliwell (London, 1845), I, 291-292. The editors remark that the poem is "Written in a hand of the time of Ed. II." The text may be found in Appendix A, below.

Is it also mikel sorwe. in song so is in salmes?
Ya, bi God! thu reddis. and so is it wel werre.
I solfe and singge after. and is me nevere the nerre;
I horle at the notes. and heve hem al of *herre*:
Alle that me heres. wenes that i erre . . .

(ll. 32-36)

The complaints of both Walter and William are taken up with
details of the names of the tones of the hexachord ("Of bemol
and bequarre. of bothe i was wol bare") and some of the more
difficult leaps from pitch to pitch, as well as problems that
seem to arise in connection with the tone *Fa* (lines 41-44
suggest that William has been having trouble with the interval
of the tritone: "*Mi contra Fa diabolus in musica*," as the verse
about the forbidden interval ran).

But even in this piece of what is really topical satire, the
musical terms are limited to those concerning the Guidonian
notation that came into use in the eleventh century; the tone
and diction of the poem link it to the literature of complaint
against political and sartorial abuses. But there is almost a
kind of delight in the display of the terminology that is used,
and in this, despite the somewhat jocular hostile tone, there is
some similarity to the verses of professional musicians at the
end of the fifteenth century that we shall examine further on.

Music as Subject: Chaucer and After

Up through the middle of the fifteenth century, with a
very few exceptions, the treatment of music in English poetry
remains confined to illustrations and descriptions of practical,
contemporary music-making, almost always from a less privileged, less technical point of view than that of the complaint
discussed above. A common occurrence is a list of instruments
given in description of the actual music occurring in a particular scene of an allegorical narrative in the late fourteenth
century.[18] Treatments of *musica speculativa*, even in English

[18] See John Gower, *Confessio Amantis*, VII, 2676-2680, for instance.

prose, are extremely rare; to those few already mentioned should probably be added only the account of Pythagoras' discovery of the intervals and proportions on the monochord, together with a brief and sketchy exposition thereof, albeit replete with diagrams, in John Trevisa's translation of Higden's *Polychronicon* (finished 1387).[19] The passage also recounts the old legend of how Pythagoras discovered the proportions by listening to the sound of hammers in a blacksmith's shop, after which he constructed a model of the different weights of the hammers in different lengths of vibrating string; then, the text continues, "whan he was konnynge of so grete priuete, he gan to fynde noumbres by þe which sownes accordeþ, and so he spedde to make þe craft of musyk. . . . Tullius . . . spekeþ of hym, and seiþ þat Pictagoras scoleres couþe brynge here mynde out of strif of þowȝtes to reste, by song and soun of strenges."[20] After this there follow a few more citations of the curative power of Pythagorean music and, finally, the little treatise on the proportions. But this account remains isolated, in Higden's comprehensive history of the world, from anything else about theoretical or actual music.

The most scrupulous reporter of different sorts of musical practice in his own day was Chaucer. Not only are there countless allusions to the actual singing and playing of both sacred and secular music by the Canterbury Pilgrims and the characters that populate the world of the stories that they tell; Clair C. Olson pointed out some years ago that throughout the corpus of Chaucer's work there were many comparisons and figures of speech based on musical examples,[21] although often these are of so general or homely a nature as to seem trivial when adduced as examples of the author's knowledge

[19] *Polychronicon Ranulphi Higden Monachi Cestrensis*, ed. Joseph R. Lumby (London, Oxford, Cambridge, Edinburgh and Dublin, 1871), The Rolls Series, No. 41, III, 203-213.

[20] *Ibid.*, p. 205.

[21] Clair C. Olson, "Chaucer and the Music of the Fourteenth Century," *Speculum*, XVI (1941), pp. 64-91.

of music. There seem to be only a few examples of Chaucer's
treatment of any of the themes or subjects of *musica speculativa*: the discussion of the nature of the physics of sound in
The Hous of Fame, ll. 765-781; the black knight's declara-
tion, in *The Boke of the Duchesse*, ll. 1160-1170, that the songs
that he composed and sang to his now deceased lady suffered
because of his lack of knowledge of speculative music ("Al-
thogh I koude not make so wel / Songes, ne knewe the art
al, / As koude Lamekes sone Tubal"),[22] followed by a brief
narration of the discovery of music by Tubal while listening
to the hammers in a smithy ("But Grekes seyn Pictagoras, /
That he the firste fynder was"); and finally, two mentions
of the music of the spheres. The first, in the fifth book of
Troilus and Criseyde, relates how Troilus, at his death, was
transported to the heaven of the eighth sphere,

> And ther he saugh, with ful avysement,
> The erratik sterres, herkenyng armonye
> With sownes ful of hevenyssh melodie.
>
> (ll. 1811-1813)[23]

The second such reference draws a specific connection between
the celestial harmony and the practical music of men on earth.
It is an exposition of the *Somnium Scipionis* of Cicero, which,
as we have seen, was known through Macrobius' commentary
and transmitted the doctrine of the heavenly music and its
earthly implications to the Medieval world. Scipio is shown
the heavens:

> Thanne shewede he hym the lytel erthe that here is,
> At regard of the hevenes quantite;
> And after shewede he hym the nyne speres,
> And after that the melodye herde he

[22] *The Boke of the Duchesse*, ll. 1160-1162. This and succeeding references are to Chaucer's *Works*, ed. F. N. Robinson, second ed. (Cambridge,
1957).
[23] *Ibid.*, p. 479. Cf. Gower, *Confessio Amantis*, IV, 2416-2420 for another
blending of Jubal, or Tubal, and Pythagoras as founders of music.

That cometh of thilke speres thryes thre,
That welle is of musik and melodye
In this world here, and cause of armonye.

(ll. 57-63)[24]

Of all these allusions, perhaps that in *The Boke of the Duchesse* is most interesting in that it brings together the two branches of music, albeit in what was a traditional academic argument that knowledge of singing alone was not sufficient to master music (in the words of the fifteenth-century theorist Tinctoris, "*Musicorum et cantorum magna est differentia*").[25]

Chaucer is perhaps the only English writer of his time with both the knowledge of academic musical speculation and the skill and desire to portray naturalistically the varieties of life of his own day. Yet his disposition to treat of practical music, instruments, and the like in one context, and knowledge such as of the music of the spheres in another, leads us to suppose that the all-embracing concerns of Tinctoris' *musicus* were perhaps not widely shared outside the musical profession. Occasional musical images appear in Chaucer's writings that represent striking musical ideas unassimilated into an overall view. In the Prologue to *The Legend of Good Women*, just after his famous lines in praise of the daisy, the poet turns to the praise of his lady, who is, he says,

The maistresse of my wit, and nothing I.
My word, my werk ys knyt so in youre bond
That, as an harpe obeieth to the hond
And maketh it soune after his fyngerynge,
Ryght so mowe ye oute of myn herte bringe
Swich vois, ryght as yow lyst, to laughe or pleyne.

(ll. 88-93)[26]

This is interesting not so much for its use of the old heart-

---

[24] *The Parliament of Foules*, ll. 57-63. In Robinson's edition, p. 311.
[25] Joannes Tinctoris, *Diffinitorium Musices* (ca. 1475), in E. de Coussemaker, *Oeuvres Théorique de Jean Tinctoris* (Lille, 1875), p. 489.
[26] Robinson's edition, p. 484.

string figure, as for the way in which the figure is applied to
even a conventional love-situation: the poet likens himself to
an instrument upon which the lady can play what tune of
feeling she chooses. This is a theme which really comes into
its own only at the turn of the seventeenth century, when
associations of music with the power to elicit passion become
a dominant principle of musical esthetics. But it merely serves
a passing purpose for Chaucer; other comparisons of people
to harps, and human actions to harp music and playing, are of
a completely different nature. (As, for example, Pandarus to
Troilus in *Troilus and Criseyde*, I, 730-735, where there is a
Boethian example of the ass as being so bestial that he is not
moved by musical sounds, or a different figure later on in
Book II, 1030-1036.) It has been observed that "either Chaucer
did not know or did not care about the theoretical aspects of
music."[27] Of course, a distinction should have to be drawn
between practical and speculative "theory" here, although
there are other grounds for disagreeing with this formulation.
But that Chaucer maintains no general view on the subject of
music is undeniable. He holds neither the scholastic notion
that music was properly part of the quadrivium and a necessary part of everyone's study, while minstrels, tavern fiddlers,
and the like were not properly musicians at all, nor the
Lollard view of the indescribable corruption effected by the
institution of music in and out of churches,[28] nor even the
position of many fourteenth-century Italian writers who went
so far into Neoclassicism as to compare actual composers of
their own day with musical heroes of antiquity. There is
nothing in Chaucer to compare, for example, with Guillaume
de Machaut's *Dit de la Harpe*, a 350-odd line allegory comparing the strings of a harp to the thirty virtues of his lady,
in fact identifying the lady with the instrument itself, praised
as being the favorite of David, Orpheus, and Apollo (there is

[27] Clair C. Olson, *op.cit.*, p. 90. But see my " 'Moedes or Prolaciouns'
in Chaucer's *Boece*," *Modern Language Notes*, LXXI (1956), pp. 397-399
for an argument against this.
[28] See below, Chapter V, pp. 250-251.

already a lyre-harp synthesis at work here). Such an instrument is unfit for Johannes de Grocheo's *musica vulgaris* and only proper for the kind of delicate, artful, polyphonic courtly song written by Machaut himself: *"Après Raison, qui la harpe gouuerne, / Ne vuet mie qu'on la porte en tauerne."*[29] The discussion of the virtues of *"Honneur, Scens, Raison et Mésure"* contains some interesting remarks[30] on the fundamental association of the stringed instrument (sometimes called "lire") with the latter two virtues, in a way almost reminiscent of and very possibly derived from the great theoretical and ethical distinction of Antiquity between the *aulos* and the lyre.

Machaut's fame and influence as a composer, of course, were as great as his literary importance, and it is not surprising to see him give a musical subject elaborate treatment, even though it is worked carefully, as subject matter, into the substance of a literary convention. There are no fourteenth-century English musicians with the status and contemporary fame of many Continental musicians until John Dunstable (c. 1370-1453), whose reputation in France was as great as was the extent of his influence on English and Burgundian music of the fifteenth century. The fourteenth-century English composer is not a figure easily conjured up and sensed, and there is no speculative or topical poetry that emerges, either from his own pen or about him, until the end of the fifteenth century. After Chaucer, and particularly in the work of the Scottish Chaucerians, there starts to flourish one of the two mutually exclusive traditions of the poetic treatment of musical subjects in England extending through the beginning of the sixteenth century. The first of these leans more toward the exposition of speculative music; the second involves more the dispraise of the practical.

Perhaps this latter tradition should be considered first, in

[29] *"Dit de la Harpe,"* ll. 251-252. Text from Karl Young, "The *Dit de la Harpe* of Guillaume de Machaut," in *Essays in Honor of Albert Feuillerat*, ed. Henri M. Peyre (New Haven, 1943), pp. 1-20.

[30] ll, 263-276.

that it involves attitudes toward music and toward all vain-glorious human enterprise that we today tend to think of as being more particularly medieval in their rejection even of study and secular knowledge as precariously worldly. It is a tradition that ignores altogether, for the most part, the very existence of *musica speculativa*, or of music's exalted place in the *quadrivium*. Music is "piping" or "minstrelsy" or "fiddling," the contemptible and lecherous activity of the world of the tavern. In an age of Humanism later on, it becomes a simple matter to bolster this traditional sort of attack on music with learned but nonetheless misleading and half-understood citations of Plato's "*Kulturkampf*" and other musical criticisms of the past. But before the Tudor era, the outright or implicit condemnation of music directed at the unlearned uses no complicated arguments. *Flesh*, in the early fifteenth-century morality *The Castle of Perseverance*, for example, announces:

> I am Mankyndis fayre Flesch, florchyd in flowris;
>   My lyfe is with lustys and lykynge i-lent;
> With tapytys of tafata I tymbyr my towris;
>   In myrthe and in melodye my mende is i-ment . . .
>   (ll. 237-240)[31]

Music is guilty by association here, as it is in the Coventry play of *The Magi, Herod, and the Slaughter of the Innocents*, where *Erode* declares that during his rest, "Trompettis, viallis, and othur armone / Schall bles the wakyng of my maieste"[32] (ll. 538-539).

The theme of the worldly vanity of music is caught up in the treatment of the musician as one of the many human roles or degrees in the *memento mori* literature of the fifteenth century. An interesting manuscript containing some moralized drawings includes a representation of a harper, being shot at with an arrow by Death, the whole surmounted by a five-line

[31] Text from *Chief Pre-Shakesperean Dramas*, ed. J. Q. Adams (Cambridge, Mass., 1924), pp. 267-268.
[32] *Ibid.*, p. 159.

musical staff, and followed by a macaronic poem whose burden
is a text from Job XXX: 31: *"Versa est in luctum cithera
mea, / Et organum meum in vocem flencium"* ("My harp is
turned to mourning, and my organ into the voice of them
that weep").[33] It begins by translating:

> Allas, ful warly for wo may I synge,
> For into sorrow turned is my harpe
> And my organ into voyce of wepynge,
> When I rememyr the deth that is sharpe.
>
> (ll. 1-4)

The harper, however, soon to be undone as all men eventually
are, seems momentarily to take on some of the gloomy, prophetic sagacity of the preacher-poet himself: "Therefore
turned is myne organ into *flencium vocem*, / When I se this
noght consyderd *in cordibus vivencium*" (ll. 23-24). In *The
Daunce of Death*, a translation from a fifteenth-century French
original, the theme is rather that all of the wisdom and craft
of the musician, being too much of the world, must go for
naught. *Dethe* says to the *Mynstralle*:

> O thow Minstral / that cannest so note & pipe
> Un-to folkes / for to do plesaunce
> By the right honde (anoone) I schal the gripe
> With these other / to go vp-on my daunce
> Ther is no scape / nowther a-voydaunce
> On no side / to contrarie my sentence
> For yn musik / be crafte & accordaunce
> Who maister is / shew his science.[34]

But if the acknowledgment of the existence of a learned study
of music is made, the tortured reply of the musician caught
up in the dance puts down his pretensions to cunning by con-

---

[33] Printed by Thomas W. Ross in "Five Fifteenth Century 'Emblem'
Verses from Brit. Mus. Addit. MS. 37049," *Speculum*, XXXII (1957), pp.
274-282.

[34] *The Daunce of Death* (Ellesmere MS.), ed. Florence Warren (London,
1931), p. 60.

fronting him with musico-choreographic complexities of a kind he has never seen before:

> This newe daunce / is to me so strange
> Wonder dyuerse / and passyngli contrarie
> The dredful fotyng / dothe so often chaunge
> Whiche now to me / is no thyng necessarie
> Zif hit were so / that I myght asterte
> But many a man / zif I shal not tarie
> Ofte daunceth / but no thynge of herte.[35]

The minstrel's art is of no avail at the end.

The poetic treatment of the minstrel reaches a peak of didactic satire in Alexander Barclay's translation, in 1509, of Sebastian Brant's *Das Narrenschiff*. Barclay concludes his section "Of nyght watchers and beters of the stretes playnge by nyght on instrumentes and vsynge lyke Folyes what tyme is to rest" with a confession that singing-by-night does not seem to be quite the national menace in England that it appears from Brant's text to be on the Continent, and that the moral equivalent is English drunkenness. He is nevertheless able to work up considerable venom over "These dronken bandes of Folys than doth Jest / About the stretis, with rumour noyse and cry / Syngynge theyr folysshe songes of rybawdry."[36] He proceeds to give vent to it in the following stanzas:

---

[35] *Ibid.*, p. 62. Another translation handles this same strophe quite differently, giving the minstrel a rather more conventional farewell to all his instruments:

> Ey benedicite / this world is freele
> Now glad / now sory / what shal men vse
> Harpe lute phidil / pipe farewell
> Sautry Sithol / & Shalmuse
> Al wordly myrthe / I here refuse . . . .

Ibid., p. 63. "Sithol" would be a variant for "cithol," "cithern," etc., a plucked string; "Shalmuse" is an earlier form for "shawm" (later, Fr. *chalumeau*), an oboe-like double-reed. The two groups of instruments parallel each other, in the two successive lines, with respect to their type, appearance, and musical function.

[36] Alexander Barclay, *The Ship of Fools*, ed. T. H. Jamieson (Edinburgh, 1873), I, 297.

The furyes ferefull spronge of the flodes of hell
Vexith these vagabundes in theyr myndes so
That by no mean can they abyde ne dwell
Within theyr howsys, but out they nede must go
More wyldly wandrynge than outher bucke or doo
Some with theyr harpis another with his lute
Another with his bagpype or a folysshe flute

Then mesure they theyr songes of melody
Before the dores of theyr lemmandere
Yowlynge with theyr folysshe songe and cry
So that theyr lemman may theyr great foly here
And tyll the yordan make them stande arere
Cast on theyr hede, or tyll the stonys fle
They nat depart, but couet there styll to be . . .

Not only the suspicious mingling of chamber and street instruments, but the use of the word "mesure" with respect to the
"songes of melody," suggests that Barclay's attack is turned
toward a broader target than merely drunken revellers. Actual
performers, capable of reading notation, and perhaps hired
out or retained by a courtier for *eine kleine Nachtmusik*, are
here brought under the abusive slop-jar.

After the middle of the sixteenth century, attacks upon
music become far more elaborate, sophisticated, and learned,
partly because of the puritan movement among the clergy
against elaborate musical services and instrumental music in
the churches, and partly because the general level of Classical
education was much higher, on the part of polemicists, than it
had been in the previous centuries. On the other hand, a growing tradition had made for the literary association of *musica
speculativa* with some of the actualities of musical practice;
even the unmusical, eventually, began to find some grounds
for treating the lute or "a folysshe flute" as something other
than an instrument of either demonic sway or universal human folly. Much earlier, William Langland, in the Prologus
to *Piers Plowman*, describes the myriad occupations of the

people in the "faire felde ful of folke," and includes mention of some that "murthes to make as mynstralles conneth, / And geten gold with here glee giltles I leue."[37] But this last comment is merely the result of Langland's own charity, and in the next lines he remembers the conventional abuse: "Ac iapers & iangelers Iudas chylderen, / Feynen hem fantasies and foles hem maketh."[38] For a real appreciation of musical art per se, and for a more understanding view of the nature of the musician, there had to develop a tradition of writing about music and of finding a place for its description in contemporary literary forms that would partake of some of the hitherto purely academic and scholarly praise of *musica speculativa*, the "minstrelsy of the study," as it were.

Such a tradition is found in the conventional fifteenth- and early sixteenth-century treatments of music as a liberal art. An early example is one from Gower's *Confessio Amantis* (ca. 1390). In the seventh book, in a discussion of the education of Alexander the Great, occurs a digression on the *quadrivium* and *trivium*, informing the reader about

> The second of Mathematique
> Which is the science of Musique,
> That techeth upon Armonie
> A man to make melodie
> Be vois and soun of instrument
> Thurgh notes of acordement,
> The which men pronounce aloft
> Nou scharpe notes and nou softe,
> Nou highe notes and noe lowe,
> As be the gamme a man mai knowe,
> Which techeth the prolacion
> Of note and the condicion.
>
> (VII, ll. 151-162)[39]

---

[37] William Langland, *Piers the Plowman*, Prologus, ll. 33-34, ed. W. W. Skeat, tenth ed. (Oxford, 1900), p. 2.

[38] *Ibid.*, ll. 35-36.

[39] John Gower, *Confessio Amantis*, in *Complete Works*, ed. G. C. Macaulay (Oxford, 1901), III, 237-238.

The zeal of the portrayal is not matched here, particularly, by any precision in the use of the musical terminology. Although "Armonie" and "melodie" remained synonymous with "musical sounds" through the middle of the fifteenth century, the "gamme" or *gamut* (the whole compass of the notated musical range) would have nothing whatever to do with "the prolacion / Of note," which is a purely rhythmic, rather than a tonal notion.[40] Gower's mistake here is over a point of practical rather than of speculative theory; that is, *prolation* is a technical notion in the music of the fourteenth century, and not the kind of thing that would be studied in a required set of readings for a university degree. Even in the fifteenth century, the academic study of music would involve reading Boethius rather than the theorists of contemporary music.[41] Encyclopedias and compendia of general knowledge could instruct a reader no more accurately than does Gower: the French fourteenth-century encyclopedia and gazetteer translated by Caxton under the title of *The Mirrour of the World* (1481) treats of music, for example, in a rather peculiar way. Following a discussion of geometry, the association of music and medicine, which is only one of the corollary points of speculative music, dominates the exposition and leads to another point entirely: "Of this science of musyque cometh alle attemperaunce, and of this arte procedeth somme physique; ffor like as musyque accordeth alle thinges that dyscorde in them, and remayne them to concordaunce, right so in lyke wyse trauaylleth physique to brynge Nature to poynt that disnatureth in mannes body, whan ony maladye or sekenes encombreth hit."[42] But, the encyclopedist continues, medicine is not one of the seven "sciences of philosophy," the reason being that it attends to the health of the body, to maintain it "whiche ellis oftentymes myght lightly perysshe." And there-

---

[40] See " 'Moedes or Prolaciouns' in Chaucer's *Boece*," p. 398.

[41] See the introduction to Stephen Hawes, *The Pastime of Pleasure*, ed. William Edward Mead (London, 1928), p. lxi n.

[42] *Caxton's Mirrour of the World*, ed. Oliver H. Prior (London, 1913), p. 38.

fore, he concludes, there is "nothyng liberal ne free" about medicine or any of its works; "and for as moche as science that serueth to mannes body leseth his franchise, but science that serueth to the soule deserueth in the world to haue the name liberal; ffor the sowle ought to be liberal as thyng that is of noble beyng, as she that cometh of God, and to God wille and ought retorne; and therfor ben the vii sciences liberall, ffor they make the soule all free."[43] Finally having established, by means of a clever and sound scholastic argument the true nature of the liberal arts, the author goes on to music itself: "Of this arte is musyque thus comune that she accordeth her to euerich so well that by her the vii sciences were sette in concorde that they yet endure. By this science of musyque ben extrayt and drawen alle the songes that ben songen in holy chirche, and alle the accordaunces of alle the instruments that haue diuerse accordes and diuerse sownes. And where ther is reson and entendement of somme thinges, certes who can wel the science of musyque, he knoweth the accordance of alle thinges. And alle the creatures that payne them to doo wel remayne them to concordance."[44] This is no more than an essay on *harmonia mundi*, taking music as model for all the "liberal," or *liberating*, arts.

Rather different from sources like this one is the elaborate treatment of speculative and practical music in *The Court of Sapience*, a long didactic allegory hitherto ascribed to John Lydgate.[45] In a rather conventional, dream-allegory frame, the author is led on a journey by Dame Sapience and comes to the court of Dame Philosophy, who is accompanied by her seven ladies in waiting. In the description of Dame Musyk enthroned, the reader is offered a course of musical instruction starting out, in the approved manner of many musical treatises of the preceding centuries, with the division (going back to

[43] *Ibid.*, pp. 38-39.
[44] *Ibid.*, pp. 39-40.
[45] *The Court of Sapience*, ed. Robert Spindler (Leipzig, 1927), pp. 97-103, 105-114.

Cassiodorus and Isidore of Seville) of music into rhythm, harmonics, and metrics:

> A lyte besyde wythyn a place of blys
> Dame Musyk sate, and wyth her ladyes thre;
> The furst hyght Dame Armonica y wys,
> The secund Rithmica, a lady fre,
> The thryd hyght Metrica, full of beaute;
> The song she prykyd, she nombred notes trew,
> That melody formyd an heuyn new.
>
> The furst delyted in hyr rewnys swete;
> The secund mesuryd the dytee wyth the note;
> The thryd nombryd her song wyth certayn fete,
> And whyche bene theyr boundes ryght well she wrote,
> And wyth them were good clerkis, that thus wrote.
> And sayd that Musyk was the pure connyng
> And verray wey of true parfyte lyuyng.
>
> They wrote also, who that furst musyk fonde;
> Som sayd Tuball, som Lynus Tibeus,
> Som Zetus, Amphion, as they dyd vnderstonde,
> Som sayde also hit was oone Orpheus,
> Som playnly sayd, for ought they cowde dyscus,
> That by the sowne of hamers in a forge
> Pyctagoras furst musyk gan to forge.
>
> (ll. 2017-2037)[46]

The problem, as far as the three ladies are concerned, is indeed "whyche ben theyr boundes," since the tripartite division of categories could mean very little to a post-classic world with measured music and stressed vernaculars, and had become merely formulaic during the centuries of its repetition in countless musical treatises. The presence of the "clerkis" is of some interest here; they set the bounds of each of the branches of music, discuss its general ethical importance (more in the way

---

[46] The text of this and the following passages occupies pp. 203-206 of the edition cited above.

of a kind of *paideia* here, it seems, than in terms of the traditional effects upon the soul), and argue about the origins of music, in a way that suggests that the poet was well aware of such inconsistencies of lore as the Tubal-Pythagoras legend. There is an almost Chaucerian humor and wryness in "Som sayde also hit was oone Orpheus," the "oone" taking on a certain degree of sarcasm. The important thing is that Dame Musyk and her handmaids are accompanied by students of speculative music. The beautiful melody played by Metrica which "formyd an heuyn new" is not being praised merely in an extravagant way at this point, for it must be remembered that this is an allegory of universal music in all its forms and that the sounds capable of creating a new heaven by their very presence are those which are already established in the traditional one.

The following stanzas recount how Dame Musyk began "one her craft to recorde" by demonstrating the basic intervals on a monochord, out of whose single string "dyuerse tewnes she brought, / And thus the ground of musyk furst she sought."[47] She also "taught syx syllabes, whyche we notes clepe," the names of the tones of the Guidonian hexachord that were still employed, although the notational system for which they were invented had long since passed on: ". . . Ut, Re, my, fa, sol, la; / These syllabes sex yseth Dame Musica." We are told how "She taught these nootes by hyr monycord, / As she dyd the stryng towche or gon pulle,"[48] with much detail about this process and, finally, we learn that

> She taught theym than, whyche were tewnes perfyte,
> And yaue theym lust to here theyre concordaunce,
> Whyche tewnes eke byn clepyd imparfyte,
> And whyche in song shuld be theyre gouernaunce,
> Proporcion she had in remembraunce,
> Diapason wyth Diapente eke,
> And Diatesseron was nat to seke.

[47] II, 2043-2044.　　　　[48] II, 2053-2055.

Whyche laarge, whyche long, whyche brefe, whyche
    semybrefe,
Mynim, crochet, in rewle and eke in space,
All thys she taught, but, for I must be bryef,
In thys matere I nyl no ferther pace;
For thow I wold, therto I haue ho space;
But whoso lyst of Musyk for to wyt,
For verray ground to Boece I hym remyt.

And to a clerk, which cleped is Berno,
Johan de Muris, and John de Musica,
To Guydo eke, in his Micrologo,
There mayst thou see of Dame Armonyca,
Of Dame Metryk, and of Dame Rithmica;
Of al Musyke the veray ground parfyte
There shalt thou fynd with blysse and al delyte.

                    (ll. 2066-2086)

The teaching of the proper consonances is quite conventional
here, although the eagerness of the supposed pupils to hear
the beautiful concords of the octave and fifth, after undoubtedly having had explained their surpassing splendor in glow-
ing mystical terms, is a rather good touch. Then follows, as
we see, the question of rhythm, and finally the limits of the
redactor's patience begin to show. He refers the reader to a
number of theorists; it may be observed that only one of
them, Jean de Muris, lived after the twelfth century at all,
and that even so, that famous writer on the *ars nova* died
more than a hundred years before *The Court of Sapience* was
written.[49] The writer's acquaintance with practical music and
its teaching, it must be admitted, is of an extremely school-
bookish sort. He closes his section on music with a rather
conventional list of instruments:

[49] Excluding Boethius, and, of course, Jean de Muris (d. 1351), all of
the writers on music mentioned in this stanza, from Guido d'Arezzo to one
John Cotton were of the eleventh and twelfth centuries.

And these with Musyke were in ioye and blysse,
And helped her prouynce with her armonye,
And with them was ecche instrument ywys
That is of Musyk and of mynstralcye,
Harp, lute, pype, trump, fydel, regals, sautry,
The rote, the orgons, and the monycord,
The gyterne, symbale and the clauycord.

(ll. 2087-2093)

And here at least the poet has referred to the actual music of the world about him, for the instruments mentioned form a pretty good contemporary list (with the exception of the monochord, purely a teaching device, which is probably there for the rhyme in any case).

This studied, academic exposition of what was really part of the university curriculum nevertheless serves the function of associating "mynstralcye" with a liberal art and with ancient wisdom rather than with "iapers and iangelers." Thus it constitutes a step forward in the direction of the attitudes toward music taken by the sixteenth-century Northern Humanist educators, who, as we shall see, encouraged the study of practical music for many of the same reasons that the Scholastics had continued to urge the study of the speculative.

But the role of practical music in long allegorical works was also an important one. In Lydgate's adaptation of part of the French *Les Echecs Amoureux* called *Reason and Sensuality*, made about 1408, the garden of *Deduit* or Pleasure is described at length, and a rather long section is devoted to rehearsing "the Mynstralcyes that Weren in the gardyn of Deduit." From the very beginning, it is made clear that these are no ordinary festivities, for not only "folke of al condicion / Duellede in that mansion," but "goddys also of the hevene, / For merthe oonly and solace, / Soiourned in that lusty place." Then, following an allegorist's convention, Lydgate cannot restrain himself from painting details:

And yt syt nat me to be stille
But telle, how they were devyded,
And also how they wer provyded
Of Instrumentys of Musyke,
For they koude the practyke
Of al maner Mynstralcye
That any man kan specifye;
For ther wer rotys of *Almanye*
And eke of *Arragon* and spayne,
Songes, stampes, and eke daunces,
Dyuers plente of plesaunces,
And many vnkouth notys newe
Of swiche folkys as lovde trewe,
And Instrumentys that dyde excelle,
Many moo than I kan telle:
Harpys, fythels, and eke rotys,
Wel accordyng with her notys,
Lutys, Rubibis, and geterns,
More for estatys than taverns,
Orgnys, cytolys, monacordys.
And ther wer founde noo discordys,
Nor variaunce in ther sovns,
Nor lack of noo proporsiouns,
Ther was so noble accordaunce.

(ll. 5564-5587)[50]

The reservation that was noted in connection with Machaut about the proper use of the noblest plucked and bowed stringed instruments is preserved here as well ("More for estatys than taverns"); and while the lack of discord and the surfeit of good proportions are each pretty much of a tag here, the whole picture does fall into some kind of place. It is elaborate, courtly music which is being described, of the sort and degree of splendor that came to be associated, in the fifty-year period

[50] John Lydgate, *Reason and Sensuality*, ed. Ernest Sieper (London, 1901). The whole musical passage runs from p. 146 to p. 147 of Volume I of this edition.

following Lydgate's poem, with the courts of Burgundy.[51]
As Lydgate goes on, he gets even more specific; having mentioned all the "indoor" or chamber instruments (i.e., those
with a natural dynamic level and range to best suit them for
the quieter kind of singing and playing in relatively small
rooms), he next proceeds to the "outdoor" ones (he distinguishes between them as being "lowe" and "high," respectively), and to their function, and finally passes on to his
praise of the music heard in Pleasure's garden, "In honour
of the god *Cupide*":

> And for folkys that lyst daunce
> Ther wer trumpes and trumpetes,
> Lowde shallys and doucetes,
> Passyng of grete melodye,
> And floutys ful of armonye,
> Eke Instrumentys high and lowe
> Wel mo than I koude knowe,
> That I suppose, ther is no man
> That aryght reherse kan
> The melodye that they made:
> They wer so lusty and so glade.
> They do no thing but pley and syng
> And rounde aboute goo dauncyng,
> That the verray heuenly son
> Passed in comparison
> The harpis most melodious
> Of David and of Orpheous.
> Ther melodye was in all
> So heuenly and celestiall

[51] Thurston Dart, in *The Interpretation of Music* (London, 1954),
pp. 156-157, gives an account of the elaborate musical entertainments held
at a feast for the Order of the Golden Fleece at Lille in 1454, in which the
mixture of sacred and secular music of various forms and styles, and the
profusion of instrumental and vocal combinations used in the performance
(the musical compositions were performed by musicians from a huge model
church and a monstrous mock pie, alternately), suggest something of the
descriptions of the musical activities in the Gardens of Love in French and
English love-allegories.

> That ther nys hert, I dar expresse,
> Oppressed so with hevynesse,
> Nor in sorwe so y-bounde,
> That he sholde ther ha founde
> Comfort hys sorowe to apese
> To a-sette his hert at ese.
>
> (ll. 5588-5612)

The reiterated designation of "heuenly" and "celestiall," the reference to the linked figure of David and Orpheus, and the final insistence that the power of this music is sufficient to lighten the burden of all cares, lead one to suspect that the musical scene elaborated by Lydgate is no mere decorative arrangement, based perhaps as much on Lorris' portion of the *Roman de la Rose* as on Lydgate's original. *Les Echecs Amoureux* continues the story long after the unfinished *Reason and Sensuality* breaks off, and moves into an encyclopedic account of practical ethics;[52] in the English version, the garden of Pleasure is more of a narrative goal than a temporary scene of the chess game that is later allegorized so elaborately in the French poem. It is a heaven of Love that Lydgate is depicting, and he employs some of the attributes of the Christian heaven in painting his scene. If these are courtiers at their *fêtes* (and we have been told that the gods are among them), they also seem to produce, like the Blessed, a celestial music. Granted that in the courtly poetry of the fifteenth century the adjective "heavenly," like so many others, becomes a kind of automatic tag of praise,[53] the word seems to

[52] See Sieper's commentary on the relationship of the two poems in his edition, II, 59-76.

[53] See H. S. Bennett, *Chaucer and the Fifteenth Century* (Oxford, 1947), p. 130. For a possibly more significant use of what is avowedly a formula, see the fable of the fox and the raven in Lydgate's endless, translated *Pilgrimage of the Life of Man*, ll. 14261-14272, where the fox, as Flattery, sings a typical praise of delightful music in fawning over the raven's voice,

> Whych ys so fful of melodye
> And off hevenly Armonye;
> ffor trewly, as I kan dyscerne,
> Ther ys ne harpe nor gyterne

function here with a force rare in Lydgate. It serves to relate the extremely accurate picture of practical music, incredibly lavish withal, to the more exalted and general praises of music in the oldest books. To a certain extent, the allegory supports this extravagance of praise; connecting the music in the garden with heavenly harmony is an intensification of the same kind of effect that was gained by careful mention of the nobility of the lute and rebec. The garden of Pleasure thus prefigures the garden of Love, which, as C. S. Lewis has remarked, "like the Celestial City, comes at the end of his story instead of at the beginning."[54]

An extremely interesting adaptation of the traditional musical festivities in the love-allegory occurs in Gavin Douglas' *The Palice of Honour* (1501), a poem which, although coming almost at the end of the era in which that form flourished, can in no way be said to represent lack of invention or a decadent hyper-conventionality. In the course of Part 1 of the poem, the poet observes from his hiding place the triumphs of Minerva, Diana, and finally, Venus, in the most magnificent chariot of all. The splendor of the procession is not only visual, however:

> Bot it thair mirth and solace nevertheles
> In musick tone and menstralsie expres
> Sa craftelie with curage aggreabill,
> Hard never wicht sic melodie, I ges.[55]
>
> (1, st. 40)

Because of its tag phrases ("I ges," and the use of "menstralsie"), we might expect another catalog of musical instru-

---

> Symphonye, nouther crowde,
> Whan ye list to synge lowde . . .

The fox continues by asking the raven to sing "A lytel motet with your grace," with the well-known results. But throughout this whole poem, music is treated as an instrument either of Pride (ll. 14300-14308), or of Youth and Idleness.

[54] C. S. Lewis, *The Allegory of Love* (Oxford, 1938), p. 274.

[55] Gavin Douglas, *The Palice of Honour*, in *Poetical Works*, ed. John Small (Edinburgh and London, 1874). This whole section is from 1, 20-21.

mentation, in imitation of the French. Instead, a display of general musical learning, à la *The Court of Sapience* follows:

> Accompanyit lustie yonkeirs with all
> Fresche ladyis sang in voice virgineall
> Concordis sweit, diuers entoned reportis,
> Proportionis fine with sound celestiall,
> Duplat, triplat, diatesseriall,
> Sesqui altera, and decupla resortis,
> Diapason of mony sindrie sortis,
> War soung and playit be seir cunning menstrall
> On lufe ballatis with mony fair disportis.
>
> In modulatioun hard I play and sing
> Faburdoun, pricksang, discant, countering,
> Cant organe, figuration, and gemell,
> On croud, lute, harp, with mony gudlie spring,
> Schalmes, clariounis, portatiues, hard I ring.
> Monycord, organe, tympane, and cymball.
> Sytholl, psalterie, and voices sweit as bell,
> Soft releschingis in dulce delivering,
> Fractionis diuide, at rest, or clois compell.

(1, st. 41-42)

This is no mere display of misunderstood terms, but instead a carefully constructed exposition of the nature of music. It proceeds, according to all the traditions of musical specula-tion, from proportion, in the Pythagorean manner; in the list of terms in the first of these stanzas are both names of inter-vals, the fourth, fifth ("sesqui altera" is really the name of the proportion ³⁄₂, by which both the interval of the fifth and the rhythmic signature or "proportion" were known), and the names of purely rhythmical relationships. In the general interest in mathematical problems that had been the heritage of speculative music from Boethius and Cassiodorus on, the overall notion of "proportion," of "harmony" in the abstract, came to be reinterpreted in terms of the two leading topics of practical music which, throughout the history of "measured music," required mathematical consideration: the intervals and the rhythmic proportions. Both of them are treated in Douglas' exposition. "Decupla" is the note-value proportion of ten to one; and "diatesserial" may be both the interval of the fourth and the proportion later known in its Latin form of "quadrupla."

So, too, are the forms of musical composition, both those *passé* and those contemporary with Douglas, and the instruments that follow, carefully ordered. "Cant organe" is the chant of the *organum*, and not an instrument at all;[56] and *organum* was as obsolete at the beginning of the sixteenth century (even in musically retarded England) as the term "pricksang" for written-out (and later printed) part-music was properly up to date. "Relesching" and "spring" probably refer to a device of ornamentation and to a fast tune, respectively. The instruments are a typically mixed list, including both the portative (organ) and the monochord (which one would have played music upon no sooner than one would today upon a pitch pipe).

But the display of practical knowledge of musical theory is no end in itself here. Douglas then proceeds to evaluate the music, and to praise it in terms of the two principal epitomes of Renaissance *musica speculativa*, the celestial music revealed to Cicero's Scipio in his dream, and the fabled effectiveness of the music of Greece as symbolized in the figure of Orpheus:

> Not Pan of Archaid sa pleasandlie playis,
> Nor king David quhairs playing as men sayis,
> Coniurit the spreit the quhilk Saul confoundit,
> Nor Amphion with mony subtell layis,
> Quhilk Thebes wallit with harping in his dayis,

[56] Small, *op.cit.*, mis-glosses this and several other musical terms, leaving a reader with the conviction that Douglas does not know whereof he writes at all. Despite his disclaimer to having understood the "nombers fine" of the music, his use of musical terminology, both speculative and practical, is not misinformed.

Nor he that first the subtell craftis foundit,
Was not in musick half sa well igroundit,
Nor knew their measure tent daill be na wayis, /so to
At thair resort baith heuin and eird resoundit. deal with

Ne mair I vderstude thir numbers fine
Be God, than dois a gekgo or a swine,
Saif that me think my labour will I tine,   /lose
Ne mair I will thir verbillis sweit define, /warblings
How that thair musick tones war mair cleir,
And dulcer than the mouing of the spheir,
Or Orpheus harp of Thrace with sound diuine, . . .

(I, st. 43-44)

Douglas finishes up this encomium with a reference, paralleling the one to Orpheus, to a famed border harper, Glasgerion.
It is not enough for Douglas, as it was for Lydgate, Guillaume
de Lorris, and the author of *Les Echecs Amoureux*, to assure
the reader by reiteration that the music was of a celestial
quality. He must instead compare it favorably with the healing and effective playing of David, Amphion, and Orpheus,
and insist that the poet himself was so awe-stricken at the
spectacle and the sound (again, this suggests Scipio when confronted by the music of the spheres) that he was incapable of
understanding "thir numbers fine," which should in any case
probably have proved too subtle for mortal ears. Although
the power of the music to elevate the soul of the hearer to its
former high state, and the correspondence between *musica
humana* and the universal harmony are absent from this
account, Douglas' description may be said to be a prototype
of late Renaissance treatments of music in English poetry.

One other theme in the non-professional attitude toward
music that began to emerge in the early sixteenth-century era
of secular Humanism is that of the role of music in education,
on the one hand, and in the list of accomplishments demanded
of any courtier, on the other. The roots of the former lie in

[84]

the study of speculative music in the Medieval universities, and of the latter, probably as far back as the sense of courtly *techne* of the troubadours, who would write and compose the texts and melodies of their *lais* and *sirventes*, but would always have a *jongleur* to play the accompaniments and introductions of the *vielle* and sometimes to sing the songs. The role of music in what I shall call Renaissance *paideia* finds its canonical delineation, from the courtly point of view, in Castiglione, as its place in the total scheme of human knowledge may be said to have been most elaborately expounded in Ficino. But it is Northern Europe, and England in particular with which we are concerned here, and the time-lag between England and Italy with respect to the development of what we might distinguish as courtly and scholarly Humanism (which were locked together in Italy, almost from the beginning, by a bond of patronage) is considerable. It is only with the Tudor courts that we see either of these branches of Renaissance enlightenment flourishing at all (notwithstanding the possible accomplishments of Henry V as a composer).[57] It is for this reason that an extended discussion of the educative function of music dating from the last quarter of the fifteenth century can be of such interest for us here, as much because of its precociousness as for the role of the digression on music in the overall theme of the poem in which it occurs.

This poem is the *Orpheus and Eurydice* of another "Scottish Chaucerian," Robert Henryson; a retelling of the story of the Thracian musician, it concludes with a lengthy "Moralitas" or allegorization translated from the Latin, Henryson admits, of the late thirteenth-century Dominican, Nicholas Trivet. The poem commences with an account of Orpheus' lineage, including a description of "memoria" and her daughter muses, many of whom are praised for musical skills ("The secound maid clippit melpomyne, / As hony sueit in modela-

<hr>

[57] Compositions signed "Roy Henry" are among those in the fifteenth-century Old Hall Manuscript. See Manfred Bukofzer, "The Music of the Old Hall Manuscript," in *Studies in Medieval and Renaissance Music* (New York, 1950), pp. 78-79.

tioun,"[58] etc.). Finally, the poet mentions the last of these, and returns to Orpheus' mother herself:

> Urania, the nynt and last of all,
> In greik langage, quha cowth it rycht expound,
> Is callit armony celestiall,
> Reiosing men with melody and sound.
> Amang their nyne calliope was cround,
> And maid a quene be michty god phebuss,
> off quhome he gat this prince schir orpheouss.
>
> No windir wes thocht he was fair and wyse,
> gentill and gud, full of liberalities,
> his fader god, and his progenetryse
> a goddess, finder of all armony:
> quhen he wes borne scho set him on hir kne,
> and gart him souk of hir two paupis quhyte
> The sueit lecour of all musik perfyte.
>
> (ll. 57-70)

The final couplet leaves no doubt as to the divine nature of Orpheus' musical gifts. Henryson then goes on to tell of the young lord's love for the "quene euridices," of her mishap with the serpent's bite and her descent to hell. After lamenting her loss in complicated ten-line stanzas, Orpheus goes to seek his wife, and gets the aid of "his fadir phebus," who leads the young man through all the spheres of heaven in search of her. He has just left Mercury "quhilk callit is the god of eloquens," all unsuccessful, to return to earth,

> Yit be the way sum melody he lerd.
>
> In his passage amang the planeitis all,
> he hard a hevinly melody and sound,
> passing all instrumentis musicall,
> causit be rollyn of the speiris round;

[58] II, 38-39. In Robert Henryson, *Poems and Fables*, ed. H. Harvey Wood (Edinburgh and London, 1933), p. 136.

Quhilk armony of all this
     mappamound, /mappa mundi: the world
Quhilk moving seiss unyt perpetuall,   /cease[59]
Quhilk of this warld pluto the saule can call.

Thair leirit he tonis proportionat,
as duplare, triplare, and emetricus,
enolius, and eik the quadruplait,
Eppodeus rycht hard and curius;
off all thir sex, sueit and delicius,
rycht consonant fyfe hevinly symphonyss
componyt ar, as clerkis can devyse.

ffirst diatesserone, full sueit, I wiss
And dyapasone, semple and dowplait,
And dyapenty, componyt with the dyss;
Thir makis fyve of thre multiplicat:
This mirry musik and mellefluat,
Compleit and full of nummeris od and evin,
Is causit be the moving of the hevin.

               (ll. 218-239)

Here the music of the spheres is seen as educating the questing
Orpheus even more completely, and imparting more precious
arcana than he had received so literally at his mother's breast.
Here again are overtones of Scipio's dream-journey and the
celestial music which he heard upon it; it is the perfect Pythagorean revelation in that the "mirry" and "mellefluat"
qualities of the music result from the fact that the music is
"compleit and full of numeris od and even," which, in turn,
is caused by the celestial revolutions. Henryson, a school-
master of Dunfermline (as Dunbar refers to him in his famous
lament for dead poets), protests his ignorance of any practical
music:

[59] The text is corrupt at this point, and various conjectures as to the
meaning of this line are all tentative. Following Wood's suggestion
(p. 260), we might ignore the "Quhilk," and read it "until the motion of
this perpetual unity ceases."

Off sic musik ot wryt I do bot doit,
Thairfoir of this mater a stray I lay,
For in my lyfe I cowth nevir sing a noit.

(ll. 240-242)

But aside from a few uncertainties, dialectal, scribal, or otherwise, his exposition makes excellent sense; so does his description of Orpheus' playing in the underworld, later on in the
poem:

Than orpheus befoir pluto sat doun,
And in his handis quhit his herp can ta,
And pleyit mony sueit proportioun,
With baiss tonis in Ipotdorica,
With gemilling in yporlerica;
quhill at the last for rewth and grit petie,
Thay weipit soir, that cowth him heir or se.

(ll. 366-372)

Allowance must be made for the fact that the hypodorian and
hypolocrian modes were not being intoned and played at the
same time, and for the fact that "gemilling" referred to a kind
of *organum* in parallel thirds perhaps first described by
Giraldus Cambrensis (unless an actual harp style in parallel
thirds or sixths existed as late as this under that name). But
the importance of Henryson's excursions into musical theory
lies in the relationship shown between the celestial harmony,
the careful schooling in all the mathematical secrets of musical
proportions, and the final power to so affect an audience that
"for rewth and grit petie, / Thay weipit soir." It is the first
treatment in an English poem of what becomes in the sixteenth century the basis for the literary praise of music, and
for its polemical defense from many attackers.[60]

[60] Henryson's long *Moralitas* to the story of Orpheus and Eurydice allegorizes it in an utterly Medieval fashion, and copies Nicholas Trivet's analysis
of the tale, "rycht full of fructe and seriositie." Orpheus is "the pairte
intelletyfe / Off manis saule, and undirstanding fre, / And seperat fra
sensualite" (ll. 428-430). Eurydice is "our effectioun / Be fantesy oft
movit up and doun" (ll. 431-432). The serpent that bites her is sin, etc.
etc. The conclusion is simple: "Than orpheus hes wone euridices / Quhen

Of the allegory of Dame Musyke in Stephen Hawes' *The Pastime of Pleasure* (1505-1506) not much of interest is to be observed. Hawes' poem comes at the end of an era, as does *The Palice of Honour*, but its allegorical frame seems too much a mere excuse for its encyclopedism. Graunde Amoure, its hero, in search of La Bell Pucell, is advised to look for her in the tower of music, where indeed he goes to find "a temple / made of crystall,"

> In whiche musyke / the lady excellent
> Played on base organs expedyent
> Accordynge well / vnto dyopason
> Dyapenthe / and eke dyetesseron
>
> (ll. 1467-1470)[61]

Dame Musyke plays in proper tune. Nine stanzas later, we see her enthroned; after a description of the appearance of her chamber, comes a record of "all her mynstralsy,"

> As taboures / trumpettes / with pypes melodyous
> Sakbuttes / organs / and the recorder swetely
> Harpes / lutes / and crouddes ryght delycyous
> Cymphans / doussemers / *with* clarycymbales gloryous
> Rebeckes / clarycordes / eche in theyr degre
> Dyde sytte aboute / theyr ladyes mageste.
>
> (ll. 1528-1533)

If the list of attendant instruments looks backward to the former century, the reply of the lady to Grande Amore, upon his request for instruction in her "noble scyence," does so to an even greater degree. What follows is not so much a treatment of even speculative music, but more the prospectus for an academic course of study. Dame Musyke is a personification of one fourth of the *quadrivium* and little else:

---

our desyre with ressoun makis pess" (ll. 616-617). Trivet's moralization is a traditional one, and widely followed. See below, Chapter IV, pp. 167-173.

[61] Stephen Hawes, *The Pastime of Pleasure*, ed.cit. (n 41, above).

> It is she sayde // ryght gretely prouffytable
> For musyke doth sette // in all vnyte
> The dyscorde thynges // which are varyable
> And deuoydeth myschefe // and grete inyquyte
> Where lacketh musyke // there is no pleynte
> For musyke is concorde // and also peace
> Nothynge without musyke // maye well encreace
>
> The .vii. scyences // in one monacorde
> Eche vp on other // do full well depende
> Musyke hath them // so set in concorde
> That all in one // maye ryght well extende
> All perfyte reason // they do so comprehende
> That they are waye // and perfyte doctryne
> To the Ioye aboue // whiche is celestyne.

(ll. 1541-1554)

Music's greatest virtue is its role as an institution of harmony, of concord;[62] but in Hawes' exposition, it seems limited to the according powers of a not-over-assertive Dean of the Faculties. The only sections of the five hundred lines which are devoted to the doings in the tower of music that seem to hint of their author's contemporary world are those in which, on several occasions, the poet-hero is commanded "with all pleasaunce / To daunce true mesures // without varyaunce" (1586-1587). The dance as a courtly entertainment becomes associated with music in general only during the sixteenth century in England; previously, the actual dancing (aside from its music, which was not considered at all as anything but popular music of the lowest kind) would have been considered a branch of games rather than of music. It is only during the sixteenth century, also, that dance music becomes an important and influential branch of instrumental music generally. The bouts of dancing that go on in Hawes' tower of music would not

---

[62] But see also lines 1576-1583 on the solace, moral uplift, and wit-sharpening qualities of music, in a stanza that ends in Hawes' worst, flattest, and, unfortunately most typical way: "It is good recreacyon / after study."

have occurred so prominently in connection with an earlier treatment of one of the liberal arts. But in no other respect does this treatment of music as a liberal art look forward to the rest of the century.

Ethical Music and Musical Ethics

The roles of music and dance in the education and deportment of gentlemen, on the one hand, and as practical instances of a universal spiritual and intellectual order, on the other, were being prepared, perhaps, in *quattrocento* Florence and Urbino, but only in the next hundred years did those roles become public in England. There is no English speculative writer on music to compare with Ficino, or later with Zarlino, as the propounder of a complete *organum* of musical philosophy. Neither is there in England a Castiglione to delineate so nicely the boundary between courtly accomplishment in music and dancing, and virtuosity offensive for its affinities with the skill of professionals. But under the Tudor courts there gradually develops a set of attitudes toward music that only come together, in the works of poets and speculative writers on many subjects, in the last two decades of the sixteenth century. The acceptance of music as *paideia* (whether by Humanist educators or writers of courtesy literature) and the implications for metaphysics and ethics of Humanist musical theory may be observed in scattered instances, however, early in the 1500's. Even earlier, the listing of music as an "accomplishment" occurs in Caxton's *Book of Curtesye* (1477):

> It is to a godly child wel fyttynge
> To vse disportis of myrthe & plesaunce
> To harpe or lute or lostely to synge
> Or in the prees right manerly to daunce
> Whan men se a chyld of suche gouernaunce

> They saye glad may this chyldis frendis be
> To haue a chylde so manerly as is he.[63]

This falls, of course, far short of Count Ludovico's learned and eloquent defense of music in *The Courtier*,[64] in which the physical and spiritual benefits of music are expounded at length, with many examples from Classic authors, in a manner which would become standard practice for the following hundred years and more. But it is plainly a beginning. Of the musical activity at the courts of both Henry VII and his son enough is known to lead one to infer that music was beginning to be cultivated as a courtly practice encouraged, in the latter case, by the king himself.[65]

A growing association of music with manners, at any rate, seems to be responsible for the extended string of musical images in a lively piece of satire by John Skelton, probably written while he was tutoring the future king at his father's court.[66] Later, in his self-congratulatory *The Garlande of Laurell* (1523), Skelton was capable of writing about the music of Orpheus in the manner of Lydgate. He describes a vision in which

> Orpheus, the Traciane, herped meledyously
> Weth Amphion, and other Musis of Archady:
>
> Whos heuenly armony was so passynge sure,
> So truely proporsionyd, and so well did gree,
> So duly entunyd with euery mesure,

[63] *Caxton's Book of Curtesye*, ed. F. J. Furnivall (London, 1868), p. 31.
[64] Baldassare Castiglione, *The Courtier* (1528), tr. Thomas Hoby (1561), Everyman Edition, pp. 75-77.
[65] For a brief discussion of the music of the Tudor court, see Ernest Walker, *A History of Music in England*, third edition, ed. and enlarged by J. A. Westrup (Oxford, 1952), pp. 18-52; also, Gustave Reese, *Music in the Renaissance* (New York, 1954), pp. 763-815; and Wilfred Mellers, *Music and Society* (New York, 1950), pp. 65-85.
[66] At some time between 1495 and 1499, at any rate, if line 14 ("Lord, how Perkyn is proud of hys pohen [peahen]") does indeed refer to a still living Perkin Warbeck and the wife he married in 1495, four years before his hanging for treason.

> That in the forest was none so great a tre
> But that he daunced for ioye of that gle.
>
> (ll. 272-278)[67]

But the earlier tirade is rather different stuff. It is written "*Agaynste a comely coystrowne* [bastard], *that curyowsly chawntyd, and curryshly cowntred* [sung a part], *and madly in hys musykkys mokkyshly made agaynste the ix Musys of polytyke poems and poettys matryculat.*"[68] Perhaps the target of Skelton's mockery actually used courtly musical activity as a ladder for his social climbing; perhaps, however, the whole musical conceit is merely metaphoric, like several specific references to the duties of the stable (whether or not for some literal, biographical reason) mentioned in connection with the later line "For Jak wold be a jentylman, that late was a grome." The poem starts out with Skelton's statement of his profound annoyance at those who commit the eighth sin of "peuyshnes," and turns immediately to his victim who, he says, "When he is well, yet can he not rest" (l. 7). The second of the poem's ten rhyme-royal stanzas compares court baked-goods and those made for horses, concluding with the general observation that "But for in his gamut carp that he can, / Lo, Jak wold be a jentylman!" The third stanza makes some passing references to popular songs of the period and their refrains, supposedly sung by the victim. But the next strophe opens up mercilessly the long musical comparison:

> He can not fynd it in rule nor in space:
> He solfyth to haute, hys trybyll is to hy;
> He braggyth of his byrth, that borne was full bace;
> Hys musyk withoute mesure, to sharp is hys my;
> He trymmyth in hys tenor to counter pyrdewy;
> His dyscant is besy, it is withoute a mene;
> To fat is hys fantsy, hys wyt is to lene.

[67] John Skelton, *Poetical Works*, "principally according to the edition of" Alexander Dyce (Boston, 1856), II, 182.
[68] *Ibid.*, I, 19-22.

He lumbryth on a lewde lewte, Roty bully joyse,
  Rumbyll downe, tumbyll downe, hey go, now, now!
He fumblyth in hys fyngeryng an vgly good noyse,
  It semyth the sobbyng of an old sow:
  He wold be made moch of, and he wyst how;
Wele sped in spyndels and turnyng of tauellys;
A bungler, a brawler, a pyker of quarellys.

Comely he clappyth a payre of clauycordys;
  He whystelyth so swetely, he makyth me to swete;
His descant is dasshed full of dyscordes;
  A red angry man, but easy to intrete:
  An vssher of the hall fayn wold I get,
To poynte this proude page a place and a rome,
For Jak wold be a jentylman, that late was a grome.

Jak wold jet, and yet Jyll says nay;
  He counteth in his countenaunce to checke with
      the best:
A malaperte medler that pryeth for his pray,
  In a dysh dare he rush at the rypest;
  Dremyng in dumpys to wrangyll and to wrest:
He fyndeth a proporcyon in his prycke song,
To drynk at a draught a larg and a long.

                              (ll. 22-49)

The flexibility of the musical imagery here is most interesting.
Skelton puns upon the musical term to refer to his victim's
ancestry ("full bace"), and, later on, to embellish the theme
of his gluttony (a "larg" and a "long" are the two longest
note values in the so-called "white mensural notation" of the
period; the more common name was "maxima"). On the
other hand, the faults of musicianship that the victim commits
in the poem are treated at face value, as breaches of manners
or worse. In "Comely he clappyth a payre of clauycordys,"
either the line and the following one are completely sarcastic,
or the second following is a somewhat strained metaphor (of

which Skelton is quite capable), not about the poor man's playing, but about his "upper part," or head, perhaps. The general theme of overreaching, social climbing, is figured wonderfully in "He solfyth to haute, hys trybyll is to hy," and the constant harping on busy-ness applies to that lack of courtly *sprezzatura* which betrays the base origin. The conclusion of the main portion of the satire (the last two stanzas are a conventional exhortation to improve and to "come fight it out," possibly with a "flyting") betrays some of the personal animosities of an academic, jealous either of the standards of his profession, or of his own situation and status:

> Nay, iape not with hym, he is no small fole,
>   It is a solemnpne syre and a solayne;
> For lordes and ladyes lerne at his scole;
>   He techyth them so wysely to solf and to fayne,
>   That neyther they synge wel prycke songe
>   nor playne:
> Thys docter Deuyas commensyd in a cart,
> A master, a mynstrell, a fydler, a farte.
>
> (ll. 50-56)

Throughout this torrent of raillery, Skelton refers always to practical music; and whether or not his target was an actual teacher or style-setter, it is not the academic discipline that is being discussed, but rather the actual singing and playing that would be heard at court. "Countering," "knacking" (l. 17), "wrangling," "wresting," are all terms for singing a rather complicated vocal part; "solfing" is still "solfa-ing" today, and "fayn" may possibly designate either *musica ficta* or improvisation, in the same sense that is indicated by a modern musician's use of "to fake." The distinction between "pricksong" and "plainsong" is the old one that concerns Walter and William in the fourteenth-century poem discussed earlier in this chapter. And the "Dremyng in dumpys" may be the earliest use of the word "dump" in a printed source: it has, at any rate, no "doleful" meaning at all, a "dump" at this time probably being a musical composition with a recurrent, *ostinato*-like figure in the bass ("Pastime with Good Company," a song ascribed to Henry VIII himself, might be called a dump).[69] Whether or not Skelton is using music to stand for all the learning that he felt privileged to impart,[70] or whether his victim's musical activities are being pilloried with no worse a distortion than that of caricature, the figurative association of bad music and bad behavior is clear.

Dating from about the same time is one of the most elaborate (as well as one of the most puzzling) musical-ethical treatises of the Northern Renaissance. The so-called "Leckingfield Proverbs," some sixty-six couplets arranged into groups of four lines, were once ascribed to Skelton, but since the beginning of the present century the most likely candidate has appeared to be one William Peeris (fl. ca. 1520), family chaplain of Henry Percy, Fifth Earl of Northumberland. The proverbs were originally found written "In the garet at the New Lodge in the parke of leckingfelde," as a slightly later MS tells us,[71] and they go to make up one of the most complete treatises on vocal, instrumental, and basic theoretical practice in English before the later decades of the century. These verses are given complete in an appendix to this study;[72] the curious moral tone must be remarked upon here, however. The opening lines start out with the invention of music, and make no attempt to adjudicate the Tubal-Pythagoras dispute:

[69] See John Ward, "The Dolfull Domps," *Journal of the American Musicological Society*, IV (1951), pp. 111-121.

[70] There is a possibility that, even as early as this, an equation of music and learning in general is conventional. See, for example, Caxton's Preface to *The boke of Eneydos compyled by Vyrgyle* (1490), in which he says of Skelton: "And also he hath redde the ix. muses and vderstande theyr musicalle scyences, and to whom of them ech scyence is apropred. I suppose he hath dronken of Elycon's well." Quoted in Skelton, *Works, ed.cit.*, I, xix.

[71] The text here used is from Ewald Flügel, "Kleinere Mitteilungen aus Handschriften," *Anglia*, XIV (1891-1892), pp. 477-480; all the Leckingfield proverbs are also printed in F. Grose, *Antiquarian Repertory* (London, 1808), IV, 332ff.

[72] See below, Appendix B.

1. When the philosophers putagoras and tuball.
   From the pure sympill hammer and stethe svbstanciall.
   The celestiall soundes of musyk first made & dyd expres
   They fet them not from curiosite nor grete riches.

2. Oute of the trew plaine songe they Judgyde the
          melody
   Curious conueyinge hydithe much armanye
   Therfore of the playne nottis to sette a sure grounde
   Makithe a modulacion of moste parfyte sounde.
   In curiosite oftyme trowthe slippith by.
   And in the playne trew nottis all the swetenes
          dothe lye.

After this, stanzas 3 through 9 concern themselves with details
of singing; then stanzas 10-20 take up specific problems of
playing and (particularly) tuning the harp, clavichord, lute,
monochord, virginal, trumpet, shawm, organ, and recorder,
in that order. Next a discourse on notation and the perils of
misunderstanding it and consequently getting proportions
wrong follows (21-29), replete with specific, sometimes symbolic references to the "colors" of notation, the names of the
parts of a musical composition ("meane"), etc. The concluding
quatrains again emerge into the more general air of *musica
speculativa*:

30. Musike is a science and one of the seuyn
    Withe swete sowndes to prays the plasmator of heuyn
    They that of protervite will not tewne well
    Ve. Ve. Ve. theyre songe shalbe in hell.

31. He that lystithe his notis to tune welle and tyme
    Muste measure in melpomene one of the muses ix
    If he meddyll withe megera infernall is the sounde
    Ibi erit fletus malange to confounde.

32. The modulacion of musyke is swete and celestiall
     In the speris of the planettis makynge sownde
            armonicall
     If we moder oure musyke as the trew tune is
     In heuyn we shall synge *Osanna in excelsis.*

The poem thus ends, quite properly, with mention of the music of the spheres. All along, however, it has been drawing dire conclusions about the moral evil of playing badly, miscalculating a change of rhythm, or not keeping an instrument in proper tune, or being so "curious" that the "playne trew nottis" are betrayed by over-fancy but not really good, musicianly playing.

The stress on tuning in these verses, as well as their nods toward the Greek world (in occasional words, references, and spellings), seem peculiar perhaps; but there does seem to have been a kind of Pythagorean spirit about the last days of the court of Henry VII, involving particularly a number of composers.[73] It must also be remembered that problems of tuning and temperament were crucial to musical theorists throughout the sixteenth century, and that a great interest was taken in mathematical proportion (this time because of rhythmic considerations), by the theorists of the *ars nova* in the fourteenth century. The peculiarly retarded state of English music being what it was, such a movement might seem to lie in a kind of twilight world between the Medievalism of one set of concerns and the Neoclassicism of the others. A musician like William Cornyshe, composer and actor in and arranger of court theatricals for Henry VII, was capable of

[73] John E. Stevens, in "Rounds and Canons from an Early Tudor Songbook," *Music and Letters*, XXXII (1951), pp. 29-37, suggests that such a group centered about William Cornyshe, and that it was highly hermetic, devoted to Pythagoras (whom they meant by "The Philosopher," rather than Aristotle), and much given to the use of what Greek they had. Their musical activity, as a group, involved the writing of the elaborate puzzle canons typical of the fifteenth century in Northern Europe, but with Greek terms in the clues and descriptions, and a suggestion of Humanism in their attention to the New Learning.

writing something that looks very much like the Leckingfield Proverbs, and twisted about so as to allegorize the musical *caveat* in a completely ethical way, with polemical application.

In "A parable betwene enformacion and musike," formerly printed in editions of Skelton up through the eighteenth century, the injunctions about instruments, singing, and notation from the other set of proverbs are suddenly turned into what is almost a scene from a morality, when wily "Enfirmacion" attempts to play the part of the good musician.[74] He ends up, however, the victim of musical-moral complaint much more in the philosophical tone of the Leckingfield Proverbs than in the excited, belligerent one of Skelton.

A second generation of Humanist scholar-musicians seemed more interested in making public advertisement of the virtues of their discipline than in conducting private wars or in giving coterie advice. Interesting examples of this appear in two dramatic interludes of the period before 1530. The first of these is less specifically propagandistic than the second, although the author's intention is made quite clear through the allegory. John Rastell's *The Interlude of the Nature of the Four Elements* has been of most interest to scholars because of its extended treatment of recent geographical explorations and discoveries;[75] at one point, however, Rastell, no musician himself (he was a lawyer and member of Parliament, and translated the *Celestina*), contrives to work some musical discussion into what a modern playwright would consider a brief scene of build-up for a song. Sensuall Appetyte, a common figure in interludes and late moralities, and his troupe of

[74] This is part of a longer "Treatise Between Truth and Information," an attack on Sir Richard Empson, who had had Cornyshe imprisoned in the Fleet jail. For text and comment see below, Appendix C; also, Flügel, *op.cit.*, pp. 466-471. Cornyshe seems to have been at the center of the group discussed by Stevens; his secular compositions include settings of Skelton and verses attributed to Wyatt. The association of Peeris, Skelton, and Cornyshe was through the Percy family, as well as through the Court. See Skelton's *Works, ed.cit.*, I, xvii.

[75] See E. M. Nugent, "Sources of John Rastell's *The Nature of the Four Elements*," *PMLA*, LVII (1942), pp. 74-88.

dancers have just sung an *a cappella* three-part vocal piece and
then Sensuall Appetyte has performed a solo. It is suggested
that a "kyt or taberet" (stringed instrument or drum) to
accompany the singing, in the hands of a minstrel, would make
the whole thing sound better, at which suggestion Sensuall
Appetyte and his crew leave in search of a tavern and minstrels, *"exeunt cantando."* Left on stage are Humanyte and
Yngnorans, a well-known pair in school-plays. The former
begins:

Hu.   Now yf that Sensuall Appetyte can fynd
      Any good mynstrelles after hys mynd,
      Dout not we shall have good sport.

Yng. And so shall we have for a suerte:
      But what shall we do now, tell me,
      The meane whyle for our comfort.

Hu.   Then let us some lusty balet syng.

Yng. Nay, syr, by the Hevyn King!
      For me thynkyth it servyth for nothyng,
      All suche pevysh prykyerd song!

Hu.   Pes, man, pryksong may not be dispysyd,
      For therwith God is well plesyd,
      Honowryd, praysyd and servyd
      In the churche oft tymes among.

Yng. Is God well pleasyd? trowst thou therby?
      Nay, nay for there is no reason why,
      For it is not as good to say playnly,
      Gyf me a spade,
      As gyf me a spa, ve, va, ve, va, ve, vade?
      But yf thou wylt have a song that is good,
      I have one of Robyn Hode,
      The best that ever was made.[76]

[76] John Rastell, *The Nature of the Four Elements,* facsimile prepared by
J. S. Farmer (London: Tudor Facsimile Texts, 1908), sig. E7^v.

Then the song is sung. Yngnorans' argument against "prykyeryd song"—that is, composed music written in mensural notation (as usually opposed to "plain song" or any one of a number of oral traditions, such as plain chant, folksong, popular dance tunes, etc.)—is one which we will find about sixty years later incorporated into Puritan polemic against elaborate church music. Here he is allowed to clown it up a bit. The joke would be turned against fancy, learned music with its melismatic treatment of words (note also his piety about it all), were it not for Humanyte's little encomium about the exalted nature of prick-song, and for the fact that Yngnorans is, as always, to be put down finally. The objection (that music "servyth for nothyng") and the defense (that it honors, praises, and serves God) contain in germ much later musical debate. What is interesting is that even here Yngnorans' objections are religious. But it should not be forgotten that this little scene has the effect of introducing another kind of song (a plain song of Robin Hood, instead of a "lusty balet"—we will be misled if we use the latter term in our sense: the "balet" was a part-song).

Rastell, however, unlike many other early court dramatists, was no musician. John Heywood, perhaps the most famous of these playwrights, was master of an organization of singing boys; and John Redford, with whom he may have been associated, had become Master of the Children at St. Paul's in 1534. Redford's morality *Wyt and Science* (probably about 1530) concerns the tribulations of Wyt, a student engaged to Lady Science and obligated by a promise to her parents, Reason and Experience, to make a journey to Parnassus, overcoming Tedyiousnes on the way. He sets off, with his companions named Instruccion, Study, and Dylygence; all of these are eventually lost by the wayside, either through their own vagrancy or through the interference of the Vice, Tedyiousnes; the latter mauls Wyt with his club, knocking him out. Then enters Honest Recreation, a gentle lady sent, we learn later, by Reason. She and her attendants sing a part-song, kneeling about the unconscious Wyt, and revive him with the inspirational effects of their text, probably, more than with the medicinal value of the singing. Wyt, revived, forgets his Lady Science, and makes a pass at Honest Recreation, who rebuffs him, but in the end suggests a dance, only to have Wyt fall, at the end of it, into the lap of Idellnes, a whore. Honest Recreation warns the student of the monster into whose clutches he is falling, and Idellnes replies with a long vituperative speech, calling the excellent lady who revived Wyt after he had been attacked by Tedyiousnes a harlot herself. Part of Idellnes' harangue is of considerable interest:

Under the name of Honest Recreation
She, lo! bryngth in her abhominacion!
Mark her dawnsyng, her maskyng, and mummyng.
Where more concupyscence then ther cummyng?
Her cardyng, her dycyng, dayly and nyghtlye—
Where fynd ye more falcehod then there? Not lyghtly!
Wyth lyeng and sweryng by no poppetes,
But teryng God in a thowsand gobbetes.
As for her syngyng, pypyng and fydlyng,
What unthryftynes therin is twydlyng!
Serche the tavernes and ye shall here cleere
Such bawdry as bestes wold spue to heere.

(ll. 371-382)[77]

But this is the harlot, herself, talking; the whole device is part of a noble tradition of Humanist satire in which the Enemy is put down by means of his own (purported) words. Additional point is gained by the fact that there is considerable actual music in the interlude itself, with Redford's choir boys being shown off to good advantage, and their Master's best secular compositions as well. Later on in the play, Favor, Fame, and Ryches, emissaries of the World, come to serenade Lady Science, and they too sing, accompanied by their own

[77] John Redford, *Wyt and Science*, in *Chief Pre-Shakespearean Dramas*, p. 331.

viols. Two more elaborate part-songs of reconciliation come at the end of the play, by which time the kind of traditional allegorical objections to music formerly associated with such situations[78] is completely put down, as far as the audience is concerned. Both as a dramatic device to introduce an extra song, and as a piece of strongly felt personal polemic ("pypyng and fydlyng" was the kind of phrase that grated against the ears of a learned and well-placed dramatist and musician), the episode seems eminently successful.[79]

But neither the spread of knowledge as a result of the efforts of the committed leaders of the New Learning, nor the encouragement of musical and dramatic activities in the court of Henry VIII (and of liturgical music in the cathedrals), could stem two slowly developing traditions of the dispraise of music that would receive constant voice throughout the remainder of the century. This dispraise was not only to call forth eloquent defense but would serve to bring together for polemical (and later, poetic) purposes many previously scattered and separate themes of speculative music that had never been united in any one speculative or literary work. The process of refuting pious attacks on music, both sacred and secular, and of countering courtly objections to the feminizing influence of music and dance in the education of a

---

[78] As, for example, in the *Pilgrimage of the Life of Man* again (see above, n. 53), where the girl Yowthe and the temptress Ydelnesse both give long recitals of their musical activities, replete with the customary list of instruments and musical forms, all mingled together. See ll. 11200ff. and particularly, 11610-11620, in the text edited by F. J. Furnivall (London, 1901), II, 307, 317.

[79] The abuse even of academic musicians of the highest standing got rather fierce in England in the sixteenth century; see Ernest Brennecke, "A Singing Man of Windsor," *Music and Letters*, XXXIII (1952), pp. 33-40. For more of Redford's writing on specifically musical subjects, see *The Moral Play of Wit and Science*, ed. J. O. Halliwell (London, 1848), pp. 62-65, where there appears reprinted a manuscript poem on the difficulty of learning to sing "pevysh pryk song," to be sung or recited by a small boy. It is largely a complaint against the master (Redford himself?) for his demands and beatings ("Out of our buttokes we may pluck the stumpes thus longe!"). Also see Arthur Brown, "Two Notes on John Redford," *Modern Language Review*, XLIII (1948), pp. 508-510.

future prince or nobleman, served to organize the diverse materials of inherited Medieval musical lore and knowledge, and to bring to bear on them the newfound knowledge of the Classics. And, finally, by extension in various ways, the defense of music was eventually to have an important role in the defense of poetry itself.

Music Praised and Blamed

The very height of venom in attacking music-makers was probably attained long before the middle of the sixteenth century, if not by zealous patristic writers condemning secular music in order to belabor the flute-girls of the theaters, then certainly by Medieval churchmen like the twelfth-century Aelred, Abbot of Rievaulx, Yorkshire, who in a famous passage in his *Speculum Charitatis* attacked the liturgical music of his own day.[80] The Gothic retribution meted out by Hieronymus Bosch in the "Hell of the Musicians" panel of his great triptych, "The Garden of Earthly Delights," may perhaps, as one rather unorthodox interpreter has suggested, be no anti-musical representation at all.[81] Yet at no more than first glance, it is a fiendish and ingenious assembly of tortures and perversions of the use of instruments that seems, except for the uniqueness of the symbolic imagination behind it, not

[80] Aelred is quoted at length by William Prynne. See below, Chapter v, pp. 257-260.

[81] See Wilhelm Fränger, *The Millennium of Hieronymus Bosch*, tr. Eithne Wilkins and Ernst Kaiser (Chicago, 1951), pp. 84-91. Fränger bases his interpretation of this lurid scene upon his general theories about the significance of the doctrines of the Adamite cult for the iconography of his paintings, and also upon some Neoplatonic musico-theology in the philosophy of Erigena, which he feels to be relevant here. But there is too much to be said about this here, other than to note the interesting combination of harp and lute in the treble instrument of the three in the center of the scene (a figure is crucified in its strings, and it may comment very literally upon the evil of making a synthesis of the divine harp and the vulgar lute, a synthesis whose prevalence we have already observed). It should also be added that the opening interval in the upper line of the music printed in a book placed beneath the harp-lute is that of the dreaded tri-tone, the "*diabolus in musica*" of all Medieval and Gothic musical theory (see the transcription in Fränger, p. 87, where this is not commented upon).

unconventional. From the medieval moralist's condemnation of minstrels to the complex series of struggles for status by professional musicians in the sixteenth century,[82] a constant stream of attack aimed at the practitioners themselves often eclipsed any more sophisticated arguments against music pure and simple. Just as the courtly and religious attacks on music in the sixteenth century must be distinguished, so must the learned and unlearned sorts of deprecation. The latter distinction often cuts at right angles, as it were, to the former. By and large, two or three polemical devices are constantly employed by the "learned" writers: in the first place, every bit of Classical or Christian lore about music that hints of a judgment against any one musical form or type or institution (the Greek philosophers' distrust of the *aulos*, for example, or Plato's and Aristotle's preference for certain scales) was taken as an implied synecdoche. The part, that is, was taken for the whole, and used as evidence that all of music (or the specific contemporary musical institution under fire) was thus condemned. Confusions about instruments and their names were put to good use, so that any instrumentalist could become a "fiddler" or a "piper." And there was always some venerable text to condemn either of these.

The cleverest confounder of music in the Elizabethan era is one of the few who grant the increasingly common Neoclassic premise that the music of Antiquity was far superior to that of his own day. Stephen Gosson, in *The Schoole of Abuse* (1579), levels his attack against music, stage-playing, and poetry ("Cosen germans," he calls them) with this historical degeneration in mind. After listing in a typical anecdotal fashion the virtues of Ancient music and poetry, he asks

[82] See the excellent study by Walter L. Woodfill, *Musicians in English Society* (Princeton, 1953), particularly pp. 201-239, for additional comment and examples of the subject discussed below. The whole volume should be consulted for a historical record of the changing role of the professional and amateur musician at the end of the sixteenth century. The traditional abuse of the professional musician continues well on into the seventeenth century, as represented by character books like John Earle's *Micro-Cosmographie* (1628), ed. E. Arber (London, 1868); see pp. 51, 69.

"Thinke you that those miracles could bee wrought with play-ing of Daunces, Dumpes, Pauins, Galiardes, Measures Fancyes or new streynes?" He then urges his readers to forgo practical music for its speculative branch: "*Pythagoras* bequeathes them a Clookebagge, and condemnes them for fooles, that iudge Musicke by sounde and eare. If you will bee good Scholars, and profite well in the Arte of Musicke, shutte your Fidels in their cases, and looke vp to heauen: the order of the Spheres, the vnfallible motion of the Planets, the iuste course of the yeere, and varieties of seasons, the concorde of the Elementes and their qualyties, Fyre, Water, Ayre, Earth, Heate, Colde, Moysture and Drought concurring together to the constitu-tion of earthly bodies and sustenance of euery creature."[83] After considering the concord of "well gouerned common wealthes" Gosson declares with the fervor of a staunch de-fender of practical music for partaking of these qualities, "this is right Musicke, this perfecte harmony." C. S. Lewis has sug-gested[84] that Gosson's delight in his own literary style may have obscured an interest in the position he was defending. This seems certainly true in a passage which utilizes the old, Medieval objection to newfangledness, but where the typically euphuistic list and paraphrased proverb seem themselves to have occasioned the whole point. Just after mentioning the Greek anecdote about Terpander and the punishments he incurred for adding extra strings to the lyre, Gosson continues: "Were the *Argiues* and *Pythagoras* now aliue, and saw how many frets, how many stringes, how many stops, how many keyes, how many sharps, how many rules, how many spaces, how many noates, how many restes, how many querkes, how many corners, what chopping, what changing, what tossing, what turning, what wresting and wringing is among our Musitions, I beleue verily that they would cry out with the

[83] Stephen Gosson, *The Schoole of Abuse*, ed. Edward Arber (Birming-ham, 1868), pp. 25-26.
[84] C. S. Lewis, *English Literature in the Sixteenth Century* (Oxford, 1954), p. 395.

countryman: *Heu quod tam pingui macer est mihi in aruo.*
Alas, here is fat feeding, and leane beastes. . . ."[85]

Roger Ascham, in the first dialogue of *Toxophilus* (1545),
brings up music mostly in order to discredit it in favor of his
chosen subject, archery. But his objections, or rather, those of
his protagonist, Toxophilus, are confined to a number of illustrations and conclusions drawn from Classical authors about
the weakening, relaxing effects of music. Since his main theme
throughout has been the *corpus sanum* part of the famous
dualism, he sees these effects of music as a kind of moral sub-
version. Toxophilus discusses the Greek philosophers' disapproval of the Lydian scale because of its laxness and voluptuousness; he acknowledges what appear to have been just those
virtues of the Dorian for which he is arguing but goes on to
employ one of the devices used by almost every "classicizing"
musical attacker: "Nowe wether these balades and roundes,
these galiardes, pauanes and daunces, so nicelye fingered, so
swetely tuned, be lyker the Musike of the Lydians or the
Dorians, you that be learned iudge. And what so euer ye
iudge, this I am sure, yat lutes, harpes, all maner of pypes,
barbitons, sambukes, with other instruments euery one, whyche
standeth by fine and quicke fingeringe, be condemned of
Aristotle, as not to be brought in and vsed among them,
which studie for learning and vertue."[86] There is almost a
kind of calculated know-nothingism about Ascham's list of
instruments, in which contemporary and Classical names are
strung together in a careless-sounding way. Toxophilus' real
objection, it turns out, is that "the minstrelsie of lutes, pipes,
harpes, and all other that standeth by suche nice, fine minikin
fingering (suche as the mooset parte of scholers whom I knowe
vse, if they vse any) is farre more fitte for the womannishnesse
of it to dwell in the courte among ladies, than for any great
thing in it, whiche shulde helpe good and sad studie, to abide
in the vniuersitie amonges scholers."[87]

[85] Gosson, *op.cit.*, p. 27.
[86] Roger Ascham, *Toxophilus*, ed. Edward Arber (London, 1868), p. 39.
[87] *Ibid.*, p. 41.

It is interesting to note that Philologus, the dialogue's antagonist and pupil, retorts with an impassioned defense of singing (rather than instrumental music), for many of the reasons that Toxophilus has condemned music in general, and laments several times the decline of music-teaching to children: "I wysshe from the bottome of my heart, that the laudable custome of Englande to teache chyldren their plaine-song and priksong, were not so decayed throughout all the realme as it was."[88] Philologus' encomium of singing is based on arguments common in the sixteenth century: its "natural-ness," the physical benefits accruing therefrom (a good voice was called a "good breast"), etc. But Ascham's overall attack on what he feels to be mincing, courtly music is hardly miti-gated either by this or by his subsequent remarks in *The Scholemaster* (1570) to the effect that "the Muses, besides learning, were also Ladies of dauncinge, mirthe and minstrel-sie: *Apollo*, was god of shooting, and Author of cunning playing upon Instruments."[89] But this admission is qualified by the context of the argument in which it occurs, under the rubric, that is of "learnyng joyned with Pastime"; in Apollo's case, the shooting was the learning, the music the "mirthe."

With only a few exceptions, verse is not employed as a medium by music's detractors in the sixteenth century. A fairly long dispraise of music by a poet of some gifts occurs in "The Fourthe Songe" of George Gascoigne's *The Grief of Joye Certeyne Elegies: Wherein the doubtfull delightes of manes lyfe, are displaied*, published in 1576. This work is in Gas-coigne's moralizing vein, and is only a little less gloomy than his rewriting of the Medieval *De Contemptu Mundi* which he did in the same year. In the fourth of the "songs" of this work addressed to the Queen herself, Gascoigne announces his intention to show how "the mynde" "Can seldome be, so

---

[88] *Ibid.*, p. 41. This gets to be a common cry after 1570, too. See Morison Comegys Boyd, *Elizabethan Music and Musical Criticism* (Philadelphia, 1940), pp. 13-36. Also, Woodfill, *op.cit.*, p. 241.

[89] Roger Ascham, *English Works*, ed. W. A. Wright (Cambridge, 1904), p. 216.

bridled from the badd, / But that delight, maie draw one
foote tofarre, / Whils vayne excesse, the mery meane dothe
marre."[90] He continues:

13 To prove this trew, who shall the game Begynne?
Must musicke first, bewraye her vayne delight?
And must she saye, that as the fowlers gynne,
Dothe lye full close in depthe of dangers dight,
Whiles yet his pype, dothe playe in plesaunt plight:
Even soe, her sweete consents beguyle sometymes,
The highest harte, in harmonye that clymes? /

For fourteen rhyme-royal stanzas he continues his deprecation, all directed to this initially stated theme and employing
a wealth of Classical allusion. At times, his diction attains
the realm of the best Elizabethan wit, with musical puns and
personal anecdote skillfully applied to a purpose often calling
for rant:

19 Amongst the vaynes, of variable Joyes,
I must confesse, that Musicke pleasd me ones
But whiles I searcht, the semyquaver toyes,
The glancing sharpes, the halfe notes for the nones;
And all that serves, to grave owre gladsome grones;
I found a flatt, of follye owt of frame,
Whiche made me graunt my Musicke was but lame.

20 I meane I fownde, that (ravished thereby)
My wandring mynde, sometyme forgott yt selfe /
And reason ranne, his cowrce so farre awrye,
That ere I wyst, my wytts were sett on shelfe
Of trothe my braynes, so full were of suche pelfe,
That some reporte, contynually dyd ryng
Within myne eares, and made me seeme to singe.

---

[90] George Gascoigne, *The Glasse of Government and other Works*, ed.
John W. Cunliffe (Cambridge, 1910), pp. 550-554. No line numberings
are given; these lines are from stanza 12.

21 I coulde not reade, but I must tune my words/
   I coulde not speake, but as yt were by note/
   I coulde not muze, but that I thought some byrds,
   Within my brest did rellease all by rote . . .

Gascoigne's diction comes closest to the actually elegant, yet still obviously early-Elizabethan tone of his best verse, in a stanza in which he moralizes the myth of the swan-song for his own purposes. After invoking Nero as a sweet singer who died in the midst of his foolish music, he goes on:

24 And lyke the Swanne, he soong before his deathe/
   Whiche maie suffise, to prove the tyckell trust,
   That can be buylt, upon our fading breathe/
   Yt may suffise to shewe that all oure lust,
   At last will leave us, yn the depthe of dust/
   Yt serves to prove, that no man synges so sweete,
   As can eschewe, withe bytter deathe to meete./

This disapproval of music as a distraction, as the irresistible Siren song that lures the helpless conscience to its wreck, or simply as a more subtle version of the lascivious fiddling decried by many Medieval writers, finds few advocates in verse, as was previously remarked. Before passing over to the question of the defense of music, however, we might examine a most subtle use, not of these themes aimed at the dispraise of music, but of the tradition of that dispraise for larger narrative and allegorical purposes.

There is no overabundance of musical reference or imagery in *The Faerie Queene*. Just as its rare occurrences in the actual narrative have a kind of decorative role, as music of festivity or celebration, so does the poetic representation of the musical sounds, their manner of production, and their effects follow a course rather more of embroidery than of lengthy, interpolated catalogs or disquisitions on musical lore and doctrine. There is triumphal music at Redcrosse Knight's return and his engagement to Una (*F.Q.*, I.xii.7, 13), and at the occasion

of their marriage, when "all the while sweete musicke did
apply / Her curious skill, the warbling notes to play,"[91] and
which terminates in the answering echoes of heavenly harmony, producing an ecstatic effect upon the assembled hearers:

> During the which there was an heavenly noise
> Heard sownd through all the pallace pleasantly,
> Like as it had bene many an angels voice
> Singing before th' Eternall Majesty,
> In their trinall triplicities on hye;
> Yett wist no creature, whence that heavenly sweet
> Proceeded, yet each one felt secretly,
> Himselfe thereby refte of his sences meet,
> And ravished with rare impression in his sprite.
>
> (F.Q., I.xii.39)

But this is no earthly music that has such spiritual effects.
Earthly music is a different matter. The most obvious comparison is with the music in Castle Joyeous, where there is a
kind of parallel to the wedding music mentioned above:

> And all the while sweete musicke did divide
> Her looser notes with Lydian harmony;
> And all the while sweet birdes thereto applide
> Their daintie layes and dulcet melody,
> Ay caroling of love and jollity,
> That wonder was to heare their trim consort.
> Which when those knights beheld, with scornefull eye,
> They sdeigned such lascivious disport,
> And loath'd the loose demeanure of that wanton sort.
>
> (III.i.40)

The Lydian scale of Antiquity, with all of its associations of
voluptuousness, marks the music for what it is. What is most
interesting here is that the birds, the natural singers as opposed

---

[91] *F.Q.*, I.xii.38. The text is from Spenser's *Complete Works*, ed. R. E.
Neil Dodge (Cambridge, Mass., 1908).

to the artificial music-makers of human song, are here depicted as forming a "trim consort" or well-balanced instrumental ensemble with Malecasta's musicians. There is some enchantment about all this, and it echoes the earlier evil music in the Bower of Bliss, where not only birds but all the other sounds of nature "had for wantonesse ensude / Art, and that Art at Nature did repine," as in the case of the visual appearance of the Bower itself. The full description of this music bears out C. S. Lewis' contention[92] that it is the very artificiality of the Bower of Bliss (as opposed to the *natural* beauty of the Garden of Adonis, where, incidentally, there is no music at all), that signifies its role as the evil paradise:

> Eftsoones they heard a most melodious sound,
> Of all that mote delight a daintie eare,
> Such as attonce might not on living ground,
> Save in this paradise, be heard elswhere:
> Right hard it was for wight which did it heare,
> To read what manner musicke that mote bee:
> For all that pleasing is to living eare
> Was there consorted in one harmonee;
> Birds, voices, instruments, windes, waters, all agree.
>
> The joyous birdes, shrouded in chearefull shade,
> Their notes unto the voice attempred sweet:
> Th'angelicall soft trembling voyces made
> To th'instruments divine respondence meet:
> The silver sounding instruments did meet
> With the base murmure of the waters fall:
> The waters fall with difference discreet,
> Now soft, now loud, unto the wind did call:
> The gentle warbling wind low answered to all.

> (II.xii.70-71)

[92] *The Allegory of Love*, pp. 324-332. Lewis draws an important distinction between the moral significance of Malecasta's castle and Acrasia's Bower (pp. 339-344), but this does not affect the function of the music in any way. It is quite similar in both.

Guyon and the palmer follow the music to where "it seemed heard to bee" and find Acrasia and her enchanted lover surrounded by her musicians, "Many faire ladies and lascivious boyes, / That ever mixt their song with light licentious toyes" (these last would signify "fancies," and perhaps musical free composition). The picture calls to mind a scene done by a painter of the School of Fontainebleau, perhaps; but the moral import of the music is quite clear throughout. The pun on "bass," a very frequent one in Elizabethan and Metaphysical musical conceits, is here used admirably to indicate that art and nature are so confused, have so interchanged their roles, that the water-music (bearing, it is true, the bass part in the consort) is something lower and less exalted than the "silver sounding," artificially wrought playing of the instruments. Since the Art in the Bower of Bliss is hardly like that art "which in their piedness shares / With great creating Nature" in Perdita's garden, the amalgam is necessarily a noxious one. And the blending of natural and contrived musical sounds, while it depends on this notion of the latent evil of the artful and artificial, nevertheless harks back in essence to many Medieval attacks on music itself.[93]

The defense of music throughout the sixteenth century

[93] In general, Spenser is much less interested in music than is Sidney, and there are relatively few musical images or references in his entire corpus of work. The minstrelsy in *Epithalamion*, ll. 129-147 is clearly intended to represent folk rather than courtly music. It is described and praised, however, in the most conventional sixteenth-century terms. Mentioned are "The pipe, the tabor, and the trembling croud, / That well agree withouten breach or jar": there are no Orphean lyres or noble lutes here, and the instruments are all those of the tavern. Yet the music is as tuneful as if it were the heavenly harmony. The damsels dancing and singing with timbrels are so traditionally effective "That all the sences they doe ravish quite." Even the cries of boys in the street are harmoniously composed, "As if it were one voyce." The combined sounds finally reach heaven and *become*, in a sense, the cosmic music. In the equation of *song* and *poem* in that poem ("Song, made in lieu of many ornaments"), and in the treatment of musical terms in *The Teares of the Muses*, as well as in E. K.'s extended comments on the music of Antiquity in the October eclogue of *The Shepheardes Calender*, we have examples of musico-poetic blendings that may have been influenced by the musical experiments of the *Pléiade*, but which in any case reflect a generally Neoclassicist interest in the music-poetry of the ancient world.

contributed many opportunities for its formal praise, either in prose or in verse. The tradition of the *encomium musicae* which has been so enlighteningly traced through a number of Renaissance writers back to roots in Classical and Christian musical speculation by Professor James Hutton,[94] came after a while to be characterized as a more or less polemical one. The framework of the musical encomium is laid, from a formal point of view, in such relatively straightforward arguments in favor of including music in educational curricula as those of Sir Thomas Elyot and, later on in the century, Richard Mulcaster. The former, in the seventh chapter of Book I of *The Boke Named the Gouernour* (1531), urges the study of both speculative and practical music. For the latter, particularly in connection with learning to play an instrument, musicians of Antiquity are invoked. But there is more than one *caveat* to be displayed here; the playing of instruments, says Elyot, "moderately used and without diminution of honour, that is to say, without wanton countenance and dissolute gesture, is nat to be contemned."[95] There are other warnings, too; the dreadful example of Nero, who allowed himself to become so involved in his own deficient playing that he maltreated his captive audiences for insufficient adulation, is waved aloft: "O what misery was it to be subiecte to suche a minstrell, in whose musike was no melodye, but anguisshe and dolour?"[96] Elyot also seems to recall an argument similar to Lord Julian's in *The Courtier*, Book III (against those "hard and often divisions that declare more cunning than sweetness"[97] in playing an instrument), in tell-

---

[94] James Hutton, "Some English Poems on Praise of Music," *English Miscellany*, 2 (1951), pp. 1-63. Professor Hutton treats the *laudes musicae* as a tradition in itself, and tends to ignore either the poetic conventions in which a musical reference is embodied, or the ultimate function, within the poem or play (particularly in the case of Shakespeare), of the account of music's effects. He also neglects the polemical tradition in which the defense of music seemed necessary.

[95] Thomas Elyot, *The Boke Named the Gouernour* (Everyman Edition), p. 25.

[96] *Ibid.*, p. 27.

[97] *The Courtier*, tr. Hoby, *ed.cit.*, p. 194.

ing how "Kynge Philip, whan he harde that his sonne Alexander dyd singe swetely and properly, he rebuked him gentilly, saynge, But, Alexander, be ye nat ashamed that ye can singe so well and connyngly? whereby he mente that the open profession of that crafte was but of a base estimation."[98] The speculative part of music is to be learned because it leads to "the better attaynynge the knowledge of a publike weale; whiche, as I before haue saide, is made of an ordre of astates and degrees, and, by reason therof, conteineth in it a perfect harmony. . . ."[99] This last theme in particular, rather than a more general one of the elevating quality of the universal harmony and of the study of it, bears directly on Elyot's own subject. It is a theme which will get much fuller treatment, in this specifically political context, by Shakespeare and in Sir Richard Knolles' translation of Jean Bodin at the beginning of the seventeenth century.[100]

The worthy head of the Merchant Tailors School, however, in his *The First Part of the Elementarie* (1582), invokes no speculative side of music and no world harmony to bolster his purely pragmatic argument. Putting down what were evidently some of the usual objections, Mulcaster asks, "When Musik shall teach nothing but honest for delite, and pleasant for note, comlie for the place, and semelie for the person, sutable to the thing and servicable to circumstance, can that humor corrupt, which bredeth such delite . . .?"[101] Further on, he makes specific recommendations: sight-reading is to be taught first, the lute and virginal are the best instruments to be studied early "because of the full musik which is to be vttered by them & the varietie of fingring," a uniform notational system is to be encouraged, etc.[102] It is significant that his whole argument and exposition of the musical curriculum

[98] Elyot, p. 27.
[99] *Ibid.*, p. 28.
[100] See above, Chapter II, p. 41.
[101] Richard Mulcaster, *The First Part of the Elementarie*, ed. E. T. Campagnac (Oxford, 1925), p. 24.
[102] *Ibid.*, pp. 65-67.

follows the model of basic grammar, and enforces an analogy by the use of grammatical terms throughout.

But Mulcaster's thoroughly pragmatic approach is the general exception to the growing convention of the use of speculative music to defend the practice. Such is the case with prose defenses such as Thomas Lodge's answer to Gosson[103] and John Case's lengthy *apologia* in *The Praise of Musicke* (1586), which, followed by a Latin version of the same two years later, set forth arguments for music's virtues that are steeped in references to Greek music and philosophy.[104] This also seems to be the rule for laudatory poems of the later part of the century, which tend to expound musical doctrine rather than to generate conceits involving musical imagery, although this last is common practice in personal, commendatory poems prefixed to songbooks. A well-known example of the more expository style is that of a poem by Richard Edwards in the *Paradise of Dainty Devices* (1576), and quoted by Peter in *Romeo and Juliet*, IV, v, 128ff.:

> Where gripyng grief the hart would wound & dolfull
>   domps the minde oppresse
> There Musick with her siluer sound, is wont with
>   spede to giue redresse,
> Of troubled minde for euery sore, swete Musick hath
>   a salue therfore.
>
> In ioye it make our mirth abound, in grief it chers
>   our heauy sprights,

[103] Lodge addresses himself to "your second abuse, Gosson, your second abuse; your disprayses of Musik, which you unadvisedly terme pyping," and proceeds from the music of the spheres, through the fabled effects of music in Antiquity, finally drawing a distinction between praiseworthy music and blamable "pipers" and "harpinge merye beggers." See "A Reply to Stephen Gosson's Schoole of Abuse," etc. (1579), reprinted in *Elizabethan and Jacobean Pamphlets*, ed. George Saintsbury (New York, 1892), pp. 22-30.

[104] See *The Praise of Musicke* (London, 1586) and *Apologia musices cum vocalis quam instrumentalis et mixtae* (London, 1588). Also see M. C. Boyd, *op.cit.*, pp. 29-32, 292-300.

The carefull head release hath found, by Musicks
    pleasant swete delights
Our sences, what should I saie more, are subiect vnto
    Musicks lore.

The Godds by Musick hath their praie, the foule
    therein doeth ioye,
For as the Romaine Poets saie, in seas whom Pirats
    would destroye,
A Dolphin saued from death moste sharpe, Arion
    plaiyng on his harpe.

A heauenly gift, that turned the minde, like as the
    sterne doth rule the ship,
Musick whom the Gods assignde to comfort man,
    whom cares would nip,
Sith thou both man & beast doest moue, what wiseman
    then wil thee reproue.[105]

The general tenor of these lines is not so much music's power
to modulate behavior or feeling as, specifically, its power to
quicken despair into joy or at least well-being. The anecdote
of the third stanza is framed to this effect: the Olympians can
hunt with music, for the quarry delights even to die because
of the "silver sound";[106] and as birds, so with fish, for Arion
charmed his Dolphin into a willing craft. But there is no
appeal to *harmonia mundi* at all here. Only a few years later,
however, some stanzas from George Whetstone's elegy for
Sir James Dyer, an eminent jurist and husband of Sir Thomas
Elyot's widow, could turn a mere point of sentimental biography into an epitome of public virtue:

For publique good, when care had cloid his minde,
    The only ioye, for to repose his sprights,

---

[105] From *The Paradise of Dainty Devices* (1576-1606), ed. Hyder
Rollins (Cambridge, Mass., 1927), p. 63.
[106] Both Rollins and Hutton (*op.cit.*, p. 32n.) seem to misunderstand
the significance of "praie" and "foule," although Hutton corrects Rollins
with respect to the latter's suggested emendation of "soule."

Was musique sweet, which showed him wel inclind;
  For he that dooth in musique much delight,
A conscience hath disposed to most right;
The reason is, her sound within our eare,
A sympathie of heaven we think we heare:

And therefore, calde the image of the soule,
  Forth of the hart which care and greefe doth wrest:
The swan in songs, her passing-bell doth knowle;
  The nightengale, with thornes against her brest,
  Dooth wake to singe when other birds doo rest,
(As showen before) for to deceive their paine,
Whose torments else would make them crie amaine.[107]

Here the theme of music as the solace of grief is blended
with the more general function of universal harmony.

But perhaps no single musical *apologia* sums up this tradition as nicely as does "A Hymne in Prayse of Musicke"
appearing in Davison's *Poeticall Rhapsody* (1602) and most
often ascribed to Sir John Davies. It is unusual not so much
for the completeness of its stock of allusion, cosmological,
ethical, and heroic references, as for the excellent schematic
arrangement of these traditional materials within the frame
made by the tripartite distinction of its initial stanza:

Prayse, Pleasure, Profit, is that three-fold band,
Which ties mens minds more fast then Gardions knot.
Each one some drawes, al three none can withstand,
Of force conjoyn'd, Conquest is hardly got.
  Then Musicke may of harts a Monarcke bee,
  Wherein Prayse, Pleasure, Profit, so agree.[108]

The author then goes on to prove music's possession of these
three attributes:

[107] George Whetstone, "A Remembraunce of the Precious Vertues of the
Right Honourable and Reverend Judge, Sir James Dier, Knight . . ."
(1582). Quoted in Thomas C. Izard, *George Whetstone, Mid-Elizabethan
Man of Letters* (New York, 1942), pp. 241-242.
[108] In *A Poetical Rhapsody*, ed. Hyder Rollins (Cambridge, Mass., 1931-
1932), I, 201ff.

> Praise-worthy Musicke is, for God it prayseth,
> And pleasant, for brute beasts therein delight:
> Great profit from it flowes, for why it raiseth
> The minde ouerwhelmed with rude passions might.
>> When against reason passions fond rebell
>> Musicke doth that confirme, and these expell.

Music's role as a reasonable, leavening force on "rude passions" is different from another traditional view of its powers as exciting and controlling, rather than merely damping, the passions. The latter view, we shall discover, emerges triumphant during the seventeenth century. But Davies' music is the well-ordered, Dorian singing that Plato and Aristotle permitted.

The remainder of the poem employs traditional references to the heavenly music, the care-soothing powers of music over the woes of all creatures, examples from Antiquity, and the example of the natural music of birds:

> If Musicke did not merit endlesse prayse,
> Would heaun'ly Spheres delight in siluer round?
> If ioyous pleasure were not in sweet layes,
> Would they in Court and Country so abound?
>> And profitable needs wee must that call,
>> Which pleasure linkt with praise doth bring to al.

> Heroicke minds with praises most incited,
> Seeke praise in Musicke, and therein excell:
> God, man, beasts, birds, with Musick are delighted;
> And pleasant t'is, which pleaseth all so well.
>> No greater profit is then selfe content,
>> And this doth Musick bring, and care prevent.

> When Antique Poets Musicks praises tell,
> They say it beasts did please, and stones did moue:
> To proue more dul then stones, then beasts more fel,
> Those men, which pleasing Musick did not loue.

They fain'd, it Cities built, and States defended,
To shew the profit great on it depended.

Sweet birds (poore mens Musitians) neuer slake
To sing sweet Musicks prayses day and night:
The dying Swans in Musicke pleasure take,
To shew, that it the dying can delight;
    In sicknes, health, peace, war, wee do it need,
    Which proues, sweet Musicks profit doth exceed.

But I, by niggard praysing, do disprayse
Prayse-worthy Musicke in my worthles Ryme:
Ne can the pleasing profit of sweet layes,
Any saue learned Muses well define.
    Yet all by these rude lines may clearly see,
    Prayse, Pleasure, Profit, in sweet Musicke bee.

Of course, this argument does not proceed by means of mere exposition alone. There is much word-play here, particularly in the last five stanzas, where the scheme is the same throughout: the first two lines treat of *praise*, the second two of *pleasure* and the third pair, of *profit*. The concluding stanza is the most playful in this respect, and the most contrived and highly figured; and while the overall presentation of what is not very original musical doctrine moves along from point to point in a demonstrative fashion, the texture of the verse and the use of verbal knacks to clinch points is a far cry from the prosaic presentations of the earlier Humanist defenses of music in verse. Davies himself (if these verses indeed be his—the signature "I. D." in the miscellany and the diction of much of Davies' minor poetry suggests that they are), expounds traditional speculative musical lore on the subject of the soul as a harmony and of music as reason elsewhere. And here the tone and method are completely expository save for the metaphorical instruments. In the second part of *Nosce Teipsum* (1599), "Of the Soule of Man and the Immortalite Thereof," Davies declares that

> Her harmonies are sweet, and full of skill,
>   When on the Bodie's instrument she playes;
> But the proportions of the *wit* and *will*,
>   Those sweet accords, are euen the angel's layes.

> These tunes of *Reason* are *Amphion's* lyre,
>   Wherewith he did the *Thebane* citie found;
> These are the notes wherewith the heauenly *quire*,
>   The praise of Him which spreads the heauen doth
>   sound.[109]

There is a mixture of metaphorical musical instruments here, and the body becomes an instrument operated by the soul, only to be dropped in the next stanza in favor of the traditional allegorization of Orpheus' lyre (in this case, given to Amphion). But both figures are traditional ones, and Davies is merely expounding Platonist doctrine. The transition to the heavenly music is rather abrupt in the second of these stanzas, but such brisk identifications represent the typical sixteenth-century method of unifying disparate elements of musical lore.

Two important late sixteenth-century treatments of *musica speculativa* must be mentioned here. Davies' *Orchestra, or a Poem of Dauncing* (1596) actually substitutes a vision of cosmic dance for universal music, and the concepts of "time" and "measure," as expressed in the poem's subtitle, correspond to the more usual *harmonia mundi*. The role of music per se in the work is a relatively minor one (as in references to "sweet *Musicke*, Dauncing's onely life"). But the treatment of cosmology (with its frequently cited fence-straddling of the Copernican and Ptolemaic models in the fifty-first stanza) is figured forth in terms of the formal court dance of Davies' time. Any prolonged study of the poem would necessitate a thorough consideration of the role of dance in Renaissance *paideia*. In *Orchestra* two ideas come together in the image of dancing: the instilling of grace and discipline, and the par-

---

[109] Sir John Davies, *Complete Poems*, ed. Alexander B. Grosart (London, 1876), I, 35.

taking by the dancer in the universal order (through the association of "measure" in the abstract sense and "measure" = "dance"). But the treatment of these ideas in the poem, and of their association with Platonic love would be too long for parenthetical inclusion here.

Likewise, the consideration of *auditus* in George Chapman's *Ovid's Banquet of Sense* (1595) poses too many special problems to allow for extended comment at this point. In the poem Ovid, hearing his Corynna sing to her lute "t'enamoure heuenly eares," is led to consider the pleasure arising through the sense of hearing, and thence to the other senses as well. Stanzas 15-30 are concerned with hearing, perhaps derived from some speculations of Ficino's; they are of interest here primarily because there occurs in them the use of musical terms in rather elaborate conceits, such as where the Lady's appearance is said to sing more sweetly "Where songs of solid harmony accord / Rulde with Loues rule; and prickt with all his strings." But here, as elsewhere in the poem, the musical imagery digresses from the central line of exposition.

Music as Image

If Davies' metaphors are traditional, however, and if most Humanist poetry in praise of music seems to draw upon little more than a stock of allusion, it is not to suggest that there was no invention in the treatment of musical themes by Elizabethan poets. The purely technical problems dealt with by practical musicians in their own occasional verses, and the speculative essays of the non-professional musician in polemical or philosophical poems tend to keep to separate styles of diction and separate vocabularies and stocks of allusion. But even early in the century we can see occasional uses of musical imagery that prefigure later poetic styles.

An early sixteenth-century poem on "The Armonye of Byrdes" first printed ca. 1551, for example, contains some interesting mixtures of old and new devices. The poem describes a gathering of birds and proceeds to treat of each species in a separate stanza; the lines are often macaronic in a late-Medieval manner. The puns are occasionally arresting and graphic, as, for example, the play on "parte" in the lines depicting the song (and flight) of the lark, where the word is used in its specifically musical sense as well as in the more general one of "task" or "role":

> Than sayd the larke
> Because my parte
>> Is upward to ascend,
> And down to rebound
> Toward the ground
>> And singing to discend . . .[110]

An unusual interlingual pun of almost a Joycean type occurs in the last two lines of a later stanza:

> Than all in one voyce
> They dyd all rejoyce
>> *Omnes vos iste,*
> Chaungyng their key
> From ut to rey
>> *Et tu rex glorie Christe.*[111]

But perhaps the most remarkable figure in the whole piece is one which seems almost to adapt the turns made on the colors of musical notation in the Leckingfield Proverbs and in Cornyshe's poem; here the black and red ink become the colors of mourning and of blood, respectively, as if suggested by an implied pun on the word "pricke":

> The osyll dyd pricke
> Her notes all thycke
>> With blacke ynke and with red;

[110] *A proper new Boke of the Armonye of Byrdes* (1551?), ed. J. Payne Collier, The Percy Society Series, vol. VII (London, 1842), p. 6.
[111] *Ibid.,* p. 10.

> And in like facyon
> With Christe in his passyon,
>   From the fote to the crown of the head.[112]

There is an almost Baroque grotesquerie to these lines, however, which is by no means typical of its period.

One of the most common sources of musical imagery in the early Tudor period, on the other hand, consists in the punning use of musical terms which is made to extend the length of a poem. The best example of this is probably that of some verses by John Redford on the subject of "the meane." This term is employed, in connection with English music of the fifteenth through the seventeenth centuries, to designate the middle part in a polyphonic composition; in the earlier period, the three voices of the most common compositional scheme were designated *treble, mean,* and *tenor,* reading from top to bottom. Redford's poem suggests that the mean part, often notated in a black notation as opposed to the white of the other parts, was often used to conceal some basic compositional device, such as a *cantus firmus.* The general intention of the whole word-play is to associate the musical part with the Aristotelian ethical mean; the point is driven home again and again throughout the long and rather pedantic verbal quibble, not unworthy, at times, of Shakespeare's Holofernes:

> Long have I bene a singyng man,
>   And sondry partes oft have I soong,
> But one part, sins I fyrst began,
>   I cowld nor can syng, old nor yong;
> The meane I mene, whych part showth well
> Above all partes most to excell.

> The base and treble are extrems;
>   The tenor standyth sturdely;
> The cownter rangyth then, me sems;
>   The mene must make our melodye;

---

[112] *Ibid.,* p. 11.

Wherby the mene declaryth well
Above all partes most to excell.

Marke well the maner of the mene,
   And therby tyme and tune our songe
Unto the meane, where all partes lene,
   All partes ar kept from syngyng wrong;
Thowghe syngyng men take this not well,
Yet doth the mene in thys excell.

The mene in cumpas is so large,
   That evry parte must joyne therto;
Yt hath an ere in evry barge,
   To syng, to say, to thynke, to doo;
Of all these partes this part showth well
Above all partes most to excell.

The mene is so commodious,
   That sang we but that part alone,
The mene is more melodious
   Then all those partes, lackyng that one;
Wherby the mene comparyth well
Among all partes most to excell.

The mene in losse, the mene in gayne,
   In welth or in adversytye;
The mene in helth, the mene in payne,
   The mene menyth allwayes equitye:
This is the mene who menyth well,
Of all our partes most to excell.

To me and myne, with all the rest,
   And God grant grace with harty voyce
To syng the mene that menyth best,
   All partes in the best to rejoyce;
Whych mene in menyng menyth well,
The mene of menes that doth excell.[113]

[113] Text from *The Moral Play of Wit and Science and Early Poetical Miscellanies*, ed. James Orchard Halliwell (London: printed for the Shake-

Through the notion of the mean, a general point about *mousike biou kybernetes* is being made, a point made elsewhere by Redford himself and by other early Humanist writers on music and on education. By the second stanza, the metaphoric value of the statements about the mean takes over completely, so that "The mene must make our melodye" and, later on, "The mene is so commodious / That sang we but that part alone" are ethical statements, rather than musical trivia.

During the course of the century, musical imagery in non-didactic poetry, particularly in those poems where music is not the formal subject, tends to confine itself more to the use of figures involving instruments and some of their traditional associations than it does to the use of those drawn from the more abstract musical conceptions. Nevertheless, there are many examples of these general musical metaphors in both verse and prose of the Elizabethan era. One of the simpler types involves the literalization of abstract "concord" or "harmony" into musical consonance, much in the same way that Redford used the notion of the mean; the musical notion is employed almost as an allegorical figure of *"Concordia"* might, with "sweet harmony" ("sweet" because in tune, rather than merely gentle and pleasant) serving an abstract purpose. Thus, in one of the songs from Sir Philip Sidney's *Arcadia* (1593), a shepherd refers to his old music (i.e. poetry) teacher as follows:

> He said, the Musique best thilke powers pleasd
> Was jumpe concorde between our wit and will:
> Where highest notes to godlines are raisd,
> And lowest sinke not downe to jote of ill.[114]

"Jumpe" is "exact" or "even," and the concord that mediates

---

speare Society, 1848), pp. 80-82. Also see Carl F. Pfatteicher, *John Redford* (Kassel, 1934), pp. 63-65. This poem is sometimes ascribed to John Heywood.

[114] Sir Philip Sidney, *Complete Works*, ed. Albert Feuillerat (Cambridge, 1912-1926), II, 74.

between "our wit and will," or reason and feeling, is the traditional harmony of the soul. But the ethical point here connects specifically with music, and not for the purpose of praising music and displaying its virtues to some attacker, but to associate both music and ethics with poetry. We shall presently examine this tradition, particularly in Sidney's writing.

But more elaborate conceits were based on concepts of musical speculation or practical theory. A common device at the turn of the seventeenth century is the localization of the *harmonia mundi* in contemporary contrapuntal practices; and if the *locus classicus* of this may be found in Kepler's demonstration of the counterpoint sung by the heavenly bodies, other applications seem more effective for remaining outside. what purports to be empirical demonstration. In Godfrey Goodman's treatise on the decay of the cosmos, *The Fall of Man* (1616), the whole of Creation is seen as participating in a great consort, marred only by humankind: "The little chirping birds (The Wren, and the Robin) they sing a meane; the Goldfinch, the Nightingall, they joyne in the treble; the Blacke bird, the Thrush, they bear the tenour; while the foure footed beasts with their bleating and bellowing they sing a bass. . . . Only man, as being a wild and fierce creature, hath no certaine note or tune . . . his instruments are the guts of dead creatures, a token of his crueltie, and the remainder of his riot."[115] The contrast between natural and artificial music here is made to stand for another one between innocency and the craft and creative power born of experience: musical instruments produce sounds only at the price of the death of a natural singer.

A familiar passage in Gervase Markham's pamphlet on *Countrey Contentments* (1611) gives detailed suggestions for the arrangement of hunting hounds' voices to form a three-part chorus of bass, counter-tenor and mean;[116] it has often

[115] Godfrey Goodman, *The Fall of Man* (London, 1616), p. 78.
[116] Quoted in *Life in Shakespeare's England*, ed. J. Dover Wilson, third ed. (London, 1944), p. 37.

been cited as a practical analogue of the discussion between Theseus and Hippolyta in *A Midsummer Night's Dream*, IV, i, following upon the former's call to "mark the musical confusion / Of hounds and echo in conjunction." But the point here is Theseus' claim that his own hounds, whose "cry more tunable / Was never hollowed to, nor cheered with horn," are musically superior to the sound of the Cretan hounds heard once by his wife, who reports that she never heard

> Such gallant chiding; for, besides the groves,
> The skies, the fountains, every region near
> Seemed all one mutual cry. I never heard
> So musical a discord, such sweet thunder.
>
> (IV, i, 119-122)

This is no mere modish inclusion of the niceties of county sporting, but a hyperbolic description of musical, and hence of hedonic, perfection.

But by far the most common musical images in sixteenth-century poetry are those connected with musical instruments, and among these the figure of the lute is the most prevalent of all. We have already seen how the combined lute-harp-lyre could, in the Renaissance, combine Classical, Biblical, and contemporary instruments into a kind of universal string, possessing the ethical and esthetic values of the Greek *kithara*, as well as having other symbolic functions. Aside from the figure of the world-lute in its various forms, and of the political instrument that we noted in the previous chapter, there began to develop in the lyric poem an explicit association of the lute with the Muse, culminating in the highly conceited use of this image in the sonnet sequences of the 1590's.

Possibly the earliest use of such a figure is the implicit lute-muse identification in two of the best-known poems of Sir Thomas Wyatt. It has been customary to treat the musical instrument referred to in both "My lute, awake" and "Blame not my lute" as an actual lute to which Wyatt sang his songs, presumably in settings by Cornyshe and other composers of the court of Henry VIII;[117] and while evidence corroborating the practice of accompanied monody at Henry's court is not hard to find,[118] the possibility that a literary convention is being invoked and continued has not been generally voiced. The covert invocation of the muse or of some other inspiring deity through a reference to the poet-musician's lyre is very common in Classical poetry, and goes along with the use of the string or wind instrument to stand for poetry itself. From the Anacreontic that complains of its author's lyre and how it could only play songs of love, despite his desire to sing epic (*"he lyre gar / monous erotas adei"*),[119] through the use of *"tibia"* by Virgil in his eighth eclogue (*"Incipe, Maenalios mecum, mea tibia versus"* and subsequently, as a refrain),[120] in imitation of Theocritus' line in which "muse" corresponds to "pipe," the convention maintains itself. Employing a mixture of Biblical harp, lyre, and pastoral pipe, the Carolingian poet and courtier, Angilbert, could indite an eclogue to Charlemagne beginning *"Surge, meo domno dulces fac, fistula, versus / David amat versus, surge et fac, fistula, versus."*

---

[117] See, for example, Sir Thomas Wyatt, *Collected Poems*, ed. Kenneth Muir (London, 1949), pp. xxvii, xxix; also, E. M. W. Tillyard, *Sir Thomas Wyatt* (London, 1929), pp. 15-16.

[118] See John H. Long, "Blame Not Wyatt's Lute," *Renaissance News*, VII (1956), pp. 127-130. It should be mentioned that Long commits an error in the transcription of some lute tablature which renders his conclusion false.

[119] *Elegy and Iambus, with the Anacreonta*, ed. J. M. Edmonds (Loeb Edition, London, 1931), II, 50. Frequently translated in the seventeenth century by Cowley, Philip Ayres and other poets, this little poem is given in translation from *A Poetical Rhapsody, ed.cit.*, I, 181:

> Of *Atreus* Sonnes faine would I write
> And faine of *Cadmus* would I sing:
> My Lute is set on Loues delight,
> And onely Loue sounds ev'ry string.
> Of late my Lute I alt'red quite,
> Both frets and strings for tunes aboue,
> I sung of fierce *Alcides* might,
> My Lute would sound no tune but Loue,
> Wherefore yee worthies all farewell,
> No tune but Loue my Lute can tell.

[120] See the comment on this refrain line by H. J. Rose in *The Eclogues of Vergil* (Berkeley, 1942), p. 148.

Later on, when David has been thoroughly identified with Charlemagne, the good Angilbert himself can become his court poet: *"Vatis Homerus amat David, fac, fistula versus."*[121] But it is the arousing of the sluggish instrument-muse which is of consequence here. The similarity of Wyatt's refrain to other such instances seems hard to discount:

> My lute awake! perfourme the last
> Labor that thou and I shall wast,
>   And end that I have now begon;
> For when this song is sung and past,
>   My lute be still, for I have done.
>
> As to be herd where ere is none,
> As lede to grave in marbill stone,
>   My song may perse her hert as sone;
> Should we then sigh, or syng, or mone?
>   No, no, my lute, for I have done.
>
>   (ll. 1-10)[122]

And throughout the poem it is the poet's power of articulateness that is intended by the instrumental reference. Even if a literal allusion to an instrument being played and sung to is present, it detracts not at all from the implied metaphor.

Similarly, the more or less explicit reference to an instrument actually played by the courtier-poet in the other lyric becomes identified, in the course of the poem, with the poet's own "voice." He starts out by insisting on full responsibility for the content of his "songes":

> Blame not my lute for he must sownde
>   Of thes or that as liketh me;
> For lake of wytt the lutte is bownde
>   To gyve suche tunes as plesithe me:

[121] *Monumenta Germanicae Historica. Poetae Latini aevi Caroli*, ed. E. Duemmler (Berlin, 1884), I, 360.
[122] Wyatt, *Collected Poems*, pp. 49-50.

> Tho my songes be sume what strange,
> And spekes suche wordes as toche thy change,
>   Blame not my lutte.
>
> (ll. 1-7)[123]

And as he proceeds to embroider the image, the weight of that responsibility grows heavier:

> My lute and strynges may not deny,
>   But as I strike they must obay;
> Brake not them than soo wrongfully,
>   But wryeke thy selff some wyser way:
> And tho the songes whiche I endight
> Do qwytt thy chainge with rightfull spight,
>   Blame not my lute.
>
> (ll. 15-21)

But this is only that he may turn on the lady who has injured him ("Blame but the selffe"), and finally conclude with the warning that if she break the strings of his instrument in wanton revenge, he has already possessed himself, for the lady's benefit, of "Stringes for to strynge my lute agayne." The lute seems to be identified not with a muse here, but with the poetry of complaint itself, and the whole lyric might be said to sum up the defense of the kind of courtly poetry whose only esthetic was the justice of its accusations and ethical prescription.[124]

In the sonnet sequences of the last decade of the century, however, the implicit image of Wyatt becomes an overt one. But the sonnet describing or invoking a lute would also tend to generate and attempt to extend for as long as possible a musical conceit employing as many general musical terms as possible. For example, Sonnet XLVII from Samuel Daniel's *Delia* (1592), also set as a lute song in his brother John

---

[123] *Ibid.*, pp. 122-123.
[124] Wyatt's other references to an instrument, or to singing (in anything more than a casual fashion) are more like the muse-invocation of "My lute, awake" than this last poem. See *Collected Poems*, pp. 38, 39, 64-65.

Daniel's book of ayres of 1606, starts out with the stated comparison and proceeds to work in other musical expressions:

> Like as the Lute that ioyes or els dislikes,
> As is his arte that playes vpon the same:
> So sounds my Muse according as she strikes
> On my hart strings high tun'd vnto her fame.
> Her touch doth cause the warble of the sound,
> Which heere I yeeld in lamentable wise,
> A wailing deskant on the sweetest ground,
> Whose due reports giue honor to her eyes.
> Els harsh my style, vntunable my Muse,
> Hoarce sounds the voyce that prayseth not her name:
> If any pleasing realish heere I vse,
> The iudge the world her beautie giues the same.
> O happie ground that makes the musique such,
> And blessed hand that giues so sweete a tuch.[125]

Here it is the poet who is his Muse's instrument, of course, and he describes his bondage to his lady-muse in a manner quite the reverse of Wyatt's relationship to his lute in "Blame not my lute." The conventional figure of heart-strings is almost a cliché even at this period,[126] and the punning use of "touch" to designate both a passage of musical sound and a caress is almost in the process of becoming one. But the association of music with the poetry that comprises the sonneteer's sole discourse is unmistakable, and in this a link with the less fictional world of Wyatt's lyrics of complaint may be discerned.

The figure of the sonneteer himself as his lady's instrument becomes an almost automatic one, enriched only by the addi-

[125] Samuel Daniel, *Poems and a Defence of Ryme*, ed. A. C. Sprague (Cambridge, Mass., 1930), p. 34. Also see *English Madrigal Verse*, ed. E. H. Fellowes (Oxford, 1929), p. 402 for the slightly different version from the songbook (the last quatrain's first two lines change places with the last two, and there are one or two other minor alterations).

[126] See "Upon his Ladies buying strings for her Lute," in *A Poetical Rhapsody*, I, 162, which also contains the equally conventional pun on "fret."

tion of more musical terms to the conceit, and by embellishing tropes to the diction. In the 1599 version of Michael Drayton's *Idea*, the ninth sonnet shows just such an elaboration:

Love once would daunce within my Mistres eye,
And wanting musique fitting for the place,
Swore that I should the Instrument supply,
And sodainly presents me with her face:
Straightwayes my pulse playes liuely in my vaines,
My panting breath doth keepe a meaner time,
My quau'ring artiers be the Tenours straynes,
My trembling sinewes serue the Counterchime,
My hollow sighs the deepest base doe beare,
True diapazon in distincted sound:
My panting breath the treble makes the ayre,
And descants finely on the musiques ground.
Thus like a Lute or Violl did I lye,
Whilst the proud slaue daunc'd galliards in her eye.[127]

There is a close connection between the conceit in this poem and the use of organic correspondences between instruments and their parts and portions of the universe or members of the human body, as used by speculative writers. But the point in sonnets like these is always the insistence on the love relationship as figured forth in the instrument-performer situation. And well it might be, for the love of the Petrarchan sonneteer for his lady puts him always in a passive role. Elsewhere, Drayton uses the lute-muse metaphor rather than one of the instrument as self: "My faire, had I not erst adorned my Lute / With those sweet strings stolne from thy golden hayre";[128] and by this he means to start out, "Had you not been my *real* muse. . . ."

This figure of the instrument as the self maintains itself not only in the love-sonnet literature at the close of the six-

[127] Michael Drayton, *Minor Poems*, ed. Cyril Brett (Oxford, 1907), p. 30.
[128] *Ibid.*, p. 3.

teenth century, but continues to be even more common in devotional poetry, particularly that of the Metaphysicals, in the next hundred years. The relationship of poet to lady is simply transferred to one of prayer to God. But at the beginning of the seventeenth century, the instrumental conceit takes on an interest of its own, as in the following sonnet of John Davies of Hereford from his *Wittes Pilgrimage* (1610):

No plaies my *Mind* vpon his *Instrument*,
(Thought-wasted *Body*, Organ of my *Minde*)
No *Parts* but such as wholy discontent,
My *Parts* are so vntun'd, by Thee, *Vnkinde!*
My *Longues* (the Bellowes) draw in naught but *Aire*,
That *filles* my Wind-pipes but with harshe Complaints
Tending to *Diapasens* of *Dispaire*,
Which often die, for, that Winde often faints.
My *Hart* and *Braines* (the *Stoppes*, that cause the Moode)
Do often stopp: sith oft such *Moodes* they cause
As by the *Pangs of Death* are oft with-stood,
Through which the *Organs* Voice doth, sinking, pause:
But if thou (SWEET) will haue It sweetly rise,
Then, breathe sweet Aire into It as It dies.[129]

Here the relationship of player to instrument is seen as that of psyche to body, and the conceit is that of an organ. But the puns are many and varied, including those on "Parts," "Stoppes," "Aire," "Sweet," and the quibble on the two senses of "Moode" (*mode*, or key, vs. *mood*, or feeling).[130] The whole notion of "organ" is itself taken in a specifically musical and a general sense also: the body is the *organ* or *instrument* of the mind, and the limitation of these terms to their musical sense provides the basis of the metaphor. Whether in the case of abstractions such as "harmony" or of terms like "instrument," this process of localizing the musical

[129] John Davies of Hereford, *Complete Works*, ed. Alexander B. Grosart (London, 1878), p. 11.
[130] For a discussion of this, see below, Chapter IV, pp. 206-211.

application of a more general term forms the broadest connection between speculative and practical music in both poetry and prose of the Renaissance.

That the instrument conceit became conventional in its own right, apart from its use in either the poet-muse or poet-lady relationship, can be seen in the great frequency of knacks and quibbles on terms denoting parts of instruments throughout the corpus of Shakespeare's plays, for example,[131] and in the eagerness of certain inferior sonnets to go to work upon all the old puns. Thus William Percy's *Coelia* (1594), number eight, which starts out "Strike up, my Lute! and ease my heavy cares," concludes lamely:

> Ay me! what warbles yields mine instrument!
> The basses shriek as though they were amiss!
> The Means, no means, too sad for merriment!
> No, no! the music good, but thus it is
>   I loathe both Means, merriment, Diapasons;
>   So She and I may be but Unisons.[132]

The only addition to the received pun on "mean" is the additional layer of reference to the use of the word to designate the middle courses of lute stringing.

The wish to be accepted as the lady's lover invites an instrumental comparison in Shakespeare's Sonnet No. 128. But here the conventional lute is replaced by the popular virginals, giving the sonnet more of the flavor of a *genre* scene than of a literary exercise:

> How oft when thou my musike musike playst,
> Vpon that blessed wood whose motion sounds
> With thy sweet fingers when thou gently swayst,
> The wiry concord that mine eare confounds,
> Do I enuie those Iackes that nimble leape,

---

[131] See Gretchen L. Finney, "A World of Instruments," *ELH*, xx (1953), pp. 87-120.

[132] Text from *An English Garland*, ed. Edward Arber (Birmingham, 1883), VI, 143.

To kisse the tender inward of thy hand,
Whilst my poore lips which should that haruest reape,
At the woods bouldnes by thee blushing stand.
To be so tikled they would change their state,
And situation with those dancing chips,
Ore whome their fingers walke with gentle gate,
Making dead wood more blest then liuing lips,
    Since sausie Iackes so happy are in this,
    Giue them their fingers, me thy lips to kisse.[133]

There has been considerable discussion among commentators about the virginal jacks, and whether the wooden part of the action that held and activated the quill is actually being referred to here (the problem is how, unless the lady were adjusting or repairing the quills, the rail usually holding them in place would have been removed at the time). It is still possible that Shakespeare refers, either by mistake or by a kind of metonymy, to the wooden keys themselves; by calling them "jacks" he is able to consider them as his lips' almost personified rivals. But, in any case, the use of the musical instrument here is typical of the treatment of lutes, viols, keyboards, and recorders simply as common objects that, as such, are candidates for potential treatment in a conceit. Had the instrument here been instead a set of combs, and the lady's fingers her hair, the essentially non-musical character of the image would be more obvious, but no stronger. The opening line is hardly developed in the ensuing quatrain, and the second quatrain's point becomes the important one.

The musical figure in Sonnet No. 8, on the other hand, expands a truism of *musica speculativa* that remains an extremely popular poetic image throughout the seventeenth

[133] Text from the Quarto of 1609. For the comments referred to below, see the Variorum Edition, ed. Hyder Rollins (Philadelphia, 1944), I, 326-328. The common, domestic quality of a lady playing her virginals is nicely shown in a line from some experimental Classical iambics sent in a letter from Spenser to Gabriel Harvey, in which "mirthe" is designated by the mention of his mistress "Playing alone careless on hir heavenlie virginals." In Spenser, *ed.cit.*, p. 769.

century. The reference to the phenomenon of sympathetic
vibration (which can be observed in the production of a tone
by a free string if another one, placed at some distance, but
tuned to exactly the same frequency, is struck), appears in
the third quatrain as a concrete image of concord, or abstract
harmony. In this case, that harmony is represented by the
three-part polyphony of a familial unit, and the effect of the
whole poem is to urge the Young Man to marry and beget
"breed to brave" Time:

> Musick to heare, why hears't thou musick sadly,
> Sweets with sweets warre not, ioy delights in ioy:
> Why lou'st thou that which thou receaust not gladly,
> Or else receaust with pleasure thine annoy?
> If the true concord of well tuned sounds,
> By vnions married do offend thine eare,
> They do but sweetly chide thee, who confounds
> In singlenesse the parts that thou should'st beare:
> Marke how one string sweet husband to an other,
> Strikes each in each by mutuall ordering;
> Resembling sier, and child, and happy mother,
> Who all in one, one pleasing note do sing:
> > Whose speechlesse song being many, seeming one,
> > Sings this to thee thou single wilt proue none.[134]

The Young Man is sad for very different reasons than is
Jessica, in *The Merchant of Venice*, v, i, when she says, "I am
never merry when I hear sweet music." In each case the very
harmoniousness of the musical sounds is ultimately responsible
for the feelings of the listener. But what for Jessica is the
great solemnity resulting from an intimation of the harmony
of the world, is for the Young Man little more than a kind
of sulky guilt, insists the sonneteer; he is only bearing a solo
part in life, where he should imitate abstract harmony by
marrying, and thus producing a real union. The sounds of
harmonious music must abash anyone, so runs the argument,

[134] See Variorum Edition, pp. 23-25.

who remains single in a travesty of harmony, rather than bearing his proper part in a true consonance. Although attempts have been made to prove that the reference is to the double strings, or courses, of a lute in the third quatrain, I think that there can be no doubt that the "married" strings resonate because of their "mutuall ordering," each setting the other in motion. The pair of strings in a lute course would vibrate only as a result of being struck simultaneously by a player's finger. But over-nice insistences here may be more than a rather general image will bear. What is most important is that the music is being considered for its harmoniousness rather than for the feelings and actions which, Orpheus-like, it induces in the hearer. The whole sonnet is directed toward twitting the Young Man, and the tone is extremely ironic ("obviously you're sad about something, listening to the music, but what you *should* be worrying about in your selfishness is the loneliness of your life and the fruitlessness of your death"). The implication of the couplet is clear: "the song of the choiring family rebukes you by the many-ness of its blended parts, for your single-ness will end in death and will thus 'proue none.' " The conceit is based upon the truism that a harmony is a "marriage" of discrete sounds, and in the final line "single" again insists upon the identification of marital and musical aloofness, chiming as it does with the opening syllable of the line.

But consistent musical conceits like this one were an exception, rather than a rule in the sonnet literature of the turn of the seventeenth century. Very often the poet's "lute" would be addressed not as a muse, nor as a courtly or modern counterpart of a pastoral poet's pipe (which is much the same thing), but rather simply as a companion. There is a beautiful French model for such treatments in *Sonnet XII* of Louise Labé, originally published in Lyon in 1555, which begins

> Lut, compagnon de ma calamité,
> De mes soupirs témoin irréprochable,

De mes ennuis controlleur véritable,
Tu as souvent avec moy lamenté . . .[135]

To this same genre belongs the lute of the lady in the poem of George Gascoigne, who, "being wronged by false suspect," gives vent to her grief by demanding, "Give me my Lute in bed now as I lie, / And lock the doores of mine unluckie bower"; the poem concludes

But thou my Lute, be still, now take thy rest,
Repose thy bones uppon this bed of downe:
Thou hast discharg'd some burden from my brest,
Wherefore take thou my place, here lie thee downe.[136]

This conclusion is not as extravagant as it may seem, for lutes were indeed kept in, or sometimes on beds (when they were not put in cases) as protection against the cold and damp as much as against breakage.

Similarly, the lute upon the belly of which Gynecia inscribes her unexpressed complaint in the third book of Sidney's *Arcadia* is not actually a muse or genius of expression, so much as a confidante: under a veil, Sidney says, "she contended to cover her never ceassing anguish, has made the Lute a monument of her minde." The inscription begins, "My Lute which in thy selfe thy tunes enclose, / Thy mistresse song is now a sorrow's crie."[137] The couplets which conclude both of the poem's stanzas employ figures from musical practice. The first uses the notion of an inaudible ground bass, or continuous theme for variations or "divisions": "And though my mones be not in musicke bound, / Of written greefes, yet be the silent ground." The final couplet moralizes the fact that the tauter, thinner treble strings of a sixteenth-century lute were relatively louder than were the heavier bass courses, and that on all stringed instruments, as the strings are stopped "lower

[135] Louise Labé, *Love Sonnets*, tr. F. Prokosh [sic] (New York, 1947).
[136] George Gascoigne, *Works*, ed. J. W. Cunliffe (Cambridge, 1907), I, 338.
[137] Sidney, *Complete Works*, II, 35-36.

down" (closer to the bridge), the string length is diminished and the pitch of the resulting sound raised: "Thus in thy selfe, least strings are loudest founde, / And lowest stops doo yeeld the hyest sounde." This thought has followed, and paralleled a similar figure about the injustice of deserts in a wicked world: "Thus noble golde, downe to the bottome goes, / When worthlesse corke, aloft doth floting lye."

Other instances of musical figures of such a type, employing either the lute or some more general musical phenomenon or myth, are too frequent to discuss here.[138] Purely instrumental figures throughout the sixteenth and early seventeenth centuries tend by and large to substitute lute, harp, and lyre for each other, even in translation; a rare exception is in a commendatory poem of Hugh Holland's, prefixed to Sir Thomas Hawkins' translation of Horace, 1625:

> I knew before thy dainty tuch,
> upon the Lordly Violl:
> But of thy Lyre who knew so much
> Before this happy triall?
> So tuned is thy sacred Harpe,
> To make her eccho sweetly sharpe.
>
> I wote not how to praise inough
> Thy Musick and thy Muses. . . .[139]

[138] A few might be mentioned only: see Barnabe Googe, *Eglogs, Epytaphes, & Sonettes* (1563), ed. Edward Arber (London, 1871), p. 108; the cycle of poems on love and music from Thomas Watson's historically important sonnet sequence *The* 'ΕΚΑΤΟΜΠΑΘΙΑ (1582), in *Poems*, ed. Edward Arber (London, 1870), pp. 37-52; Giles Fletcher's *Licia* (1593), No. xxx, in *Elizabethan Sonnets*, ed. Sidney Lee (London, n.d.), p. 49; Richard Linche, *Diella* (1596), No. xvi, in *Elizabethan Sonnets*, p. 309; Spenser, *Amoretti*, No. xxxviii. Also see Sidney, *Complete Works*, IV, 270, 286, 288, etc.

[139] Text from Louise Imogen Guiney, *Recusant Poets* (New York, 1938), I, 369. This should be contrasted to the mixture of the three instruments in such poems as Ronsard's "A sa Lyre" (*Odes*, I, xxii), where the "lyre dorée" becomes a "luth," and finally the instrument of the French national bard, "Harpeur François," Ronsard himself. Also see Ben Jonson in No. LXXIX of *Under-wood* for a collation of harp, lute, lyre, and theorbo.

Here the lyre, as the Classical instrument, is distinguished from the lute, or contemporary one, and the contrast is made to correspond to that between various sorts of poetry. The "sacred Harpe" may very possibly refer to Hawkins' translation of a sacred text at some earlier time. But the use of various sorts of instruments to symbolize their appropriate poetic modes is unmistakable in the other two cases.

Holland's use of the instruments to indicate poetry itself, of course, belongs to a tradition of Neoclassical poetry in which, following both the Latin practice of using *"carmen"* for "poem" and the Renaissance's developing knowledge of Greek music and musical theory, poetry and music are identified. It is improper, I feel, to consider this a case of musical imagery as such. The bardic harp and juggler's fiddle were always taken, in a received synecdoche, for the whole of their art, all Classical traditions aside. It is particularly in connection with the Neoclassicism of the French *Pléiade* (as well as Jean de Baïf's *Académie*), and of the Sidney circle in England, that the music-poetry identification takes on much importance in later sixteenth-century poetry. It is true that much of the controversy over prosody that was being waged at the turn of the seventeenth century either touched upon or alluded to musical questions, although it is strange that Thomas Campion, a strong advocate of quantitative scansion over the debased practice of stressed scansion and rhyme, never applied his knowledge both of musical theory and practice to this question in the manner of Baïf's *vers* and *musique mesurées*.[140] Sir Philip Sidney used "music" to mean "poetry" perhaps as much as any Elizabethan man of letters, but he was also capable of perceiving the independent course which poetry was to take, separated from music in the modern world. Throughout the *Defence of Poesie* he employs music both

[140] See below, Chapter IV. Also see John Hollander, "The Music of Poetry," *Journal of Aesthetics and Art Criticism*, XV (1956), pp. 234-238, for a discussion of the relationship between prosodical theories and views of music.

as symbol and analogy, on the one hand, and as a separate art, on the other.

The most impressive of all these references to music comes in the course of Sidney's discussion of the quantitative-accentual controversy in an analysis of "auncient" and "moderne" methods of versifying. After having described them both, he continues: "Whether of these be the more excellent, wold bear many speeches, the ancient no doubt more fit for Musick, both words and time observing quantitie, and more fit, lively to expresse divers passions by the low or loftie sound of the well-wayed sillable."[141] Sidney here makes use of an argument traditionally applied to music itself; and, like the composers and writers of the Baïf circle, he finds quantitative verse best adapted to music. But in his next sentence Sidney makes a point which, rendered slightly more general, is crucial to the understanding of the post-Classical divergence of music and poetry. Of the modern, accentual prosody he remarks, "The latter likewise with his rime striketh *a certaine Musicke to the eare*" (italics mine), thus delineating for the first time, perhaps, the notion of the "music of poetry" which remains a commonplace even today. About the quantitative-accentual question, Sidney concludes "and in fine, since it dooth delight, though by another way, it obtaineth the same purpose, there being in either sweetnesse, and wanting in neither, majestie." One commentator has remarked that Sidney's interest in Classical prosody resulted from his "attempt to accomodate verse to music."[142] Rather, one might say, both his concern over prosodical matters and his interest in the music-poetry analogue stem from a common source in his larger attempt to accommodate some of the esthetic standards and models of antiquity to the exigencies of what he already saw as a national literature in a national language.

Sidney's views on the subject of poetry and music are most

[141] Sidney, III, 44.
[142] John Buxton, *Sir Philip Sidney and the English Renaissance* (London, 1954), pp. 113-116, argues this in some detail.

elaborately set forth in a dialogue between Dicus, favoring quantity, and Lalus, a partisan of accentual scansion, inserted into the Queen's College manuscript of *Arcadia*. In it, what approaches very closely to the doctrines of the Baïf circle, *mutatis mutandis*, are expounded for English poetry by Dicus, while Lalus uses extremely sophisticated arguments to hold that "Dicus did muche abuse the dignitie of *Poetrye* to applye yt to musicke since rather Musicke is a servante to poetrye, for by thone the eare onelye, by thother the mynde is pleased." Lalus goes on to argue that if ever the text and setting of a song do not fit each other, "yt is the musicions faulte and not the poettes." The controversy is settled by the ponderous Basilius, who concludes that "in bothe kindes he wrote well that wrote wisely and so bothe commendable."[143]

It is obvious that Sidney's interest here is not vested in either side, but rather in the nature of the arguments themselves, and it is indeed unfortunate that no particular group of composers centered about him as formed around Count Giovanni di Bardi in Florence in the 1580's. The experiments in advanced musical Neoclassicism that led to the development of Baroque music might have changed radically England's musical history in the next hundred years.

In the last analysis, then, the identification of music and poetry in literary language must be construed not so much as a figure of language as a kind of esthetic ideal. Similarly, the use of the stringed instrument to stand for the literary art is a Neoclassic literary convention having little to do with the history of the literary use of *musica speculativa*.

We might, before leaving the subject of sixteenth-century instrumental imagery, glance at a figure from the exposition of universal music in Joshua Sylvester's translation of Du Bartas. At the end of the second day of the second week, an

---

[143] This material is inserted into the Oxford MS R. 38/301, facing page 86 of the original version of *Arcadia*. It is discussed by R. H. Zandvoort in *Sidney's Arcadia: A Comparison between the Two Versions* (Amsterdam, 1929), p. 10.

almost medieval description of music leads to a disquisition on
the heavenly harmony. Music is unveiled as a lady, and we
are made to see

> all those Harps & Lutes,
> Shawms, Sag-buts, Citrons, Viols, Cornets, Flutes,
> Plac't round about her; prove in every part
> This is the noble, sweet, Voyce-ord'ring *Art*,
> Breath's Measurer, the Guide of supplest fingers
> On (living-dumb, dead-speaking) sinnew-singers:
> Th'Accord of Discords: sacred *Harmony*,
> And Numb'ry Law, which did accompany
> Th'Almighty-most, when first his Ordinance
> Appointed Earth to rest, and Heav'n to dance.[144]

Next follows a description of the music of the spheres, here
clearly separated from the song of the angels, although
seventeenth-century poets were to blur this distinction fairly
consistently:

> For (as they say) for supr'Intendent there,
> The supreame Voyce placed in every Sphear
> A *Syren* sweet; that from Heav'ns Harmony
> Inferiour things might learn best Melody,
> And their rare Quier with th'Angels Quier accord
> To sing aloud the praises of the Lord. . . .

Finally, we get the comparison of the heavenly harmony
to the actual sound production of an organ. The cosmic instrument is no longer representative of universal harmony because of its perfectly tuned and proportioned strings, but
because it is animated by breath, wind, air: so is the cosmos
moved by the divine afflatus:

> Where, as (by Art) one selfly blast breath'd out
> From panting bellows, passeth all-about
> Winde-Instruments; enters by th'under Clavers

---

[144] Joshua Sylvester, *Du Bartas His Divine Weekes and Workes* (London,
1641), p. 143.

Which with the Keys the Organ-Master quavers,
Fils all the Bulk, and severally the same
Mounts every Pipe of the melodious Frame;

At once reviving lofty *Cymbals* voyce,
Flutes sweetest ayre, and *Regals* shrillest noyse:
Even so th'all-quickning Spirit of God above
The Heav'ns harmonious whirling wheels doth move;
So that re-treading their eternall trace,
Th'one bears the Trebble, th'other bears the Base.

And Sylvester follows Du Bartas as he goes on to expound
the effects of music as accounted for by the structure of the
universe, the myths of musical power of Antiquity, etc., in
short, to develop a perfect model of the *encomium musicae*
convention as traced by Professor Hutton.[145]

The use of the instrumental figure seems to belong to a
different genre than do the countless quibbles on "stop" and
"fret" and "neck" and the like that comprise so many instrumental comparisons in late sixteenth-century poetry. It occurs,
of course, in a context of exposition of speculative music that
is revived later on only by Milton and Cowley in their very
different ways. But, by and large, the tradition of the poetic
praise of music itself gives way to the use of musical imagery
and thought in more complicated ways in the seventeenth
century. Not only the use of instrumental figures, but the
very notion of the heavenly harmony changes its function
radically in an age when myths about the music of the spheres
can no longer be believed, and when their metaphorical use
is no longer permitted in empirical accounts of the nature
of the universe.

Perhaps the best demonstration of how this change was to
effect itself may be made in the course of a consideration of
some occurrences of musical themes and images in Shakespeare's plays.

[145] See above, n. 94.

Shakespeare's Many Sorts of Music

When seen in the light of the richness of sixteenth-century musical thought, the modern academic question of "Shakespeare and Music" tends to be more blinding than the glittering of its generality would warrant. With the aid of the musicological studies of the past thirty years, we are better able than ever before to reconstruct the actual music performed in and referred to in Shakespeare's plays. The growth of studies in the History of Ideas has given us models for understanding how words and customs that have misleadingly retained their forms to this day reverberated differently in various historical contexts. The forays of sixteenth- and seventeenth-century poets into *musica speculativa*, consequently, can now be understood as more than either the fanciful conceits or the transmission of quaint lore that many nineteenth-century readers took them to be. But the recent critical traditions that read all of Shakespeare with the kind of attention previously devoted to other kinds of poetry have tended to create a third, queer category of symbolic music. G. Wilson Knight in particular has employed the images of tempest and music in his criticism to suggest the universal themes of disorder and resolving, reconciling order. These concepts stem largely from his invaluable early work on the last plays, in which, trivially speaking, storm and music do appear to alternate.

But Professor Wilson Knight's notion of Shakespearian "music" tends often to get out of hand. He confuses the actual practice of music on the Elizabethan and Jacobean stage with *musica speculativa* and musical imagery in the texts of the plays themselves, and both of these, finally, with his own notion of "music" as a critical term for a general condition of transcendent order. Thus he can say of music that "Shakespeare's use of it is very straightforward. No author would give directions for soft music whilst Duncan is being murdered: the music-love associations in Shakespeare are as natural as his tempests."[146]

The objections that might be raised are numerous here, but I shall content myself with observing that in the first place, Marston in *The Malcontent* seems to have done just what it is asserted that no author would do,[147] and that in the second place, a dangerous mixture of categories occurs in the last clause. While tempests as plot devices (and their noises as sound effect and stage property) remain fairly regularized throughout Elizabethan and Jacobean drama, the use of music cannot be said to do so. Instead, a great change occurs when one moves from the outdoor theaters with their elaborate use of music in signalling functions and the necessity of incorporating all music except these signals into the plot of the play itself. The small coterie theaters of the city, with their more elaborate court and chapel musical connections, followed the masque eventually in developing a musical consort whose playing was more or less a *donnée*, and whose presence need not always be explained by a cry of "Ho, the recorders" or the like. It is perhaps the influence of the coterie theaters and their musical conventions which lead to the masque-like use of music in Shakespeare's late plays, and to what Professor Wilson Knight calls "the mysterious symbolic music that accompanies Antony's failure as a soldier and his dying into love."[148]

It is essentially a romantic, if not actually a *symboliste* notion of music which Professor Wilson Knight employs, and aside from his naïve treatment of sixteenth-century music and attitudes toward it, his insistence on Shakespeare's symbolic music ignores conventions of musical imagery and exegesis in Renaissance literature. Worse than this, however, has been the effect of his failure to see exactly to what degree Shakespeare's poetic

---

[146] G. Wilson Knight, *The Shakesperian Tempest* (Oxford, 1932), p. 5.
[147] See Christian Kiefer, "Music and Marston's 'The Malcontent,'" *Studies in Philology*, LI (1954), pp. 163-171.
[148] G. Wilson Knight, *op.cit.*, p. 215.

intelligence utilized received ideas about music, both speculative and practical, analyzing and reinterpreting them in
dramatic contexts. Finally, and perhaps worst of all, some of
Shakespeare's amazingly original contributions to *musica
speculativa* have been lost sight of.

Many of the musical subjects and images that appear in
Shakespeare's plays and poems are of a more or less conventional quality. By and large, the bulk of the references in all
the plays is to practical music, which is cited, satirized, and
praised in various contexts like any other human activity. Of
particular interest to Shakespeare always was the richness of
various technical vocabularies, and much of the wit in all but
the later plays consists of puns and twisted tropes on technical
terminology, often that of instrumental music. Two well-
known passages of *musica speculativa* in the earlier plays,
however, deserve some comment.

The first of these is Richard II's great speech in Pomfret
Castle. After likening his prison to the world and to his own
body, the King hears music offstage:

> Music do I hear?
> Ha, ha! Keep time. How sour sweet music is
> When time is broke and no proportion kept!
> So is it in the music of men's lives,
> And here have I the daintiness of ear
> To check time broke in a disordered string,
> But for the concord of my state and time
> Had not an ear to hear my true time broke.
>
> (v, v, 41-48)[149]

"Proportion" here is used in its immediate sense of time-signa-
ture, and "Time broke in a disordered string" refers to the
music he hears playing. But the "disordered string" is also
himself, an emblem of the unruled, unruly state. "The concord of my state and time" invokes the musical connotations

---

[149] This and other quotations from here until the end of the chapter
employ the text of Shakespeare's *Complete Works*, ed. G. B. Harrison (New
York, 1952).

of "concord" as well—for centuries the word had reverberated with the old pun on "heart" and "string." What the King is saying is that now, in his broken state, he is sensitive to all the nuances of musical order, but formerly, lulled by the metaphorically musical order of his earlier reign, he had been unable to hear the tentative tempi in his own *musica humana*. In this passage an occurrence of practical music is interpreted in perfectly traditional terms, and human and worldly musics are made to coincide, both in Richard's own rhetoric and in the hierarchical imagery throughout the play. The conventional multiplicity of extensions of the term "music" are employed directly, and Richard, aside from the tireless progression of his thoughts, is talking like something out of an old book.

The final irony of Richard's soliloquy,

> This music mads me, let it sound no more,
> For though it have holp madmen to their wits,
> In me it seems it will make wise men mad.
> Yet blessings on his heart that gives it me!
> For 'tis a sign of love, and love to Richard
> Is a strange brooch in this all-hating world . . .
>
> (v, v, 61-66)

is reinforced by the fragmentation of "music" into its various categories. The music is maddening because its human and universal roles have not coincided for the King, whose necessary identity with the proper order of the state has been called into question by the fact of his deposition and imprisonment. Bolingbroke, the discord, the untuner, has himself become the well-tuned, regulating instrument of state. And, finally, the practical music is sundered from its speculative form in Richard's gratitude for the instrumental sounds themselves, which he takes as the evidence of someone's thoughtful care.[150]

---

[150] Cf. the musico-political metaphor in *Henry V*, I, ii:

> For government, though high and low and lower,
> Put into parts, doth keep in one consent,
> Congreeing in a full and natural close,
> Like music.
>
> (ll. 180-183)

I believe that it is this same conventional use of the emblematic stringed instrument in a political context that is at work during a moment in Brutus' tent in Act IV, scene iii, of *Julius Caesar*. The boy Lucius has fallen asleep over his instrument after singing for Brutus, and the latter has taken it away from him lest it drop to the ground and break. After the ominous appearance of Caesar's ghost, Brutus cries out, and the boy half-awakens, murmuring, "The strings, my lord, are false." Brutus, missing the import of this, comments, "He thinks he still is at his instrument," and shakes Lucius fully awake, inquiring after the phantom. But the meaning, I think, is clear, and the false strings suggest the discordant conspirators, now jangling and out of tune even among themselves. Brutus, who "in general honest thought / And common good to all, made one" of the varying faction he led, meets the prophetic truth of the boy's half-dreamed image with a benevolently naturalistic interpretation of it.

The even better-known music at Belmont in *The Merchant of Venice* shows a more dramatically sophisticated use of *musica speculativa*. In general, the dramatic structure of the whole play hinges on the relationship between Venice, the commercial city where gold is ventured for more gold, and the symbolically golden Belmont, where all is hazarded for love. Belmont is full of practical music in one of its most common sixteenth-century forms. Music used for signalling, the tuckets, flourishes, and sennets familiar to modern readers through stage directions, were not confined to the uses of dramaturgy; it was a matter of actual practice for distinguished persons to be accompanied by their private trumpeters. It is almost as a signal that the song "Tell me where is fancy bred" is employed. Like a nursery-rhyme riddle, it advises against appearances, and cryptically urges the choice of the lead. In a speech preceding the song, Portia's wit analyzes and interprets the ceremonial music she has ordered:

Let music sound while he doth make his choice,
Then, if he lose, he makes a swanlike end,
Fading in music. That the comparison
May stand more proper, my eye shall be the stream
And watery deathbed for him. He may win,
And what is music then? Then music is
Even as the flourish when true subjects bow
To a new-crowned monarch.

(III, ii, 43-50)

Here Portia makes the point that the same music can play
many roles, that the concept emerges from the fact as the
result of an intellectual process. She selects two polar concepts,
incidentally: music as signal, which plays little or no part in
traditional musical speculation, and the myth of the dying
swan, a stock image in romantic lyrics throughout the century.
Portia reaffirms this later on, when she remarks of the music
that Jessica and Lorenzo hear on the bank, "Nothing is good,
I see, without respect. / Methinks it sounds much sweeter
than by day." Nerissa replies that "Silence bestows that virtue
on it," invoking one of the dominant Belmont themes of the
deception of ornament, of the paleness more moving than
eloquence. It is the same theme that prefaces Lorenzo's initia-
tion of Jessica into the silent *harmonia mundi*:

Soft stillness and the night
Become the touches of sweet harmony.
Sit, Jessica. Look how the floor of heaven
Is thick inlaid with patines of bright gold.
There's not the smallest orb which thou behold'st
But in his motion like an angel sings,
Still quiring to the young-ey'd cherubins.
Souch harmony is in immortal souls,
But whilst this muddy vesture of decay
Doth grossly close it in, we cannot hear it.

(v, i, 56-65)

This is the vision of Plato's Er and Cicero's Scipio. It is significant that the one instance of Shakespeare's troping of the doctrine is Lorenzo's explanation of the inaudible character of the heavenly music. Neither of the traditional reasons (acclimatization, or the physical thresholds of perception) is given. Instead, the unheard music is related to immortality, and by extension to a prelapsarian condition, a world which, like heaven, need not conceal its ultimate gold, which even Belmont must do. This approaches Milton's treatment of the subject in *At a Solemn Music*.[151]

Then enter the musicians, to play at Lorenzo's bidding. "I am never merry when I hear sweet music," says Jessica, and here she uses "sweet" to mean "perfectly tuned" in the same standard sixteenth-century sense that was employed by Richard in Pomfret Castle. Renaissance musical doctrine would answer her question by reference to the gravity of the celestial harmony that is engaged by any truly tuned earthly musical proportions. Lorenzo retorts with a traditional disquisition on music and the affections, ending on a note of *musica humana* with all of its ethical and political connotations:

> The reason is, your spirits are attentive.
> For do but note a wild and wanton herd,
> Or race of youthful and unhandled colts,
> Fetching mad bounds, bellowing, and neighing loud,
> Which is the hot condition of their blood.
> If they but hear perchance a trumpet sound,
> Or any air of music touch their ears,
> You shall perceive them make a mutual stand,
> Their savage eyes turned to a modest gaze
> By the sweet power of music. Therefore the poet
> Did feign that Orpheus drew trees, stones, and floods,

[151] And see also Ronsard's *Préface sur la Musique* (1572), in *Oeuvres Complètes*, ed. Paul Laumonier (Paris, 1914-1919), VII, 16-20. Ronsard inveighs similarly against "*ceux qui sont engourdiz, paresseux, et abastardiz en ce corps mortel, ne ce souvenant de la céleste armonie du ciel, non plus qu'aux compagnons d'Ulysse d'avoir esté hommes, après que Circe les eut transformés en porceaux.*"

Since naught's so stockish, hard, and full of rage
But music for the time doth change his nature.
The man that hath no music in himself
Nor is not moved with concord of sweet sounds,
Is fit for treasons, stratagems, and spoils.
The motions of his spirit are dull as night
And his affections dark as Erebus.
Let no such man be trusted. Mark the music.

(v, i, 70-88)[152]

Innuendoes of *musica mundana*, golden, silent, and inaccessible, are intimated at Belmont, where actual music is heard, and where the Venetian incompatibilities of gold and love are finally reconciled, almost as much in the golden music as in the golden ring.

In *Twelfth Night*, however, the role of music is so obviously fundamental to the spirit of the play that it is momentarily surprising to find so little speculative music brought up for discussion. But I think that, on consideration of the nature of the play itself, the place of both active and intellectual music, and the relations between them, emerge as something far more complex than Shakespeare had hitherto cause to employ. *Twelfth Night* is, in very serious ways, a play about parties and what they do to people. Full of games, revels, tricks, and disguises, it is an Epiphany play, a ritualized Twelfth Night festivity in itself, but it is much more than this: the play gives us an analysis, as well as a representation, of feasting. It develops an ethic of indulgence based on the notion that the personality of any individual is a function not of the static proportions of the humors within him, but of the dynamic appetites that may more purposefully, as well as more pragmatically, be said to govern his behavior. Superficially close

---

[152] Again, Ronsard, *loc.cit.*, pp. 16-17: "*Car celuy, Sire, lequell oyant un doux accord d'instrumens ou la douceur de la voyx naturelle, ne s'en resjouist point, ne s'en esment point, et détesté en pieds n'en tressaut point, comme doucement ravy, et si ne scay comment dérobé hors de soie; c'est signe qu'il a l'ame tortue, vicieuse, et depravée. . . . Comment se pourroit accorder avec un homme qui de son naturel hayt les accords?*"

to comedy of humors in the characterological extremes of its
dramatis personae, the play nevertheless seems almost intent
on destroying the whole theory of comedy and of morality
entailed by the comedy of humors.

The nature of revels is disclosed in the first scene. The
materials are to be music, food and drink, and love. The basic
action of both festivity in general, and of the play itself, is
declared to be that of so surfeiting the appetite that it will
sicken and die, leaving fulfilled the tempered, harmonious
self. The movement of the whole play is that of a party: from
appetite, through the direction of that appetite outward toward
something, to satiation, and eventually to the condition when,
as the Duke hopes for Olivia, "liver, brain and heart / These
sovereign thrones, are all supplied, and filled / Her sweet
perfections with one self king." The "one self king" is the final
harmonious state to be achieved by each reveller, but it is
also, in both the Duke's and Olivia's case, Caesario who kills
"the flock of all affections else" that live in them, and who is
shown forth in a literal Epiphany in the last act.

The Duke's opening speech describes both the action of
feasting, and his own abundant, ursine, romantic temperament.
But it also contains within it an emblematic representation of
the action of surfeiting:

> If music be the food of love, play on.
> Give me excess of it, that, surfeiting,
> The appetite may sicken, and so die.
> That strain again! It had a dying fall.
> Oh, it came o'er my ear like the sweet sound
> That breathes upon a bank of violets,
> Stealing and giving odor! Enough, no more.
> 'Tis not so sweet now as it was before.
>
> (I, i, 1-8)

The one personage in the play who remains a melancholic
humors character is the one person who is outside the revels
and cannot be affected by them. Olivia's rebuke cuts to the

heart of his nature: "Thou art sick of self love, Malvolio, and taste with a distempered appetite." Suffering from a kind of moral indigestion, Malvolio's true character is revealed in his involuted, Puritanic sensibility that allows of no appetites directed outward. His rhetoric is full of the Devil; it is full of humors and elements as well. No other character tends to mention these save in jest, for it is only Malvolio who believes in them. Yet real, exterior fluids of all kinds, wine, tears, sea-water, urine, and finally the rain of inevitability bathe the whole world of Illyria, in constant reference throughout the play.

The general concern of *Twelfth Night*, then, is *musica humana*, the Boethian application of abstract order and proportion to human behavior. The literalization of the universal harmony that is accomplished in comedy of humors, however, is unequivocally rejected. "Does not our life consist of the four elements?" catechizes Sir Toby. "Faith, so they say," replies Sir Andrew, "but I think it rather consists of eating and drinking." "Thou'rt a scholar," acknowledges Sir Toby. "Let us therefore eat and drink." "Who you are and what you would are out of my welkin—I might say 'element,' but the word is overworn," says Feste, who, taking offense at Malvolio's characterization of him as a "dry fool," touches off the whole proceedings against the unfortunate steward. The plot to ridicule Malvolio is more than the frolicsome revenge of an "allowed fool"; it serves both to put down the killjoy and to affirm the psychology of appetite and fulfillment that governs the play. To the degree that the *musica humana* of *Twelfth Night* involves the substitution of an alternative view to the fairly standard sixteenth-century descriptions of the order of the passions, an application of the musical metaphor would be trivial, and perhaps misleading. But the operation of practical music in the plot, the amazingly naturalistic treatment of its various forms, and the conclusions implied as to the nature and effects of music in both the context of celebration and in the world at large all result in some musical speculation that remains one of the play's unnoticed accomplishments.

The actual music in *Twelfth Night* starts and finishes the play, occurring throughout on different occasions and in different styles. The presumably instrumental piece in which the Duke wallows at the opening dampens his desire for it very quickly, but that desire returns before the play is over. Orsino's appetite at the start of the play is purportedly for Olivia, who hungers for, and indulges herself in, her own grief. The Duke's actual love, too, is for his own act of longing, and for his own exclamations of sentiment. The desires of both are directed outward before the play is over. But until a peculiar musical mechanism, which will be mentioned later on, has been set to work, the Duke will hunt his own heart; and his desires, "like fell and cruel hounds," will continue to pursue him. The music in Act II, scene iv, is of just such a nature to appease the Duke's extreme sentimentality. Orsino makes it plain what sort of song he wants to hear:

> Now, good Caesario, but that piece of song,
> That old and antique song we heard last night.
> Methought it did relieve my passion much,
> More than light airs and recollected terms
> Of these most brisk and giddy-paced times.

(II, iv, 2-6)

This is a familiar sentimental attitude, the desire for the Good Old Song that nudges the memory, the modern request made of the cocktail pianist, the half-ironic translation in Bertolt Brecht's *Happy End*, where a singer tries to recapture better days by imploring "*Joe, mach die Musik von damals nach.*" Orsino's favorite song, he says,

> is old and plain.
> The spinsters and the knitters in the sun
> And the free maids that weave their thread with bones
> Do use to chant it. It is silly, sooth,

[156]

> And dallies with the innocence of love,
> Like the old age.

(II, iv, 44-49)

Actually, the song that Feste sings him is a highly extravagant, almost parodic version of the theme of death from unrequited love. Its rather stilted diction and uneasy prosody are no doubt intended to suggest a song from an old miscellany. "Come away" is a banal beginning, appearing at the start of four song texts in Canon Fellowes' collection. We may also presume that the setting employed was rather more archaic than that of the well-polished lute accompaniments of the turn of the century.

It is just one of these "light airs and recollected terms," however, with which Sir Toby and Feste plague Malvolio in their big scene of carousal (II, iii). A setting of "Farewell, dear heart" appears in Robert Jones' first book of airs, published in 1600. Of the other songs in the same scene, one is a catch, a more trivial form of song, certainly with respect to its text, than the sophisticated and intricate lewdness of the post-Restoration round. The other is a "love song" sung by Feste, and preferred by Sir Toby and Sir Andrew to "a song of good life," perhaps with a pious text. It is of the finest type of Shakespearean song that catches up the spirit of overall themes and individual characters, ironically and prophetically pointing to the end of a plot or bit of action. All of "Oh mistress mine" is in one sense an invocation to Olivia to put off her self-indulgent grief, her courting of her dead brother's memory. In particular, the first stanza refers to Viola, the boy-girl true love, "that can sing both high and low."

Feste's songs to Malvolio in his madman's prison are both of an archaic cast. The first is a snatch of a song of Wyatt's, "A robyn, joly robyn" that was set to music by William Cornishe during the reign of Henry VIII. The other one, a parting jibe at Malvolio's cant about the Devil, suggests the doggerel of an old morality, invoking Malvolio as the Devil himself, and continuing the game of mocking him by appealing to his own rhetoric.

All of these occurrences of practical music function in the plot as well as with respect to the general theme of feasting and revels. The one reference to *musica speculativa* is a very interesting one, however, and leads to the most important aspect of the operation of music in *Twelfth Night*. Olivia is exhorting Viola to refrain from mentioning the Duke to her, and implying that she would rather be courted by his messenger:

> I bade you never speak of him again.
> But would you undertake another suit,
> I had rather hear you to solicit that
> Than music from the spheres.

> (III, i, 118-121)

The citation of the music of the spheres here has the tone of most such references during the later seventeenth century in England. With the exception of poets like Milton and Marvell, who used metaphors from the old cosmology for intricate poetic purposes of their own, the music of the spheres became, in Cavalier and Augustan poetry, a formal compliment, empty of even the metaphorical import that the world view of the centuries preceding had given to it. Just as the word "heavenly," used in exclamations of praise, long ago became divorced from its substantive root, the music of the spheres gradually came to designate the acme of effective charm in a performer. It was often employed in compliments to ladies, for example, whose skill at singing made the spheres sound dissonant, abashed the singing angels, and so forth. As in the case of Dryden's music that would "untune the sky," references to the heavenly harmony had nothing to do with received ideas of music's importance during the later seventeenth century, which were more and more becoming confined to a rhetorical ability to elicit passion, on the one hand, and to provide ornament to the cognitive import of a text, on the other. Purcell likens music and poetry to beauty and wit, respectively; the former can unite to produce the same wondrous effects in song that the latter can in a human being, although the virtues of each are independent. The differences between music and poetry also tended to cluster about the celebrated rift between thought and feeling. Most important of all, traditional *musica speculativa* gradually ceased being a model of universal order, and was replaced by a notion of music as a model of rhetoric, whose importance lay in its ability to move the passions, rather than in its older role of the microcosmic copy of universal harmony. The Apollonian lute-harp-lyre constellation, once an emblem of reason and order, became an instrument of passion in the hands of Caravaggio's leering boys, and in the hands of Crashaw's musician who slew the nightingale by musically ravishing her, as even her avatar Philomela was never so ravished, to death.

With these considerations in mind, the crucial role of Viola as an instrument of such a rhetorical music becomes quite clear. It is unfortunate that we have no precise indication of an earlier version of the play, presumably rewritten when the superior singer Robert Armin entered Shakespeare's company, in which some of the songs may have been assigned to Viola. She declares herself at the outset:

> I'll serve this Duke.
> Thou shalt present me as a eunuch to him.
> It may be worth thy pains, for I can sing,
> And speak to him in many sorts of music,
> That will allow me very worth his service.
>
> (I, ii, 55-59)

She will be the Duke's instrument, although she turns out to be an instrument that turns in his hand, charming both Olivia and himself in unexpected fashion. Orsino is given an excess of music in Viola. As Caesario, she wins Olivia for her *alter ego* Sebastian; the latter is, himself, in his few scenes, rhetorically effective almost to the point of preciosity, and is likened to the musician Arion, who charmed his way to safety. Viola represents affective, instrumental, prematurely Baroque music in *Twelfth Night*, and it is she whose charm kills off the gourmandizing sentimentality in both Orsino and Olivia, directing their appetites of love outward, in fact, toward herself. Among the characters to whom Malvolio refers as "the lighter people," it is Feste, the singer and prankster, whose pipe and tabor serve as a travesty of Viola's vocal cords. The operation of Viola's "music" involves charming by the use of appearances; the effects of the trickery instigated by Feste are to make Malvolio appear, until he is undeceived, to be Olivia's ridiculously amorous swain. (It is, of course, the phrase "To be Count Malvolio" that appears on his lips after reading the forged letter.) Through the mechanism of fooling, the travesty of music below stairs, Sir Andrew is chastened, Sir Toby is soberly married to Maria, Malvolio is made to act out the madness of which he falsely accused Feste, and "the whirligig of time brings in his revenges."

The music that brings about the conclusion of the revels is thus a figurative music. It pervades the symbolic enactment of indulgence and surfeit in the plot as the actual music, relegated to its several uses and forms with considerable eye to details of practice in Shakespeare's own day, pervades the spectacle of *Twelfth Night*. The play is about revelry, and, in itself, revels; so too, there is music in it, and a working out of a theme in speculative music that strangely coincides with later views on the subject. The *Ursprung* of Viola's music is certainly in the action of the play; it is not to be implied that *Twelfth Night* is anything of a formal treatise. The music in Illyria all serves its immediately dramatic purposes. Within the context of the play's anti-Puritan, anti-Jonsonian treatment of moral physiology,[153] the role of music seems to have become inexorably defined for Shakespeare. Set

---

[153] This notion of the play as an anti-Jonsonian comedy is treated more fully in my "Twelfth Night and the Morality of Indulgence," *Sewanee Review*, LXVII (1959), pp. 220-238.

in a framework of what, at this point, it might be almost coy to call a study in *musica humana*, practical music becomes justified in itself. Free of even the scraps of traditional musical ideology that had been put to use in the plays preceding it, *Twelfth Night* represents a high point in one phase of Shakespeare's musical dramaturgy. It is not until *Antony and Cleopatra* and the last romances that the use of an almost supernatural music, perhaps, as has been suggested, imported to some degree from the musical *données* of the masque, comes to be associated with the late, great themes of reconciliation and transformation.

CHAPTER IV · "WHAT PASSION CANNOT MUSIC RAISE AND QUELL?"

What Passion cannot MUSICK
raise and quell?
When Jubal *struck the corded*
Shell,
His listening Brethren stood a-
round,
And, wond'ring, on their Faces
fell
To worship that Celestial Sound:

The Guises of Orpheus

$\mathcal{T}$HE power of musical sounds to affect a hearer has always been, as we have seen, as much a literary idea as an observed phenomenon. The transmission to Humanist Europe of Classical notions of musical and abstract harmony entailed a fundamental distortion of the basic concept of harmony itself; and all the important notions of musical speculation in general remained unchanged despite those sweeping changes in musical practice that could render matters of fact into points of belief. But it was always the fundamental question of the immediate operation of sounds upon a hearer that elicited the attention of received opinion as well as of legitimate speculation. In the compendia of Renaissance musical thought, the question of music's effects played an ordered part in the organic world of earthly and cosmic musical sounds. The one unfinished task of a writer or transmitter of the doctrines of musical humanism was that of working out a reconciliation between Classical lore of musical *ethos* and Christian ideas of universal harmony and love as figured forth in music. But, by and large, considerations of music's fabled ability to manipulate human behavior remained subordinated to a general cosmological scheme in which *musica mundana* and *musica humana* remained in the relation of macrocosm to microcosm, and in which the effects of practical music upon human actions resembled more the workings of season and climate than of goads, shackles, or the strings of a marionette.

But there was always some strength in an independent literary tradition of the fabulous powers of music, a tradition independent of medieval schemes of universal order or scholarly, Neoclassical attempts to understand the puzzles of Greek musico-ethical theory. The mythological figures of Arion, Amphion, and the seductress Sirens; the perversely associated Marsyas and Linus, musical martyrs in their way, behind whom stood the historical Terpander, punished by the Spartan court for adding extra strings to the then supposedly tetrachordal lyre; and, finally, the predominant personage of Orpheus himself had always stood for the ideal and the model of the poet-musician. The art of Orpheus and his instrument, that object of the hatred of his frenzied destroyers, were always taken, in an unbroken tradition from Classic times on, as representations of eloquence. This figurative notion of eloquence, effective utterance in the abstract, always clung to allusions to and moralizations about the Thracian hero. Through him something approaching the intermediate sense (as far as the modern meanings of "poetry" and "music" are concerned) of the Greek *mousike* was retained long after the cultural practices supporting such a sense had so changed as to limit its meaning.

The association of Orpheus with abstract eloquence and concurrently with the power of actual secular music can be seen very early. Indeed, the fourteenth-century text of the Florentine *ars nova* composer, Francesco Landini's *madrigale*,

"*Sy dolce no sono chol' lir' Orfeo*" represents this tradition in almost its fully developed form:

> *Sy dolce no sono chol' lir' Orfeo*
> *Quand' assetrasse fier', u-cel e boschi*
> *D'amor cantando d'infante deo*
> *Come lo gallo mio di fuor da boschi*
> *Con nota tale che gia m'audita*
> *Non fu da filomena in verdi boschi*
> *Non piu Febo canto quando schernita*
> *Da Marsia fu suo tibia in folti boschi*
> *Dove vincendo lo spoglio di vita. . . .*

(So sweetly did not Orpheus sound with his lyre / When he drew towards himself beasts, birds and woods, / Singing of the divine child of Love, / As did my rooster from out the woods / With such sound as was never heard / From Philomel in the green woods; / No more did Phoebus sing when his flute was scorned / By Marsyas in the verdant woods / Where victorious he deprived him of his life.)[1]

The association of certain peripheral figures may be noted here, such as the nightingale, Marsyas and Apollo, Amphion. The fact that Orpheus' attractive music is compared unfavorably, here, with the poet's prized *gallo* only indicates his status as a conventional touchstone. Orpheus continues, throughout the centuries, to be used in this way. Often, as in the famous

[1] Text from Willi Apel and Archibald T. Davison, *Historical Anthology of Music*, revised edition (Cambridge, Mass., 1949), pp. 57-59. There is a corrupt text of the *ritornello* which mentions Amphion, moving the stones; "*facto fa contrario al gorgone*," says the text, implying that the musical animation of the rock was the opposite process to a gorgon's petrifying stare.

song in *King Henry VIII*, III, i, the whole point of the reference will turn upon an exposition of the Classical material:

> Orpheus with his lute made trees,
> And the mountain tops that freeze,
>   Bow themselves, when he did sing.
> To his music, plants and flowers
> Ever sprung, as sun and showers,
>   There had made a lasting spring.
>
> Everything that heard him play,
> Even the billows of the sea,
>   Hung their heads, and then lay by.
> In sweet music is such art,
> Killing care, and grief of heart,
>   Fall asleep, or hearing die.[2]

"Take thy lute, wench," says Queen Katherine; "my soul grows sad with troubles. / Sing and disperse 'em, if thou canst. . . ."; and in the song she sings, the Queen's waiting-woman specifically emphasizes the relaxing, rejuvenating power of music. The substitution of "lute" for "lyre" or some other more accurate name is, as we have seen in a previous chapter, conventional throughout the Renaissance. Yet it has become such a commonplace by this time that the clear indication, in both the dialogue and the action, that the song itself is being accompanied by a lute, helps to support the self-reference of the text.[3] That self-reference, a soothing, care-killing song whose text concerns the soothing, care-killing powers of song, operates in somewhat the same way as does the frequent assurance, in so many nineteenth-century lullabies, that "Mother will sing a lullaby."

While Orpheus is traditionally associated with inducing

---

[2] This song is almost universally assigned to Fletcher, and I see no reason not to concur.

[3] We might almost say that there is an implied emphasis on "*his* lute" here. See the remarks on this, also, in Richmond Noble, *Shakespeare's Use of Song* (Oxford, 1923), pp. 112-113.

activity in inanimate rocks, trees and animals, and, finally, men, it is as a governor of feelings that he comes primarily to be used in English poetry of the seventeenth century. The role of Orpheus in a rare case like that of *Lycidas* is as complicated as is the notion of poetry itself in that poem; far more usual is the simple open or covert Orphean allusion. The former case might be illustrated by an almost random example. This is by William Strode (1600-1645):

SONG

When Orpheus sweetly did complayne
Upon his lute with heavy strayne
How his Euridice was slayne,
    The trees to heare
    Obtayn'd an eare,
And after left it off againe.

At every stroake and every stay
The boughs kept time, and nodding lay,
And listened bending all one way:
    The aspen tree
    As well as hee
Began to shake and learn'd to play.

If wood could speake, a tree might heare,
If wood could sound true griefe so neare
A tree might dropp an amber teare:
    If wood so well
    Could ring a knell
The Cipres might condone the beare.

The standing nobles of the grove
Hearing dead wood so speak and move
The fatall axe began to love:
    They envyde death
    That gave such breath
As men alive doe saints above.[4]

[4] William Strode, *Poetical Works*, ed. Bertram Dobell (London, 1907), pp. 1-2. Also see below, Chapter VI, n. 38.

This is typical of seventeenth-century poetic treatments of Orpheus if only because of the way in which it employs an elaborate conceit, almost an end in itself in this poem, to *account* for the emotive and motivating powers of the hero's music. Here also is a slightly submerged reference to actual musical facts: the "shake" of "Began to shake and learn'd to play" puns on the seventeenth-century lute ornament (also called a "beat" or sometimes "sweetening"—today, what we would term a mordent). The contrast between the "dead wood" of the lute and the living sighs and musical complaints of the growing trees is also a seventeenth-century commonplace; in the wit of much pre-Augustan poetry it figures forth the kind of contrast between the Natural and the Artificial that is so elaborately treated, as we shall see further on in this chapter, in Crashaw's "Musicks Duell."

Again, the Orphean allusion can be a covert one, as in these lines from Waller's "At Penshurst":

> While in the park I sing, the listening deer,
> Attend my passion, and forget to fear.
> When to the beeches I report my flame,
> They bow their heads, as if they felt the same.
> To gods appealing, when I reach the bowers
> With loud complaints, they answer me in showers.
> To thee a wild and cruel soul is given,
> More deaf than trees, and prouder than the heavens![5]

Here the poet's linking of himself with Orpheus fades out into a more general treatment of the sympathy of nature; it is almost as if the Orphean power to charm all creation with music were the mechanism through which the pathetic fallacy might be held to operate.

But before Orpheus could emerge as the sublime shaper of human feeling, rather than merely of universal activity, as the raw material of the myth provides, there would be several stages of quasi-allegorical treatment of the story by

[5] Edmund Waller, *Poems*, ed. G. Thorn-Drury (London, 1893), p. 64.

Medieval and Renaissance writers. A modern critic has remarked on the amazing imaginative richness of that same raw material, however, and on how well it could adapt itself to various purposes. Joseph Kerman remarks in his *Opera as Drama* that "The myth of Orpheus, furthermore, deals with man specifically as artist, and one is drawn inevitably to see in it, mirrored in a kind of proleptic vision, the peculiar problems of the opera composer. Initially Orpheus is the supreme lyric artist. In the classic view he is the ideal of the prize-winning *kitharista*—or, in Christian allegory, the evangelical psalmist who charmed the melancholy Saul. To the fourteenth century, he is the minstrel who exacts his boon from the Fairy King; to the sixteenth, perhaps, the madrigalist; to the nineteenth, proud Walther who persuades the German pedants. The eighteenth century painted him, tremulously, as the amiable singer of Metastasio's faint verses who entranced the King of Spain. . . ."[6] And if the figure of the Thracian musician undergoes so many changes of guise, the interpretation of the power of his music takes many differing forms as well. An important source for Medieval treatments of Orpheus is Boethius' *De Consolatione*, translated into Old English by King Alfred, which, however, gives no account of the reasons for the wondrous effects of the music upon its hearers. We have seen how Henryson's Orpheus partook of the benefits of a good scholastic education: he studied his *quadrivium* so well as to learn the lessons of, and hence to master, the powers of universal harmony.[7] It was to the advantage of Humanism, however, to allegorize the Orphean music into rational discourse. The almost propagandistic gloss, in a 1525 printed version of John Walton's fifteenth-century verse translation of Boethius, in Book III, Metrum XII, is a good early example of this: "By Orpheus ys understand the hyer part of the soule / that ys resonabeltye enformed with wysdom and eloquence. Thys Orpheus by the swetnesse of hys harpe /

<hr/>

[6] Joseph Kerman, "Orpheus: the Neoclassic Vision," in *Opera as Drama* (New York, 1956), p. 27.

[7] See above, Chapter II.

that ys to say bestly men and savage broght into the rule of reson."[8] This kind of moralization, in which the Orphean music is rational and calming, stresses not so much the power of his playing to incite and inflame either feelings, deeds, or even thoughts, as its power to bring the soul into the adjusting climate of wisdom, "the rule of reson." This power is conceptually related to the traditional notion of *musica humana*, which defines the harmonious composition of the soul by saying that it is in perfect tune or harmony with the universal music. The music of "thys Orpheus," rather than inducing "worldely lustes" or feelings, subdues them by leading them into the magnetic field, as it were, of universal reason.

In allegorizations like this one, the destroying Maenads in "the rout that made the hideous roar" become all the forces of unreason. Francis Bacon describes them in his allegorization of the story in *De Sapientia Veterum* (1609), "And all this went on for some time with happy success and great admiration; till at last certain Thracian women, under the stimulation and excitement of Bacchus came where he was; and first they blew a hoarse and hideous blast upon a horn (*cornu*) that the sound of his music could no longer be heard for the din: whereupon the charm being broken that had been the bond of that order and good fellowship, confusion began again; the beasts returned each to his several nature and preyed one upon the other as before. . . ."[9] Bacon's moralization of the story is one of Philosophy. Orpheus' singing, he continues, has two distinct powers; one of these is the power to propitiate infernal forces, and the other is the traditional affective influence of the music upon animate and inanimate entities. In the allegory, the former is natural philosophy (our natural science), the latter, moral and political philosophy. Bacon follows platonistic tradition as carried on by Jean Bodin and others, as well as in emblem literature, by equating the harmonious

---

[8] Boethius, *De Consolatione Philosophiae*, tr. John Walton, ed. Mark Science (London, 1927), p. 372.

[9] Francis Bacon, *De Sapientia Veterum* (1609), tr. J. Spedding, in *Philosophical Works*, ed. J. M. Robertson (London, 1905), pp. 835-836.

structure of the lyre, as well as of its music, with a model of human order. The Bacchic Maenads become the disorders of ungoverned nature: "For so it is that after kingdoms and commonwealths have flourished for a time there arise perturbations and seditions and wars; amid the uproars of which, first the laws are put to silence, and then men return to the depraved conditions of their nature and desolation is seen in the fields and cities."[10] Without the civilizing influence of the Orphean music, humanity lapses into barbarism. It takes little straining of analogy for us to see how, *mutatis mutandis*, this purely civil effect may be seen as Christian grace, saving rather than civilizing. While Bacon's twofold allegory of natural and moral philosophy is definitely his own and his own age's, it lies close in some ways to Classical notions of music as *paideia*, and to the distinction between the music of the Orphean lyre and the Maenads' *auloi* as a difference between the conventional rational and irrational associations of their respective instruments.[11]

The traditional Neoclassic linking of music and poetry having been made, apologies for poetry readily take this same course. Thus Henry Peacham in the 1634 edition of *The Compleat Gentleman* can ask in his chapter "Of Poetry," "And what were the songs of *Linus, Orpheus, Amphyon, Olympus*, and that ditty *Iopas* sang to his harpe at *Dido's* banquet, but Naturall and Morall Philosophy, sweetned with

[10] *Ibid.*, p. 836.

[11] In allegorizations of the Orpheus myth that are of this type, it is generally forgotten that Orpheus was the son of Dionysus, rather than of Apollo (which is never stated, but almost implicitly suggested often). His lyre, at any rate, is the instrument sacred to Phoebus, and his music was, in Greek terms, a rational music, as opposed to the textless sound of the *aulos*. The whole Dionysiac aspect of the Orpheus legend, and the Orphic religious cult (I employ the adjective "Orphean" throughout to avoid confusion with this), are a thing apart from what we have been discussing. See W. K. C. Guthrie, *Orpheus and Greek Religion* (London, 1935), pp. 39–48, for a good account of some of the origins of the legend and its early variants and parallels. Also, D. P. Walker, "Orpheus the Theologian and Renaissance Platonists," *Journal of the Warburg and Courtauld Institutes*, XVI (1953), pp. 100–120; pp. 101–102 of the latter summarize the Orphic doctrines of the affections and passions.

the pleasance of Numbers, that Rudenesse and Barbarisme might the better taste and digest the lessons of civility?"[12] This notion of sugar-coating, while peculiarly appropriate to a courtesy book, seems strangely premature as an oversimplification of one theme in Augustan poetics. Also of incidental note here is the way in which Iopas' "*cithara . . . aurata*" of *Aeneid* I, 740 becomes a minstrel's "harpe" (rather than the Psalmist's one).

Perhaps of greatest concern to us here is the allegorization of the powers of Orpheus' music to be found in what Douglas Bush has called "the greatest repository of allegorized myth in English,"[13] George Sandys' commentary on Ovid. This work contains some rather interesting reflections on several of the stock musical figures of Antiquity: Marsyas, Orpheus, Amphion, the Sirens, Philomel, and Procne, etc. Commenting, for example, on Midas' disfiguring breach of taste (in Book XI of the *Metamorphoses*), Sandys remarks as follows on the musical contest which prompted the foolish king's unfortunate judgment: "But to sore more high: the contention betweene these musitians, and the event thereof, exhibits a healthfull doctrine, which may restraine our vaineglory and judgments with sobriety. For there is a twofold harmony or musick; the one of divine providence, and the other of humane reason. To humane judgment (which is as it were to mortall eares) the administration of the World, of the Creature, and more secret decrees of the highest, sound harsh and disconsonant; which ignorance, though it be deservedly marked with the eares of an asse, yet is it not apparant, or noted for a deformity by the vulgar."[14] This dichotomy is somewhat reminiscent of Bacon's two functions of rational music; however, Sandys'

[12] Henry Peacham, *The Compleat Gentleman* (second edition of 1634) (reprinted Oxford, 1906), p. 79.

[13] Douglas Bush, *Mythology and the Renaissance Tradition in English Poetry* (Minneapolis, 1932), p. 243. Also see R. B. Davis, *George Sandys, Poet Adventurer* (London, 1955), pp. 198-226.

[14] G[eorge] S[andys], *Ovid's Metamorphoses Englished, Mythologiz'd and Represented in Figures* (1632), p. 390.

view is much more Elizabethan than is Bacon's, whose system allows for the investigation by human reason of those realms of "the administration of the World, of the Creature" that Sandys feels are beyond reason's grasp. Sandys' dichotomy also suggests comparison with a widely circulated seventeenth-century distinction between "divine and civil" musical practice.[15] On Marsyas, Sandys keeps pretty close to traditional views about the nature of wind instruments, combining a Greek distrust of the *aulos* with the Medieval and Renaissance use of the trumpet as an emblem of fame: "Marsyas, the inventor of wind instruments, may resemble ambition and vaine glory, which delight in loud shouts and applauses: but virtue and wisdom have a sweeter touch, though they make not so great a noyse in popular opinion."[16] It should only be remarked here that "sweeter touch" means, literally, "more harmonious sound"; the distinction between the loud and uncontrolled and the soft and well-tuned is one of the traditional ones in the string-wind polarity—a distinction drawn both from the doctrines of antiquity and from the difference in Renaissance musical practice, between the "indoor" and "outdoor" instruments and even pitches.

In his fairly long section on Orpheus himself, however, we find Sandys giving expression to what was to become a dominant theme of seventeenth-century musical and esthetic theory in general. After discussing the Orphean music as poetry and as eloquence, and making some traditional points about the function of texts in song, Sandys continues:

"Yet musick in it selfe most strangely works upon our humane affections. Not in that the Soule (according to the opinion of the *Platonists*) consisting of harmony, & rapt with the sphericall musick before it descended from Heaven to inhabit the body, affects it with the like desire (there being no nation so barbarous, or man so austere and stupid, which is not by the melody of instruments and numerous com-

[15] See below, Chapter v.
[16] Sandys, *op.cit.*, p. 225.

posures, either incited to pleasure or animated to Virtue) but because the Spirits which agitate in the heart, receave a warbling and dancing aire into the bosome, and are made one with the same where with they have an affinity; whose motions lead the rest of the Spirits dispersed through the body, raising or suppressing the instrumental parts according to the measures of the musick; sometimes inflaming: and againe composing the affections: the sense of hearing stricking the Spirits more immediately, then the rest of the sences."[17]

And here we have indication of a new phase in the history of musical thought. The older tradition of world harmony and its consequences for the effects of music upon individuals are here specifically repudiated, and the powers of music are accounted for in terms of a quasi-mechanistic model. The isolation of these powers from their prior position in the organism which embraced universal and human music—what Leo Spitzer calls "the disappearance of the one (semantic) field" uniting "world-harmony" and "well-temperedness"[18]—begins to manifest itself both in speculative accounts of a more literary nature and in the writings and interests of musicians and technical theoreticians, toward the beginning of the seventeenth century. In such a scheme, Orpheus abandons his role as philosopher and takes up one as exhorter, for a combination of notions widely differing in origin and function comes to assign to musical sounds the power over the passions, and to assign to language alone the ability to excite reason and the workings of the intellectual faculties.

These notions might all be said to comprise a shift from an interpretation of music as an *imitative* art to that of music as an *expressive* one. We shall see during the course of the present chapter the implications of this shift for both poetry and musical practice. The first of these notions is of the greatest general historical importance: it concerns the development of

[17] *Ibid.*, p. 356.
[18] Leo Spitzer, "Classical and Christian Ideas of World Harmony" (Part II), *Traditio*, III (1945), p. 315.

rationalist psychology. Descartes, in conceiving of the passions or affections as being capable of immediate agitation by sensually received stimuli, completely bypassing the governing function of the intellectual or rational soul, paved the way for an interpretation of music's effects that could ignore completely the older, organic view. What we might call the Renaissance para-physiology of correspondences between microcosmic humors and macrocosmic elements had been able to support the musical views of "the Platonists" that Sandys so casually puts down. Within the framework of the Cartesian psychology, not only does music operate directly upon the passions, but correspondences between qualities of the musical stimuli and their effects upon the agitations of the nervous system can be demonstrated without appeal to metaphysics and cosmology. This application of the theory of the passions to musical esthetics—what we shall henceforth refer to, together with certain corollary musical ideas soon to be discussed, as the doctrine of the affections—can virtually be said to have completely replaced the older theories of *musica speculativa* by the end of the seventeenth century. "Replaced *as an account of music's powers*," it should be added, for certainly the literary use of the older lore perpetuates itself; it is equally true that the very demands that were beginning to be made of what we would now call "scientific" *accounts* of any phenomena precluded the older speculative treatment of either the fabulous skill of Orpheus or the actual events at an opera.[19]

A second idea that underlay the new notions of musical expression was much more a strictly literary one. One of the basic doctrines of musical Neoclassicism, as it began to manifest itself in the 1580's in Florence with the group of musical theorists known as the Camerata, involved the recognition that the music of Ancient times, about which so little was actually known (save for the corpus of speculative theory),

[19] See Katharine Everett Gilbert and Helmut Kuhn, *A History of Esthetics* (Bloomington, 1953), pp. 205-215. Also see Arthur W. Locke, "Descartes and Seventeenth Century Music," *Musical Quarterly*, XXI (1935), pp. 423-431.

was far superior to that of debased modern days. An important consequence of this notion was the interpretation of the Greek fables of music's powers, such as the Orpheus myths, in the light of the notion that only in the perfect music of a high and far-off Classical epoch could such powers demonstrate themselves. By the end of the seventeenth century, for example, when the doctrine had become a commonplace, Jeremy Collier could write: "That the Musick of the Antients could command further than the Modern, is past Dispute. Whether they were Masters of a greater Compass of *Notes*, or knew the Secret of varying them more artificially: Whether they adjusted the Intervals of Silence more exactly, had their hands or their voices farther improved, or their Instruments better contrived: Whether they had a deeper Insight into the Philosophy of Nature, and understood the *Laws* of the *Union* of the Soul and Body more thoroughly; and from thence were enabled to touch the Passions, strengthen the *Sense*, or prepare the *Medium* with greater advantage: Whether they excell'd us in all, or in many of these ways, Is not so Clear. However this is certain, That our Improvements of this kind are little better than an Ale-house-Crowds, with respect to theirs."[20]

Early seventeenth-century theorists, however, thought that they had the answer that Collier, writing in the penultimate decade of the century, could not claim to isolate. The relative importance of text and melody in all sung music became a basic question for much of the early Baroque music. It began to be generally agreed among theorists and composers of Italian music of the new *stilo recitativo* or *stilo rappresentativo* that not only the entire rational or affective content of music, but its very *raison d'être* as well, lay in the way in which it underlined the emotional content of a text in the setting of it. The experiments in a monodic style, accompanied only by a bass line (or by a thin realization of it on an archlute) led to the triumph of expressive rather than imitative

[20] Jeremy Collier, "Of Musick," from *Essays Upon Severall Moral Subjects*, second edition (London, 1697), II, 22-23.

music, in the development of opera. But the general effect of the stressing of music's commitment to the expressive elaboration of the meaningful text was to help enforce a distinction between the ability of music and language to operate only upon human feeling and human reason respectively.[21]

A third notion that lies behind the seventeenth-century affective theory of music's power is an identification of music with rhetoric, rather than with philosophy, or rational discourse in general, that becomes increasingly common during the first half of the century. If music is considered as one of the arts of persuasion, along with rhetoric, or even as rhetoric itself, its independent influence over human feeling is assured by virtue of that connection with the arts of rhetoric, which, said Locke, "are for nothing else but to insinuate wrong ideas, move the passions, and thereby mislead the judgment, and so indeed are perfect cheats."[22] And here the allegorized role of music might be said to have come full circle, for Locke's condemnation of the persuasive arts sounds very much like Bacon's complaint against the anti-rational Maenads, the monstrous, frenzied destroyers of Orpheus and his sublimely affective music.

But let us look, for a while, at some of these ideas in a little more detail. It is the intention of this chapter, among other things, to associate the doctrine of the affections with the musical style (and its expression, in the poetic style) of the Baroque. In order better to demonstrate that association, we might look somewhat more closely at the grounds upon which the role of music as an influence over passion was laid.

Music and the Passions

Descartes' theories of music in particular are interesting not so much for their comprehensiveness, nor for the strength

[21] See Manfred Bukofzer, *Music in the Baroque Era* (New York, 1947), pp. 1-19; also below.
[22] John Locke, "An Essay Concerning Human Understanding," III, x, No. 34, in *Philosophical Works*, ed. J. A. St. John (London, 1913), II, 112.

with which they are argued, as for their influence and timeliness. They are first set forth in his *Compendium Musices* (1618, shortly thereafter translated into French), and later, throughout his life, in his voluminous correspondence with Marin Mersenne on musical and acoustical subjects. Opening in a very different manner from the encyclopedic musical treatises of the Renaissance, which served as real compendia of musical lore as well as of information about acoustics and modish practice, Descartes' little book dismisses the historical, metaphysical, and cosmological synthesis of *musica speculativa* in its very announcement of intention. At the very start, in an English version of the middle of the seventeenth century, he declares that "The OBJECT of this Art is Sound. The END; to delight and move various Affections in us. For songs may bee made dolefull and delightfull at once: nor is it strange that two divers effects should result from this one cause, since thus Elegiographers and Tragoedians please their Auditors so much the more, by how much the more grief they excite in them."[23] Descartes continues to rule out the operations of metaphysics in accounting for music's effects by assuring his readers that the means to the previously stated end are confined to differences of duration and pitch only (this is *simpliste*, even for a mechanistic account, of course). Then, no doubt attempting to confront the commonplace of *musica speculativa* which held, as William Byrd had put it, that "There is not any Musicke of Instruments whatsoever, comparable to that which is made of the voyces of Men. . . ,"[24] and which went on to justify this with appeals to the celestial music and to over-literal constructions of passages in Plato

---

[23] *Renatus Des-Cartes Excellent Compendium of Musick: With Necessary and Judicious Animadversions Thereupon.* By a Person of Honour (London, 1653), p. 1. The person in question was probably Lord Brouncker, President of the Royal Society, mentioned in a musical connection by Pepys in his diary. See below, Chapter VI, pp. 386-387; also see E. D. Mackernesse, "A Speculative Dilettante," *Music and Letters*, XXXIV (1953), pp. 236-252.

[24] William Byrd, *Psalmes, Sonets and Songs of Sadness and Pietie* (1588), *Preface*, in E. H. Fellowes (ed.), *English Madrigal School* (London, 1913-1924), vol. XIV.

and Aristotle about the difference between sounds produced by air columns with souls behind them and those produced by inanimate instruments only,[25] he continues as follows: "This only thing seems to render the voice of Man the most gracefull of all other sounds; that it holds the greatest conformity to our spirits. Thus also is the voice of a Friend more gratefull then of an enemy, from a sympathy and dispathy of Affections: by the same reason, perhaps, that a Drum headed with a Sheeps skin yields no sound, though strucken, if another Drum headed with a Wolfs skin bee beaten upon in the same room."[26] What seems almost amazing, incidentally, is that Descartes should here perpetuate an old wives' tale of the most suspicious variety in the course of an argument aimed at dispelling mysteries in previous explanations of the power of music.

Throughout his early treatise, Descartes tends toward the view that the more elaborate musical configurations become invested with emotional significance because of conditioned associations surrounding the circumstances of their reiterated hearing. He does feel that purely rhythmic phenomena tend automatically and almost *naturally* to operate on certain passions, the faster movements upon the "higher" spirits (joy, anger, etc.), the slower upon the heavier affections. Only in this does his account suggest the humoral interpretations of Humanist theories. But in general he aims at a rejection of the views that supported most of the views of imitation, "tonepainting," the emotional effects of major, minor, augmented, and chromatic chordal configurations, held by sixteenth-century theorists. And in 1630 we can find Descartes writing to Mersenne that if an auditor had only been able to listen to the lively, triple rhythms of a galliard under painful condi-

---

[25] Aristotle's point in this frequently referred to passage (*De Anima*, 420b-421a) is more involved with a justification of the view that only textually governed music can be rational, probably, than with anything else. *Rational* music, produced by a sounding instrument with a soul, will be ordered by *language*, an implicit criterion for soul-possession here.

[26] *Compendium, ed.cit.*, p. 2.

tions, the formal elements of the dance could not help but assume a painful character.[27] In the *Compendium*, Descartes also refuses to evince one shred of interest in the Pythagoreanism of fifteenth- and sixteenth-century imitative counterpoint, or, indeed, in the practice itself. Of through-composed canon, he remarks that "In such Compositions where that Artifice is observed perpetually from beginning to the end: we conceive, that may belong not more to Musick, than *Acrosticks* or retrograde Verses to *Poesie*, which was invented to charm the respective Passions, as well as Musick."[28]

It is, I think, quite significant that Descartes concerns himself neither with the music of Antiquity (except with respect to a few acoustical questions) nor with the matter of the relationship between text and musical setting in vocal music. For him the essence of music is instrumental sound, or the vocal intonation of sound modelled on the former, the voice being treated as merely another instrument. For him, in short, the effects of music upon feelings are purely matters of acoustics and physiology. The affective theory of music takes no account of the workings of language accompanying or, as Aristotle might have it, informing, a sequence of musical sounds. A seventeenth-century writer fully convinced of the truth of that theory, like Jeremy Collier (a man who wondered "whether there may not be some *Counter Sounds*; which may give the Mind as high a Disgust, as the other can a Pleasure")[29] could view this new theory with some distrust: "Though the Entertainments of Musick are very Engaging; though they make a great Discovery of the Soul; and shew it capable of strange Diversities of Pleasure: Yet to have our

[27] Descartes goes on to anticipate Pavlov to a certain extent, and to lay the groundwork for a notion of phonic norms established by means of conditioning: "*Ce qui est si certain, que je juge que si on avoit bien fouetté un chien cinq ou six fois, au son du violon, si-tost qu'il oiroit une autre fois cette musique, il commenceroit à crier & à s'enfuir.*" René Descartes, *Oeuvres*, ed. Adam et Tannery (Paris, 1902), p. 134. See also, André Pirro, *Descartes et la Musique* (Paris, 1907).

[28] *Compendium*, p. 54.

[29] Jeremy Collier, "Of Musick," *ed.cit.*, II, 23-24.

Passions lye at the Mercy of a little Minstrelsy; to be Fiddled out of our Reason and Sobriety; to have our Courage depend upon a *Drum*, or our Devotions on an *Organ*, is a sign we are not so great as we might be. If we were proof against the charming of Sounds; or could we have the Satisfaction without the Danger; or raise our Minds to what pitch we pleas'd by the Strength of *Thinking*, it would be a nobler Instance of Power and Perfection."[30]

Text and Melody: Neoclassicism

Throughout the sixteenth century, however, the proper relationship between word and tone had been the concern of musical theorists; and, as we have already remarked, the perfection of the music of Antiquity began to be measured against a rule of textual-musical cooperation. As early as 1515, a non-musician like Sir Thomas More could express this notion in his comments on the one truly superior quality of the liturgical music of his Utopians: "Then they sing prayses unto God, whiche they intermixt with instrumentes of musicke, for the moste parte of other fassions then these that we use in this parte of the worlde. And like as some of ours bee muche sweter then theirs, so some of theirs doo farre passe ours. But in one thinge doubtles they goo exceding farre beyonde us. For all their musike bothe that they playe upon instrumentes, and that they singe with mannes voyce dothe so resemble and expresse naturall affections, the sound and tune is so applied and made agreable to the thinge, that whether it bee a prayer, or els a dytty of gladnes, of patience, of trouble, of mournynge, or of anger; the fassion of the melodye dothe so represent the meaning of the thing, that it doth wonderfullye move, stirre, pearce and enflame the hearers myndes."[31]

It would be extremely misleading to suggest, as was done

[30] *Ibid.*, II, 24.
[31] Thomas More, *Utopia*, Book II, tr. Raphe Robynson, ed. J. Rawson Lumby (Cambridge, 1940), p. 158.

by certain later seventeenth-century writers,[32] that the sixteenth-century tradition of what came to be called the musical
stile antico was not at all interested in serving the interests of
the text set by the music. It was a principle of Renaissance
musical esthetics in general, and of what was known as the
musica reservata of Josquin des Pres, Lassus, etc., that the
musical setting must imitate or "represent" the dominant
affective tone of the text. The difference between the older
and newer approaches to this problem of musical expression
lay in the attitudes of the founders of the so-called *nuovo
musiche* of the beginning of the seventeenth century toward
polyphony, and in the matter of their construction of, and
attitude toward, the music of Antiquity. We have already
remarked on such devices as the "tone-painting" of the Italian
madrigalists that were used for expressive purposes in the
earlier style; the basis of the controversy waged by Bardi,
Caccini, Vincenzo Galilei, Jacopo Peri, and others at the end
of the sixteenth century in Italy was the seeming fact that
polyphonic music betrayed, obscured, and falsified the content of a text, by virtue of the fact that an inactive hearer
(rather than a *participant*: this cannot be too strongly underlined) could not understand the words of an intricately tex-
tured polyphonic setting.[33] The ideal of the newer attitude
toward the text approached Greek practice or, rather, what
little was known about the practice, aside from theory, of
Ancient times.[34] A setting for a solo voice, accompanied only

[32] See Bukofzer, *op.cit.*, pp. 4-9.

[33] See John Hollander, "The Empire of the Ear," unpublished Columbia
master's essay (1952), pp. 23-26, 80-83.

[34] Vincenzo Galilei was responsible for uncovering the first piece of
actual Greek music known to the post-Classic world, but he could not
decipher the notation. This was in 1581. Thereafter there was much experi-
ment with Greek tuning and temperament, always a consuming question in
the sixteenth century, but the debate on the question of how best to secure
the proper *effetti* from music remained active. It can be readily understood
after even a cursory perusal of the arguments for the new monodic music
that the debate did not depend on confusion as to Classic practice so much
as upon a disagreement over historical theory: If Greek practice consisted
of *x*, *y*, *z*, etc., can it best be resurrected in a wholly different age by

by a simply figured bass line, and known as *recitativo*, became the pure type of the expressive setting. It is extremely significant, I feel, that the almost immediate result of the stylistic experiments of the Florentine Camerata and others was the use of the new style in the earliest operas. The attitude toward the text and its latent emotional content which proscribed polyphony went very well indeed in a courtly, and later a public, musical drama in which it was the passive audience's function to be acted upon (in an extension of the purely dramatic notion of *katharsis*) by the expressive music of the singers.

A crude but illuminating distinction between the affective theories of the Humanist and Baroque musicians might be drawn with respect to this quality of action or passion in the audience. For the older *musica speculativa*, music was an activity, and it is almost tacitly assumed that when one is drawing benefits from practical music (with the important exception of a *patient* in need of the legendary curative powers of music), one is oneself producing this music or, better, a single harmonious part of it. Polyphony was an almost perfect model for the notion of universal harmony, and for the corollary idea of the musical linking of the smaller and greater worlds. The early theorists of Baroque music, however, disregarding this whole aspect of *musica speculativa*, found the model of the musical relationship not among the cooperating vocal lines in a polyphonic composition, nor among the dancers going through their complicated, Pythagorean fig-

---

doing *x*, *y*, *z*, or by attempting to compensate for the historical shift by deriving the proper *x'*, *y'*, and *z'* to be used? This seems to lie behind much of the debate. D. P. Walker in the first part of his excellent and comprehensive long article, "Musical Humanism in the Sixteenth and Early Seventeenth Centuries," *The Music Review*, II (1941), pp. 1-13, distinguishes between three different positions with respect to the problem of reconstituting the music of the Ancient World, a conservative view that retained a purely academic interest in the classic music, while approving of modern polyphony (Artusi, Solinas); the radical reform position of the Camerata; and a centrist position, which he associates with figures as disparate as Zarlino and Mersenne. Also see part V of Walker's article, in *The Music Review*, III (1942), pp. 55-71.

ures in a court dance or masque, but in the metaphorical ravishment of the senses of an auditor by the emotive power of an expressive song.

Another point of difference here concerns the practical applications of the ideological differences of the older and newer styles concerning the use of instruments. In the sixteenth century, with the exception of lute and keyboard music, which had notational systems and distinct instrumental styles of their own, vocal polyphony was the ideal model for all music; and while *a cappella* singing was only one of many styles of performance, and instruments were freely used to double and to substitute for vocal parts, the instruments were by and large forced to take vocal roles. Their styles, that is, were not distinctive, and there was no canonical instrumentation for any piece of music. The occasion determined whether the louder dynamics of winds, or the softer volume of plucked and bowed strings, would be employed for an indoor or outdoor performance. But with the beginnings of what is called by historians the music of the Baroque, the role of the instrument becomes extremely important. In practice, instrumental styles for purely textless music grow more and more individualized, just as, later on, the role of the human voice becomes more and more that of a string or wind instrument. In esthetic theory, the instrument (and particularly the string, probably as much because of the tradition of the Orphean lyre as for any other reason) becomes the expressive, ravishing, feeling, and active musical being. The movement which had started off by demanding a closer cooperation of text and melody ended in helping to reinforce the notion that textless music alone could elicit the feelings of a hearer which the text could never quite muster enough magic to provoke.

The music of recitative sought in many ways to approach the expressive inflections of actual (that is, colloquial Italian) speech; and since it is obvious that intonation patterns reflecting rhetorical and emotive qualities vary considerably from language to language, it seems natural that the Italianate *recitativo* style should maintain itself as a purely musical one when used to set other languages, and that no matter how successful it might have been in engaging the inflectional significances of the Italian tongue, its apparent rhetorical and persuasive effectiveness became a purely academic or ideological point in other cases. The first notable examples of the actual use of recitative in English is in 1617, in Ben Jonson's *Vision of Delight* and *Lovers Made Men*, the former masque containing an introductory speech, and the latter being through-composed in the Italian manner, "stylo recitativo, by Master Nicholas Lanier."[35] And while the English accompanied monody of the ayres or lute songs flourished to the eventual exclusion of the polyphonic madrigal in later Jacobean days, it was only with the Caroline masque composers Lanier, the brothers Lawes, Matthew Locke, and others that recitative came into its own.[36] It would be the Italianate style in vocal music, and the French in dance music, that would prevail after the Restoration; and despite the flurry of controversy that arose at the beginning of the eighteenth century about the whole question of Italian opera in England,[37] both

[35] Ben Jonson, *Lovers Made Men*, opening stage direction, in *Works*, ed. C. H. Herford and Percy and Evelyn Simpson (Oxford, 1925-1952), VII, 454. Aside from its ethical implications, the remark to the effect that the dance *raises up* the observers refers very literally to the masque scene itself: it is calling up the audience to join the masquers in the final revels, when actors and spectators will all join in "the general dance." Another such situation occurs in a song in Campion's *The Lords Maske*, devoted much to the subject of music and poetry, in the second stanza of which Orpheus enjoins the masquers both figuratively and literally:

> Courtship and Musicke suite with love,
>   They both are workes of passion;
> Happie is he whose works can move
>   Yet sweete notes helpe perswasion.
> Mixe your words with Musicke then,
>   That they the more may enter;
> Bold assaults are fit for men,
>   That on strange beauties venture.

(In Campion, *Works*, ed. Percival Vivian [Oxford, 1909], p. 97.)

[36] See Bukofzer, *op.cit.*, pp. 182-186. Bukofzer makes the point (p. 184) that the English recitative composers were unable to grasp the essential method used by the Italians in intensifying effects.

[37] See below, Chapter VI.

recitative and the esthetic that justified its practice were commonplace in the later part of the seventeenth century. Thus, Philip Ayres, in an epigram of compliment "On Cynthia, Singing a Recitative Piece of Music," can write some time before the end of the sixteen-eighties:

> O thou angelic spirit, face, and voice,
> Sweet Syren, whose soft notes our souls rejoice,
> Yet when thou dost recite some tragic verse,
> Thy tone and action make it sweetly fierce.
>
> If thou soft, loud, sad or brisk note dost hit,
> It carries still our hearts along with it;
> Thou canst heat, cool, grieve us, or make us smile
> Nay, stab or kill, yet hurt us not the while.
>
> Thy gesture, shape and mien so pleasing are,
> With thee, no human being can compare;
> Thy passions, all our passions do excite,
> And thy feign'd grief does real tears invite.
>
> List'ning to thee, our bodies seem as dead,
> For our rapt souls then up to Heav'n are fled;
> So great a Monarch art thou, that thy breath
> Has power to give us either Life, or Death.[38]

Here the doctrine of recitative's affective power is expounded rather systematically, if somewhat pedestrianly (with the exception of the neat conclusion of the third quatrain); but it is complete, even to the figurative ecstasy recorded in the ultimate stanza, which, as we shall shortly see, became a conventional device in the Baroque poetic treatment of music's effects.

Skepticism and dissent, of course, accompany the promulgation and preservation of any doctrine, and the new music and its esthetic justifications were no exceptions to this. Aside from

[38] Philip Ayres, *Lyric Poems, Made in Imitation of the Italians* (London, 1687), in *The Caroline Poets*, ed. G. Saintsbury (Oxford, 1921), II, 281-282.

the attacks of professional musicians and theorists like G. M. Artusi,[39] there were the relatively unusual positions taken by Galileo Galilei, the famous son of the sixteenth-century Neo-classicist Vincenzo, who held rather premature views about "pure" music exclusive of a text; but even this heterodox view implicitly supported the growing equation of music with the epitome of all stimuli that elicit passion. If a song is to be admired more than actual sobs in representing a sighing lover, Galileo argued, just so must a musician be superior to a singer in such a representation if he achieved his aims "solely by dissonances and passionate musical accents."[40] It is rare that the skepticism concerning music's ability to affect grief, for example, evidenced by the nurse in Euripides' *Medea*,[41] is met with in the seventeenth century. But often a poet, or even a musician expressing his objections in verse, will condemn the new expressive music in no uncertain terms.

The great English polyphonic composer, Orlando Gibbons, published only one set of madrigals, and that in the year 1612, when the fullest production of the Italianate madrigal (but natively perfected, in its own way) had passed its peak. It was a point in the history of English music after which accompanied songs were to form by far the greater part of what were published as songbooks, and at a time when the Italian monody had begun to be heard of in England. Gibbons' first two madrigals are settings of rather polemical texts; I have tried to show elsewhere that the first of them, "The Silver Swan," refers in its setting to the homophonic texture of the part-arrangements that usually appeared with the accompanied lute songs.[42] The text is clearly modelled on that of a madrigal

[39] See Oliver Strunk, ed., *Source Readings in Music History* (New York, 1950), pp. 393-404; also, pp. 290-322 and 363-415, for translations of many important theoretical treatises in the history of early Baroque musical esthetics. Also see Bruce Pattison, *Music and Poetry of the English Renaissance* (London, 1948), pp. 121-128.

[40] See Erwin Panofsky, "Galileo as a Critic of the Arts," *Isis*, XLVII (1956), pp. 3-15.

[41] Euripides, *Medea*, ll. 190-203.

[42] See my "The Empire of the Ear," pp. 61-66.

by Orazio Vecchi appearing in the second edition (1597) of Nicholas Yonge's *Musica Transalpina*, "*Il bianc' e dolce Cigno*":

> The silver swan, who living had no note,
> When death approached her silent throat;
> Leaning her breast against the reedy shore,
> Thus sung her first and last, and sung no more:
> Farewell, all joys; O death come close mine eyes;
> More geese than swans now live, more fools than wise.[43]

The swan is dying of more than Jacobean melancholy, of more than early-Baroque *Weltschmerz*. The geese are the newer crop of anti-polyphonists, of those secular composers who, like Thomas Campion in his *A New Way of Making Fowre Parts in Counter-point*, were willing to reduce the polyphonic art to rule-of-thumb harmonizations, and whose primary interests were monodic lute-songs. Likewise, the text of Gibbons' second madrigal castigates poets for a concomitant lack of seriousness. It must be remembered here that Gibbons' most elaborate compositions were for the Anglican Service, and that Puritan attacks upon church-music may have been stimulating his ire somewhat. At any rate, the association of religious poetry (perhaps Gibbons, in choosing or writing this text, may have had in mind something as specific as metrical versions of the psalter) with polyphonic church music seems to lurk behind these lines:

> O that the learned poets of this time,
> Who in a love-sick line so well can speak,
> Would not consume good wit in hateful rhyme,
> But with deep care some better subject seek.
> For if their music please in earthly things,
> How would it sound if strung with heavenly strings?[44]

---

[43] E. H. Fellowes, ed. *English Madrigal Verse* (Oxford, 1929), p. 97.
[44] *Ibid*. On both of these poems, as well as on the texts and settings of the other madrigals in Gibbons' collection, see Jean Jaquot, "*Lyrisme et Sentiment Tragique dans les Madrigaux d'Orlando Gibbons*," *Musique et Poésie*

Stranger perhaps is the complaint of the lutenist-composer John Daniel, brother of the poet Samuel, who, although a writer of monodic accompanied songs, seems to have resented the directions being taken by the English ayre of the Jacobean period. It was the custom of the composers of lute songs to set successive strophes of stanzaic poems to the same melody that had been originally composed for only the first of them. Thus, it often occurred that what constituted an admirable setting for the first stanza jarred exceedingly against the rhythmical variations of successive ones, even though the prevailing metrical scheme would purport to render all corresponding lines in all the stanzas rhythmically identical: a startling, but typical case of this is that of Alfonso Ferrabosco's setting of Donne's "So, So, Leave off this Last Lamenting Kiss" (in his *Book of Ayres*, 1609), in which the second verse cannot under any circumstances be sung to the setting that should, ideally, do for both of them. The madrigalists, on the other hand, except in what were called "ballets" or "fa-la's" and which were of a rather frivolous character, usually set the successive stanzas of strophic poems in a set or group of madrigals to avoid such lack of "fit," or even distributed the sections of a longer piece among several settings. This is the practice followed by Daniel in his book of lute songs, many of which are long, elaborate, repetitive (as far as the text is concerned), and highly chromatic in texture, utilizing many of the harmonic devices of the English madrigal as it flowered under the masterful skill of Thomas Weelkes and John Wilbye. These ayres of Daniel (or Danyel, as he usually spelled it) also seem occasionally, probably because of their rather extreme chromaticism, to approach some of the melodic lines of later seventeenth-century vocal monody.

The cycle of songs generally called "Chromatic Tunes" consists of the songs numbered xiii through xv in Daniel's

*au XVI*e *Siècle*, Colloques Internationaux du Centre National de la Recherche Scientifique, Sciences Humaines, v (Paris, 1954), pp. 140ff.

Songs for the Lute, Viol, and Voice (1606). They set successive portions of the following text, which may very well be either Daniel's own, or, like others in the book, the work of his famous brother:

> Can doleful notes to measured accents set
> Express unmeasured griefs that time forget?
> No, let chromatic tunes, harsh without ground,
>   Be sullen music for a tuneless heart;
>
> Chromatic tunes most like my passions sound,
>   As if combined to bear their falling part.
> Uncertain certain turns, of thoughts forecast
> Bring back the same, then die, and, dying, last.[45]

The "measured accents" might refer generally to the four-square strophic settings of the lute songs of Campion, or to something as specific as the French *musique mesurée*, the experiments in musico-poetic rhythms of Lejeune and Baïf which tried to approximate quantitative scansion. Perhaps both are implied, or rather, the apparent connection between the two: Campion studied medicine in France in his younger days, and may very well have come into contact with the writings of the left wing of the *Pléiade* most interested in these particular questions of imitating Classical prosody. He may, in fact, have been thus influenced in his own extreme prosodic theories. At any rate, Daniel's verses, while clearly falling in a tradition of melancholic Jacobean madrigal texts that were becoming rather modish,[46] make their stylistic proscriptions and recommendations on purely expressive grounds. What is odd in them is the particular kind of fence-straddling manifested by their attachment to the English polyphonic tradition, on the one hand, and to the ideology of the new music, on the other. The vivid turns and bare oxymoron of the text are set in apt ways suggestive of the most advanced monodic

---

[45] *English Madrigal Verse*, p. 405.
[46] See Wilfrid Mellers, "*La Melancolie au Debout du XVIIe Siècle et le Madrigal Anglais,*" in *Musique et Poèsie au XVIe Siècle*, pp. 153-165.

style: the line about the "unmeasured griefs that time forget" is wonderfully contrived, in the setting, to allow a chromatic change on "un" of "unmeasured," and to allow the words "which time forget" literally to "forget time" in the sense that they are all set to a sharply syncopated phrase, moving on all the off-beats, and in strong contrast to the six quarter notes of "Express unmeasured griefs." The "dying fall" suggested in the final line is the cadential pattern referred to as such in the sixteenth and seventeenth centuries; but it also aligns itself with the languorous dying and the ecstatic death that become commonplaces in much Baroque musical poetry.

Aside from a certain amount of intransigency upon the part of polyphonic composers, however, the new vocal style and the notions about the relationship between word and note that helped to give it ideological support were rapidly becoming entrenched. If the newer theories affected a basis of devout Neoclassicism for their own justification, however, it must be remembered that this Neoclassicism *per se* is not to be taken as an earmark of early Baroque music or its esthetic backgrounds. Two closely related points suggest themselves here. In the first place, the musico-poetic theories of Jean-Antoine de Baïf, perpetuated in the Academy which he formed to put these into practice,[47] were closely related, in some places, to those of the Camerata and their successors. At other crucial points, particularly on the question of the interpretation of "musical expression" and the adherence to many traditions of sixteenth-century *musica speculativa* such as Pythagoreanism, macro-microcosmic correspondences, etc., the esthetics of the French Academies sharply distinguishes itself from the monodic theories. The Neoclassicism, the attempt fully to realize the promises of recreating the fabulous effects of the music-poetry of Antiquity that the scholarship of Humanism had opened up, is surely there. But the sentiments expressed by

[47] For the fullest account of Baïf's Academy, its history and thought, as well as its affiliations with other groups such as the *Pléiade*, see Frances A. Yates, *The French Academies of the Sixteenth Century* (London, 1947), pp. 1-35.

Baïf, in his introductory sonnet to a songbook of Costeley's in 1570, for example, concern themselves with the Classical unification of music and poetry for far more general reasons than merely the increased emotional effect that could be gained by imitation of it: "*Jadis Musiciens et Poetes et Sages,*" he complains "*Furent mesmes auteurs; mais la suite des ages, / Par le temps qui tout change, a separe les troys.*"[48] Baïf's Orpheus is more Bacon's than it is that of Sandys.

One of the most interesting accomplishments of the Baïf Academy was that of the so-called *vers* and *musique mesurée.*[49] In an attempt to purify lyric poetry and its settings of prosodical barbarisms, a pseudo-quantitative verse form in poetry was set to a homophonic (chordal, *not* monodic) musical composition in which half and quarter notes would be used to set long and short syllables respectively. Latent in this practice were some of the Florentine group's objections to the rhythmic confusions of polyphonic settings of texts, but the direct, quasi-erotic relationship of performer and auditor that lay behind the monodic settings was as yet undeveloped here. The musical ideal of the French Academies still lay in the earthly imitation of the *harmonia mundi*; and although its theorists were extremely interested in such phenomena as Classical modal *ethos* and its implications with respect to sixteenth-century theories of character, their psychology was not that of the affections, nor was their musical doctrine the one that we see developing in the following century.

A related distinction must be made, I feel, in connection with the masque, particularly in Jacobean and Caroline England. Insofar as it is a prototype of opera, the later English masque, even if not through-composed, does seem to fall within the range of the newer esthetic theories. But insofar as the music in the masque is much more a question of pageantry

---

[48] Quoted by D. P. Walker, "Musical Humanism" (part 1), p. 6.

[49] Yates, *op.cit.*, pp. 36-76 gives a definitive account of both the theory and practice of the measured poetry and music of the sixteenth century in France. See also an account of the earlier German Horatian Ode settings in Gustave Reese, *Music in the Renaissance* (New York, 1954), p. 705.

than of actual drama, we must class the masque as a thing very much apart from opera, and perhaps not a real predecessor of it at all. Masque songs are certainly monodic set-pieces, and they are often operatic in character; but the *action* of a masque (the anti-masque aside) is essentially a symbolic representation rather than an expressive musical dramatization. Even more important, however, is the crucial role of the dance in all masques. The masque dances involve the masquers both as mythological or fictional characters, and in their real identities as patron-audience; the conclusion of the masque in the general measures only helps to reinforce, rather than to destroy the symbolic, even allegorical connections between court ladies, the Virtues and Vices they are appropriately turned out to represent, and their own real ethical world in which "literary" allegory must indeed be interpreted in the actualities of morality.

Here too must be mentioned the role of the dance in sixteenth-century *musica speculativa*, both as *paideia* and as a counterpoint-like concrete representation of the universal harmony. Miss Yates, in *The French Academies of the Sixteenth Century*, has given us an elaborate account of the part played by speculative notions of world harmony, of the Pythagorean mathematical relationships geometrically expressed, etc. in some of the French court entertainments of the later decades of the sixteenth century, such as the *Ballet Comique de la Reine*.[50] Movement, abstract pattern and floor-plan, and the symbolic significance of "the general dance" were all utilized to make the dance in such pageants truly imitate the universal dance of all parts of the organism of Nature. So, too, in the English masques did the symbolic function of the dancing intertwine with its use as a formal convention of the entertainment. Perhaps the best analysis of the complicated multiple functions of the masque dancing occurs in Ben Jonson's great late masque, *Pleasure Reconcild to Vertue*. While the masquers arrange themselves for the first dance, and at the

[50] Yates, pp. 236-274.

conclusion of it, Daedalus sings two songs of advice and guidance to the dancers, allegorizing their already allegorized dance in a nest of complication leading almost to the proverbial Chinese boxes. Daedalus, after having been introduced as helping the masquers so that "They may securely prove / then, any laborinth, though it be of Loue," begins:

> Come on, come on; and where you goe,
>   so enter-weaue the curious knot,
> as eu'n the' obseruer scarce may know
>   which lines are Pleasures, and which not.
> First, figure out the doubtfull way
>   at which, a while all youth shold stay,
>   where she and Vertue did contend
>   which should haue Hercules to frend.
> Then, as all actions of mankind
>   are but a Laborinth, or maze,
>   so let your Daunces be entwin'd,
>   yet not perplex men, vnto gaze.
> But measur'd, and so numerous too,
>   as men may read each act you doo.
> And when they see the Graces meet,
>   admire the wisdom of your feet.
> For Dauncing is an exercise
>   not only shews the mouers wit,
> but maketh the beholder wise,
>   as he hath powre to rise to it.[51]

(ll. 253-272)

The concluding quatrain moves dance into the domain of the united figure of *musicien*, *poète*, and *sage*, by invoking a didactic function (and thus, ultimately, an ethical one) for dancing, but without ever bringing it under the control of affective theory. Here, too, as in the case of the prosodic and musical theories of the French theorists and Thomas Campion,

---

[51] Ben Jonson, *Pleasure Reconcild to Vertue*, in *Works*, ed. Herford and Simpson, VII, 488-489.

we have a case of a kind of pre-Baroque musical Neoclassicism that sought perhaps the same ends as the doctrine of the affections, but without appeal to the notion that only through the passions are men activated from without. It was aided by a retention of the organic, hierarchical world view whose gradual replacement in the early seventeenth century could cause Donne to bemoan a world with "all coherence gone." The masque is truly a peculiar sort of transitional form in the history of musical thought as well as in the history of musical drama. In Florence in 1589, a number of masques played before and constructed by the Camerata of Count Bardi, which utilized some of the monodic experiments and theories of the group, had as their subjects some of the most conventional topics of *musica speculativa*. As one commentator remarks, "It is enough to quote the titles of some of the masques: *The Harmony of the Spheres, The Rivalry of the Muses, The Song of Arion, The Descent of Apollo and Bacchus together with Rhythm and Harmony*. Three of them represent the supreme harmony of the cosmos, three others the power of human harmony. . . . *These masques conclude, and in a sense symbolize, a cycle of abstract theorizing and Platonic longings for the music of antiquity which survived more in fable than in reality*."[52]

Music and Rhetoric

After summing up a considerable quantity of Classical and more recent lore concerning the civilizing effects of music in a chapter of his *The Compleat Gentleman*, Henry Peacham remarks, "Yea, in my opinion, no Rhetoricke more perswadeth, or hath greater power over the mind: nay: hath not Musicke her figures, the same which Rhetorique? What is a *Revert* but her *Antistrophe*? her reports, but sweet *Anaphora's*? her counterchange of points, *Antimetabole's*? her passionate Aires but *Prosopopoea's*? with infinite other of the same nature."[53]

[52] Nino Pirotta, "Temperaments and Tendencies in the Florentine Camerata," *Musical Quarterly*, XL (1954), pp. 175-176 (my italics).
[53] *The Compleat Gentleman*, ed.cit., p. 103.

The identification of music with rhetoric that became quite common throughout Europe in the early seventeenth century seems to have been no mere carry-over of a fragment of *musica speculativa*, nor of Humanist moralizing of the study of music as a model of all knowledge, but rather a direct concomitant of the affective theories. We observed earlier in this chapter that Bacon, allegorizing Orpheus as philosophy, gave to his music a quasi-rhetorical function; but in a similar, earlier passage in *The Advancement of Learning*, he makes of that Orphean music much less a rational philosophy than an actual oratorical art. Bacon claims that as long as men "give ear to precepts, to laws, to religion, sweetly touched with eloquence and persuasion of books, of sermons, of harangues, so long is society and peace maintained; but if these instruments be silent, or that sedition and tumult make them not audible, all things dissolve into anarchy and confusion."[54] The musical allusion in "sweetly touched" means simply "harmoniously accompanied," and the implication here is clearly that the controlling instruments of rhetoric are the persuasive, effective melody to laws' and religion's important text, necessary because that text, no matter what its truth, cannot establish its principles in the actual behavior of men without some means of affecting their feelings as well as their intellects.

This general treatment of affective music as a rhetorical art becomes so much a seventeenth-century commonplace that Shaftesbury, writing just over a hundred years after Bacon, could treat that relationship as axiomatic, and go on to analyze it in a somewhat naturalistic fashion:

"It may be easily perceived from hence that the goddess PERSUASION must have been in a manner the mother of poetry, rhetoric, music, and the other kindred arts. For 'tis apparent that where chief men and leaders had the strongest interest to persuade, they used the highest endeavours to please. So that in such a state or polity as has been described, not only

[54] Francis Bacon, *The Advancement of Learning*, ed. William A. Wright, fifth edition (Oxford, 1926), pp. 52-53.

the best order of thought and turn of fancy, but the most soft and inviting numbers, must have been employed to charm the public ear, and to incline the heart by the agreeableness of expression.

"Almost all the ancient masters of this sort were said to have been musicians. And tradition, which soon grew fabulous, could not better represent the first founders or establishers of these larger societies than as real songsters, who, by the power of their voice and lyre, could charm the wildest beasts, and draw the rude forests and rocks into the form of fairest cities. Nor can it be doubted that the same artists, who so industriously applied themselves to study the numbers of speech, must have made proportionable improvements in the study of mere sounds and natural harmony, which of itself must have considerably contributed towards the softening of the rude manners and harsh temper of their new people."[55]

Here again, although the passions in general have become the standard Augustan notion of "pleasure" as that which is produced by these persuasive arts, the author must conclude with the observation that pure music itself must, despite the exaggerations of "fabulous" traditions, have been employed to tame the wilder passions of primitive men, at least to some degree. Shaftesbury was no mechanist at bottom; elsewhere, he is capable of the extremely platonistic observation that "harmony is harmony by nature, let men judge ever so ridiculously of music. So is symmetry and proportion founded still in nature, let men's fancy prove ever so barbarous, or their fashions ever so Gothic in their architecture, sculpture, or whatever other designing art."[56] But his treatment of musical and rhetorical persuasion, and in particular his measured attitude toward the promulgation of musical mythology, mark the culmination of a whole century's development.

But aside from this general linking of music and rhetoric, in which the ability of each to move men's actions and passions

[55] Anthony Ashley Cooper, 3rd Earl of Shaftesbury, *Characteristics*, ed. J. M. Robertson (New York, 1900), I, 154.
[56] *Ibid.*, I, 227.

affords grounds for their association, many more specific parallels were drawn. In the remarks of Henry Peacham on the subject quoted above, what appeared to be inventive comparisons of rhetorical tropes and figures to musical devices actually represent a widely established seventeenth-century convention. Particular instances of the direct comparison of individual musical and rhetorical devices appear even earlier than do the more systematic treatments: thus Peacham himself, in a rhetoric text called *The Garden of Eloquence* (1593), remarks of his figure of *symploce*, "This figure may serve to any affection, and is a singular ornament, pleasant to the eare, which of some is called the *Rhetoricall* circle, and of others the Musicall repetition. . . ."[57] And Bacon, again in *The Advancement of Learning*, in arguing the priority of one general speculative discipline which he calls *philosophia prima*, inserts in a list of principles of order that appear and reappear from phenomenon to phenomenon and from one kind of human activity to other related ones: "Is not the precept of a musician, to fall from a discord or harsh accord upon a concord or sweet accord, alike true in affection? Is not the trope of music, to avoid or slide from the close or cadence, common with the trope of rhetoric of deceiving expectation?"[58]

But elaborate and systematic attempts to enforce all manner of musico-rhetorical parallels make such observations as Bacon's and Peacham's look casual and trivial. In 1606, Joachim Burmeister published a Latin treatise entitled *Musica Poetica* dealing with all manner of parallels between the two arts. In Chapter XII, "*De Ornamentis sive de figuris Musicis*," he gives elaborate musical analogues of the following rhetorical figures, arranged in two groups, according to whether the musical patterns involve harmonic or melodic devices: (1) Harmonic: 1. "*Est fuga realis*"; 2. *Metalepsis*; 3. *Hypallage*; 4. *Apocope*; 5. *Noema*; 6. *Analepsis*; 7. *Mimesis*; 8. *Anadiplosis*; 9. *Symblema*; 10. *Syncopa*; 11. *Pleonasmus*; 12.

[57] Henry Peacham, *The Garden of Eloquence* (London, 1593), p. 44.
[58] *The Advancement of Learning*, ed.cit., pp. 107-108.

Auxesis; 13. *Pathopoeia*; 14. *Hypotyposis*; 15. *Aposiopesis*; 16. *Anaploce*. (II) Melodic: 1. *Parembole*; 2. *Palillogia*; 3. *Climax*; 4. *Parrhesia*; 5. *Hyperbole*; 6. *Hypobole*. Finally listed are those figures *"tam Harmoniis, quam Melodiis communibus"*: 1. *Congeries*; 2. *"De simul Procedentibus sive Faux Bourdon"*; 3. *Anaphora*; 4. *"Fugi imaginaria."*[59]

This interest in the musical analogues was by no means confined to Germany, but spread to Italy and elsewhere as well.[60] It seems almost as if the eventual interest in purely structural devices for their own sake in the seventeenth century were a direct descendant of the fifteenth-century Flemish composers' interests in notational puzzles, crab and inverted canons, and the like, or a parallel of the interest in "figure" poems displayed theoretically by George Puttenham in his *Arte of English Poesie* (1589),[61] or occasionally in practice by Joshua Sylvester in his translation of du Bartas and George Herbert in such poems as "Easter Wings." The impetus behind these seventeenth-century musico-rhetorical figures is clearly not the covert Pythagoreanism of the Netherlands composers, nor the justification by Puttenham of the use of complicated visual devices, "whereby the maker is restrained to keepe him within his bounds, and sheweth not only more art, but serveth also much better for briefenesse and subtiltie of device. . . ."[62] Rather does the strained attempt in the seventeenth century to equate musical devices with rhetorical

[59] Joachim Burmeister, *Musica Poetica: Definitibus et Divisionibus breviter delineata,* . . . etc. (Rostock, 1606). See Martin Ruhnke, *Joachim Burmeister (Schriften des Landesinstitut für Musikforschung, Kiel, Band 5.)* (Kassel and Basel, 1955.) There is a good summary of evolving theories of music and rhetoric on pp. 135-139 of this study. For what is probably the most elaborate of these seventeenth-century treatises on musico-rhetorical correspondences, see Jan Albert Ban, *Dissertatio Epistolica De Musica Natura* (Leyden, 1637).

[60] Simon Towneley Worsthorne, *Venetian Opera in the Seventeenth Century* (Oxford, 1954), pp. 15-16 comments on musico-rhetorical theories in Italy, among the Camerata, etc., as well as mentioning the widespread use, later in the century, of overly ornate figures and patternings.

[61] See Chapter XII, entitled "Of Proportion in Figure."

[62] George Puttenham, *The Arte of English Poesie*, in G. G. Smith, ed. *Elizabethan Critical Essays* (Oxford, 1904), II, 95.

patterns seem to be based upon a desire to identify the persuasive powers of the first and the second. If music was to conform to its image in the mythology of Antiquity, its very structural devices and building-blocks must be seen as operating directly upon the feelings of its auditors, rather than as merely serving the more idealized and abstract interests of organic structure. Each convention of the musical language had to appear to be capable of the same sort of quasi-behaviorist analysis, as far as the correspondence between its own structure and its direct effects was concerned, as was traditionally given to the figures and tropes of rhetoric.

Not completely identical with this traditional association of music and rhetoric, but running in an obviously parallel path to it, is the seventeenth-century reinterpretation of the traditional theme of music's healing powers. We shall have reason to examine this in greater detail a little further on, but we might dwell for the moment upon the specific association of music with the specific passion of love. Thomas Ravenscroft in 1614 declares, "I have heard it said that Love teaches a man Musick, who ne're before knew what pertayned thereto: And the Philosophers three Principall Causes of Musick, 1. Doulour, 2. Joy, 3. Enthusiasme or ravishing of the Spirit, are all found by him within Loves Territories. Besides, we see the Soveraignty of Musicke in this Affection, by the Cure and Remedy it affoords the Dispassionate, and Infortunate Sonnes of Love, thereby to asswage the turmoyles, and quiet the tempests that were raised in them."[63] Music's ability to produce feelings of love, its effect of "Enthusiasme or ravishing of the Spirit" can be traced back to the earliest roots of platonist musical speculation; the traditional *piercing* of the spirit through the ear, and the subsequent plucking of the soul from out the confines of the body is an old notion, implicit

[63] Thomas Ravenscroft, *A Briefe Discourse of the true (but neglected) use of Charact'ring the Degrees* . . . etc. (1614), quoted in Morison Comegys Boyd, *Elizabethan Music and Musical Criticism* (Philadelphia, 1940), p. 35.

in all doctrine relating macrocosmic and microcosmic musics.[64] "But whilst this muddy vesture of decay / Doth grossly close it in, we cannot hear it" says Lorenzo to Jessica of the heavenly music in *The Merchant of Venice*. It rightly follows that, in order to affect the soul at all, practical, earthly music must penetrate that "muddy vesture of decay" and push through to the passive soul which, in responding to it, casts off the dull, gross weight of the body. But in the early seventeenth century, this musical ecstasy becomes associated with either an erotic or a religious situation, and casts off its associations with more general musical speculation to the extent of being confined to practical music alone. It is natural that the various meanings of the word "ravish" (violent sexual possession, bewilderment, ecstatic separation of soul from body—in a platonist or Christian sense, its "release"), all equally well established in English by the fourteenth century, should tend to cluster more about the erotic sense when applied to music. The overtones of "rape" become increasingly prominent in its more generally applied cognates, "ravish" and "rapture."[65]

[64] For an account of some of the history of the notion of the musical ecstasy, as well as a citation of many examples of its occurrence in English poetry of the period in which we are interested here, see Gretchen L. Finney, "Ecstasy and Music in Seventeenth Century England," *Journal of the History of Ideas*, VIII (1947), pp. 153-186.

[65] Or the modern "carried away" in its various figurative senses. In erotic poetry, the use of "ravish" generally tends to preserve the sense "rape" in a covert way, while appearing to use it only in an accepted figurative tradition in which the soul is "ravished" by the sights and sounds of another person, just as the body is ravished by the violent touch. Thus, the words to the famous *Pavane* in Thoinot Arbeau's treatise on dancing, *Orchésographie* (Langres, 1589):

> *Belle, qui tiens ma vie*
> *Captive dans tes yeux,*
> *Qui m'as l'ame ravie*
> *D'un souris gracieux . . . .*

Here there is an implicit conceit of the lady holding the poet captive in a castle and forcing him to submit to her indignities, although "ravie" has a completely conventional figurative sense here as well. The point here is that in the doctrine of the affections and in Baroque esthetics generally, "ravish" carries the senses of "generally causing to be ecstatic" and "sexually violate" (with regard to the latter, we have the full recognition of these sexual-musical overtones in Joyce's "Sir Tristam, violer d'amores" in

The relationship between music as rhetoric and music as erotic action is, I think, quite obvious. In each case the musician is the active performer upon the passive listener. In one instance, the listener is persuaded, convinced, deterred, exhorted, and generally moved; in the second, the listener responds as it were to the arousing caresses of the music. The musical instrument which in the hands of the rhetorical musician remains the active means of persuasion (literally, the "organ" or "instrument"), becomes identified in the erotic scheme more with the passive auditor-victim-beloved. Just as the performer plays upon his instrument, so does the music play upon the instrument of the listener's spirit. And just as the end of the musico-rhetorical process is the emergence of the auditor's response in the desired *action* (which, of course, can consist of some active demonstration of feeling as well), so does the erotic musical experience conclude in the ecstasy of the hearer's ravished soul, treated more or less as religious frenzy or sexual climax and often, in the seventeenth century, as an inseparable blend of the two.

The primary difference between sixteenth- and seventeenth-century theories of musical treatment of the emotions, then, might once again be referred to a difference between *representation* or *"imitation"* and *expression,* between the notion of a musical setting as an appropriate and sympathetic background for a text, and the idea of music as a vehicle for a piercing of the hearer with that which will agitate the passions within him and cause *him* to "imitate" or "represent" within himself the desired feeling.[66] The end of the process that led from the literary use and treatment of one view to that of

---

Finnegans Wake, New York, 1947, p. 3). Also, for example, see Richard Barnfield's famous sonnet, "To His Friend Master R. L. in Praise of Music and Poetry," ll. 5-6: "Dowland to thee is dear, whose heavenly touch / Upon the lute doth ravish human sense."

[66] See Brewster Rogerson, "The Art of Painting the Passions," *Journal of the History of Ideas,* XIV (1953), pp. 68-94, especially pp. 81-87. In volume X (1949), pp. 344-356 of the same periodical, P. Albert Duhamel in "The Function of Rhetoric as Effective Expression" fills in some of the general background on the psychology of rhetoric in Ancient times.

the other seems almost to lie in the identification of music with that feeling itself. A twentieth-century poet might be quoted here to show this limit, this end of the growing identification of music with the affections:

> Just as my fingers on these keys
> Make music, so the selfsame sounds
> On my spirit make a music too.
>
> Music is feeling, then, not sound;
> And thus it is that what I feel
> Here in this room, desiring you,
>
> Thinking of your blue-shadowed silk
> Is music.[67]

The poetic allusion to the fabled powers of the music of Antiquity, frequent in the sixteenth century, and the actual utilization of the newer doctrines of music's power over human feelings, however, are two different matters. Shakespeare, as we have previously seen, affords the greatest rewards to a student of this change in musical thought and its literary interpretations; he employs almost every kind of musical imagery, and in almost every way, that we find in use during the sixteenth century. In general, we find that seventeenth-century English poets take immediately to the newer notions of affective music, while yet clinging to the imagery of Christian speculative music, notably that of the heavenly harmony, the singing of the angel-spheres, etc. In a future chapter, we shall indeed see how the promiscuous use of this imagery tends to trivialize all but its complimentary and decorative import from about 1640 on. But we might at this point examine one or two cases of the poetic treatment of expressive music before that date, with a view to showing what literary conventions and styles tend to associate themselves with the newer musical theories.

[67] Wallace Stevens, "Peter Quince at the Clavier," *Harmonium* (1923), in *Collected Poems* (New York, 1956), pp. 89-90.

A rather nice distinction between an Elizabethan and a more seventeenth-century handling of a musical theme can be drawn in the case of two poems of Thomas Campion, both texts from his songbooks. In his first book of ayres "Contayning Divine and Morall Songs" (undated, but no earlier than 1612),[68] the first strophe of number VII reads as follows:

> To Musicke bent is my retyred minde,
> And faine would I some song of pleasure sing;
> But in vaine joys no comfort now I finde,
> From heav'nly thoughts all true delight doth spring.
> Thy power, O God, thy mercies to record,
> Will sweeten ev'ry note and ev'ry word.[69]
>
> (ll. 1-6)

This is the plain, straightforward exposition of what C. S. Lewis miscalled the "drab style" of the English Renaissance; the sententious conclusion drawn in the immediately following lines is almost predictable: "All earthly pompe or beauty to expresse, / Is but to carve in snow, on waves to write." Moving away from this explicitness toward a more conceited, epigrammatic style, incidentally, the song that follows this one directly in Campion's book seems to lie midway between Sidney's first *Astrophel and Stella* sonnet ("I sought fit words to paint the blackest face of Woe") and George Herbert's "Jordan II," which may be a comment upon the Sidney sonnet; it certainly directs itself to the same subject as the other two poems.

> Tune thy Musicke to thy hart,
> Sing thy joy with thankes, and so thy sorrow:
> Though Devotion needes not Art,
> Sometimes of the poore the rich may borrow.
>
> Strive not yet for curious wayes:
> Concord pleaseth more, the lesse 'tis strained;

---

[68] See Edmund H. Fellowes, *English Madrigal Verse*, p. 608.
[69] Thomas Campion, *Works*, ed. Percival Vivian (Oxford, 1909), p. 120.

> Zeale affects not outward prayse,
> Onely strives to show a love unfained.[70]
>
> (ll. 1-8)

This poem, in which music becomes synonymous with prayer, really belongs to a seventeenth-century convention of private devotional poetry that we shall examine in a later chapter. In the sharp paradoxes of lines four and six, however, and in the abrupt way in which the terms of the fourth line are associated with those of the third, these verses leave the flat devotional tone of the preceding poem far behind.

It is with both of these, perhaps, that another poem of Campion's should be contrasted, not so much for its style (it is in no way closer to the Metaphysical style, and perhaps less so, than "Tune thy Musicke to thy hart"), as for the musical ideology it represents:

> When to her lute Corrina sings,
> Her voice revives the leaden stringes,
> And doth in highest noates appeare,
> As any challeng'd eccho cleere;
> But when she doth of mourning speake,
> Ev'n with her sighes the strings do breake.
>
> And as her lute doth live or die,
> Led by her passion, so must I,
> For when of pleasure she doth sing,
> My thoughts enjoy a sodaine spring,
> But if she doth of sorrow speake,
> Ev'n from my hart the strings doe breake.[71]

In the first place, "to her lute" is really a punning construction here, meaning both *"accompanied by* the instrument" (its immediate and most usual sense), and in the simplest sense of singing *at* or *towards* it (as if it were a person). What starts out as merely a rather extravagant compliment to the lady turns out to be somewhat more than this, as the implications

[70] *Ibid.,* p. 121.   [71] *Ibid.,* p. 9.

of the second sense of the phrase are explored in the comparison: When Corinna accompanies herself upon her lute, it is almost as if the inanimate instrument were responding to her voice itself, rather than to her fingers. The instrument also responds sympathetically to her mood, and it seems to be the receptive audience to her very feelings. Like the lute, I am moved almost immediately by her feelings, rather than by her voice (as the instrument is by her voice, rather than by her fingers). This metaphorical association of instrument played upon and adoring audience affected is enhanced not only by the almost outworn heart-strings parallel (in the setting, there is a hocket in the voice part before "the strings doe breake," followed by a harsh, probably arpeggiated tonic chord that "imitates" the breaking in each strophe), but by a possible pun on "spring," which may suggest an overtone of the seventeenth-century use of "springer" for an extremely common lute ornament. And upon closer inspection, the old heart-string association is itself revivified through the metaphor of breaking; while the poet's snapped heart-strings here are by no means as ingeniously contrived as are the tiny mirror-like shards of heart, reflecting the lovers in little, that Donne gives us in his treatment of heartbreak. The fact that more than a stock image is at work in Campion's poem is undeniable.[72]

In any case, the Corinna poem is a model of the affective musical event. "And as her lute doth live or die, / Led by her passion, so must I": the ravished hearer is like the instrument in that the adored performer is master of them both.

---

[72] Rosemond Tuve, in *Elizabethan and Metaphysical Imagery* (Chicago, 1947), p. 15, comments on this lyric and insists that "The images reveal a man moved, but writing what the rhetorics call 'a praise' of the lady and the music, rather than examining the nature of his emotional experience." Miss Tuve wishes to contrast Campion's method with that of Donne or Herbert here, but from my comments it will appear obvious that I feel she has underestimated the strength of the conceit. And one has only to compare this poem with some of the Cavalier and early Augustan "praises" of ladies singing and playing (see above, Chapter VI) to realize exactly how much real "examination" is actually at work in it.

The fact that both can be spoken of as *played upon,* of course, reflects an older tradition. We may recall here Hamlet's little moral emblem for the benefit of Rosencrantz and Guildenstern, which likens the manipulation of the recorder to the crudely contrived attempts of the Danish sycophants to control him.[73] The figure of the self as instrument is traditional in Christian meditation; the petitioner asks God to "tune up" or "play upon" him—a motif which will be discussed in the next chapter. But the situation that Hamlet alludes to, in which the active performer plays upon the passive auditor in a way which is likened to that in which the performer's instrument is controlled, is characteristic of the doctrine of affective music. Music becomes, in Campion's little poem, the vehicle or medium for the transmission of feeling. The way in which this association is made is vastly different from what we might expect in a more typically Elizabethan appeal to the phenomenon of sympathetic vibration (for example, two lutes, perfectly in tune, will remain such that each will sound if the other is plucked: even as you and I, etc.). It is, incidentally, perhaps faintly ironic that the musical esthetic embodied in the text is far more advanced, with respect to Continental musical practice and thought, than is Campion's rather pedestrian setting.

Mode and Mood

The two extremes of feeling used almost schematically in Campion's poem are that of "pleasure" and "sorrow." The point is stressed that the appropriate feeling in Corinna, the singer, *expressed* in the proper musical configurations, will elicit the identical feelings in the listening poet. For a modern listener whose experience had been confined to Classic and Romantic music, it would be easy to imagine Corinna as sing-

[73] "Call me what instrument you will," the extended conceit concludes, "though you can fret me, yet you cannot play upon me." *Hamlet,* III, ii, 360-388 in Shakespeare, *Complete Poems and Plays,* ed. Neilson and Hill (Cambridge, Mass., 1942).

ing in a major key to make her auditor's thoughts "enjoy a sodaine spring," and in a minor one to break his heart. Exactly why a triad, embracing an interval differing only by the position of a semitone from another, should produce a feeling of sadness in a hearer as opposed to the feeling of resolution occasioned by the other, opens up the whole notion of modality and *ethos*. That this subject became more and more important in the new musical esthetic seems almost inevitable when one remembers the widely separating functions it ascribed to music and text. Modality concerns the ability of certain musical configurations, or groups and orders of configurations, to elicit particular active or emotive responses in their hearers; and, as we have seen, the speculative music of Antiquity that was transmitted to the Medieval writers on music contained much discussion of the various tonal systems and keys and their various effects.

Just as the twentieth-century listener mentioned above might have great difficulties in presenting a persistent questioner with a plausible account of *why* the minor passage was sad, or even of why it made him feel sad to such an extent that he was willing to ascribe that sadness to the music itself, so the musical theorists of both the Ancient and Medieval worlds found it difficult to explain the nature of the correspondence between certain musical patterns and certain human feelings conventionally associated with them. In the fully developed cosmological interpretation of music that combined Christian and Classical doctrines, or of the Chinese or Hindu or Arabic musical systems in the East, the correspondences of pattern and feeling were provided for in terms of elaborate metaphysical identifications of elemental substances, bodily and emotional humors, seasonal patterns, mathematical, musical, and prosodical structures, etc. But, aside from these connections, established almost by fiat, there remained always an essential core of mystery. "The several affections of our spirit, by a sweet variety, have their own proper measures in their voice and singing, *by some hidden correspondence wherewith they are stirred up*,"[74] writes St. Augustine, who elsewhere goes on to interpret that correspondence, in a way that was assiduously followed for centuries, in terms of what might be called a kind of Christian Pythagoreanism. The analogy that most immediately presents itself to a modern reader in connection with the whole theory of mode or pattern and feeling elicited in the hearer is that of a communication system of any electrical kind. In such a system, a *message* or spoken statement is "encoded" into electrical impulses and transmitted along a *channel* to the receiver of the message, for whom it is *decoded* back into speech again. In the analogy with affective music, the feeling corresponds to the *message*, and the music to the *code*. In the mythology of the fabulous effects of music that descended from Antiquity, the proper response of any sentient being to any particular musical mode was considered to be as automatic and predictable as the vocal response of a loudspeaker or headphone receiver to the electrical impulses fed into it. But with no empirically derived and substantiated set of hypotheses like those of physics to account for the intervening process, both Classical and Modern thinkers had to resort either to such metaphysical systems as could embrace the notion of modal correspondences, or to a final and underlying mystery.

The Greek modal system (and I shall use throughout the term "mode" to refer to all such ethically informed musical patterns as the Greek *harmoniai*, the *tones* of Christian liturgical chant in the Middle Ages, the modern major and minor modes, etc.) was preserved in *musica speculativa* long after any music had ceased to resemble that of the Attic world. We have seen already how some of the confusions between that modal system and the Medieval church tones resulted from the purely literary transmission of musical lore.[75] For the

[74] St. Augustine, *Confessions*, x, xxxiii, tr. E. B. Pusey (Everyman Edition), p. 235 (italics mine).
[75] See above, Chapter II, pp. 37-38. Also see Curt Sachs, *The Rise of Music in the Ancient World* (New York, 1943), pp. 216-238, 248-252; Egon Wellesz, *A History of Byzantine Music and Hymnography* (Oxford, 1949), pp. 38-47.

Renaissance, so much interested in recapturing the lost, fabled glories of the perfectly effective Classic music, the descriptions of the modes and their effects in Plato, Aristotle, Plutarch, and other writers tempted theorists to construct all sorts of speculative models for the effects of modes and scales. But for the most part, the casual ability to refer blithely to the acknowledged fact of the Phrygian "mode" as having warlike and exciting effects, the Lydian as being voluptuous and relaxing, the Dorian as being straightforward, just, and manly, and with never a touch of wonder, remained a literary possession.

As far as English poets and speculative writers are concerned, the problem of modality is of special interest because of a fortuitous linguistic circumstance. The English derivatives of the Anglo-Saxon *"mod"* (originally "pride," "courage," finally becoming "feeling" generically) and the Latin *"modus"* ("measure," "manner," "means," "structure," "pattern") fell together in spelling and pronunciation at some time in the fourteenth century. The resulting form, "moode" (up through the seventeenth century's end), was used in both senses; this accounted for the current spelling of "mood" for what should systematically be called logical and grammatical "modes," as opposed to what have for the most part crystallized into usages of "mood" for "feeling." Up through the later fourteenth century, there can be found practically no occurrence of *moode < modus*, partially because treatises on grammar, logic, and music were all written in Latin, in which the homonymic conflict could not occur, and partially because the musical sense of *"modus"* was reserved for a purely rhythmical and mensural purpose (the ecclesiastical "modes" were called *"toni"* in Latin).[76] But with the renewed interest of the Renaissance in the music of Antiquity, the use of "moode" to refer to the keys and transposing scales (the *tonoi* and

[76] See John Hollander, " 'Moedes and Prolaciouns' in Chaucer's *Boece*," *Modern Language Notes*, LXXI (1956), pp. 397-399, for what I suspect to be the first case of this homonymic conflict in English, occurring in Chaucer's translation of Boethius.

harmoniai) of Greek music became increasingly common in English.

With respect to the problems of musical esthetics, however, the confusion of "mode" and "mood" brought together two notions whose conceptual association constituted a basic doctrine rather than merely the strained connection afforded by a pun. In some verses of John Davies of Hereford "In the most just Praise of Musicke" prefixed to Ravenscroft's *Briefe Discourse*, a familiar notion is embroidered with a repetition containing a phrase that can only be read as illustrating this association:

> But no man is so ill that hath no good:
> So, no man in the Abstract can be nought:
> Then 'tis no man that hates sweete Musickes moode,
> But something worse than all that can be thought.[77]
>
> (ll. 13-16)

With this blending of "mode" and "moode," the same sort of semantic entity is generated, suggesting the same sort of false etymological relationship, as has been seen to arise in the case of the *cor, cordis,* and *chorda* association in words like *concors,* etc.[78] Just as the latter could serve as the basis for images like that of *heart-strings,* and for allegorizations of the phenomenon of sympathetic vibration, as well as for the very notion of harmony in the abstract as well, so the "mode"-"mood" connection could assist in the gradual development of the esthetic notion that the feeling evoked by a musical (or, by extension, a poetic or even pictorial) work, *resided in the work itself.*[79] And in addition to this, the unusual association of the

[77] John Davies of Hereford, *Complete Works*, ed. A. B. Grosart (Edinburgh, 1878), II, 9.
[78] See Leo Spitzer, "Classical and Christian Ideas of World Harmony," Part II, *Traditio*, III (1945), pp. 307-325.
[79] To speak of the "moode of a song," for example, would be to refer to its tonality, but to suggest that it was sad in the same sense that a singer or hearer of it might be; in short, that the song itself could "feel sad," or be characterized as having a *mood* (in our sense) *of sadness.* Thus, by means of the mood of the musical or poetic work, the gulf between the feelings of singer and hearer is bridged.

two English words helped, in general, to urge the further identification of successions of musical sounds with passion. For the doctrine of the affections could appeal to the music of Antiquity for its stress on the unmediated activity of musical progressions and patterns upon the feelings of the hearer; without the necessity of appeal to any universal harmonic system, the eternal power of music could be shown forth.

It was generally agreed throughout the Renaissance that the effects proper to each of the old Greek names were consistent; no one seemed to have the faintest idea what the ancient scales sounded like, however, and the inherited confusions about the liturgical scales only contributed to greater misunderstanding.[80] But at every turn, during the course of the late sixteenth and early seventeenth centuries, an interest in finding analogues and equivalents for the old modal systems flourished. In the so-called Archbishop Parker's Psalter of 1568,[81] the great Elizabethan composer Thomas Tallis composed a series of eight four-part settings in a fairly homophonic style for the metrical versions of the psalms therein contained. Each of the psalm tunes (the tenor in all the harmonizations contained the melody) was written to one of the old church-tones (or "tunes": here again two words fell together), a very common practice then as later on, even when liturgical music freed itself completely from any sacred *cantus firmus* as the basis of its structure. What is significant here, however, is the set of verses expounding the *ethos* of each of the melodies (which, it must be remembered, served somewhat as "modes" or "scales" or other tonal formulae might, in that many possible texts were to be sung to them):

The nature of the eyght tunes

1. The first is meeke: devout to see,

[80] See D. P. Walker, "Musical Humanism in the 16th and Early 17th Centuries," Part III, *The Music Review*, II (1941), pp. 220-227.

[81] *The whole Psalter translated into English Metre, which contayneth an hundred and fifty Psalmes. Imprinted at London by Iohn Daye . . .* No date. See M. C. Boyd, *op.cit.* (note 63, above), pp. 41-42.

2. The second sad: in majesty.
3. The third doth rage: and roughly brayth.
4. The fourth doth fawne: and flattry playth,
5. The fyfth delighth: and laugheth the more,
6. The sit bewayleth: it weepeth full sore,
7. The seventh tredeth stoute: in froward race,
8. The eyghte goeth milde: in modest pace.[82]

The tunes are grouped, by the use of the symbols printed at the left of each, and above the tunes and many of the psalm texts themselves, into those proper to psalms of trust, rejoicing or lamentation respectively. The similarity of these marks to the Greek accents is quite obvious (the "grave" and "acute" marks indicating gravity and elation, respectively).[83] Tallis himself seems to have followed the pattern prescribed here by his editor (or by himself, perhaps), in that only the second and sixth "tunes," the truly dolorous ones, employ a chord containing an E. Even more significant is the order of the assigned temperaments: giving the tunes the misleading Greek names that became attached to the tones in which they are composed, the "second" would be the "Dorian"; the "third," "Phrygian"; then "Lydian," "Mixolydian," etc. The appropriate *ethos*, grave, excited, lascivious, pleasant, and convivial, can thus be seen to have been adapted in the verses on "The nature of the eyght tunes." Even within the strict confines of the world of four-square psalm-settings, the Classical modality appears to be at work.

By the end of the seventeenth century, when much more was known about Ancient musical practice than had been understood a hundred years previously, the predominantly literary quality of most information about the Classical modes was fairly well recognized. Thus Richard Blome, in a courtesy book called *The Gentleman's Recreations*, gives some indication of how a rather poorly informed and unmodish popu-

---

[82] Quoted in Boyd, p. 44.
[83] Boyd, p. 44n., seems to overlook this, referring to them as "arbitrary symbols."

larizer could appear nonchalantly learned: "The most usual *Moods* of the *Greeks* (for *Alipius* names fifteen) were five, the *Dorick*, the *Lydian*, the *Aeolick*, the *Phrygian*, and the *Ionick*. What the Use and Nature of these *Greek Moods* was, is not certainly determined . . . only thus much is generally noted, That the *Dorick* is most graver and solid; the *Lydian* the most sprightly, and what we now-a-days call Air."[84] The variant forms "Ionick," etc., are of some interest in that they reflect the association of musical modality with metrical schemata (in the case of "Ionic," a Classical meter), or with the architectural orders; "Dorick" itself becomes, as we shall see in the next chapter, almost a synonym for "solemn." Blome might have been familiar with the Phrygian warlike and agitated feeling as well, for he would certainly have been made familiar with it in much casual poetic allusion, even in Milton alone, for example.

But two cases of the application of the Classical "modes," or some musical derivative thereof, seem more significant in the general picture of seventeenth-century musical thought than almost any other ones. Both of these, interestingly enough, are French rather than English or Italian. The first instance, it is true, does depend upon an analogy drawn previously by Zarlino in his great sixteenth-century compendium of musical knowledge, but the application of that analogy by a real painter is a rather different matter from that of a digression in a speculative account that purported to embrace every conceivable area of possible musical relevance. Nicholas Poussin, in a letter to his friend and patron, Chantelou, dated November 24, 1647, opened up the whole question of extending the Neoclassic *effeti*, the modern versions of the fabled effects of Ancient music, to the art of painting as well. In answer to Chantelou's objection that he had admired strongly a painting that Poussin had made for someone else, the great Baroque painter replied:

[84] Richard Blome, *The Gentleman's Recreations*, second ed. (London, 1710), p. 248.

"Do you not see that, along with your own disposition, in the nature of the subject lies the cause of this effect, and that the subjects which I am treating for you have to be done in a different manner? All artifice in painting depends upon this . . .

"That is why I wish to bring to your attention one important thing that will teach you what to observe in the subjects depicted.

"Our wise ancient Greeks, inventors of all beautiful things, found several Modes by means of which they produced marvellous effects.

"This word 'Mode' means actually the rule or the measure and form, which serves us in our productions. This rule constrains us not to exaggerate by making us act in all things with a certain restraint and moderation; and, consequently, this restraint and moderation is nothing more than a certain determined manner or order, and includes the procedure by which the object is preserved in its essence.

"The Modes of the ancients were a combination of several things put together; from their variety was born a certain difference of Mode whereby one was able to understand that each one of them retained in itself a subtle variation; particularly when all the things which entered into combination were put together in such a proportion that it was made possible to arouse the soul of the spectator to various passions. Hence the fact that the ancient sages attributed to each style its own effects. Because of this they called the Dorian Mode stable, grave, and severe, and applied it to subjects which are grave and severe and full of wisdom.

"And proceeding thence to pleasant and joyous things, they used the Phrygian Mode, in which there are more minute modulations than in any other mode, and a more clear-cut aspect. These two styles and no others were praised and approved of by Plato and Aristotle, who deemed the others superfluous; they considered this (Phrygian Mode) intense, vehement, violent, and very severe and capable of astonishing people.

"I hope, before another year is out, to paint a subject in this Phrygian Mode. The subject of frightful wars lends itself to this manner.

"They [the ancients] also decided that the Lydian Mode lends itself to tragic subjects because it has neither the simplicity of the Dorian nor the severity of the Phrygian. . . ."[85]

Poussin proceeded to go on and discuss the Hypolydian and Ionian modes in a similar manner. What is interesting about his account is not so much the peculiar confusions and awkwardnesses in his exposition of the ancient doctrine (the notion of "a combination of several things together," or *harmony* in the abstract, Poussin applies to the *harmoniai*, of scales, for example). Instead, it is to the relationship between *style* and *subject matter* in painting that our interest should direct itself here. After presenting his question-begging description (failing to give any explanation at all) of how the modes actually affected feelings, Poussin remarks that the Dorian mode was applied to grave and severe *subjects*, by which he could only have been referring to the character of the *text* set, or of the *occasion* on which the scale was used. In any case, the analogue of these in painting becomes for him subject matter, and he conceives the notion of a proper style to fit the dominant feeling or mood of any particular subject. It is not so much in his misleading assignment of the warlike or, at best, frenzied Phrygian to the "pleasant and joyous things" that we can see a non-musical sensibility at work, as in his rather unorthodox analysis of its "more minute modulations" and "clear-cut aspect." These have no possible application to the actual Phrygian *harmonia*, but they represent very clearly, I think, the visual interests of a painter.

He never actually outlines the modalities of painting style, however. Perhaps it is only fair to treat Poussin's use of the

[85] Quoted and translated in Elizabeth Gilmore Holt, *A Documentary History of Art* (New York, 1958), II, 154-156.

notion of mode and affection as a kind of elaborate metaphor, supported in some measure by the vagueness and abstract quality of his discussion of modality in music (the notion of "variation," for instance). Other analogies drawn between musical elements and the techniques of painting, even in Poussin's own days, are much more specific. Marin Mersenne, in his voluminous and comprehensive *Harmonie Universelle* (1636) treats of painting in Proposition III of his *"4ᵉ Livre de la Composition,"* devoted to determining *"si la Basse est le fondement, & la principale parti de la musique."* He connects the technique of underpainting with a dark brown or a black with the notion of a bass in music ("ground" in seventeenth-century English usage): *"Et les Peintres, dont les tableaux réprésentent une Musique muette, se servent du brun, ou du noir, pour le fondement des autres couleurs, quoy qu'il ne soit pas si excellent."*[86] But Poussin makes no such specific suggestions for the pictorial or even painterly reinterpretation of the notion of musical modality. Perhaps his inability or unwillingness to describe precisely the ways in which modes of painting might be established is to be ascribed to a sense of craft or jealously guarded technique that clung to painting long after any vestiges of it had disappeared from the attitudes toward their art of composers (but perhaps not of instrumentalists). But, in any event, the modal analogue for painting is a clear step in the direction of linking the pictorial to the musical and poetic arts in their common role as expressive instruments of emotion.

[86] Marin Mersenne, *Harmonie Universelle, Contenant la Théorie de la Musique* . . . etc. (Paris, 1636). Mersenne, following his general program of qualifying and demonstrating the inconsistencies of the *musica speculativa* of the previous centuries (such as the overly literal musical-political metaphors derived by Jean Bodin from Plato), consigns to a dismissive notice in a corollary older notions of correspondences between modes, colors, planets, elements, humors, etc. of the older theories of world harmony. See Cor. I to Prop. IV, Bk. IV. For additional material on analogies between painting and music, see Poussin's further correspondence (particularly for such notions as the modality of the three architectural orders which shows up in the illustrations to *La Rhétorique des Dieux*); also, Frances A. Yates, *The French Academies of the Sixteenth Century*, pp. 131-152.

Another use of the notion of modality in seventeenth-century France is a purely musical one, and, as such, not so startling as that of Poussin. Yet it draws together many of the separate strands of musical and esthetic tradition that we have observed to operate in the environment of the doctrine of the affections and of the expressive, as opposed to the imitative, theory of art generally. Denis Gaultier (1597?-1672) was one of the greatest lutenists of the seventeenth century. The lute, which during the sixteenth century had remained perhaps the most numerous and ubiquitous of stringed instruments, began in England and Italy during the rise of Baroque music to suffer a decline at the expense of the keyboards. But a great rejuvenation of the lute and its music occurred in France during the early decades of the seventeenth century when the traditional stringing of the instrument was altered to permit of a much greater range in the bass (by the addition of many extra bass courses or strings), and, even more important, to allow of a much greater flexibility of tonality. The characteristic music of the French lutenists consisted of *suites*, or groups of dances (and later of little program pieces) in the same or related keys, and *tombeaux*, or short commendatory pieces in memory of someone famous or dear to the composer. All of these, of course, were purely instrumental; the delicate, arpeggiated, highly ornamented style of these lute pieces eventually influenced the French keyboard style of the later part of the century. Gaultier, even among a flourishing and highly praised group of composers (his surname is a famous one in the history of French lute music), achieved an outstanding fame. A manuscript collection of some sixty-nine of his compositions for lute was compiled, between the years 1664 and 1672, and illustrated copiously by Abraham Bosse, Robert Nanteuil, and Eustache Le Sueur. Entitled *La Rhétorique des Dieux*, it consists of the lute pieces, arranged into *suites* according to their keys, and grouped under the headings, not of the key designations, but of the names of the Greek modes. In fact, Gaultier himself refers to the keys as modes, and never once in the conventional manner. In justification of his title, the elaborate preface declares, "*Ceux qui possèdent la Musique y trouveront une entière satisfaction, en ce que cet Autheur s'exprime avec tant d'art, tant d'adresse et des termes si choisis, que de toutes les parties du Corps il attire l'Ame à l'oreille: qu'il représente très parfaitement la nature des Passions: & qu'il élève les Esprits les plus abbaissez, aux plus sublimes vertus; Cette façon de s'exprimer La Rhétorique des Dieux, d'autant que l'Entendement humain ne peut conçevoir de langage plus éloquent.*"[87] But this fairly conventional praise of the affective power of music is followed by a set of detailed remarks on the subject of the "modes" in which the pieces are written, with respect to which they are grouped, and whose appropriate effects are elaborately illustrated in the accompanying wash drawings:

"*Tout cecy est suivy de douze desseins du Sieur Bosse, executez par luy mesme, qui représentent les douze Modes, dont les noms sont, le Dorien ou Dorique, le Sous-dorien, le Frigien, Sous-frigien, le Lidien, Sous-lidien . . .* [here he names the others] *& comme chacun de ces modes est propre à exciter certaines passions, & qu'ils sont propres à certains chants, l'on a réprésenté dans chacun les actions que le mode fait naistre, les Instruments tant anciens que modernes qui luy sont plus convenables, & mesmes l'on a observé d'y faire Architecture conforme à ces modes, en chacun desquels se trouve sur tout un Luth avec un Livre ouvert ou le mode est notté.*"[88]

The pieces themselves, aside from the many *tombeaux*, have mythological titles and are frequently accompanied by little narrative expositions or allegorizations of the subject, written at the end of the lute tablature. The illustrations, all of *putti* playing instruments of music of various sorts (al-

[87] Denis Gaultier, *La Rhétorique des Dieux*, ed. Andre Tessier (Paris, 1932), facsimile page 1.
[88] *Ibid.*, facsimile pp. 2-3.

though the prescription of the preface is followed in each case), also include other creatures showing the visible effects of the respective modes, and often the musicians themselves are the ones most vigorously affected. The elaborate modal scheme extends to the pieces themselves, which are all brought under the proper heading, if not by the title, then by the explanation following the composition.

The whole enterprise of the manuscript of *La Rhétorique des Dieux* involves the representation of the doctrine of the affections in its fully developed seventeenth-century form. The fact that these are textless, purely instrumental pieces is quite important, I think, for it is the expressive, non-verbal effects of music itself, completely split off from the "rational" powers of the text (in both Greek and Humanist musical theory) that is being celebrated. The lute itself is allegorized by the whole book as the gods' rhetorician. In the book's schematic grouping of pieces into their actual keys (completely aside from the literary-esthetic treatment of them as "modes"), Gaultier might be said to have been exploring the potentialities of his tuning; like Bach in the *Well-Tempered Clavier*, he might have been attempting to demonstrate the creative advantages annd potentialities engendered by a purely mechanical flexibility recently introduced. But the strength of the literary apparatus is undeniable, and its importance for the overall conception of the book cannot be overestimated. The notion of *ethos* in its Baroque version of the power of music over the passions (notably, of war and love) is literally treated and pictorially represented. The persuasive but wordless instrument, associated with the highest type of rhetoric (that of feelings), is all but deified itself in a great monument to musical expression.

It was not until the eighteenth century that musical theorists like Mattheson and other later German writers on what became known as the *Affektenlehre*, and the English estheticians Avison, Beattie, and Brown, thoroughly explored this notion of *expression* that was at the time of Poussin being formulated with respect to painting.[89] It was also not until the Augustan period in English literature that notions of literary expression began to be connected with those of painting, in particular, and began to come under the domination of rules of order and decorum that seem somehow to characterize the art of the earlier seventeenth century in France, rather than in England and Italy. But it is perhaps only in the earlier period that the expressive theory of music's power is treated in such an appropriate literary fashion. Taking the power of music as a *subject* to be represented, itself emotionally, in a literary style proper to it (to use Poussin's example), we can find the perfect marriage of poetic form and theme in the wild, "uncontrolled" Baroque style of Richard Crashaw, rather than, perhaps, in the more measured Neoclassicism that is always the other side of the coin of seventeenth-century cultural history.

Crashaw: The Baroque Expressive Strife

The literary application of the art-historical term "Baroque" has had a highly controversial but by now firmly established history.[90] The controversy has resulted, perhaps, chiefly from

---

[89] Or shortly thereafter, at any rate. See Charles Le Brun's *Méthode pour apprendre à dessiner les passions proposée dans une conférence sur l'expression générale et particulière* (1698), excerpts from which are printed and translated in Holt, *A Documentary History of Art*, pp. 161-163; also see Brewster Rogerson, *op.cit.* (note 63, above). For some remarks on the imitation vs. expression problem in eighteenth-century theory, see Meyer Abrams, *The Mirror and the Lamp* (New York, 1953), pp. 51 ff. Also see Herbert M. Schueller, "The Use and Decorum of Music as Described in British Literature, 1700 to 1780," *Journal of the History of Ideas*, XIII (1952), pp. 73-93.

[90] See René Wellek, "The Concept of Baroque in Literary Scholarship," *Journal of Aesthetics and Art Criticism*, V (1947), pp. 77-109, for an exhaustive account of the use of the word and the notion in literary studies. In the same number of the journal, pp. 109-128, may be found contributions on the subject from musicologists and art historians. Also, the same journal, Volume XIV (1955), pp. 143-174, again takes up the question of the usage of "Baroque," this time with an enlightening essay by a historian, Carl J. Friedrich (himself the author of a general history of *The Age of the Baroque* in the "Langer Series"). A lucid and forceful examination of the concept coupled with an attempt to use it practically, is that of Lowry

the fact that one can never be sure whether the word's extension is a historical period or a style. If the historical period is meant, the boundaries set by a pair of initial and terminal dates allow of a fairly good procedure for the use of the term. When a style is designated, there has tended to be much more disagreement among musicologists, art historians, and literary scholars over whether or not a particular work or artist represents the definitive Baroque qualities, over whether or not these qualities remain the same or related in all three fields.

In the preceding pages, the term "Baroque" has been introduced primarily in its historical sense, and particularly with respect to the esthetic theories underlying and accompanying the music of a clearly defined epoch. By the Baroque musical ideology, whether invoked by composer-theorists, painters, or poets, we have meant the affective doctrines of the seventeenth century, freed almost completely from their role in theories of universal music, and concentrating primarily upon the effects of music upon the more spectacular passions, love and violence in particular. It would be with some hesitation that I would introduce at this point a set of purely stylistic criteria for Baroque poetry in English. But many recent writers have already evidenced this hesitancy; Odette de Mourgues, in *Metaphysical, Baroque and Précieux Poetry*, suggests that a solely stylistic criterion is as misleading in this case as a purely historical one would be empty. Her final decision, serving best her purposes of literary history, represents what seems to be a general trend of usage. "I

Nelson, Jr. in "Gongora and Milton: Toward a Definition of the Baroque," *Comparative Literature*, VI (1954), pp. 53-63. The most extended recent attempt to utilize not only this notion, but the art-historical term "Mannerist" as well, is that of Wylie Sypher in his perceptive but often forced *Four Stages of Renaissance Style* (New York, 1955); his distinction between "Baroque" and Neoclassical "Late Baroque" is of some considerable interest and possible use, however. Also see M. M. Mahood, *Poetry and Humanism* (New Haven, 1950), for a series of studies of seventeenth-century English poetry which make excellent use, with hardly any Procrustean manipulation, of both "Mannerist" and "Baroque"; also, Curt Sachs, *The Commonwealth of Art* (New York, 1946), pp. 99-162.

should like," she concludes her discussion of this problem, "to limit the meaning of the term baroque and to apply it only to the poetry in which, although the problems of the age are reflected, the perfect poise between intelligence and sensibility is either destroyed or not achieved or not attempted, with the result that the poet has a distorted vision of life, distorted through imagination and sensibility, without any apparent care for proportions or balance."[91] She follows this statement with a decision to analyze the following aspects of Baroque poetry: "the mystical, the morbid, the macabre, the cosmic, the apocalyptic, the absurd." Perhaps one of her strongest points is an insistence on differentiating "Baroque" style from Metaphysical writing among English poets.[92] It might be observed, with respect to our own interest in the poetic representation of the power of music, that the Metaphysical style (considered in Dr. Johnson's original sense as embracing the "Tribe of Ben" as well as the followers of Donne) never served the doctrine of the affections particularly well. We shall see in the following chapters how two common types of seventeenth-century English musical poem tended either to preserve the notions of Humanist *musica speculativa* for religious purposes or to maintain them as stuffed, mounted relics, unanimated by any belief in them, for use in complimentary, epigrammatic poems. For example, Drummond of Hawthornden, adapting an epigram of Marino on the subject of a marble statue of the affective-musical hero, Amphion, manages to turn the same implicit Gorgon conceit used in the fourteenth-century text of a madrigal by Francesco Landini.[93] But in the course of his poem, the real point about the independent power of music becomes submerged in the wit of his comparison, which seems to exist for its own sake:

> This Amphion, Phidias frame,
> Though senceless it apeare

[91] Odette de Mourgues, *Metaphysical, Baroque and Précieux Poetry* (Oxford, 1953), p. 74.
[92] *Ibid.*, pp. 67-75.   [93] See above, note 1.

Doth live, and is the same
Did Thebes towres upreare;
And if his harpe be tuichte not to your eare,
No wonder, his harmonious sounds alone
Would you amaze, & change him selfe in stone.[94]

If ever an elaborate, even overexpressive representation of the musical theory of the passions seems to stand out above all others, however, it is surely in the work of an avowedly Baroque poet, Richard Crashaw.[95] His treatment of it occurs in *Musicks Duell*, generally regarded as its author's most successful secular poem. Crashaw's adaptation of the frequently translated Latin verses of the Jesuit rhetorician Famianus Strada avoids most of the proverbial excesses of such religious work as *The Weeper*: it remains a model of a kind of propriety seldom attained by the practice of so extravagant a style. The subject of the poem is a contest of technical musical skill between a lutenist and a nightingale. Readers with a nineteenth- or twentieth-century notion of virtuoso musical performance find little difficulty in allowing of the rightness of the poem's elaborate rhetoric in consideration of its subject. Indeed, commentators from Grosart to Austin Warren have tended to consider the poem itself as a virtuoso performance, as a splendid pyrotechnical display in which, contrary perhaps to the opinions about virtuosity of the past few decades, there is some investment of the heat of real feeling.

Instrumental virtuosity has a long history of literary celebration. The popular figure of a daemonic Paganini, playing on strings made from the gut of a defunct mistress, has its counterpart in diabolic myths surrounding the Elizabethan keyboard composer and performer, John Bull.[96] The blind

[94] "Amphion of Marble," number xviii in the group of posthumous poems in William Drummond of Hawthornden, *Poetical Works*, ed. L. E. Kastner (Manchester, 1913), II, 236.

[95] See Mario Praz, "The Flaming Heart: Richard Crashaw and the Baroque," reprinted in *The Flaming Heart* (New York, 1958), pp. 204-263; also see below, note 105.

[96] Anthony à Wood, in his *Fasti Oxonienses*, mentions these tales of Bull

Francesco Landini, a fourteenth-century organist-composer, was celebrated as an avatar of Orpheus.[97] By the end of the sixteenth century, many famous musical figures were more generally celebrated as performers than as composers: John Dowland, who, in the words of Barnfield's sonnet, "Upon the lute doth ravish human sense," had garnered such praises as a virtuoso lutenist on the Continent that he remained an expatriate in the Danish court for several years. During the seventeenth century, professional vocal and instrumental soloists became more and more common.[98] Although the lute was throughout this period undergoing replacement by various keyboard instruments, we have already seen how such performers as the Frenchman Denis Gaultier and others revivified the lute and created for it new idioms that were eventually to influence significantly French baroque keyboard styles.

It is perhaps significant that for Strada's neutral terms *"cithara"* and *"fidicen,"* used in Renaissance Latin to designate any stringed instrument and a performer upon one, respectively, Crashaw, William Strode, Ford, and Sir Francis Wortley all give "lute" and "lutenist" in their adaptations. In one anonymous translation only do the words "viol" and "fidler" appear;[99] and we may guess that the lute remained as

---

in two entries for 1586 and 1592. Under the first year, he quotes an anecdote of Bull's prowess as a composer, ending with a comment by another musician that "he that added these 40 parts must be either the Devil or Dr. Bull." In an entry under the later date, Wood records that, when chief organist to James I, Bull "was so much admired for his dextrous hand on the Orgon, that many thought that there was more than Man in him." See also Percy Scholes, *The Puritans and Music* (London, 1934), pp. 278-279, for a quoted account of how a musician, witnessing the performance of the violinist Thomas Baltzar, stooped "downe to Baltzar's Feet, to see whether he had a Huff on, that is to say, whether he was a Devil or not, because he acted beyond the parts of a man."

[97] See Leonard Ellinwood, "Francesco Landini and his Music," *Musical Quarterly*, XXII (1936), pp. 190-216.

[98] See below, Chapter VI, pp. 346-354; also, Marc Pincherle, "Virtuosity," *Musical Quarterly*, XXXV (1949), pp. 226-243.

[99] These are all reprinted, in full or in great part (with the exception of Strode's version) in A. B. Grosart's edition of *The Complete Works of Richard Crashaw* (London, 1872-73), I, 203-206. Strode's may be found in his *Works, ed.cit.* (note 4, above), pp. 16-18.

archetypal a stringed instrument as it was a common one up through the 1640's at least. But while it is important to remember that Crashaw must have been personally acquainted with skillful contemporary lute-playing, it is quite obvious that *Musicks Duell* is no mere example of either *laus musicae* or *laus fidicinis*, neither a poem in praise of music generally, nor a commendation of a particular or ideal performer.

Aside from conventions of the hyperbolic praise of virtuoso performers, it might be observed that Strada's original poem falls into other musico-poetic traditions as well. The swan and nightingale have from the period of Classical Antiquity been mythically celebrated: the first, to culminate a life of silence just before death; the second, symbolically bemoaning her pre-metamorphosed state's outrage. Plato evinced considerable skepticism about the singing of the fabled birds in the *Phaedo* ("But men, because they are themselves afraid of death, slanderously affirm of the swans that they sing a lament at the last, not considering that no bird sings when cold, or hungry, or in pain, not even the nightingale, nor the swallow, nor the hoopoe").[100] In St. Augustine and in many other medieval writers, the singing of the nightingale and of birds in general becomes the type of *natural* as opposed to *artificial* music, of singers who "sing well under the guidance of a certain sense, that is, do it harmoniously and sweetly, although if they were questioned about those numbers or intervals . . . they could not reply."[101] The seventeenth-century fondness for the most poetic of birds is attested to by the frequency of the nightingale's celebration in verse.[102] It is not quite clear whether

[100] *Phaedo*, 84b-85a, quoted in Jowett's version. The swallow and hoopoe were the transformations of Procne and Tereus in the Philomel myth.

[101] St. Augustine, *De Musica*, I, v, tr. Robert Catesby Taliaferro in *Writings of St. Augustine*, ed. Ludwig Schopp et al. (New York, 1947), II, 177. See also Leo Spitzer, *op.cit.*, Part I, *Traditio*, II (1944), pp. 457-459 for a discussion of other treatments of birds' songs and "natural" music.

[102] Patrick Hannay's 1600-odd line *Philomela* (1622), reprinted in *The Caroline Poets*, I, 620-642, and itself provided by the author with a melody to which all the verses of the poem were to be sung (as was done in earlier times with Tasso, for example) is only one spectacular case. See

George Sandys' allegorization of Ovid's bird reveals an independent tradition, or, indeed, actually depends on Strada's theme of the nightingale as pathetic over-reacher. Sandys' false etymology of the bird's name from φιλω-μέλος (lover of melody), instead of from φιλω-μῆλον (lover of fruit) is undoubtedly his own, however:

"The Nightingall chanting in the solitary woods; deservedly called *Philomela*, or a lover of musicke, in that no bird hath so sweet a voice among all silvan musitians: singing fifteene days and nights together, when the leaves begin to afford her a shelter, with little or no intermission. So shrill a voice in so little a body, and a breath so long extended, is worthy admiration; shee alone in her songs expressing the exact art of Musicke in infinite variety. Neither have all the same tunes and divisions, which shewes their skill to be more than naturall. They strive among themselves in fervent contention: the vanquished not seldome ending her life with her song, through griefe or over-straining. . . ."[103]

Thus does the nightingale become a little heroine of musical expression. While Sandys goes on to point out the intricate musical schooling to which nightingales put their young (thus carrying out his notion that the birds are rather "civilized" than *supernatural* in their skill), the Medieval idea of the silvan and untutored quality of the bird's music still overshadows his interpretation, as it does both Strada's text and Crashaw's version. Furthermore, the notion of the nightingales being contentious singers is reflected in numerous literary sources,[104] pitting of the bird and the instrumentalist against

---

also the nightingale poems of Philip Ayres reprinted in *The Caroline Poets*, II, 297, 303, 334, and countless other examples.

[103] George Sandys, *op.cit.*, p. 227.

[104] From the medieval *débat* of *The Owl and the Nightingale* onward, contentions of birds are fairly common. Du Bartas (first week, fifth day) records a contest of nightingales; an actual one is reported as having been seen by Thomas Coryate, in *Coryats Crudities Hastily Gobled up in Five Moneths Travells* (London, 1611), p. 253. See also the elaborate allegory of the Nightingale as musician, full of the most specific musical references (to instruments, modes, meters, and styles), and rivaling only Sandys in

each other, and setting the scene for an almost perfect Baroque battle of expression.

No wonder, then, that Crashaw's poem has been made a case in point by many critics arguing for its author's position as the English poet to manifest most typically the sensibility of the Italian Baroque.[105] Qualities usually mentioned are the sensuousness of the imagery, the fundamental use of decorative elaboration to assist rather than to impede the forward motion of the narrative, and the final emblematic denouement of the story itself, wherein disembodiment and ecstatic death fulfill the effects of a perfect art. One would wish always to be chary in pushing stylistic analogies too far. But if one can agree with Professor Wylie Sypher that one of the basic devices of Baroque style in both painting and poetry was the sensuous analogue of the Incarnation, that, as he puts it, "the flesh did not become spiritual—the spiritual became fleshly,"[106] then one must accept *Musicks Duell* as a triumph, if not a model, of Baroque writing. Its effect is to materialize, in its treatment of Strada's little fable, a particular view of the nature of music in terms of a figurative reconstruction of its actual performance and sound. It effects a fleshly transformation of the spiritual by representing the abstract effects upon each other of competing Apollonian virtuosi in imagery which invoked the domains of both Mars and Eros, and ends in a love-death of one of the contenders that blends and transcends the two.

When considered in such a light, however, *Musicks Duell*

---

its comprehensiveness, in Henry Hawkins' emblem book, *Parthenia Sacra* (London, 1633), pp. 138-148. There is an interesting reference to "the lusory and death of the nightingale, that hath furnished so many rare poets with matter for excellent verses" in Mary Burwell's *Instruction Book for the Lute* (ca. 1670), a MS. transcribed by Thurston Dart, *The Galpin Society Journal*, XI (1958), p. 50. The text goes on to tell the Strada-Crashaw story.

[105] See for example, Austin Warren, *Richard Crashaw: A Study in Baroque Sensibility* (Baton Rouge, 1939), pp. 63-76; Praz, *op.cit.*; T. O. Beechcroft, "Crashaw and the Baroque Style," *The Criterion*, XIII (1934), pp. 407-425; Wylie Sypher, *op.cit.*, pp. 189-190, 238-239.

[106] Sypher, p. 188.

presents a pair of interpretive problems that have been generally overlooked. The first of these concerns the precise range of sensuousness, as well as the function, of the elaborate imagery. The second, which cannot perhaps be answered until the first has been understood, concerns the overall nature of music itself as treated in the poem. A convenient approach to the first of these may be found in a rare lapse of insight in Austin Warren's splendid book on Crashaw. In arguing for a specific view that Crashaw "sought, by onomatopoeia and subtler forms of tone color, to create a poetry approximating music," he observes as follows: "Crashaw's technical terms, his *praeludium, divisions, diapason,* are fewer than those to be found in Marino or Milton and can be matched by many of his contemporaries in an age when musicianship, to the extent of reading at sight one's part in a madrigal and playing the lute, was an expected accomplishment of gentlemen."[107]

One might object to the last part of this remark on the grounds that the late Elizabethan and Caroline periods were quite different with respect to the extent and distribution of musical accomplishment. But my main point is that *Musicks Duell* fairly overflows with technical musical language, ranging from items of general musical usage to terms which remain today in the arcana of the lutenist's specialized vocabulary.[108]

[107] Warren, p. 107.

[108] Strode's excellent and much more "faithful" version, while making use of many musical puns ("shee draweth out / Her tone at large. . . ," the last word being a notational term, etc.), makes no particular effort to employ visual descriptions, nor the technical vocabulary, of lute playing in particular. More interesting in this regard is a commendatory poem, "To Mr. *LILLY,* Musick-Master in *Cambridge,*" from Nicholas Hookes' *Amanda* (1653), reprinted (New York, 1927), pp. 56-58. Some of it deserves quotation here, if only as a case of what may have been an imitation of some of Crashaw's effects:

> Sir, I have seen your scipjack fingers flie,
> As if their motion taught *Ubiquitie*:
> I've seen the trembling Cat'lin's smart and brisk
> Start from the frets, dance, leap, and nimbly frisk
> In palsie capers, pratling (a most sweet
> *Language* of *Notes*) *Curranto's* as they meet:
> I've heard each *string* speak in so short a space
> As if all spoke at once; with stately grace

And not denying for a moment the varied effects of rhythmic and syntactical elaboration in the poem's texture, there occurs a considerable amount of grotesquely synesthetic imagery, reflecting not the visual and aural associations of a Rimbaud, as some have suggested,[109] so much as actual references to the practice of lute playing, and even to the visual phenomena of written notation. The general musical terms are most often used in punning ways. The Nightingale, at the beginning of the contest,

> Trayles her playne Ditty in one long-spun note,
> Through the sleeke passage of her open throat:
> A cleare unwrinckled song, then doth shee point it
> With tender accents, and severely joynt it
> By short diminutives. . . .
>
> (ll. 37-41)[110]

"Playne Ditty" would suggest a *cantus firmus*, a basis, in earlier musical styles, for invention. It undoubtedly refers here to the opening thematic statement of a set of divisions or variations, the common seventeenth-century form of improvisation that both bird and Lutenist employ. The "points," "accents," and "diminutives" indicate that the Nightingale

---

> The surley tenour grumble at your touch,
> And th' ticklish-maiden *treble* laugh as much,
> Which (if your *bowe-hand* whip it wantonly,)
> Most pertly chirps and jabbers merrily;
> Like frolick *Nightingals*, whose narrow throats
> Suck *Musick* in and out, and gargle notes. . . .
>
> I've heard your *base* mumble and mutter too,
> Made angry with your cholerick hand, while you
> With hastie jirks to vex and anger't more
> Correct its stubbornnesse and lash it o're:
> I've heard you *pawse*, and dwell upon an *aire*,
> (Then make't i' th' end [as loft to part it were]
> Languish and melt away so leasurely,)
> As if 'twere pity that its *Eccho* die. . . .

[109] Warren, pp. 109-110, and Beechcroft both tend to imply this.

[110] My text and line numbering are from the 1646 edition of *The Delights of the Muses*, as given in L. C. Martin's edition of Crashaw's works (Oxford, 1927), pp. 149-153.

has gone on to develop her divisions. "Unwrinckled" is a typical case of the synesthesia mentioned before, evoking an image of the half and quarter notes in which a simple ground might be written, as opposed to the "wrinkled" appearance of rapid division passages as they were sometimes written out. Crashaw's eye, ever alert for emblems, alights on written notation elsewhere:

> His nimble hands instinct then taught each string
> A capring cheerefulnesse; and made them sing
> To their owne dance; now negligently rash
> He throwes his Arme, and with a long drawne dash
> Blends all together. . . .
>
> (ll. 27-31)

A "long drawne dash" in the tablature notation used for lute music indicated the holding of a note, usually in the bass, while chordal or polyphonic change continued above it. The dash of the Lutenist's arm motion, the notational pun, and the final image expressive of the sound itself, all indicate that the Lutenist has reached a cadence.

The most flamboyant figure of this type occurs in the Nightingale's most strenuous performance. A whirlwind of effort suffuses her

> And makes a pretty Earthquake in her Breast
> Till the fledg'd notes at length forsake their nest;
> Fluttering in wanton shoales, and to the Sky
> Wing'd with their owne wild Eccho's pratling fly.
>
> (ll. 89-92)

The feathered tails on the notes of smaller value cluster across the page, and the fluttering trills and roulades of the typical contemporary solo *aria* style, dipping and soaring, fuse momentarily. This ornithological image is drawn from immediately perceptible materials. One is tempted to disagree here with a critic who remarks that such images, typical of the poem, "are not sense images";[111] that "by picturing sound as having shape or light (according to a descriptive principle which is characteristically modern)" they "cannot be said to appeal primarily to either sense"; and finally that these figures represent "a kind of *ideal* image, abstracted from the object." On the contrary, throughout *Musicks Duell* one is continually faced with the object, the musical fact. As in emblem books, where the *impresa* or picture was said to stand to the motto written above it as the body stands to the soul,[112] Crashaw's concrete, even naturalistic musical references are employed in more general images—quarrelsome, warlike, pastoral, and passionate. Such terms as "flourish," "fancies," "Aires," "lesson," "ground," "grave," "close," "grace," "measure," "fall," and many others are all transformed into parts of momentary figures, their strictly musical *designata* resonating in the background.

Perhaps the most intricate series of transformations of observed musical practice occurs in the Lutenist's final bout. The lute's strings are first invoked as the Muses, with particular attention to their clearly visible vibrations. Then they become the hairs of Apollo, and immediately thereafter, the blood vessels of Music personified. In a bit of allegorized pastoral which follows, there is an obviously anatomical treatment of the lute itself; the rosette, or sound-hole, is invoked, as well as the peculiar soft sound which results from plucking the half-damped strings, below the rosette and close to the bridge. The whole passage begins with the Lutenist's prelude to his final and triumphant fit of playing. "With a quavering coynesse" he "tasts the strings," and here both the "quavers," or eighth-notes, and the *tastar de corde* or preliminary fingering of the strings are employed to introduce the openly erotic imagery which eventually follows. Then come the strings as Muses:

[111] Beechcroft, p. 416.
[112] See William S. Heckscher, "Renaissance Emblems," *Princeton University Library Chronicle*, xv (1954), pp. 56-57.

The sweet-lip't sisters musically frighted,
Singing their feares are fearfully delighted.
Trembling as when *Appollo's* golden haires
Are fan'd and frizled, in the wanton ayres
Of his owne breath: which marryed to his lyre
Doth tune the *Sphaeres*, and make Heavens selfe
     look higher.   (ll. 113-118)

(This last almost blasphemous reversal of the notion of the music of the spheres, incidentally, eventually becomes a received device in Cavalier and Augustan poetry. Usually employed in praise of a particular performer of whom it is said that he, or more often, she, shamed the spheres by her playing, this conventional hyperbole makes a grand appearance in Dryden's *Ode for St. Cecilia's Day*, where it is Music itself that "shall untune the sky.")

After this point, the erotic imagery is elaborated, and then brusquely and nervously gives way to an image of the strings as quarreling scholars:

From this to that, from that to this hee flyes,
Feeles Musicks pulse in all her Arteryes,
Caught in a net which there *Appollo* spreads,
His fingers struggle with the vocall threads,
Following those little rills, hee sinkes into
A Sea of *Helicon*; his hand does goe
Those parts of sweetnesse which with *Nectar* drop,
Softer then that which pants in Hebe's cup.
The humourous strings expound his learned touch,
By various Glosses; now they seeme to grutch,
And murmur in a buzzing dinne, then gingle
In shrill tongu'd accents, striving to bee single. . . .
                       (ll. 119-130)

Lute strings, it may be remembered, were strung in double courses, tuned either in unisons or octaves. When a particularly vehement broken chord is played upon such strings, buzzing and jingling may result. The strings vibrate against each other and produce a din of discord and struggle for independence that Crashaw suggests even within the music's harmony itself.

Throughout this remarkable section, the physical facts of lute-playing are employed in a wide range of metaphorical contexts to carry the narrative description forward and to build up to a number of rhetorical climaxes. One of these heightened moments occurs further on, when "musick's ravisht soule" is invoked. This notion is simply an extension of the Lutenist's figurative erotic play upon his instrument. But it also brings to fruition a growing identification of music with transcendent passion. At the beginning of the poem, Crashaw follows closely Strada's text in suggesting that the Lutenist and the Nightingale represent Art and Nature respectively. The Lutenist is the master of the Apollonian strings, of the sounds they produce, and of the emotions elicited in turn from all listeners. "What passion cannot music raise and quell?" asks Dryden in the St. Cecilia's Day ode, invoking the old tradition of rhetorical, affective music which, in the seventeenth century, began to replace older established notions of music in general as a metaphor for cosmological order. The Lutenist, "in whose gentle aires" the Sun "lost the Dayes heat, and his owne hot cares" is first presented as one who quells, rather than raises, the passions. The Nightingale's voice, however, is a natural one; she is described as "The sweet inhabitant of each glad Tree, / Their Muse, their *Syren*, harmlesse *Syren* shee"—harmless because of her innocence, because she seems to possess none of the rhetorical power of the Lutenist. At best, she is able to affect him in a passive way, as might a seduced and betrayed girl, when "Shame now and anger mixt a double staine / In the Musitians face."

The distinction between Art and Nature as embodied in the two contestants rapidly becomes a far more general one. Their respective bouts of playing are treated in contrasting modes of imagery. In the second such bout, the Lutenist's playing is described in figures of quarrel, command and war:

The tatling strings (each breathing in his part)
Most kindly doe fall out; the grumbling Base
In surly groanes disdaines the Trebles Grace.
The high-perch't treble chirps at this, and chides,
Vntill his finger (Moderatour) hides
And closes the sweet quarrell, rowsing all
Hoarce, shrill, at once; as when the Trumpets call
Hot Mars to th' Harvest of Deaths field, and woo
Mens hearts into their hands . . .

(ll. 48-56)

In such images as the chirping of the "high-perch't treble,"
a hint of the imagery used to describe the Nightingale's performance appears. Her answer to the music just mentioned
is narrated in a pastoral vein:

this lesson too

Shee gives him backe; her supple Brest thrills out
Sharpe Aires, and staggers in a warbling doubt
Of dallying sweetnesse, hovers oer her skill
And folds in wav'd notes with a trembling bill,
The plyant Series of her slippery song.
Then starts shee suddenly into a Throng
Of short thicke sobs, whose thundring volleyes float,
And roule themselves over her lubricke throat
In panting murmurs, still'd out of her Breast
That ever-bubling spring; the sugred Nest
Of her delicious soule, that there does lye
Bathing in streames of liquid Melodie;
Musicks best seed-plot, whence in ripend Aires
A Golden-headed Harvest fairely reares
His Honey-dropping tops, plow'd by her breath
Which there reciprocally laboureth
In that sweet soyle.

(ll. 56-73)

This is the bird's great round. It continues for thirty-two
more lines, ending on a major climax:

[234]

Shee opes the floodgate, and lets loose a Tide
Of streaming sweetnesse, which in state doth ride
On the wav'd backe of every swelling straine,
Rising and falling in a pompous traine.
And while shee thus discharges a shrill peale
Of flashing Aires; shee qualifies their zeale
With the coole Epode of a graver Noate,
Thus high, thus low, as if her silver throat
Would reach the brasen voyce of warr's hoarce Bird;
Her little soule is ravisht: and so pour'd
Into loose extasies, that shee is plac't
Above her selfe, Musicks *Enthusiast*.[113]

(ll. 93-104)

This central image of ravishment and enthusiasm points to
music's true nature for Crashaw. The Nightingale, it must be
remembered, is the incarnation of Philomela, the girl who
was raped and silenced, only to be metamorphosed into a
musical bird. In *Musicks Duell*, still a victim, she is violated
by the intensity of her own feeling. She is placed "above," not
"beside" herself by the passion into which her musical performance seems to merge.

At this point, the Lutenist is enraged and abashed; he
embarks on his last great bout of playing, employing all his
virtuosity. Toward the end of the long passage mentioned
before, his soft playing is described. Crashaw accounts for the
low sweet sounds as

complaining his sweet cares
Because those pretious mysteryes that dwell,
In musick's ravish't soule hee dare not tell,
But whisper to the world: thus do they vary
Each string his Note, as if they meant to carry

---

[113] "Wav'd," both here and in the foregoing passage (l. 60), is used in
a way similar to "wrinckled." Reaching the "brasen voyce of warr's hoarce
Bird" is a figure that competes with the Lutenist's martial imagery in the
preceding bout.

> Their Masters blest soule (snatcht out at his Eares
> By a strong Extasy) through all the sphaeres
> Of Musicks heaven; and seat it there on high
> In th' *Empyraeum* of pure Harmony.
>
> (ll. 142-150)

The Lutenist himself undergoes a figurative enthusiasm here, but he remains always master of his music. His playing is ravishing to music itself; the Nightingale, striving to outdo him, is ravished by her own overflowing feeling. The Lutenist's long *bravura* passage comes to an end, finally, when

> At length (after so long, so loud a strife
> Of all the strings, still breathing the best life
> Of blest variety attending on
> His fingers fairest revolution
> In many a sweet rise, many as sweet a fall)
> A full-mouth *Diapason* swallowes all.
>
> (ll. 151-156)

After this cadential octave that "swallowes all" as it sweeps across the strings, cancelling out any residual vibrations, the bird finds herself too weak, too spent to answer:

> for while (sweet soule) she tryes
> To measure all those wild diversities
> Of chatt'ring strings by the small size of one
> Poor simple voyce, rais'd in a Naturall Tone;
> Shee failes, and failing grieves, and grieving dyes.
> Shee dyes; and leaves her life the Victors prise,
> Falling upon his Lute; o fit to have
> (That liv'd so sweetly) dead, so sweet a Grave!
>
> (ll. 161-168)

The Nightingale dies, not as a direct result of the Lutenist's playing, but because of her overtaxed passive powers, her magnificent, but finally inadequate capacity for feeling.[114] The

---

[114] L. C. Martin's edition, p. 326.

Lutenist is clearly the conqueror, having remained master of his own music and passions throughout the contest. He has figuratively ravished his instrument, his musical mistress; the Nightingale, herself her own instrument, has remained the passive sufferer. But undergoing such an ecstasy is certainly, for Crashaw, a kind of triumph. In *The Flaming Heart*, he expresses this seeming paradox as follows:

> For in loue's feild was neuer found
> A nobler weapon then a WOUND.
> Loue's passiues are his actiu'st part.
> The wounded is the wounding heart.
>
> (ll. 71-74)[115]

In this sense, the Nightingale has surely won. She is music's martyr, as Teresa of Avila is Crashaw's great martyr of Love. And the music by which she is undone becomes inseparable from her own passion. There is a categorical difference between the Lutenist's music at the beginning of the poem, which is more like rhetoric than the emotions it elicits, and the more general realm of feeling at the end. The poem's imagery too, having run its wildest course, dissolves, in the plainer statement of the outcome, into the more conventionally heroic tone of its Latin model.

The conflict in *Musicks Duell*, then, is between active and passive feeling, between expression and response, both seen as epitomized in music. Both Milton and Marvell have left us their poetic anatomizations of music: their concerns with it are peculiarly theological and political, respectively. It was Crashaw's accomplishment not only to record increasingly a current view of music as passion, but to imitate its production and effects, transforming material facts of music-making and

---

[115] Compare Habington, *Castara* (1634), "To *Castara* Softly Singing to her Lute," where the lady is deemed so effective and Orphean a singer that the poet can conclude with the Strada-Sandys overstrained-bird effect:

> "And ravisht Nightingales, striving too high
> To reach thee, in the emulation dye . . ."

human feeling in another domain, none the more ethereal for being more general.

Cowley's Rich Science

We can find in Crashaw's translation of Strada's passionate musical duel a high point in the history of seventeenth-century poetical representations of the doctrine of the affections. But perhaps we ought, before concluding this chapter, to expend a passing glance on what is, in many senses, a low point in that same tradition. It has been previously observed that the gradual emergence of the expressive musical esthetic from the imitative one of the sixteenth century was accompanied by a gradual change, if only by reason of the general historical contingencies involved, in the poetic treatment of music as a subject. The exposition of some portion of *musica speculativa*, the use of a musical scene as a kind of genre set-piece in the course of sonnet sequences, and the often tortured utilization of the phenomena and terminology of practical music were all extremely common in sixteenth-century poetry. The Baroque musical esthetic, on the other hand, with its great stress upon the quasi-erotic relationship between performer and audience, and its insistence upon a passion-eliciting power of music that needed no accounting for in terms of the elaborate theories of a Ficino or a Zarlino, eventually called forth a new poetic convention. The Metaphysical (and eventually, the Augustan) complimentary epigram, addressed to a singer or instrumentalist, attempted to praise the excellence of the effectiveness of a particular musician by employing, in hyperbolic or epitomizing ways, notions such as that of the heavenly harmony and the music of the spheres. The purely *literary* quality of the use of these notions can be measured by the fact that for very few, if any, writers did there remain a conceptual scheme of the universe sufficient to give such notions at least a metaphorical significance. Their use was utterly empty of any belief.

Perhaps the outstanding late seventeenth-century occurrence of a poetic treatment of music's expressive powers that seeks to expound, in the old way, the place of practical music in the universe, is that of Abraham Cowley's digression on music in Book 1 of his *Davideis*. In that ambitious and exasperating religious epic Dr. Johnson could find "wit and learning unprofitably squandered";[116] the completed four books of the poem are, at any rate, over-documented, even if part of the intention that manifested itself in so much unassimilated learning was to create at once an epic and its *scholia*. Toward the beginning of the first book, David's harping that assuaged the madness of Saul is described, a theme always of great interest to Christian and Humanist allegories connecting Christ and Orpheus with the Psalmist. The actual narrative is almost brusque:

> In treacherous hast he's sent for to the King,
> And with him bid his charmful *Lyre* to bring.
> The King, they say, lies raging in a Fit,
> Which does no cure but sacred tunes admit;
> And true it was, soft *musick* did appease
> Th' obscure fantastick rage of *Sauls* disease.[117]

This event is the *locus classicus* for much discussion of the healing powers of music in the Christian era, and served to give Biblical justification for serious consideration of the lore about the therapeutic effects of music that had descended from Antiquity.[118] In such seventeenth-century compilations of this

[116] Samuel Johnson, "Life of Cowley" in *Lives of the English Poets* (Everyman Edition), I, 37.

[117] Abraham Cowley, *Davideis, A Sacred Poem of the Troubles of David* (1656), in *Poems*, ed. A. R. Waller (Cambridge, 1905), p. 253. Line numberings are not provided in Waller's edition; I use page references throughout.

[118] See Bruno Meinecke, "Music and Medicine in Classical Antiquity," in *Music and Medicine*, ed. Dorothy M. Schullian and Max Schoen (New York, 1948), pp. 47-95; also, in the same volume, Henry E. Sigerist, "The Story of Tarantism," pp. 96-116; and the essay by Armen Carapetyan, "Music and Medicine in the Renaissance and in the 17th and 18th Centuries," pp. 117-157, also contains some enlightening discussion of the relationship of the humoral theories of character to those of the affections.

lore as Burton's section on "Musick a remedy" in the *Anatomy of Melancholy*, David's psychiatric playing becomes merely one in a long list of examples: "Who hath not heard how David's harmony drove away the evil Spirits from King Saul; and Elisha, when he was much troubled by importunate Kings, called for a Minstrel, *and, when he played, the hand of the Lord came upon him. . . .*"[119] For Cowley, writing in 1638-1640 or thereabouts, and still up at Cambridge, the incident gave excuse for a learned dissertation on the subject of *musica speculativa* and the relationships of human and universal musics:

> Tell me, oh *Muse* (for *Thou,* or none canst tell
> The mystick pow'rs that in blest *Numbers* dwell,
> Thou their great *Nature* know'st, nor is it fit
> This noblest *Gem* of thine own *Crown* t'omit)
> Tell me from whence these heav'nly charms arise;
> Teach the dull world *t'admire* what they *despise*.[120]

Then follows an account of the creation of the world in musico-poetic terms; and while the general theme is that of *harmonia mundi*, yet the celebration of poetry, of David as poet, and of the whole of creation as a monumental epical composition, serve to aggrandize the author's own epic ego:

> As first a various unform'd *Hint* we find
> Rise in some god-like *Poets* fertile *Mind,*
> Till all the parts and words their places take,
> And with just marches *verse* and *musick* make;
> Such was *Gods Poem,* this *Worlds* new *Essay*;
> So wild and rude in its first draught it lay;
> Th' ungoverned parts no *Correspondence* knew,
> An artless *war* from thwarting *Motions* grew;
> Till they to Number and fixt Rules were brought
> By the *eternal Minds Poetique Thought.*[121]

[119] Robert Burton, *The Anatomy of Melancholy*, Part II, Sect. 2, Member VI, Subsection 4, ed. Floyd Dell and Paul Jordan-Smith (New York, 1951), p. 480.

[120] *Davideis*, p. 253.   [121] *Ibid.*

The initial epic simile connecting *poesis* and Creation seems to work in the wrong direction and to liken the greater thing to a lesser one (a kind of bathos, really); the connection, at any rate, does not support the Metaphysical couplet about "Gods Poem" and its foul papers. In the following lines, however, Cowley takes up in earnest the treatment of speculative music, only returning to his subject of poetic composition after a while:

> *Water* and *Air* he for the *Tenor* chose,
> *Earth* made the *Base*, the *Treble Flame* arose,
> To th' active *Moon* a quick brisk stroke he gave,
> To *Saturns string* a touch more soft and grave.
> The motions *Strait*, and *Round*, and *Swift*, and *Slow*,
> And *Short*, and *Long*, were mixt and woven so,
> Did in such artful *Figures* smoothly fall,
> As made this decent measur'd *Dance* of *All*.
> And this is *Musick*; Sounds that charm our ears,
> Are but one *Dressing* that rich *Science* wears.
> Though no man hear't, though no man it reherse,
> Yet there will still be *Musick* in my *Verse*.[122]

This poetic "Musick" will be not the beauty of numbers, but the *musica speculativa* of knowledge and learning that Cowley hopes will crown his solemn undertaking. The insistence on the importance of the speculative branch of music with almost a medieval theoretician's fervor is interesting. The metaphor of sounds (feeling) being but the dress of musical speculation (thinking and learning), itself rich enough to afford many such clothes, is interesting also in its implications for what Cowley felt that his sacred epic should really be. Not so much in the account of musical-universal Creation, which is simply culled from a host of ancient and modern authors,[123] but in this sharply maintained distinction between the two branches of music, can a real conflict of attitudes be suspected on Cow-

[122] *Ibid.*
[123] See Cowley's elaborate notes to this section, printed in Waller's edition, pp. 274-276.

ley's part. For one thing, there lurks about this passage the older Humanist rule that it is the text (the "*Science*" of music itself) that justifies the sounds. In the version of Cowley's contemporary, Joseph Beaumont,

> Gentiler Spirits in Music place
> A soveraigne Pleasure;
> But yet ye Cords are vext to grace
> The nimble Measure.
> The sweetest Harmonie
> With *Sharps* must temper'd be.
> Some tunes are heavnly; but tis when they meet
> A sacred Thing
> Whereon to sing;
> And then ye Dittie makes ye Musick sweet . . .[124]

On the other hand, Cowley's digression concerns the traditional explanations of the power of pure sound to cure and heal. It is almost as if he were bootlegging his arguments for the power of poetry itself into his praise of therapeutic music. Even in the description of the Creation, God is implicitly likened, in the lines about the moon and Saturn, to a performer on the lyre, a singer (poet) rather than a framer and shaper.

Cowley concludes his musical *excursus* with an excited invocation of the heart of the world-harmony idea. "There is so much to be said of this subject, that the best way is to say nothing of it,"[125] he remarks in his note on the first couplet below, realizing, perhaps, the extremely commonplace character of this whole argument:

> In this *Great World* so much of it we see;
> The *Lesser, Man,* is all o're *Harmonie.*
> *Storehouse* of all *Proportions! single Quire!*
> Which first *Gods Breath* did tunefully inspire!

[124] Joseph Beaumont, "Reasonable Melancholy," from *Minor Poems,* ed. Eloise Robinson (London, 1914), p. 5.
[125] *Davideis,* Book I, note 37, *ed.cit.,* p. 276.

THE TEMPLE OF SPECULATIVE MUSIC. An illustration from Robert Fludd's *Utriusque Cosmi Historia* (1617). The structure is composed of different branches of study: the division of the monochord, the church tones, proportions, counterpoint, etc.

		Generis Duri				Generis Mollis		
		In Tenſione Graviſ-ſima.	Acutiſ-ſima.			In Tenſione Graviſſi-ma.	Acutiſſi-ma.
		Sc. pr. ſec.	Sc. Pr. Sc.			Sc. pr. ſec.	Sc. Pr. Sc.
d ♄ij.		342. 18	351. 24.		d ♄ij.	342. 18.	351. 24
h ♄ij.		285. 15	292. 48.	☿ h ♄ij.		273. 50	280. 57
g ♄j		228. 12	234. 16.		g ♄j	228. 12.	234. 16.
d ♄j		171. 9	175. 42.		d ♄j	171. 9.	175. 42.
Venus hic ob-	c♄	95. 5	97. 37	Venus ob-	c♄	95. 5	97. 37.
ſtrepit				ſtrepit.			
Ter. g iiij		7. 3	58. 34.	Ter. g iiij		57. 3.	58. 34.
♂ b iiij		35. 39.	36. 36.	♂ b iiij		34. 14.	35. 8.
g iij		18. 31.	29. 17.	g iij		28. 31.	29. 17.
♃ d j		5. 21.	5. 30.	♃ d j.		5. 21.	5. 30.
h j			4. 35.		b		
♄ b		2. 13.		✝ b		2. 8.	2. 12.
G.		1. 47.		G		1. 47.	1. 50.

Hic in graviſſima tenſione concurrunt Saturnus, Terra, apheliis; in media Saturnus perihelio, Jupiter aphelio; in acutiſſimâ, Jupiter perihelio.	Hic non tolcratur aphelius Jovis, at in acutiſſima tenſione concurrit Saturnus perihelio proxime.

HARMONICIS LIB. V. 207

mnia (infinita in potentiâ) permeantes actu : id quod aliter à me non potuit exprimi, quam per continuam ſeriem Notarum intermedia-

Saturnus   Jupiter   Mars ferè   Terra

Venus   Mercurius   Hic locum habet etiam ☽

THE MUSIC OF THE SPHERES. Two diagrams from Kepler's *De Harmonices Mundi*, showing the melody "sung" by each heavenly body, and the way in which they join in six-part counterpoint, a Renaissance version of Universal Harmony.

Hic autem monochordum mundanum cum suis proportionibus, conso-
nantiis & intervallis exactiùs composuimus, cujus motorem extra mundum esse
hoc modo depinximus.

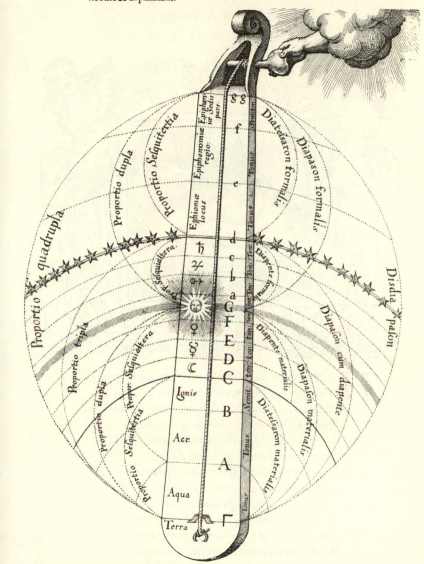

THE TUNING OF THE WORLD. In this diagram from Robert Fludd's *Utri-usque Cosmi Historia*, correspondences between the Pythagorean intervals, the planets, the elements and the metrical proportions may be seen. The whole instrument is being brought into tune from the region of the *primum mobile*.

Fœdera.

Ad Maximilianum Mediolani Ducem.

EMBLEMA X.

H ANC citharam, à lembi quæ forma halieutica fertur,
     Vendicat & propriam Musa Latina sibi,
Accipe Dux: placeat nostrum hoc tibi tempore munus,
     Quo noua cum socys fœdera inire paras.
Difficile est, nisi docto homini, tot tendere chordas:
     Vnaq; si fuerit non bene tenta fides,
Ruptave (quod facile est) perit omnis gratia conchæ,
     Illeq; præcellens cantus, ineptus erit.
Sic Itali cœunt proceres in fœdera: concors
     Nil est quod timeas, si tibi constet amor.
At si aliquis desciscat (vti plerumque videmus)
     In nihilum illa omnis soluitur harmonia.

ALCIATI'S LUTE EMBLEM: THE STRINGED INSTRUMENT AS
POLITICAL CONCORD. From Andrea Alciati's *Emblemata*. The source
of many subsequent allegorizations of stringed instruments. See p. 47f.

W HILE I lay bathed in my natiue blood ,
      And yeelded nought saue harsh , & hellish soundes :
And saue from Heauen , I had no hope of good ,
Thou pittiedst (Dread Soueraigne) my woundes ,
      Repair'dst my ruine, and with Ivorie key ,
      Didst tune my stringes , that slackt or broken lay .

Now since I breathed by thy Roiall hand ,
And found my concord , by so smooth a tuch ,
I giue the world abroade to vnderstand ,
Ne're was the musick of old Orpheus such ,
      As that I make , by meane (Deare Lord) of thee ,
      From discord drawne , to sweetest vnitie .

Basil : Doron .
           Cum mea nativo squallerent sceptra cruore ,
            Edóque lugubres vndíque fracta modos :
          Ipse redux nervos distendis (Phœbe) rebelles ,
            Et stupet ad nostros Orpheus ipse sonos .

                                        Pænitentia

PEACHAM'S HARP EMBLEM. A metamorphosis of Alciati's lute, in which the contemporary instrument becomes the
Gaelic harp, the political concord a specifically Jacobean one.
From Henry Peacham's emblem book, *Minerva Brittana*
(1612). See p. 49f.

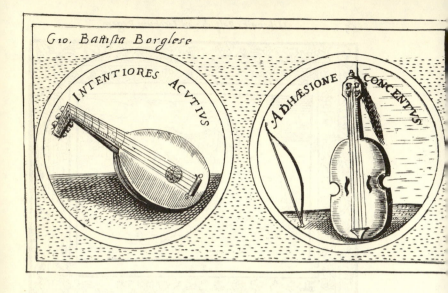

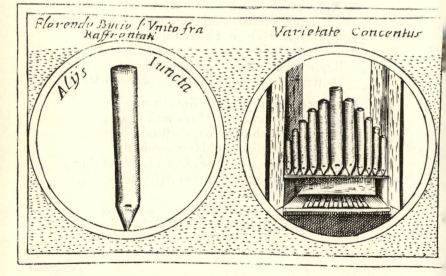

VARIOUS INSTRUMENTAL ALLEGORIES. From Giovanni Ferro's *Teatro d'Imprese* (1623). The single organ pipe is "joined to others"; the whole rank represents the agreement of differences. Of the two stringed instruments, the lute signifies high-tuned *tonus*, moral, psychological, etc. The *viola da bracchia* stands for general concord in the most traditional way.

Zu hoch gespannt/zerbricht den Bogen.

Lautenschlagen vnd Bücher lesen/
Ist zweiffels ohn ein lustig Wesen/
Doch spann die Saiten nicht zu viel/
Seh zu / hüt dich für falscher Brill.

D   Erklä-

THE HIGH-STRUNG LUTE: A WARNING. A lute emblem from Andreas Friedrichen's *Emblemata Nova* (1644), in which the traditional notion of the tuned string's *tonus* becomes a specific caveat against too much devotion to "*Lautenschlagen und Bücherlesen*."

THE mortall ſtrifes that often doe befall,
 Twixt louing Bretheren, or the private frend,
Doe proue (we ſay) the deadlieſt of all :
Yet if * compoſ'd by concord, in the end
 They reliſh ſweeter, by how much the more,
 The Iarres were harſh, and diſcordant before.

How oft hereof the Image I admire,
In thee ſweete *MVSICK*, * Natures chaſt delight,
The * Banquets frend, and * Ladie of the Quire;
Phiſition to the melancholly ſpright:
 Mild Nurſe of Pietie, ill vices foe;
 Our Paſſions Queene, and * Soule of ALL below.

* The firſt Diſcord here taken is from the eleuéth to the tenth, that is from b fa b mi, vnto alamire, a tenth to f fa vt in the Baſe, The ſecond from the ninth, or ſecond to the 8 . or vniſon.

χαῦρε * φυλῶ
ἀερέατα * χο
ϵϊνιπα * δυι
ϳω ἐταιϵν.
Homer : in Hymnus , Muſicam alloquens.

* According to the opinion of Pythagoras,

MUSIC HERSELF. In this emblem from *Minerva Brittana*, music is pictured as notation standing for actual two-part counterpoint, resolving the "jarres" into sweet concord. Music is not represented here by an instrument, a mythological figure, etc., but rather in the pure abstract.

LOVE AS SYMPATHETIC VIBRATION. An emblem from Jacob Cats'
Silenus Alcibiadis (1618 ed.), showing two lutes, tuned together, the second
vibrating when the first is plucked.

XXVI.

D e H A R P.

Zonder geluit nutteloos.

Wat baat een Harp, die tot vermaak van de ooren,
Door's meesters konst haar snaaren niet laat hooren?
Wat baat een mens zyn wysheid en verstand,
En rykdom, hem zo mild van 's hemels hand
Geschonken, die, zyn gaaven zonder luister,
Laat by zich zelfs verroesten in het duister?
Maar die, geraakt van Godlyke yver, 't goed
Dat hy bezit naar 't lichaam en 't gemoed,
Voor 's naastens dienst en welstant nimmer spaarde,
Verstrekt de lust, de rechte vreugd van de aarde.

H 2   *De*

THE MUTE HARP IS VANITY. From an eighteenth-century
Dutch emblem book, the *Zinnebeelden* of A. Houbraken. The moralization has become a homely one: "What benefits a harp to go un-
played by artful hand?" the motto asks; "What benefits a man's
reason and wisdom to be abandoned, bereft in darkness?"

EUTERPE, WITH CHITARRONE AND NIGHTINGALE. A mid-seventeenth-century allegory of music by Laurent de La Hire (1606-1656). Courtesy of the Metropolitan Museum of Art, Charles B. Curtis Fund, 1950.

"WHILE SHE SINGS, 'TIS HEAV'N HERE." Arabella Hunt, the subject of Congreve's ode. Mezzotint by John Smith, after Kneller. By permission of the Trustees of the British Museum. See p. 353f.

THE LUTE EXALTED AS RHETORICIAN. The first illustration by Abraham Bosse for Denis Gaultier's manuscript collection of lute pieces, *La Rhétorique des Dieux* (1652?), representing a lute, crowned with Laurel, Myrtle and Olive, and inscribed: "The Arbiter of Love, Peace and War."

THE WARLIKE PHRYGIAN MODE. An allegory of the Phrygian mode from *La Rhétorique des Dieux*. Although the *putti* play trumpet and drum, the lute remains prominent as the emblem of rhetoric itself, here crossed with a trumpet to signify the bellicose temperament. Another figure, at left, is moved to arms by the mode's effects.

THE AMOROUS MYXOLYDIAN MODE. The Myxolydian mode, also by Bosse, from Gaultier's book. Two *putti* play a reconstructed classical lyre and some sort of keyboard, while two others respond in character with the supposed *ethos* of the mode. Here, again the lute dominates the foreground.

MVSICAM AMOR DOCET

ILLVSTR. XX.   Book.2

IF to his thoughts my *Comments* have assented,
By whom the following *Emblem* was *invented*,
I'le hereby teach you (*Ladies*) to discover
A true-bred *Cupid*, from a fained *Lover*;
And, shew (if you have *Wooers*) which be they,
That worth'est are to beare your *Hearts* away.
As is the *Boy*, which, here, you pictured see,
Let them be *young*, or let them, rather, be
Of *suiting yeares* (which is instead of *youth*)
Not in the common and disguised *Clothes*,
Of *Mimick-gestures, Complements*, and *Oathes*.
Let them be *winged* with a swift *Desire*;
And, not with *slow-affections*, that will tyre.
But, looke to this, as to the principall,
That, *Love* doe make them truly *Musicall:*
For, *Love's* a good *Musician*; and, will show
How, every faithfull *Lover* may be so.
Each *word* he speakes, will presently appeare
To be melodious *Raptures* in your eare:
Each *gesture* of his body, when he moves,
Will seeme to *play*, or *sing*, a *Song of Loves:*
The very *lookes*, and *motions* of his eyes,
Will touch your *Heart-strings*, with sweet *Harmonies*;
And, if the *Name* of him, be but exprest,
T'will cause a thousand *quaverings* in your breast.
Nay, ev'n those *Discords*, which occasion'd are,
Will make your *Musicke*, much the sweeter, farre.

    And, such a mooving *Diapason* strike,
    As none but *Love*, can ever play the like.

Thy

ILLVSTR. III.   Book.2

O *Musicke*, and the Muses, many beare
Much hatred; and, to whatsoever ends
Their *Soule-delighting-Raptures* tuned are,
Such peevish dispositions, it offends.
Some others, in a *Morall way*, affect
Their pleasing *Straines* (or, for a sensuall use)
But, in *Gods Worship*, they the same suspect;
(Or, taxe it rather) as a great abuse.
The *First* of these, are full of *Melancholy;*
And, Pitty need, or Comfort, more then blame;
And, soone, may fall into some dangerous *folly,*
Vnlesse they labour, to prevent the same.
The *Last*, are *giddie-things*, that have besoul'd
Their Iudgements, with beguiling-*Fantasies,*
Which (if they be not, by discretion, school'd)
Will plunge them into greater *Vanities.*

    For, *Musicke*, is the *Handmaid* of the L O R D,
And, for his *Worship*, was at first ordayned:
Yea, therewithall she sitly doth accord;
And, where *Devotion* thriveth, is retayned.
Shee, by a nat'rall power, doth helpe to raise,
The *mind* to God, when joyfull Notes are sounded:
And, *Passions* fierce Distemperatures, alaies;
When, by grave *Tones*, the *Mellody* is bounded.
It, also may in *Mysticke-sense*, imply
What *Musicke*, in our-selves, ought still to be;
And, that our *jarring dives* to certifie,
Wee should in *Voice*, in *Hand*, and *Heart*, agree:

    And, sing out, *Faiths* new-songs, with full concent,
    Vnto the *Lawes*, ten-stringed *Instrument.*

L 2   *Marke*

AMOROUS LUTE AND DIVINE HARP. Notice the disposition of instruments to divine and erotic functions in these plates from George Wither's *A Collection of Emblemes, Ancient and Moderne* (1635).

ILLVSTR. X.   *Book.* 1.

When fome did feeke *Arion* to have drown'd,
He, with a dreadleffe heart his Temples crown'd;
And, when to drench him in the Seas they meant,
He playd on his melodious *Inftrument*;
To fhew, that *Innocence* difdayned Feare,
Though to be fwallow'd in the *Deeps* it were.
Nor did it perifh : For, upon her Backe
A *Dolphin* tooke him, for his *Mufick's* fake :
To intimate, that *Vertue* fhall prevaile
With *Brutifh* Creatures, if with *Men* it faile.
    Moft vaine is then their Hope, who dreame they can
Make wretched, or undoe, an *Honeft-Man* :
For, he whom *Vertuous Innocence* adornes,
Infults o're *Cruelties* ; and, *Perill* fcornes.
Yea, that, by which, Men purpofe to *undoe* him,
(In their defpight) fhall bring great *Honours* to him.
    Arion-like, the Malice of the World,
Hath into *Seas of Troubles* often hurl'd
Deferving Men, although no Caufe they had,
But that their *Words* and *Workes* fweet *Mufcke* made.
Of all their outward Helps it hath bereft them ;
Nor meanes, nor hopes of Comfort have beene left them;
But fuch, as in the Houfe of *Mourning* are,
And, what *Good-Confcience* can afford them there.
Yet, *Dolphin-like,* their *Innocence* hath rear'd
Their Heads above thofe *Dangers* that appear'd.
God hath vouchfaf'd their harmeleffe *Caufe* to heed,
And.ev'n in Thraldome, fo their Hearts hath freed,
That, whil'ft they feem'd oppreffed and forlorne;
They *Joyd,* and *Sung,* and *Laugh'd the World to fcorne.*

ILLVSTR. XXVI.   *Book.* 4.

There are a fort of people fo fevere,
That, *foolifh,* and *injurious* too, they are;
And, if the world were to bee rul'd by thefe,
Nor *Soule,* nor *Bodie,* ever fhould have eafe.
The *Sixe dayes,* (as their wifdomes underftand)
Are to bee fpent in *Labour,* by command,
With fuch a ftriCtneIfe, that they quite condemne
All *Recreations* which are us'd in them.
That, which is call'd the *Sabbath,* they confine
To *Prayers,* and all *Offices-divine,*
So wholly, that a little *Recreation,*
That *Day,* is made a marke of *Reprobation:*
And, (by this meanes) the reafon is to feeke,
When their poore *Servants* labour all the *weeke,*
(Of which, they'l bate them nothing) how it tyes
Them, to obferve the fixe-fold *Sacrifice*
By fome injoyn'd ; and gives them fuch due *Reft,*
As *God* allowed, both to *Man* and *Beaft.*
    Hee, gave the *Woods,* the *Fields,* and *Meddowes,* here,
A time to *reft,* as well as times to *beare.*
The *Forreft Beafts,* and *Heards,* have howres for *play;*
As well as time to *graze,* and hunt their prey :
And, ev'ry *Bird* fome leafure hath to fing,
Or, in the Aire, to *fport* it on her wing.
And, fure, to *him,* for whom all thefe were made,
Leffe kindneffe was not meant, then thefe have had.
The *Flefh* will faint, if pleafure none it knowes ;
The *Man* growes madd, that alway muzing goes.
    The *Wifeft* men, will *fometimes merry* bee:
And, this is that, this *Emblem* teacheth me.

                                        Live

APOLLO'S LYRE AND ARION'S VIOL. Two more emblems
from Wither's collection. The rather schematic-looking lyre is the
god's attribute in this version of the same theme treated in the
German emblem reproduced earlier. The anachronistic use of the
contemporary viol for Arion follows several Renaissance depictions.
Note, however, that this disposition of instruments is the illustrator's;
Wither's motto carelessly refers to Apollo's "Harpe."

From hence blest Musicks heav'nly charms arise,
From *sympathy* which *Them* and *Man* allies.
Thus they our *souls*, thus they our *Bodies* win,
Not by their Force, but Party that's within.
Thus the strange *Cure* on our spilt *Blood*, apply'd,
Sympathy to the distant *Wound* does guid.
Thus when two *Brethren strings* are set alike,
To *move* them *both*, but *one* of them we *strike*,
Thus *Davids Lyre* did *Sauls* wild rage controul,
And tun'd the harsh disorders of his *Soul*.[126]

Although there are some excellent couplets in this whole
section (notably the one above, in which the effects of music
are likened to besiegers who conquer through the agency of
fifth columnists, the sounds' own like within the body's walls),
it is obvious that young Cowley was neither Milton nor
Dryden. He could not, that is, manage to weave himself, his
gravest problems, his role as a poet (and hence, poetry), into
the fabric of a Biblical epic with any success. Neither could
he, like Dryden in the first St. Cecilia's Day ode, carry off an
excited rendering of a musical composition-world Creation
conceit without having the seams of his learning show. The
commonplace about the phenomenon of sympathetic vibration, for example, seems tacked on to his much more general
argument; although he cites no source but actual experience in
his notes for this information, it was an observation that appeared in practically every work on music that Cowley might
have read, and appears here almost because he thought it
was expected to do so.

In one sense, it seems natural for Cowley to have employed,
in a solemn and learned heroic poem, the kind of poetic exposition of the power of music that can be found in Du Bartas,
for example, or in Lorenzo's musical discourse in *The Merchant of Venice*. Expounding the Classical-Christian fusion
of views on world harmony and musical effect, he preserved

[126] *Ibid.*, p. 254.

in an age of Baroque esthetics a Humanist account of musical expressiveness. Perhaps his covert intention of glorifying poetry itself, and, indirectly, his own epical art, led him to the same metaphorical identification of poetic process and Biblical Creation that Milton develops so much more powerfully and movingly. Perhaps, on the other hand, the "seriousness" of his religious subject demanded a turning away from more modish views of music and styles of representation of it.[127] It will only be observed in conclusion that the maintaining of traditional ideas of universal harmony and *musica humana* throughout the seventeenth century remains as much a function of literary intention, and hence of style, as it does of belief in the *Weltanschauung* that generated those ideas. In a very real way, there is more "belief" invested in Crashaw's extravagant dramatization of music's powers than there is in Cowley's more disciplined and studied exposition.

[127] For evidence that Cowley borrowed from Crashaw, for example, and that he may have had contact with him in Cambridge, see E. M. W. Tillyard, *The English Epic and Its Background* (New York, 1954), pp. 424-425. Also see the excellent essay on Cowley in Geoffrey Walton, *Metaphysical to Augustan* (London, 1955), pp. 94-120; and Basil Willey, *The Seventeenth Century Background* (New York, 1950), pp. 205-232.

CHAPTER V · "THE SACRED
ORGANS PRAISE"

But oh! what Art can teach
What human Voice can reach
The sacred ORGANS praise?

Music Civil and Divine

IF THE course of cultural history of the intervening centuries in Europe has acted to sharpen the distinction between what we have called, in Morley's words, "speculative" and "practical" music, there are other categorical distinctions that have during the same period become quite blurred. Chief among these is the division of what Charles Butler in 1636 called in the title of his treatise "The Principles of Musik (in Singing and Setting)," "The two-fold Use thereof (*Ecclesiastical* and *Civil*)."[1] It is not, for us today, a distinction that leaps first to mind in connection with Renaissance music. This is true partly because it is our habit to think of the *a cappella* polyphonic style of the sixteenth century as embracing all music, both "divine" and "civil," serving to set with an identical attention and skill a text from the Vulgate (or, in the Protestant North, a psalm in the vernacular) or an undistinguished pastoral lyric. Our unwillingness to do any more toward isolating a "religious" music of the Renaissance than merely to distinguish the strictly liturgical from the rest of musical practice is also partially occasioned by the fact that we see how all practical music, whether liturgical or not, is accounted for and justified in the same general

[1] Charls (*sic*) Butler, *The Principles of Musik, etc.* (London, 1636). Butler was an ardent spelling reformer, and the whole treatise, like his others on grammar and bee-keeping, is written in a phonetic alphabet. I have taken the liberty of transcribing throughout.

way, with appeal to the same corpus of speculative musical knowledge.

Modern musicology has led us to understand exactly the degree to which we are misled in thinking that the *a cappella* vocal polyphony is *the* music of the sixteenth century. We have discussed in previous chapters the roles of instruments in an age when vocal music was the theoretical model, rather than the practical norm, for most music. In general, it has come to be known that the music of the sixteenth century is characterized by a number of differing musical institutions, serving different social functions, and each developing a different style.[2] At the beginning of the seventeenth century, too, national styles become even more strongly marked than they have been, and particular national genres start to flourish; thus we find the English viol-consort fantasy, the French *tombeaux* of the lutenists and *clavécinistes*, and the Italian recitative (quickly and widely disseminated), for example, retaining a typically national character throughout the seventeenth century. And we find that, by and large, the sharp cleavage between the "civil" and "ecclesiastical" practices tends to blur under the pressure of other differentiations, of style, of method of performance, and of use.

But by the end of the sixteenth century, particularly in England, both religious and musical history had combined to make Butler's distinction a cogent one. Almost immediately after Elizabeth's accession, the English church recoiled sharply from the liturgical practices of Catholic Mary's reign, and the musical service, together with the training of choirs and organists, suffered considerably.[3] But even with the new flowering of liturgical and secular music in the late eighties

[2] See Edward Lowinsky, "Music in the Culture of the Renaissance," *Journal of the History of Ideas*, XV (1954), pp. 509-553. For detailed documentation of some of Lowinsky's insights, informally presented above, consult the authoritative study of Gustave Reese, *Music in the Renaissance* (New York, 1954).

[3] Morrison Comegys Boyd, *Elizabethan Music and Musical Criticism* (Philadelphia, 1940), pp. 18-24, quotes profusely from contemporary sources as evidence of this.

and nineties, the specific role of music in the liturgy began to receive its own defense, quite apart from any attempts to promote the educational or genteel study of secular singing and playing. In the fifth book of the *Laws of Ecclesiastical Polity* (1597) Richard Hooker came to grips with the objections of the *Admonitions to Parliament*, and particularly of their defender Thomas Cartwright, on the subject of music in church.[4]

The extreme puritan view ruled out not only all instrumental music, but even florid contrapuntal vocal writing and, in particular, the antiphonal singing of psalms. The great controversy of the 1570's over the nature of the Prayer Book had elicited objections from Cartwright ranging from the dismissive comment that "They tosse the Psalmes in most Places like Tennice Balles,"[5] to the same writer's more measured statements of policy. The singing of two psalms, one at the beginning of a divine service, the other at the end, were to comprise all the permissible music, and those two psalms were to be sung to a "plaine tune" which might be sung as easily by the musically ignorant as they might be comprehended by the illiterate.[6] Given the actual musical conditions which witnessed the flowering of English polyphonic music in the later sixteenth century, parallels seem to suggest themselves between the puritan and reformed objections to polyphonic anthems on the grounds that they discouraged congregational participation, and the Neoclassic doctrines of the Florentine monodists and French academicians, who held that the significant and expressive virtues of the text must be at all costs preserved and enhanced by musical setting. On the other hand, though, it was precisely the theories and experi-

[4] Richard Hooker, *The Laws of Ecclesiastical Polity*, Book v (1597), ed. R. Bayne (Everyman Edition, London, 1907), II, 146-154. The material here discussed is dealt with in questions xxxviii and xxxix of Book v.

[5] These quotations from Cartwright's replies to John Whitgift's defense of the Anglican position represented later on by Hooker are to be found in the latter's notes, from which they are here quoted. Hooker, *ed.cit.*, II, 149, n. 1.

[6] *Ibid.*, II, 147, n. 3.

ments of early Baroque esthetes that insisted so strongly upon the respectively active and passive roles of singer and hearer, and that helped to dig the huge gulf between performer and audience that has since been widened rather than filled.

The ecclesiastical musical controversies also differed from the secular in drawing upon a long tradition of abuse and defense rather than upon recent interpretations of Attic notions, based upon particular versions of what Classic practice was like.[7] A famous passage in Book x of St. Augustine's *Confessions* served as the *locus classicus* of several points which were raised by both parties in many of the musical-liturgical controversies of the succeeding centuries. After reporting with what delight he would hear the words of a sacred text *as they affected him upon being sung*,[8] he continues:

"At other times . . . I err in too great strictness; and sometimes to that degree, as to wish the whole melody of sweet music which is used to David's Psalter, banished from my ears, and the Church's too . . . Yet again, when I remember the tears I shed at the Psalmody of Thy Church in the beginning of my recovered faith; and how at this time, I am moved, not with the singing, but with the things sung, when they are sung with a clear voice and modulation most suitable, I acknowledge the great use of this institution. Thus I fluctuate between peril of pleasure, and approved wholesomeness; inclined the rather (though not as pronouncing an irrevocable opinion) to approve of the usage of singing in the church; that so by the delight of the ears, the weaker minds may rise to the feeling of devotion. Yet when it befalls me to be more moved with the voice than the words sung, I confess to have sinned penally, and then had rather not hear music . . ."[9]

Here, in a context in which notions of the significance of the music itself do not appear to be at work (the music, the

[7] See above, Chapter IV.

[8] St. Augustine, *Confessions*, x, xxxiii, tr. E. B. Pusey (Everyman Edition, London, 1907), p. 234.

[9] *Ibid.*, p. 235.

"voice" gives the sensual pleasure, as distinguished from the words of Scripture), is the classic representation of the treatment of music, even the singing of the psalms, as worldly pleasure. When combined with the attacks of earlier Christian writers on the immorality of *tibia*-playing prostitutes and actresses (becoming, in late-medieval England, "drasty fiddlers" in taverns), such a notion can be seen to yield one sort of traditional dispraise of music. But the musical attack as part of general complaints against the material world and the specific regulation of the music of the liturgy are a somewhat different matter; and while moral arguments against music's use were employed throughout the history of the Middle Ages by writers on liturgical questions, the more tactical kind of argument in favor of it emerged fully in the debates over the Anglican service in the sixteenth and seventeenth centuries. Of course, such terms as "clear voice and modulation most suitable" ("*cum liquida voce et convenientissima modulatione*") get constant stipulative and ad hoc redefinition throughout Medieval history, as the forms of musical practice develop and ramify, and as the problem of arguing for or against specific changes demands. These and other terms, such as *harmony, mode, sing, lyre*, are only a few of musical thought's stock of what Hooker himself called "bugs wordes," or words whose reference always seemed shifty and evasive;[10] the questions of theoretical debate would often turn upon different interpretations of words like them. Whatever St. Augustine might have meant by clarity of voice, the phrase could be called upon to attack anything newfangled, whether the addition of too many additional parts in the fourteenth century, the florid polyphony of the late fifteenth century in Flanders, or whatever the musical conservative (often to be identified with the musical illiterate) deemed "unclear" or in any way confusing.

[10] "There are certaine wordes, as Nature, Reason, Will, and such like, which wheresoever you find named, you suspect them presently as bugs wordes, because what they mean you do not indeed as you ought apprehend." MS. Note on *Laws*, I, vii, 6; *ed.cit.*, I, 173-174, n. 2.

The extreme Protestant attacks upon music in the liturgy, of course, had their origins in more general Medieval musical abuse. Toward the end of the fourteenth century, for example, John Wyclif can attack singing for a great variety of reasons. His first objection seems to be against music as distraction: "Also bi song the fend lettith men to studie & preche the gospel; for sith mannys wittis ben of certyn mesure and myght, the more that thei ben occupied aboute siche mannus song the lesse moten thei be sette aboute goddis lawe."[11] Then follow familiar complaints that music "stirith men to pride & iolite & lecherie & othere synnys," that God did not ordain it, that St. Ambrose disapproved for the foregoing reasons, that Augustine was appalled by his own tendency to delight in it too much, etc. Only after these objections does Wyclif maintain that "matynys & masse & even song, placebo & dirige" were evil, having to be "songen with heighe criynge to lette men fro the sentence & vderstondynge" of the texts, and, he cannot refrain from adding, "to maken men wery & vndisposid to studie goddis lawe for akyng of hedis."[12] After this, he goes on to suggest that "deschaunt, countre note & orgon & smale brekynge" "stirith veyn men to daunsynge more than to mornynge," that such fourteenth-century musical devices as embellished descant, contrapuntal practices in general, the old *organum*, or parallel singing of a plainsong melody in octaves, fourths and fifths (or possibly, in Wyclif's day, in the *fauxbourdon* style of parallel chords of the first inversion) were in themselves practices of worldly music, rather than of truly spiritual activity. Similar to this is the objection to large choirs, in which he claims that out of forty or fifty singers, two or three will sing, and the rest will merely look on, thus allowing strumpets and thieves to justify their own idle ways by appeal to the behavior of choristers.[13] Wyclif is contemptuous of all *musica speculativa*, and for the

---

[11] John Wyclif, "Of Feigned Contemplative Life," in *English Works*, ed. F. D. Matthew (London, 1880), p. 191. "*Lettith*": "prevents."

[12] *Ibid.*, p. 191.   [13] *Ibid.*, p. 192.

doctrines of *harmonia mundi* he provides this retort for his followers: "& yif thei seyn that angelis heryen god bi song in heuene; seie that we kunnen not that song"; in this, as well as in his argument that elaborate music obscures the "sentence" of a text, he anticipates the sixteenth-century position. Wyclif sadly concedes that "oure fleschly peple hath more lykynge in here bodely eris in sich knackynge and taterynge than in herynge of goddis lawe,"[14] but by and large, his arguments have been directed specifically against the clergy who, particularly in large cathedrals and abbeys, promulgate and encourage such activity.

Cartwright, writing from a very different position and in very different circumstances in 1573, has little of Wyclif's almost naïve exuberance. He is prone to argue less in contempt of the material world than in defiance of what he hastens to point out as superstition. In objecting to the antiphonal or responsive singing of psalms "by course and side after side," he insists that "although it be very ancient, yet it is not commendable." Too many of its supporters make "the world believe that this came from heaven, and that the Angels were heard to sing after this sort: which as it is a mere fable, so is it confuted by historiographers. . . ."[15]

By far the most vigorous attack on music in church was devoted to instrumental performance, the organ bearing the brunt of the attack. We have seen how, in sixteenth-century attacks on secular music and on music in general, "fiddling" or "piping" served as the model abusive epithet applied to instrumental music, particularly that of professional performers,[16] and how the notion of *piping*, in particular, would dovetail nicely with the dispraise of the *aulos* by the theorists of Antiquity. For the puritan reformers of the liturgy, the organ was as emblematical of the Roman rite as was the "curious singing" condemned in the 1572 *Admonition*.[17] Like

[14] *Ibid.*, p. 192.   [15] Hooker, *op.cit.*, II, 149, n. 1.
[16] See above, Chapter III.
[17] See Percy A. Scholes, *The Puritans and Music* (London, 1934), pp. 229-252, for a consideration of puritan attitudes toward, and activities

the "piping," the organ could provide its detractors with much Medieval authority, through the use of misunderstood dispraise of the *organum* of the tenth through the twelfth centuries, such as Wyclif's remarks quoted above. Hooker's defense of both elaborate vocal polyphony and instrumental accompaniment starts out with general arguments based on Humanist *musica speculativa*, rather than with specific answers to points made by the puritan writers:

"Touching musical harmony whether by instrument or by voice, it being but of high and low in sounds a due proportionable disposition, such notwithstanding is the force thereof, and so pleasing effects it hath in that very part of man which is most divine, that some have been thereby induced to think that the soul itself by nature is or hath in it harmony. A thing which delighteth all ages and beseemeth all states; a thing as seasonable in grief as in joy; as decent being added unto actions of greatest weight and solemnity, as being used when men most sequester themselves from action. . . . In harmony the very image and character even of virtue and vice is perceived, the mind delighted with their resemblances, and brought by having them often iterated into a love of the things themselves . . . there is that draweth to a marvellous grave and sober mediocrity, there is also that carrieth as it were into ecstasies, filling the mind with an heavenly joy and for the time in a manner severing it from the body. So that although we lay altogether aside the consideration of ditty or matter, the very harmony of sounds being framed in due sort and carried from the ear to the spiritual faculties of our souls, is by a native puissance and efficacy greatly available to bring to a perfect temper whatsoever is there troubled . . . forcible to draw forth tears of devotion if the

---

against, organs. Also see Gretchen L. Finney, " 'Organical Musick' and Ecstasy," *Journal of the History of Ideas*, VIII (1947), pp. 273-292 for a detailed consideration of the questions dealt with in the first part of this chapter.

mind be such as can yield them, able both to move and to moderate all affections."[18]

Here, *harmonia* in the abstract sense becomes synonymous with "musical sounds" in the second part of the argument, and the effects of pure sound are held to result from some unexamined "native puissance and efficacy." After this general introduction, Hooker turns to the authority of the "Prophet David" for "adding unto poetry melody in public prayer, melody both vocal and instrumental, for the raising up of men's hearts, and the sweetening of their affections towards God."[19] We must remember that, in the sixteenth century, "*sweet*" means "*well-tuned*," and that Hooker implies very specifically here that the singing of prayers will "tune" or "temper" the affections or feelings of the singers. To this point we shall have to return later. Suffice it to say here that Hooker's conclusions, while condemning "curiosity and ostentation of art, wanton or light or unsuitable harmony, such as only pleaseth the ear. . . ," nevertheless demand that "they which . . . require the abrogation of instrumental music, approving nevertheless the use of vocal melody to remain, must shew some reason wherefore the one should be thought a legal ceremony and not the other."[20]

By and large, this remains the Anglican position throughout the seventeenth century. Jeremy Taylor, for example, in his *Ductor Dubitantium* (1650), holds that "The use of psalmody or singing of psalms, because it can stir up the affections, and make religion please more faculties, is very apt for the edification of churches," an argument more purely psychological than Hooker's and less dependent on Humanist theories of harmony. Taylor reviews the case against instrumental music from Aristotle's formulation about the superiority of rational music produced by beings with souls to the sounds produced by inanimate objects,[21] all the way through the specific objec-

[18] Hooker, *op.cit.*, II, 146. (Book V, XXXVIII, 1.)
[19] *Ibid.*, pp. 146-147.   [20] *Ibid.*, p. 147.
[21] Aristotle, *De Anima*, 420^b-421^a.

tions of many patristic writers; but he finally concludes that instrumental music cannot be condemned "if it be used as a help to psalmody, yet it must not be called so much as a circumstance of the divine service, for that is all can be said of vocal music."[22]

By the time of the Restoration, with the liturgical practice of sumptuous anthems that was restored to English cathedrals, attitudes toward music in the divine service had permanently crystallized. Even so stout a cudgeller of immorality and profaneness as Jeremy Collier could conclude his essay "Of Musick" with the following practical remarks, as free from debate of points of *musica speculativa* as it is from points of theology:

"One word of *Church-Musick*, and I have done. The End of Church-Musick is to relieve the weariness of long Attention; to make the mind more chearful and composed; and to endear the Offices of Religion. It should therefore imitate the *Perfume* of the *Jewish Tabernacle*, and have as little Composition of common Use as possible. There must be no Voluntary *Maggots*, no Military Tattoos, no Light and Galliardizing *Notes*; nothing that may make the Fancy trifling, or raise an improper Thought. This would be to Prophane the *Service*, and bring the *Play-house* into the Church. Religious Harmony must be Moving, but Noble withal; Grave, Solemn, and Seraphick. Fit for a Martyr to *play*, and an Angel to hear. It should be contrived so as to warm the best Blood within us, and take hold of the finest part of the affections: To transport us with the Beauty of Holiness; to raise us above the Satisfactions of Life, and make us ambitious of the Glories of Heaven. . . ."[23]

Gravity is the notion of greatest importance here, but Collier's gravity is in no way plain, primitive, or simple. This

---

[22] Jeremy Taylor, *Ductor Dubitantium*, Book III, Chapter IV, Rule 20. In *Works*, ed. Alexander Taylor (London, 1852), X, 411-412.

[23] Jeremy Collier, "Of Musick," in *Essays Upon Several Moral Subjects*, second edition (London, 1697), II, 25. Cf., however, Owen Felltham's "Of Music" in his *Resolves* (fourth ed., 1631), where liturgical music gets a mere half-sentence of notice.

kind of "gravity" harks back to the peculiar use of the word "Doric" by Giles Farnaby in the title of a collection of Psalm settings, ca. 1630, dedicated to Henry King before the latter became Bishop of Chichester: *"The Psalmes of David, to fower / parts, for Viols and voyce, / The first booke Doricke Mottoes, / The second, Divine Canzonets, / Composed by Giles Farnaby Bachilar / of Musicke / with a prelud, before the Psalmes, Cromaticke."*[24] The literary transmission of gravity as the dominant *ethos* of the Dorian *harmonia* resulted, as we have already seen, in the adoption of the name of the "Dorian mode" by poets and even by painters in the seventeenth century in an abstract, esthetic way.[25] It has been suggested[26] that the "mottoes" and "canzonets" of Farnaby's two books differed in that *a cappella* vocal lines and instrumental parts were separated in the two sections, the sole surviving "cantus" part, with the metrical psalm texts, serving for both sections. But Farnaby makes a point, on his title page, of indicating that it is his instrumental prelude only which will be "curiously" contrived in the ever-more-popular chromatic fantasy style; his psalm settings will be "Doricke" and "Divine," and it is almost as if this sense of gravity had become transferred to a more abstract notion of a serious, pious *style*.

Charles Butler also uses the word to categorize a style, rather than merely a tonal texture, a tonality, a rhythmic scheme, or whatever else "mode" has been applied to in a technical sense in post-Classical Western music. "The Dorik

[24] This book, which exists only in the form of one single part-book in the University of Pennsylvania Library, is discussed by M. C. Boyd, *op.cit.* (note 3 above), pp. 59-61.

[25] Cf. Milton, *Areopagitica*: "If we think to regulate printing, thereby to rectify manners, we must regulate all recreations and pastimes, all that is delightful to man. No music must be heard, no song be set or sung, but what is grave and Doric." Text from John Milton, *Complete Poems and Major Prose*, ed. Merritt Y. Hughes (New York, 1957), p. 732. Also see the discussion of modality, above, Chapter IV.

[26] See Boyd, *op.cit.*, p. 60. On the other hand, the other parts may have been identical, the phrase "Doricke mottoes" testifying to Farnaby's modish fascination with the paraphernalia of emblem literature.

Mood consisteth of sober Notes, generally in Counter-point, set to a Psalm or other pious Canticle, in Meeter or Rhythmical vers," he remarks in *The Principles of Musik*.[27] We can see how, during the following decades, the notion of a separate genus of "solemn" or properly ecclesiastical music, "Moving, but Noble withal; Grave, Solemn, and Seraphick" might begin to crystallize out of the earlier uniform solution of sacred and secular "practical" music.[28]

The early puritan position on liturgical singing, combined with the history of the eventual closing of the theaters and of the cessation of masques with the expatriation of the Court, served to generate the belief, put down so efficiently by Percy A. Scholes in *The Puritans and Music*, that all musical activity ceased under the Commonwealth. The near-ironic fact of the matter is that the gravity and proper solemnity of "serious" secular vocal and instrumental music was seldom called into question.[29] The devil was incited, if at all, through the corruption of the liturgy, it seems, rather than through the lasciviousness of any secular "piping" as innocent and contemplative as a fantasy for three viols. But the devil could also be invoked by the opposition. Thus Richard Allison, in his preface to

[27] Charles Butler, *op.cit.*, p. 1.

[28] Although Medieval writers would often contrast "lewd fiddling minstrels" with the music of the spheres, the distinction there drawn was primarily between the common-active as opposed to the learned-contemplative models of music. The distinction under discussion here eventually becomes trivialized into one between the serious and the frivolous, perhaps paralleling the change in meaning of "solemn." An example of an intermediate position from the early eighteenth century might be seen in the words of "Mr. H. Wanley," writing "Of the Age of MSS. Authors, Painters, Musicians, etc." in *The Philosophical Transactions (From the year 1700 to the year 1720) Abridg'd and Dispos'd under General Heads* (London, 1749), v, ii, 9: "A young man may make a better *Minuet* or *Jigg*; but the elder a more sound Service or *Anthem*. The Music of the former (with other accomplishments) may go a great way towards enticing a foolish girl to love; but that of the latter excites the Devotion, moves the Affections, and raises the Passions of those truly religious Souls, who take pleasure in singing Praises to the Honour and Glory of His Name, who lives for ever and ever . . ." Here the doctrine of the affections is reserved for the solemn music, although it should give an adequate account of both sorts of use and effect.

[29] See Scholes, *op.cit.*, pp. 160-194.

An Howres Recreation in Musicke (1606), cites Martin Luther: "Musicke, saith he, to Divels we know is hateful and intollerable. . .";[30] or by the author of the anonymous ballad of the year 1603 who declared of the puritans that "They doe abhorre, as devills doe all, / The plesant noise of musique's sounde."[31]

It would be a mistake, of course, to identify hostile attitudes toward ecclesiastical music with Protestantism in general. One has only to think of Luther's love and practice of the art, as well as his contributions to the liturgical musical literature, his hymns and chorales, the arrangement of a German mass, etc. Luther also contributed to speculative music, with a treatise in its praise and a commendatory poem, entitled "*Frau Musika.*" While his liturgical ideal in music was that of congregational singing, he nowhere objects, as do the English puritans, to polyphony, the use of instruments, etc. Rather even was he a professed admirer of such composers as Josquin and Ludwig Senfl; many more vicious attacks on florid polyphony in ecclesiastical uses, on the other hand, may be found issuing from the Council of Trent, despite the association, during the earlier years of Elizabeth's reign, of polyphony with Roman Catholicism.

One case of an extraordinarily violent blast at music in general ties its denunciation of secular music to its primary purpose, the denunciation of the stage. William Prynne's *Histrio-Mastix* (1633), commences with its section labelled "ACTUS 5. SCENA DECIMA" to attack "the third unlawfull Concomitant of Stage-playes," "*effeminate, delicate, lust-provoking Musicke.*"[32] The use of "effeminate" as a term of abuse is of some interest, in that a term which originally was employed only with respect to the character or *ethos* of certain

---

[30] *The English Madrigal School*, ed. E. H. Fellowes (London, 1913-1924), vol. XXXIII, reprints this collection.

[31] *Old English Ballads 1553-1625*, ed. Hyder Rollins (Cambridge, Mass., 1920), p. 146.

[32] William Prynne, *Histrio-Mastix, the Players Scourge, etc.* (1633), p. 273.

modes (the Lydian, for example, relaxed and lascivious),[33] eventually becomes a generic term of musical dispraise. The Duchess of Newcastle reports in her *Memoirs* that her brothers did "very seldom or never dance, or play on musick, saying it was too effeminate for masculine spirits."[34] And as early as 1588, Abraham Fraunce in *The Arcadian Rhetorike* could implicitly apply such a predicate in his distinction between two sorts of figures: "In figures of words which altogether consist in sweete repetitions and dimensions, is chiefly conversant that pleasant and delicate tuning of the voyce, which resembleth the consent and harmonie of some well ordered song. In other figures of affections, the voyce is *more manly*. . . ."[35]

Prynne's attacks concentrate on no one point but address themselves broadside to whatever can conceivably present a target. In general, his method involves the untiring use of syllogisms in which "Stage-playes" are invariably introduced as the middle term, and in his section on music he declares plays to be "inexpedient and unlawfull unto Christians."[36] Prynne quotes heavily (and, translating, adapts considerably) from the Church Fathers, turning any attack, Ancient or Medieval, against any form of music, back on music as a whole. He quotes Clement of Alexandria, for example: "Therefore Chromatickall harmonies are to be left to impudent malapartnesse in wine, to whorish musicke crowned with flowers. . . ."[37] He then turns the second-century writer's qualification of the scales of the chromatic genus (as opposed to the enharmonic and diatonic genera, only the last of which was deemed thoroughly suitable by many writers) into an attack on "chromatickall harmonies," or what any early seven-

---

[33] See Chapter II, above, pp. 37-38.

[34] Margaret, Duchess of Newcastle, *The Life of the First Duke of Newcastle and Other Writings*, ed. Ernest Rhys (Everyman Edition), p. 191. This would have been ca. 1625.

[35] Abraham Fraunce, *The Arcadian Rhetorike* (1588), ed. Ethel Seaton (Oxford, 1950), p. 107 (italics mine).

[36] *Histrio-Mastix*, p. 273.

[37] *Ibid.*, p. 275.

teenth-century reader would take to be the chromatic harmonic texture of much music familiar to him. The translation has simply given the cognate reading, rather than the semantically equivalent one; but we have seen how, all along, *musica speculativa* was transmitted and proliferated by this method. One of Prynne's most famous adaptations is of a long passage from Aelredus, Abbot of Rievaulx in Yorkshire, in his *Speculum Charitatis* "about the yeere 1160," which condemns in lurid descriptions the evils of polyphonic church music, including specific attacks upon the "artificiall circumvolution" of the singers, and the gestures which they make in singing. In Prynne's version, it is almost as if the elaborate interweavings of independent polyphonic parts are being condemned as lustful movements in their own right, as if the musical lines themselves were being made to sin carnally: "In the meane time the common people standing by, trembling and astonished, admire the sound of the Organs, the noyse of the Cymballs and musicall instruments, the harmony of the pipes and cornets: but yet look upon the gesticulations of the Singers, the meretricious alternations, interchanges and infractions of the voyces, not without dirision and laughter: so that a man may thinke they came, not to an Oratory, or house of prayer, but to a Theater. . . ."[38] Typical of Prynne's strategy in this whole section is his assault upon dancing. After taking great pains to show how, in dancing, men break each of the Ten Commandments, he proceeds to switch the argument to a figurative level: "To the second Objection, that *Salomon* saith, *there is a time to dance.* I answer first, that by dancing in this and the other *objected Scriptures* is not meant any corporall dancing . . . *but either an inward cheerefulnesse of heart, and readiness of spirit in Gods service, or else a spirituall exultation of the soule in the apprehension of some speciall favour of God unto it, expressed in an abundant praysing of God in psalmes, in hymnes and spiritual songs.* This

[38] *Ibid.,* pp. 279-280.

and no other is the dancing intended by Salomon."³⁹ But he is capable, on the page immediately following, of applying the same scriptural passage literally: "Therefore those who spend their working, praying, reading, studying time (*which God commandes them to redeeme*) in dancing (which too many make their work, their life, their trade) dance out of *Salomon's time and measure*, who gives no allowance to their untimely rounds."⁴⁰

Prynne has much of the general pall of other-worldliness that characterizes his Medieval sources and authorities, and in calling his position on music a "puritan" one, we might be engendering a grave confusion of the kind dispelled by Dr. Scholes. It almost seems necessary to distinguish two senses of the word "puritan" here, a strict and a general one, and while Prynne surely belongs to the faction of the first kind of "puritan," as far as his musical ideology is concerned, he writes like a member of the group of the merely other-worldly. A sense of neatness about the dialectic of history might make us want to say that with the decline of the Humanist *musica speculativa* of the sixteenth century, and the subsequent history of Baroque musical practice, it was only religious music that could qualify for the high-flown *encomia* that had previously accrued to all music.

But despite cases like that of Prynne, it has been observed that the "puritan" (in the strict sense) legislation against music during the Commonwealth was directed against ecclesiastical rather than against civil uses. Charles Butler himself put as the first and chief use of music the service of God, and added that "The second and civil use is for the solace of men. The which as it is agreeable unto Nature; so is it beloved by God, as a temporal blessing, to his people."⁴¹ By "agreeable unto Nature" Butler means no more than that musical phenomena will admit of physical accounts, and in this he represents his century rather than the preceding one. Among the

³⁹ *Ibid.*, p. 254.   ⁴⁰ *Ibid.*, p. 255.
⁴¹ Butler, *op.cit.*, p. 119.

benefits of civil music he lists comfort and solace, the virtues of working together, health of body (and here he depends upon older notions that vocal music exceeds by far, in all beneficial respects, the music of instruments), the enhancement of feasting and of sadness, recreation from work, and to "increase and express the extraordinary joy and gladness" conceived by an "extraordinary prosperous event."[42] All of these benefits are represented as being of the highest sobriety, and Butler's civil music takes on much the same aspect of responsible seriousness, even in its role as an agitator of spirits in proper circumstances, that we find implicit in the official puritan attitude toward secular music.

The musical history of the seventeenth century in England is accompanied by the gradual decline, in its first fifty years, in the use of traditional *musica speculativa* to praise, defend, expound, or account for the phenomena of musical practice. We have seen in the previous chapter how the whole notion of *effect* comes to be wrenched away, in the seventeenth-century version of the doctrine of the affections, from its role in the larger, all-embracing treatment of music's place in the cosmos. Other cracks in the speculative monolith of Renaissance musical thought appear in the growing sets of distinctions separating acoustic from harmonic theory, for example, or dividing instrumental instruction from all of these. Actual treatises start to occupy one of these domains of knowledge, and one only. Charles Butler's general remarks on music, as well as some specific ones on the subject of modality and musical occasion, were widely pilfered by John Playford in his *Introduction to the Skill of Music* (1687), which went through many editions in the late seventeenth and early eighteenth centuries and represents a kind of norm of what popular speculative music there was during that period. Yet Butler himself had grown up and received his own musical and philosophical education in the world of Zarlino and Morley, rather than in that of Descartes, or even of Mersenne. Promul-

[42] *Ibid.*, p. 125. Also see pp. 122-128, *passim*.

gators and expounders of, not to say convinced believers in, the older theories became increasingly rarer throughout the century, and were usually to be found maintaining positions on music to which their general world views had led them.

Now, by and large, the extremely practical, not to say pragmatic, received puritan position on church music led to no such retention of the older cosmological theorizing about music in general. Cartwright's eschewing of the Christianized version of the sphere-music is representative of a more far-reaching attitude on the part of later writers; and, conversely, it is among some of the intransigent orthodox, as well as among holders of more grotesque Neoplatonist positions like the Rosicrucian Robert Fludd,[43] that we find the notions of cosmic harmony retained in discussions of practical music. In general, we will also find that the survival of these notions is closely tied up with religious ones, and that in poetry in particular the use of the materials of traditional speculative music will either be tied to "solemn" subjects or else undergo the absolute trivialization that is studied in the following chapter.

Sir Thomas Browne, for example, holds the older views of universal harmony; he is led to a consideration of it, in the *Religio Medici*, in a rather typically indirect way. Having put down marriage, and women in general, and sexual intercourse in particular ("it is the foolishest act a wise man commits in all his life"), he hurries to add a personal disclaimer, which leads to more general matters:

"I speak not in prejudice, nor am averse from that sweet Sex, but naturally amorous of all that is beautiful. I can look a whole day with delight upon a handsome Picture, though it be but of an Horse. It is my temper, and I like it the better, to affect all harmony; and sure there is musick even in the

---

[43] See Robert Fludd, *Utriusque Cosmi Maiori scilicet et minori Metaphysica, Physica, atque technica Historia* (1617), *Tractatus* I, *Liber* III, "*De Musica Mundana,*" and part II of *Tractatus* II, "*De Templo Musicae.*" Fludd maintains a distinct separation of speculative and practical music in this study, treating the latter in a separate section devoted to the useful arts (war, painting, etc.).

beauty, and the silent note which Cupid strikes, far sweeter than the sound of an instrument. For there is musick where ever there is a harmony, order or proportion: and thus far we may maintain the music of the Sphears; for those well-ordered motions, and regular paces, though they give no sound unto the ear, yet to the understanding they strike a note most full of harmony; which makes me much distrust the symmetry of those heads which declaim against all Church-Musick. For my self, not only from my obedience, but my particular Genius, I do embrace it: for even that vulgar and Tavern-Musick, which makes one man merry, another mad, strikes in me a deep fit of devotion, and a profound contemplation of the First Composer. There is something in it of Divinity more than the ear discovers: it is an Hieroglyphical and shadowed lesson of the whole World, and creatures of GOD; such a melody to the ear, as the whole World, well-understood, would afford the understanding. In brief, it is a sensible fit of that harmony which intellectually sounds in the ears of GOD. I will not say, with Plato, the soul is an harmony, but harmonical, and hath its nearest sympathy unto Musick: thus some, whose temper of body agrees, and humours the constitution of their souls, are born Poets, though indeed all are naturally inclined unto Rhythme. . . ."[44]

This is typical, in many respects, of the serious treatment of *harmonia mundi* in the middle and later seventeenth century. Browne's platonism insists on actualizing the metaphorical "musick" of "harmony, order or proportion"; he insists that the music of the spheres is "heard" in the understanding rather than through sense; he invokes correspondences between *musica mundana* and *musica humana* (as he does on the page following, remarking that "there is no man's mind of such discordant and jarring a temper, to which a tunable disposition may not strike a harmony");[45] he shifts his ground

[44] Thomas Browne, *Religio Medici* (1642), intr. C. H. Herford (Everyman Edition), pp. 79-81.
[45] *Ibid.*, p. 81.

to turn a joking barb against puritan writers; he takes "Tavern-Musick" for his model of music appealing to the affections, which he nevertheless equates, under the heading of actualized harmony, with even the singing of psalms. And, in his final qualification of Plato, he is doing no more than holding to Plato's original meaning (by "harmonical" he means what was originally meant by a *harmonia* in both Plato's and Aristotle's texts), and analyzing away the mistaken notion that by "a harmony" had been meant a chord.

For a platonist like Browne, then, who could insist that "that harmony, which intellectually sounds in the ears of GOD" was no metaphor, a belief in the doctrines of world-harmony was possible, and reference to many of the notions of Renaissance *musica speculativa* could be put down to no mere antiquarianism, or quaintness, or, as was very frequently the case, to the use of a purely literary convention, empty of all commitment or belief. In a passage like the one just quoted, there is less of an actual metaphorical intention, less of a desire to make music *stand for* order, than there is of an insistence upon the reality of the traditional dualism.

There seems to be more of an actual use of metaphor, for example, in a passage like the following from a sermon of Donne: "The correspondence and relation of all parts of Nature to one Author, the concinnity and dependence of every piece and joynt of this frame of the world, the admirable order, the immutable succession, the lively and certain generation and birth of effects from their Parents, the causes: in all these, though there is no sound, no voice, yet we may even see that it is an excellent song, an admirable piece of musick and harmony; and that God does (as it were) play upon this Organ in his administration and providence by naturall means and instruments. . . ."[46] Here there is an overall musical conceit, in which all of the phenomena of order and organic structure that are, at the beginning, attributed to the cosmos

[46] John Donne, *Sermons*, ed. George R. Potter and Evelyn M. Simpson (Berkeley, 1953-   ), I, 289-290.

are seen simultaneously as the properties of a piece of vocal polyphony. We might even suspect a pun, at the end, on "means," to parallel the one on "instruments"; "Organ" certainly has the additional, more general senses, not only of "instrument of any kind," but also of "organism."[47] But the strength of "(as it were)" is clear, I think, and the musical metaphors serve the purposes of homiletic elaboration here, rather than of an ontological qualification.

Musical thought like that expressed in the passage from Browne also flourishes wherever theories of music's power that depend on the modish affective interpretations are in disfavor. The view that music agitates the affections through the senses, depending as it does on the notion that knowledge in general arises "through the force of the thing known," was a false one for those who held with Ralph Cudworth that knowledge "is an inward and active energy of the mind itself, and the display of its own innate vigor from within, whereby it doth conquer, κρατεῖν, master and command its objects, and so begets a clear, serene, victorious, and satisfactory sense within itself."[48] Indeed, the whole notion of affective, rhetorical music as the ravisher of the passive soul must refer only to the most trivial sequences of sounds, rather than to what it had always been claimed that music was, for the Cambridge Platonists who regarded that "sense within itself," in Ernst Cassirer's words, "as an action, not as a passion, as a principle of spontaneity, not of receptivity."[49] To this extent, there is a current of English thought which ignores the modes of Baroque esthetics, cleaving more to views which accounted for music's effects in terms of correspondences between man and the macrocosm, and in terms of the metaphysical reso-

[47] See Leo Spitzer, "Classical and Christian Ideas of World Harmony," Part I, *Traditio*, II (1944), pp. 442-445. Also, Gretchen L. Finney, "A World of Instruments," *ELH*, xx (1953), pp. 105-116.

[48] Ralph Cudworth, *Treatise Concerning Eternal and Immutable Morality*, III, i, 1, in *The Intellectual System of the Universe*, ed. Thomas Birch (Andover, 1837), II, 401.

[49] Ernst Cassirer, *The Platonic Renaissance in England*, tr. James P. Pettegrove (Austin, 1953), p. 63.

nances between the active, sensation-producing soul and the motions generated by acoustical events in the small world, or the ordered dancing of the bodies of the large one.

The Tuning of the Soul

One theme, in particular, that is borne along by this current rather significantly engages several of the problems with which we have been dealing. We have so far treated the notion of "solemn music" as the musical setting of public prayer, and we have seen that the attitudes toward this kind of music are conditioned by overall positions in the ecclesiastical controversies of the late sixteenth and early seventeenth centuries. But there remains the widespread metaphorical equation of music with private meditation and personal prayer with which so much poetry of the middle decades of the seventeenth century in England is concerned. It is this theme which is treated by puritan and Anglican poets alike, and it remains the portion of Humanist musical doctrine that is last to be dislocated from active belief. In addition, certain particular ethical interpretations of this theme lend themselves admirably to the world views of those, like the Cambridge Platonists, who felt that the newer notions of the passivity of the soul could account for neither the fact of knowledge nor the possibility of profound utterance.

To trace the history, briefly, of this theme since Antiquity is to start with one of the basic propositions of *musica humana*, the assertion of Plato, commented upon by Sir Thomas Browne in the passage quoted above, that the soul is a harmony. Actually, while there is in *The Republic* the famous treatment of the soul as a *harmonia*, or proportioning of reason, spirit, and sensual appetite,[50] and in the *Timaeus*[51] the elaborate account of the generation of the soul of the world given in terms of the Pythagorean generation of the consonant

[50] *Republic*, IV, 442-444.
[51] *Timaeus*, 35^b-36^b. Also see Francis M. Cornford, *Plato's Cosmology* (New York, 1952), pp. 66-74, for an elaborate commentary on this passage.

intervals, there remains Socrates' lengthy and detailed refutation, in the *Phaedo*, of the assertion that the body stands to the soul as does the lyre to the harmony played upon it, and, in short, that the soul is itself a "harmony."[52] But we have already seen that the musical and more abstractly conceptual uses of the word "harmonia" are shifted back and forth even among Classical writers with considerable fluidity. What is most interesting for us here will be the way in which the specifically (and, in a historical sense, parochially) musical interpretation of "harmony" as *vertical cluster* or polyphonic constellation could provide metaphorical materials for certain seventeenth-century poets. Hand in hand with this goes the whole notion of what I shall call psychic tonus, the specifically musical reinterpretation, in a rather different way, of the doctrine of the harmony of the soul. For in this case, the "harmony" is taken to be more of what Ancient writers might have meant by it, a scale or tuning; but since this balance or proportion between the disparate elements of the soul is treated in the ethical notion of *temperance*, corresponding to the musical notion of being *tuned* or *tempered*, the overlapping and figurative reflection of these ethical and musical concepts by each other can be well understood. Leo Spitzer, in displaying the wealth of semantic history that he uncovers in the process of trying to account for the various senses of the German word "*Stimmung*,"[53] devotes several fascinating pages to what he calls the "semantic fields" of "*Stimmung*," the French "*accord*" and the English "temper"; in all of them, he finds operating the concepts both of a musical tuning and of an emotional or spiritual adjustment. We have already considered a similar situation prevailing in the association of "mode" and "mood," in our discussion of music and the affections in the previous chapter. But the particularly religious implications of the aspect of musical ethics revealed by the

[52] *Phaedo*, 86-94.
[53] See Part II of "Classical and Christian Ideas of World Harmony," *Traditio*, III (1945), pp. 307-364, especially 309-330.

notion of *temperament* are of interest here in that they tend to engage the notions of prayer, meditation, and personal, immediate communion with God.

We have already examined some of the figurative uses of the stringed instrument during the Renaissance,[54] but the various notions of the soul as an instrument, or the body as the instrument upon which the soul plays, or the soul as the melody or chordal effusion of the body's strings, have not previously come up in a specifically devotional context. Many writers after Plato employ the figure of the self as instrument in one or more of these ways. Plotinus, for example, can use it as follows: ". . . In the case of a material frame ill organized, it may check all such action (of the Soul) upon the material frame as demands a certain collaboration in the part acted upon: thus a lyre may be so ill-strung as to be incapable of the melodic exactitude necessary to musical effect."[55] Plotinus himself, like many other later writers, uses the phenomenon of sympathetic vibration to explain the efficacy of prayer in particular: "The prayer is answered by the mere fact that part and other part are wrought to one tone like a musical string which, plucked at one end, vibrates at the other also. Often, too, the sounding of one string awakens what might pass for a perception in another, the result of their being in harmony and tuned to one musical scale; now, if the vibration of a lyre affects another by virtue of the sympathy existing between them, then certainly in the All— even though it is constituted in contraries—there must be one melodic system; for it contains its unisons as well, and its entire content, even to those contraries, is a kinship."[56]

The image of the self as stringed instrument is put to slightly different use, in the same general circumstances, by

---

[54] See above, Chapters II and III. Also see Nan Cooke Carpenter, *Rabelais and Music* (Chapel Hill, 1954), pp. 1-21 for other examples.

[55] Plotinus, *Enneads*, tr. Stephen MacKenna, revised by B. S. Page (London, 1956), p. 100.

[56] *Ibid.*, IV, 4, 41, pp. 323-324. Also see Julius Portnoy, *The Philosopher and Music* (New York, 1954), pp. 42-44.

Philo: "Service pleasing to God and to virtue is like an intense and severe harmony (*entonon kai sphodran harmonian*) and in no soul is there an instrument (*organon*) capable of sustaining it, without such frequent relaxation and unstringing of the chords [should be "strings"] that it descends from the higher forms of art to the lower."[57] Here we may also see the ethico-musical ideas of *tension* and *relaxation* at work, by means of which certain psychic states were metaphorically connected with certain musical scales, originally called "tense" or "lax" by reason of their pitch,[58] and, by extension, of the tension of the strings of the kithara. The wish to be well-tuned, to have the tension of one's psychic strings, as it were, tightened up to the proper devotional pitch, thus utilizes much more linguistic convention than can be ascribed merely to the traditional metaphor of soul as instrument: it is in the history of the concepts of tonus and temperament that the actual tightening of the string is involved. In the treatise *Quod Deus Immutabilis Sit*, ¶24, Philo makes an even more elaborately extended use of this notion: "Wonderful indeed is the soul of the Sage, how he sets it, like a lyre, to a harmony (*mousikos*) not with a scale of notes low and high, but with the knowledge of moral opposites, and the practice of such of them as are better; how he does not strain it to excessive heights, nor yet relax it and weaken the concord of virtues and things naturally beautiful, but keeps it ever at an equal tension, . . . Such a soul is the most perfect instrument fashioned by nature, the pattern of those which are the work of our hands. And if it be well adjusted, it will produce a symphony the most beautiful in the world, one which has its consummation not in the cadences and tones of melodious sound, but in the consistencies of our life's actions."[59]

---

[57] Philo, *De Sacrificiis Abelis et Caini*, ¶ 37, tr. F. H. Colson and G. H. Whitaker (Loeb Edition), II, 122-123.

[58] Or more particularly, of the pitch of the dynamic *mese* of each. See Curt Sachs, *The Rise of Music in the Ancient World* (New York, 1943), pp. 248-252.

[59] Philo, *ed.cit.*, III, 22-23.

Later on, among the patristic writers, we find that the soul-instrument comparison is often treated slightly differently. Thus St. John Chrysostom on prayer, and on psalmody in particular, urges:

"Even though the meaning of the words be unknown to you, teach your mouth to utter them meanwhile. For the tongue is made holy by the words when they are uttered with a ready and eager mind. . . . Nor will anyone, in such singing, be blamed if he be weakened by old age, or young, or have a harsh voice, or no knowledge at all of numbers. What is here sought for is a sober mind, an awakened intelligence, a contrite heart, sound reason, and clear conscience. If having these you have entered into God's sacred choir, you may stand beside David himself.

"Here there is no need for the cithara, or for stretched strings, or for the plectrum, or for art, or for any instrument; but, if you like, you may yourself become a cithara, mortifying the members of the flesh and making a full harmony of mind and body. For when the flesh no longer lusts against the Spirit, but has submitted to its orders and has been led at length into the best and most admirable path, then you will create a spiritual melody. . . . Here there is no need for place or for season; in all places and at all seasons you may sing with the mind. . . . One may also sing without voice, the mind resounding inwardly. For we sing, not to men, but to God, who can hear our hearts and enter into the silences of our minds."[60]

Here the harmony of the whole being is simplified into one of accord between body and soul. It is the notion of the spiritual music of prayer, of personal devotion (as opposed to the public ceremony requiring due "place or season") that seems, more than the instrumental allegory, to affect later traditions. But perhaps we can find traces of it in the 1580's,

[60] St. John Chrysostom, *Exposition of Psalm XLI*, tr. Oliver Strunk, in *Source Readings in Music History*, ed. Oliver Strunk (New York, 1950), pp. 69-70.

as in Stephen Batman's commentary on Bartholomaeus Anglicus' medieval encyclopedia, *De Proprietatibus Rerum*. Commenting on a verse of the epistle of James (v, 13: "Is any among you afflicted? let him pray. Is any merry? let him sing psalms"), Batman maintains that "Heerby the godly are allowed to sing, whose instruments are their bodyes, and whose stoppes or strings are good intents. Unto the bodyes belong the foure Elements, the foure contemplations, and the five senses, if any of these abound or diminish the concord of the bodyes is altered. Also the minde is turned to discorde no lesse by a crabbed imagination."[61] In this case, however, it is the good intentions that cause the whole body to resound in proper hymning, although Batman adds a couple of sentences to include in his account some of the received doctrine of *musica humana*.

Some uses of the figure, on the other hand, stress not the concord of elements of the soul, or of the whole person, but rather turn immediately to the macrocosmic order and the individual's place in it, a question which is implied in other treatments, but often handled separately. Jacob Boehme speaks of the soul, at one point, as "a tuned instrument of the Harmony of God, a concert piece in God's Kingdom of Joy, which God's Spirit would play."[62] Many other such instances of the instrumental figure and its use in formal or informal pre-Cartesian moral psychology have been noted elsewhere,[63] and it has been the intention of this brief account only to show some of the ways in which the tuning of the soul-instrument was traditionally associated, not merely with a general state of health, propriety, or even grace, but specifically with the proper composition of all the faculties of body and soul so

---

[61] Stephen Batman, *Batman Upon Bartholome* (London, 1582), sig. Ccccviv. Cf. Spitzer, *op.cit.* (Part I), *Traditio* II (1944), p. 445.

[62] Jacob Boehme, *A Book of Regeneration* (1622), in *The Way to Christ*, tr. John Joseph Stoudt (New York, 1947), p. 86.

[63] Spitzer, *op.cit.* (Part I), pp. 440-445. Also see Gretchen L. Finney, *op.cit.*, pp. 90-104; D. P. Walker, "Ficino's Spiritus and Music," *Annales Musicologiques*, I (1953), pp. 131-150, especially p. 132.

that the individual might pray, and commune with the macrocosmic harmony.

The Music of Meditation

It is primarily among the poets of what Louis Martz has called the "meditative tradition"[64] that we find employed the image of the tightening of the soul's strings to express the desire of the devout to have his prayers accepted. That it was so used in connection with all writing about "solemn music" in the seventeenth century is obviously not the case. While the links between the metaphysical religious lyrics of this "meditative" cast and the whole tradition of metrical paraphrase of the psalter has been demonstrated,[65] it should be pointed out that during the Commonwealth, and even before in the case of puritan writers, the metrical psalm set to a "plain" tune comprised all the music of public prayer.

The public, broadly articulate character of general prayer is expressed in the full-blown polyphonic imagery of George Wither's frequently-quoted verses from his pamphlet, *Preparation to the Psalter* (1619):

> From the earth's vast hollow womb
> Music's deepest bass shall come,
> Seas and floods from shore to shore
> Shall the counter-tenor roar.
> To this consort (when we sing)
> Whistling winds your descant bring,
> Which may bear the sound above
> Where the orb of fire doth move,
> And so climb from sphere to sphere,
> Till our song th' Almighty hear.[66]

[64] Louis L. Martz, *The Poetry of Meditation* (New Haven, 1954), pp. 1-22.
[65] *Ibid.*, pp. 273-282.
[66] See Scholes, *op.cit.*, p. 156, from which I quote. Also see M. C. Boyd, *op.cit.*, p. 25.

Here the whole world is seen at worship, and the metaphor of vocal polyphony, of a universal vocal consort is a very different kind than can be seen in a later poem by Wither himself; and although this represents the writing produced at the brink of its author's espousal of the puritan cause, it has definite affinities with the tradition of personal devotion, of the "spiritual melody" of St. John Chrysostom. But Wither also treats of this "inner" music more directly:

FOR A MUSICIAN

Many Musicians *are more out of order than their Instruments: such as are so, may by singing this Ode, become reprovers of their own untuneable affections. They who are better tempered are hereby remembred what Musick is most acceptable to* GOD, *and most profitable to themselves.*

1. What helps it those,
     Whose skill in *Song* hath found;
   Well to compose
     (Of disagreeing notes)
   By artfull choice
     A sweetly pleasing sound;
   To fit their Voice
     And their melodious throats?
   What helps it them,
     That they this cunning know;
   If most condemn
     The way in which they go?

2. What will he gain
     By touching well his *Lute*,
   Who shall disdain
     A grave advise to hear?
   What from the sounds,
     Of Organ, Fife or Lute,

To him redounds,
    Who doth no sin forbear?
A mean respect,
    By tuning strings, he hath,
Who doth neglect
    A *rectified-path*.

3. Therefore, oh LORD,
    So tuned let me be
Unto thy word,
    And thy *ten-stringed-law*,
That in each part,
    I may thereto agree;
And feel my heart
    Inspir'd with loving awe:
He sings and plaies,
    The Songs which best thou lovest,
Who does and sayes,
    The things which thou approvest.

4. Teach me the *skill*,
    Of him. whose Harp asswag'd
Those passions ill,
    Which oft afflicted Saul.
Teach me the strain
    Which calmeth mindes enrag'd;
And which from vain
    Affections doth recall.
So, to the Quire,
    Where *Angels* musicke make,
I may aspire,
    When I this life forsake.[67]

Here, the well-tuned self is arrived at via the musician's
instrument, and some rather conventional material is em-

[67] George Wither, *Hallelujah* (1641), Pt. 3, Hymn xxviii, text from
The Oxford Book of Seventeenth Century Verse, ed. Sir Herbert Grierson
and G. Bullough (Oxford, 1934), pp. 297-298.

ployed. The "disagreeing notes," for example, are merely the old truism about harmony that we know best in the canonical remark of the pre-Socratic Philolaus of Tarentum: "Harmony is a unity of many mixed (*elements*), and an agreement between disagreeing (*elements*)."[68] Similarly, the pun in "A mean respect" engages the strictly musical sense of "mean" as "middle polyphonic part," is it was so punned upon early in the sixteenth century. The third stanza, which also brings in the Decalogue as that to which the individual must be attuned, contains the personal instrument figure, and the fourth one moves on to a consideration of David's skill as harper (and, implicitly, as psalmist), where the harp is not employed as in the preceding conceit. Wither's poem has a rather didactic tone throughout, and only moves toward meditation in the last two strophes; the peculiar meter, resulting from splitting the pentameter line and interlocking, with rhymes, the parts thereof, suggests the kind of rhythmic variation that is to be found among the many different schemes used by writers of seventeenth-century metrical versions of the psalms, Wither himself, of course, included.

Wither's verses seem to belong half to the meditative tradition, and half to a tradition of low-Protestant didacticism that is quite separate from it. We might glance for a moment at the extreme of that line that is represented, nevertheless, by the person-instrument comparison, in such a writer as Bunyan. The latter's views on music were very likely closer to the received seventeenth-century puritan position than they were to Quaker and Evangelical sects' genuinely anti-musical position in the eighteenth century:[69] "Wonderful!" says Christian, in Part II of *The Pilgrim's Progress* about the welcoming music in the Porter's house, "Music in the house, music in the heart, and music also in heaven, for joy that we are here!"[70]

---

[68] Translation from Kathleen Freeman, *Ancilla to the Pre-Socratic Philosophers* (Oxford, 1952), p. 75.

[69] See Scholes, *op.cit.*, pp. 154-156; also, pp. 345-360.

[70] John Bunyan, *The Pilgrim's Progress from This World to That*

John Bunyan, in two emblems in his collection of didactic verses for children, allegorizes the instrumentalist, both good and bad, into the golden-voiced and ineffective preacher, respectively. But number xxix of *A Book for Boys and Girls* moralizes "Upon a Ring of Bells" (a "ring" is a set of bells used in change-ringing, rather than a Continental carillon) by employing the image of the organism as *organon*:

> Bells have wide mouths and tongues, but are too weak,
> Have they not help, to sing, or talk, or speak
> But if you move them they will mak't appear,
> By speaking they'l make all the town to hear.
>   When Ringers handle them with Art and Skill,
> They then the ears of their Observers fill,
> With such brave notes, they ting and tang so well
> As to outstrip all with their ding, dong, Bell.

Comparison

>   These Bells are like the Powers of my soul;
> Their Clappers to the Passions of my mind,
> The Ropes by which my Bells are made to tole,
> Are promises (I by experience find)
>   My body is the steeple, where they hang,
> My Graces they which do ring ev'ry Bell:
> Nor is there anything gives such a tang,
> When by these Ropes these Ringers ring them well.
>   Let not my Bells these Ringers want, nor Ropes;
> Yea let them have room for to swing and sway:
> To toss themselves deny them not their scopes.
> Lord! in my steeple give them room to play.
> If they do tole, ring out, or chime all in,
> They drown the tempting tinckling Voice of Vice:
> Lord! when my Bells have gone, my Soul has bin
> As 't'were a tumbling in this paradice!

Which is to Come (1678), in *Works*, ed. George Offor (London, 1862), III, 198.

Or if these Ringers do the Changes ring,
Upon my Bells, they do such Musick make,
My Soul then (Lord) cannot but bounce and sing,
So greatly her they with their Musick take.
But Boys (my Lusts) into my Belfry go,
And pull these Ropes, but do no Musick make.
They rather turn my Bells by what they do,
Or by disorder make my steeple shake.

  Then, Lord! I pray thee keep my Belfry Key,
Let none but Graces meddle with these Ropes:
And when these naughty Boys come, say them Nay,
From such Ringers of Musick there's no hopes.

  O Lord! If thy poor Child might have his will,
And might his meaning freely to thee tell;
He never of this Musick has his fill,
There's nothing to him like thy ding, dong, Bell.[71]

The rather feeble nursery-rhyme jingle of the beginning, with the real rhythmic lapse in the eighth line, gives way, in the moralization (this is really a kind of emblem with its motto), to something closer to devotional verse. The frequent awkwardnesses, and the "tempting tinckling Voice of Vice" notwithstanding, there is a kind of vigor in these lines which almost triumphs over the insistent homeliness of the comparison: Grace operates on the soul's passions through commitments, but if lusts become entangled in those commitments, then the music of the soul is replaced by the body's unwieldy jangling, shaken by the soul's disordered motions. There is a queer blend of orthodox Christian psychology (it is the jangling of the bells which shakes the body-tower) with Bunyan's own kind of specifically moral allegory (the use of "Promises" as intermediate entities, rather than the "senses" of seventeenth-century psychology). The lines about the hoodlum lusts draw strength from the vividness of the metaphori-

[71] J[ohn] B[unyan], *A Book for Boys and Girls: or Country Rhimes for Children* (London, 1686), pp. 36-37.

cal scene (change-ringing requires the utmost attention to order in working out the permutations, and each ringer has an almost Pythagorean involvement with his role: wild, untrained ringers would produce terrible chaos). But they also owe something to the unfortunate correspondence of the sexual overtones and the specific moral import of the imagery.

Bunyan's allegorized bells, however, really serve to mark out the limits of one side of the conventional meditative instrument figure; they are too crudely, schematically emblematic, in one sense, and the imagery and diction are not in any way "Metaphysical." The poem is too long, for there has been none of the compact and compressed quality that we have come to expect of pre-Augustan poetry.

Another treatment of bells invites comparison here, not because the identification of sounding body and human frame is laid out schematically, but rather because of the way in which it is left implicit. Part 1 of Thomas Traherne's "Bells" begins with a consideration of the soul's response to completely exterior, separate bells, but moves rapidly toward a metaphorical comparison:

I.

Hark! hark, my Soul! the Bells do ring,
    And with a louder voice
Call many Families to sing
His publick Praises, and rejoice:
Their shriller sound doth wound the Air,
Their grosser strokes affect the Ear,
That we might thither all repair
    And more Divine ones hear.
      If Lifeless Earth
      Can make such Mirth,
What then shall Souls abov the starry Sphere!

Bells are but Clay that men refine
    And rais from duller Ore;

Yet now, as if they were divine,
They call whole Cities to adore;
Exalted into steeples they
Disperse their Sound, and from on high
Chime-in our Souls; they ev'ry way
   Speak to us throu the Sky:
     Thy iron Tongues
     Do utter Songs,
And shall our stony Hearts make no Reply!

From darker Mines and earthy Caves
   At last let Souls awake,
And leaving their obscurer Graves
From lifeless Bells example take;
Lifted abov all earthly Cares,
Let them (like these) rais'd up on high,
Forsaking all the baser Wares
   Of dull Mortality
     His Praises sing,
     Tunably ring,
In a less Distance from the peaceful Sky.[72]

The opening stanza of the second part of the poem elaborates
the notion of the refining of the ore and the casting of the bell
as a version of temperament or tuning:

II.

From Clay, and Mire, and Dirt, my Soul,
   From vile and common Ore,
Thou must ascend; taught by the Toll
In what fit place thou mayst adore:
Refin'd by fire, thou shalt a Bell
Of Prais becom, in Mettal pure;
In Purity thou must excell,
   No Soil or Grit endure.

[72] Thomas Traherne, *Poems of Felicity*, in *Poetical Works*, ed. Gladys I.
Wade, third edition (London, 1932), pp. 139-140.

> Refin'd by Lov,
> Thou still *abov*
> Like them must dwell, and other Souls allure. . . .[73]

Amid other scriptural references to refining fires lurks a suggestion of I Corinthians 13:1: "Though I speak with the tongues of men and of angels, and have not charity, I am become as sounding brass, or a tinkling cymbal." The basic comparison between the clay into which the Divine breath infuses life, and the ore, smelted and tempered into a sounding bell, operates ironically against the "sounding brass" of vain prayer; the implicit metaphor (as some would have it, "dead metaphor") of *the tongues of bells* is here revivified. And the final stanza of Part II brings in a reference to harmoniousness and wholeness that is perfectly in keeping with other poets' use of the organic-instrument metaphor:

> Those Bells are of a piece, and sound,
>   Whose wider mouths declare
> Our Duty to us: Being round
> And smooth and whole, no Splinters are
> In them, no Cracks, no holes, nor flaws
> That may let out the Spirits thence
> Too soon; *that* would harsh jarring caus
>   And lose their Influence.
>   We must unite
>   If we Delight
> Would yield or feel, or any Excellence.[74]

The bells that summon all, in the beginning of the poem, to public prayer, at the end of it are brought round to be summoners of unity again, but in a very different sense. The excellent possibilities for metaphorical elaboration of the bell-metal as tempered substance are obvious throughout, as is the wonderful series of uses of "above," ranging from the bells' actual elevation in a belfry, to the relative heights

[73] *Ibid.*, p. 141.   [74] *Ibid.*, p. 142.

of nobility of base metals to baser earth, or ores, and, finally, to the Heaven-earth relationship. And, at the very end, the notion of sin as flaw as perfectly contained in the conceit: it is "sounding true" that is predicated, finally, of both the well-tempered bell and the devout, praying soul. The body-soul relationship is made almost an evolutionary one, in that the soul is seen as being cast from, refined and smelted, tempered and tuned, from a coarser clay.

Traherne is elsewhere able to make use of the more conventional image of the stringed instrument, as in the second strophe of "On Christmas Day":

> Shake off thy Sloth, my drouzy Soul, awake;
>> With Angels sing
>> Unto thy King,
> And pleasant Musick make;
> Thy Lute, thy Harp, or els thy Heart-strings take,
> And with thy Musick let thy Sense awake. . . .[75]

The music is here, as elsewhere, the harmonious utterance of prayer. It is interesting to note that the "Heart-strings" are included in the list of stringed instruments, as if they completed the triad that moved from the secular lute, to the harp of David, to the final and most spiritual instrument of all (the sense of the medieval pun on *cor, cordis* and *chorda*, which would make "heart-strings" redundant, seems to be missing here completely).

Almost the *locus classicus* for the image of the well-tuned string used to introduce a devotional poem is at the beginning of Donne's "Hymne to God my God, in my sicknesse":

---

[75] *Ibid.*, p. 136. Traherne is, elsewhere, capable of meaning by "Musick" merely a pastime or distraction. See "Cards, Musick, Dice, / So much in price"; from "Christendom," ll. 24-28, *ed.cit.*, p. 133; also from *Christian Ethicks*, the following quatrain (*ed.cit.*, p. 226):

> "All Musick, Sawces, Feasts, Delights and Pleasures,
> Games, Dancing, Arts, consist in govern'd Measures;
> Much more do Words, and Passions of the Mind
> In Temperance their sacred Beauty find."

Since I am comming to that Holy roome,
　　Where, with thy Quire of Saints for evermore,
I shall be made thy Musique; As I come
　　I tune the Instrument here at the dore,
　　And what I must doe then, thinke now before.[76]

(ll. 1-5)

Here, as one might expect, the instrumental figure is treated
in a dramatic conceit: Heaven is seen as the choir of a church,
and the poet meditating on his imminent death is the performing instrumental musician, slightly anxious, but calm
because practice has taught him to tune his instrument before
entering, and to rehearse mentally what he expects the music
to be like. That rehearsal, as a matter of fact, is the meditation
on death itself, the remainder of the actual poem. And the
instrument which he tunes is that of his own intelligence, his
rational soul about to be brought to a sufficiently high pitch
as to be able to help fill with the sound the immensity of
the vaulted firmament.

In "The Second Anniversary," Donne employs a very
much more condensed conceit, which operates through puns
and avoids mentioning an actual instrument; but the instrument is implicitly present. The reader is urged to contemplate
"our state in our death-bed":

Thinke thy selfe labouring now with broken breath,
And thinke those broken and soft Notes to bee
Division, and thy happyest Harmonie.[77]

(ll. 90-92)

"Breaking," in seventeenth-century music, is the process of
figuration, of elaboration of the line of a particular melody
with rapid figures and passages; sets of figured variations
improvised on a particular melody were called "divisions."

[76] John Donne, *The Divine Poems*, ed. Helen Gardner (Oxford, 1952),
p. 50. Cf. "The Litanie," ll. 199-202, *ed.cit.*, p. 24.
[77] John Donne, "Of the Progresse of the Soule. The Second Anniversary,"
in *Poems*, ed. Sir Herbert Grierson (Oxford, 1912), I, 253-254.

The broken, strained breathing, even the death-rattle itself is turned, because it announces the blessed state of death, into "Division," sweet music; it is also, in another sense, the division of body from soul, which will allow the latter to compose itself most harmoniously in Heaven. Thus, the "broken and soft Notes" are "thy happyest Harmonie," in both a musical and an abstract sense. The missing term here is the viol upon which divisions were customarily played; it is this viol-self which is actually being addressed. Some seventy lines earlier, Donne climaxes a terribly graphic series of images representing the purely mechanical, reflex activity of a beheaded man. He compares this false animation to ". . . a Lute, which in moist weather, rings / Her knell alone, by cracking of her strings:";[78] but anyone who has ever heard the startling, ghostly (and, for the lutenist, disheartening) snap of breaking lute strings in the next room will take this image as coming more from direct experience than from a literary or speculative convention. Nevertheless, the correspondence of sound with intellectual or spiritual activity holds true: the writhing corpse is no more *living*, or *behaving*, than the briefly twanging lute is *being played*.

Other seventeenth-century uses of the stringed instrument-soul figure in its canonical form are frequent. Thus, "The Invocation" to Francis Quarles' *First Book of Emblemes* (1635):

> Rouse thee, my soul; and drain thee from the dregs
> Of vulgar thoughts: screw up the heighten'd pegs
> Of thy sublime Theorbo four notes high'r,
> And high'r yet, that so the shrill mouth'd quire
> Of swift-wing'd seraphims may come and join,
> And make the consort more than half divine.
> Invoke no muse; let heav'n be thine *Apollo*;
> And let his sacred influences hallow
> Thy high-bred strains. . . .[79]

(ll. 1-9)

---

[78] *Ibid.* (ll. 19-20), I, 251.
[79] Francis Quarles, *Emblems, Divine and Moral; Together with Hiero-*

The conventional lute or viol has become the fashionable, double-necked theorboe, with extra bass strings, that was becoming so common after 1610 in England. The tonus of the soul is raised by tightening its pegs; the "four notes high'r" is puzzling, and if it has anything more than some private numerological significance for Quarles here, only a wild guess may be hazarded. All lutes, up through the late 1640's in England, were tuned to the so-called *viel accord*, or "old tuning," running, in fourths and one interval of a third, from *G* to *g* (and more rarely, from *A* to *a*). "Four notes high'r" would bring the top and bottom strings up to *d* and *d″* respectively, and the open double octave from open bottom string to top would bracket the church tone built on *d*, or, as it was called, the *"Dorian* mode." This, confused with the "Doric" style of Farnaby and Butler mentioned earlier in this chapter, might allow the reading of the phrase to be, "Tune me up to the solemn, devotional pitch; and even beyond that." But this may be too far-fetched; what is important is that the soul is brought to the proper solemn pitch, in order that it may play in the same register with the "shrill mouth'd" heavenly music.

A rather later example is that of a manuscript poem of Clement Paman, "On Christmas Day to my Heart":

> To Day:
> Hark! Heaven sings!
> Stretch, tune my Heart
> (For hearts have strings
> May bear their part)
> And though thy Lute were bruis'd i'th'fall;
> Bruis'd hearts may reach an humble Pastoral.

---

glyphicks of the Life of Man (London, 1736), sig. A5ʳ. Cf. Quarles' epigram "On the Musick of Organs" in his *Divine Fancies* (London, 1641), pp. 1-2; also the song beginning, "A vsless pipe stop have I been" in John P. Cutts, *Seventeenth Century Songs and Lyrics* (Columbia, Mo., 1959), p. 4.

> To Day
> Shepheards rejoyce
> And Angells do
> No more: thy voice
> Can reach that too:
> Bring then at least thy pipe along
> And mingle Consort with the Angells Song. . . .

> To Day
> God honour'd Man
> Not Angells: Yet
> They sing; And can
> Rais'd Man forget?
> Praise is our debt to-day, nor shall
> Angells (Man's not so poor) discharge it all.

> To Day
> Then screwe thee high
> My Heart: Up to
> The Angells key;
> Sing Glory; Do;
> What if thy stringes all crack and flye?
> On such a Ground, Musick 'twill be to dy.[80]

The heart-strings, the lute that was "bruis'd i'th'fall," the play on the various kinds of *height* (of pitch of psychic tonus, of the pitch of the heavenly music, of the height of Heaven) are all conventional; only the final conceit of over-tightening the instrument so as to break the strings (as opposed to the strings of Corinna's lute in Campion's poem, which snap in sympathy with her words of sorrow) seems original. The conceit is completed with a pun on the musical meaning of "ground" (a thoroughbass), and with a shade of sensual

[80] B. M. Add. MS. 18220, printed in *The Oxford Book of Seventeenth Century Verse*, pp. 825-826, with a misprint in l. 7 (*Partoral* for *Pastoral*), which I have corrected after consulting the transcription in *Seventeenth Century Lyrics*, ed. Norman Ault (London, 1928), p. 317. Also see Ault, p. 486, for data on Paman, scanty as it is. Both printed versions give "fl. 1660" as a date.

ecstasy in "dy," which seems to lie almost midway between its literal meaning and the Restoration use of it to mean erotic climax; at any rate, death, figurative or literal, as a result of tightening the pegs of the heart-strings unduly, will be a music (in the sense of a delight). And finally, the "Musick" is the prayer of the poet, the highest possible form of spiritual activity.

Henry Vaughan, in "The Morning-watch" from *Silex Scintillans* (1650), makes the prayer-music equation operate through both the notion of *harmonia mundi* and that of a musical sound rather than merely a linguistic one, as spiritual utterance:

> Birds, beasts, all things
> Adore him in their kinds.
> Thus all is hurl'd
> In sacred *Hymnes*, and *Order*, The great Chime
> And *Symphony* of nature. Prayer is
> The world in tune,
> A spirit-voyce
> And vocall joyes
> Whose *Eccho is* heav'ns blisse.[81]

> (ll. 14-22)

In "Church-Service," Vaughan employs a conceit of the harmony of even the massier elements of the human frame, reminiscent in some ways of the clay and base-metal imagery in Traherne's poem about the bells. But here it is the "grones" of the poet and the answering harmonious echo from above that make a music, and it is the soul's harmonious place in the macrocosm that allows it to be held together at all:

> Blest be the God of Harmony and Love!
> The God above!
> And holy dove!

[81] Henry Vaughan, *Works*, ed. L. C. Martin (Oxford, 1914), II, 424-425.

Whose Interceding, spirituall grones
  Make restless mones
  For dust, and stones,
For dust in every part,
But a hard, stonie heart.

2.

Oh how in this thy Quire of Souls I stand
  (Propt by thy hand)
  A heap of sand!
Which busie thoughts (like winds) would scatter quite
  And put to flight,
  But for thy might;
Thy hand alone doth tame
Those blasts, and knit my frame.

3.

So that both stones and dust, and all of me
  Joyntly agree
  To cry to thee,
And in this Musick by thy Martyrs bloud
  Seal'd, and made good
  Present, O God!
The Eccho of these stones
—My sighes, and grones.[82]

Were it not for God's guiding, binding hand, distraction
would undo the tenuous concord of grains of sand; in the
final strophe, the more extreme image of the blood of martyrs
binding all up into a kind of cement is nevertheless forcibly
joined to the musical one. Here, music stands for a version
of harmony, in the abstract sense, which is more like a
coherence and a binding than an ordering.

[82] *Ibid.*, II, 426-427. Vaughan may have found inspiration for this musical
treatment of the "grones" in Herbert's "The Crosse": ". . . (the memorie /
What I could do for thee, if once my grones / Could be allow'd for harmonie)": (ll. 14-16).

Herbert's Musical Temper

Of all these poets writing in the meditative tradition who employ musical imagery to stand for personal, spiritual utterance, Vaughan's master, George Herbert, makes most prolific use of "singing" for "prayer," or communication with God generally. A passage frequently referred to in Walton's *Life of Mr. George Herbert* (1670) makes plain not only the extent of the musical activity of the rector of Bemerton, both liturgical and secular, but a sense of his moral commitment to it as well:

"His chiefest recreation was Musick, in which heavenly Art he was a most excellent Master, and did himself compose many *divine Hymns* and *Anthems*, which he set and sung to his *Lute* or *Viol*; and, though he was a lover of retiredness, yet his love to *Musick* was such, that he went usually twice every week on certain appointed days, to the *Cathedral Church* in *Salisbury*; and at his return would say, *That his time spent in Prayer, and Cathedral Musick, elevated his Soul, and was his Heaven upon Earth*: But before his return thence to *Bemerton*, he would usually sing and play his part, at an appointed private Musick-meeting; and, to justifie this practice, he would often say, *Religion does not banish mirth, but only moderates, and sets rules to it.*"[83]

If we can believe Walton, Herbert's almost constant use of "sing" for "pray" represents a personal as well as a conventional figure: it is the actual image of the poet-divine playing and singing in secluded retirement that lurks behind so many of the musical conceits in his poetry. Those conceits are many and various; and given the intricate metaphorical texture of Herbert's poetry, with its frequent rapid leaps to new figures, or to varied interpretations of those already used,

[83] Izaak Walton, *Lives*, ed. S. B. Carter (London, 1951), p. 241. Also see Walton's anecdote (*ed.cit.*, p. 243) about a rebuke delivered at one of these music meetings, using in conversational wit musical figures similar to those used in some of the poems.

one would expect to find a fairly wide range of uses of the musical images.

In "The Thanksgiving," for example, the instrument appears implicitly through mention of the strings:

> My musick shall finde thee, and ev'ry string
>   Shall have his attribute to sing;
> That all together may accord in thee,
>   And prove one God, one harmonie.[84]
>
>   (ll. 39-42)

The active, seeking music that "shall finde" God is the fairly standard reference to the ascending music-prayer that we have already encountered. Perhaps the purest example of the image of devotional "tuning" is in a poem appropriately entitled "The Temper (1)":

> Yet take thy way; for sure thy way is best:
>   Stretch or contract me, thy poore debter:
> This is but tuning of my breast,
>   To make the musick better.[85]
>
>   (ll. 21-24)

Here there is an additional pun, it seems, on "contract," by means of which the tuned psychic strings, perhaps even writhing under the pain of tuning (the alternatives are *stretching* or *contraction* in this case, not tightening or relaxation), are obligated, indebted to their tuner.[86] A cementing harmony,

---

[84] George Herbert, *The Temple* (1633), in *Works*, ed. F. E. Hutchinson (Oxford, 1941), p. 36.

[85] *Ibid.*, p. 55.

[86] I don't know whether Rosemond Tuve, in *A Reading of George Herbert* (London, 1952), p. 144, refers to this intricate interlocking of conceits, working through the pun, in her remark that the musical image is here "damaged in tone by the presence of attention-getting novelties." But although here, as elsewhere in her comments on musical imagery in Herbert (pp. 144-148), she refers rightly to a body of Medieval imagery of the soul-stringed instrument or soul-organ type, she seems to think that its seventeenth-century use is confined to Donne and Herbert. She seems also to miss the wealth of associations of the title word "Temper" here (p. 148n.), and to minimize, perhaps, the far-reaching implications of the whole figure (". . . this conceit is not, . . . a universally used and deep-

as in Vaughan's "Church-Service," is employed in Herbert's "Repentance":

> When thou for sinne rebukest man,
> Forthwith he waxeth wo and wan:
> Bitternesse fills our bowels; all our hearts
> Pine and decay,
> And drop away,
> And carrie with them th'other parts.
>
> But thou wilt sinne and grief destroy;
> That so the broken bones may joy,
> And tune together in a well-set song,
> Full of his praises,
> Who dead men raises.
> Fractures well cur'd make us more strong.[87]
>
> (ll. 25-36)

But the binding, fracture-repairing sense may be receiving reinforcement from a pun on "well-set" that would apply to the repair of broken bones. The conclusion of "Deniall," it has often been pointed out, brings together the prayer-music conceit and a marvellously imitative bit of prosodic "music":

> Therefore my soul lay out of sight,
> Untun'd, unstrung:
> My feeble spirit, unable to look right,
> Like a nipt blossome, hung
> Discontented.
>
> O cheer and tune my heartlesse breast,
> Deferre no time;
> That so thy favours granting my request,

---

reaching symbol kindling whole trains of underground meanings . . ."
p. 148). Louis L. Martz, *op.cit.*, pp. 272-273, treats the conceit under discussion as an adaptation of the conventional Elizabethan address to the lute. See also the discussion of Herbert's musical imagery in Joseph H. Summers' excellent *George Herbert* (Cambridge, Mass., 1954), pp. 156-170, to which I am indebted throughout this section.

[87] Herbert, *Works*, p. 49.

> They and my minde may chime,
> And mend my ryme.[88]

(ll. 21-30)

Throughout the poem's first five strophes, the ultimate line did not rhyme (as "Discontented," above); not only does the rhyme of the last line finally correspond to the harmonious music of the tuned soul, but the rhyme is on the words "chime" and "ryme," and the whole last line is made to echo the last two feet of the penultimate one ("my minde may chime," / "And mend my ryme."). The blatant self-reference here is very much like the high-Renaissance practice of *tone-painting* in polyphonic music, in which a particular word of the text would be set to what was felt to be a peculiarly appropriate chord, augmented, dissonant, etc.; or even more, like the startling enjambment in Ben Jonson's ode "To the Immortal Memorie, and Friendship of that Noble Paire, Sir Lucius Cary and Sir H. Morison": "To separate those twi- / Lights, the *Dioscuri*," where the *separating* is done by the words that name it.

Herbert seems to take the music-prayer figure so much for granted that he can even reverse its normal direction. In "The Quip," the clinking of money is ironically twisted into a prayer to Mammon:

> Then Money came, and chinking still,
> What tune is this, poore man? said he:
> I heard in Musick you had skill.
> *But thou shalt answer, Lord, for me.*[89]

(ll. 9-12)

In "*Ephes. 4. 30. Grieve not the Holy Spirit, &c.*," the soul is addressed, again in the stringed instrument image:

> Oh take thy lute, and tune it to a strain,
> Which may with thee
> All day complain.

---

[88] *Ibid.*, p. 80. Also see Hutchinson's note, p. 504.
[89] *Ibid.*, p. 110.

There can no discord but in ceasing be.
　　　Marbles can weep; and surely strings
　　　More bowels have, then such hard things.[90]
　　　　　　　　　　　　　　　　　　(ll. 19-24)

Here, the gut lute-strings are seen as having "more bowels"
than the proverbially hard marble, which can nonetheless
betray feeling through its secretly porous surface. In "Dooms-
day," after mentioning the response of the dead to the final
call ("Dust, alas, no musick feels, / But thy trumpet: then
it kneels,"), the last stanza calls

　　　　　　　Come away,
　　　　　　　Help our decay.
　　　　Man is out of order hurl'd,
　　　　Parcel'd out to all the world.
　　　　Lord, thy broken consort raise,
　　　　And the musick shall be praise.[91]
　　　　　　　　　　　　　　　　(ll. 25-30)

"Broken consort" as a musical term means a mixed group of
winds, plucked and bowed strings, etc., as opposed to the
normal "whole consort" of viols, or possibly, recorders. The
mixture of the final trumpet and the scattered voices of the
awakened dead would make this term applicable in its purely
musical sense, aside from the immediacy of the other meanings
in the poem.

Perhaps the most elaborate treatment of the whole musical
figure in all of Herbert, however, is in "Easter":

　　Awake, my lute, and struggle for thy part
　　　　　　　　　With all thy art.
　　The crosse taught all wood to resound his name,
　　　　　　　　　Who bore the same.
　　His stretched sinews taught all strings, what key
　　Is best to celebrate this most high day.

[90] *Ibid.*, p. 136.　　　　　[91] *Ibid.*, p. 187.

> Consort both heart and lute, and twist a song
>   Pleasant and long:
> Or, since all musick is but three parts vied
>   And multiplied,
> Oh let thy blessed Spirit bear a part,
> And make up our defects with his sweet art.[92]
>
>   (ll. 7-18)

Here, the lute is not figured forth as the soul, or heart, at all; rather it remains only the praising poet's voice, finally connected emblematically to the crucified Christ, with sinewy strings stretched tightly over a wooden frame as the dominant visual image. The proper key for celebration of "this most high day" is, of course, the highest, most painfully (as Herbert's pun suggests) *taut* one. Only in the last stanza are the lute, and the heart which was urged to rise at the beginning of the poem, brought together in a united polyphonic piece, whose triads will be completed by the addition of the "blessed Spirit" of God. In separating the lute and the heart, the organ of skilled utterance and the instrument of feeling, respectively, Herbert is drawing on some of the same considerations of *sincerity* that are promulgated in the two "Jordan" poems, even though the lute is here overtly treated as a religious "muse." Their unification in literal harmony with the Holy Spirit represents the solution of what might otherwise be separate esthetic and devotional problems; "Easter" is certainly as much *about* devotional poetry as it represents an example of it.

Further musical conceits in Herbert are too numerous to quote profitably at this point[93]; suffice it to say that, as in the

[92] *Ibid.*, pp. 41-42. Miss Tuve, *op.cit.*, p. 145, points out the relevance of the proper Easter hymn, Psalm 57 here, as well as the connection of the heart, the strings, and Christ.

[93] See also "Employment I," p. 57; "Church-musick," p. 65; "Christmas II," p. 81; "Mortification," p. 98; "Sion," p. 107; "Providence," pp. 117-118; "The Storm," p. 132; "Grief," p. 164; and "Aaron," p. 174, for example. Herbert's use of "sing" in general seems not unmediated by

cases treated above, the musical conceit is seldom unconnected with some other, more central and governing one in each poem. It is as if the image of music were always running along beneath the surface of all of Herbert's poems, breaking out here and there like the eruption of some underground stream, but exercising always an informing, nourishing function. And as a surrogate for "spiritual utterance" in general, music is the substance, and often the subject, of the poems themselves.

Doctrine Expounded: Strode and Norris

It is primarily to the problems of personal devotion, then, to the use of music as a figure for the harmony of *musica humana*, that many seventeenth-century poets put some of the inherited traditions of speculative music. It will be noticed that it is primarily a Metaphysical diction and metaphorical texture, with its ability to wrench conventional figures into new roles, that animates the poems we have been examining. The movement of English poetry, in the later part of the century, toward the full-blown Augustan diction of the Age of Dryden, did little to nourish the traditional use of such musical images. As far as the serious use of *musica speculativa* is concerned, the devotional tradition exhausts most of the cases; the versification of doctrine, or of contemporary specu-

---

metrical psalms, particularly Sidney's versions, such as "Psalm XXXIII," ll. 7-12:

> O praise with hart the Lord,
> O now accord
> Vialls with singing voice:
> Lett tenne stringed instrument
> O now be bent
> To wittnes you rejoice.

Or, "Psalm XLII," ll. 25-30:

> Then loe, then I will
> With sweete musicks skill
> Gratfull meaning show thee:
> The God, yea my God,
> I will sing abroad
> What greate thancks I ow thee.

lation, becomes a sorrier business as the century progresses. William Strode's "In Commendation of Musick," for example, is not really a traditional sixteenth-century *encomium musicae* so much as a gracefully turned piece of wit on the same theme of the harmonic composition of the soul upon which the meditative poets all based their musical conceits:

> When whispering straynes do softly steale
> With creeping passion through the hart,
> And when at every touch wee feele
> Our pulses beate and beare a part;
>> When threads can make
>> A hartstring shake
>> Philosophie
>> Can scarce deny
> The soule consists of harmony.
>
> When unto heavenly joy wee feyne
> Whatere the soule affecteth most,
> Which onely thus wee can explayne
> By musick of the winged hoast,
>> Whose layes wee think
>> Make starres to winke,
>> Philosophie
>> Can scarce deny
> Our soules consist of harmony.
>
> O loll mee, lull mee, charming ayre,
> My senses rock with wonder sweete;
> Like snow on wooll thy fallings are,
> Soft, like a spiritts, are thy feete:
>> Griefe who need feare
>> That hath an eare?
>> Down lett him lye
>> And slumbering dye,
> And change his soule for harmony.[94]

[94] William Strode, *Poetical Works*, ed. Bertram Dobell (London, 1907), pp. 2-3.

This poem, which appeared in a miscellany of 1658 (its author having died in 1645), was being written, of course, at a time when philosophy was making just such a denial.

There were some philosophers (we have already mentioned the Cambridge Platonists in this regard) who were not doing so, however; a follower of that group, himself a poet, demonstrates for us his professional philosophical competence in his exposition of the anti-Cartesian musical theory which might be said to represent that of the Cambridge group. John Norris (1657-1711) lived a full generation later than Cudworth and More; he was one of Herbert's successors as rector of Bemerton. In "A Letter Concerning Love and Musick" he discusses the question "Whether Musick be a Sensual or Intellectual Pleasure"; having distinguished between these with respect to the mediating role of the body, Norris proceeds as follows:

"7. Now according to this Measure it seems most reasonable to define the Pleasure of Musick to be properly Intellectual. For tho' Sound singly and absolutely consider'd (which is the material part of Musick) be a Sensation, that is, a Sentiment in the Soul resulting from some Movement of the Body, and so the Pleasure that arises from the hearing it be accordingly a Sensual Pleasure, as truly, tho' not so grossly, as Smelling or Tasting is, yet the Harmony and Proportion of Sounds (which is that wherein Music formally consists) is an Abstract and Intelligible Thing, and the Pleasure of it arises not from any Bodily Movement (as the other does) but from the Soul it self contemplating the Beauty and Agreement of it. To which Beauty and Agreement, that it is in Sounds is purely accidental, since the Soul would be pleased with the same Proportion wherever it finds it. Nor is it proper to say that we *hear* Musick; That which we hear is only the *Sound*, which is a Sensation in our selves, but the *Music-part* we properly think and contemplate as an intelligible Beauty, in like manner as we do the Beauty of Truth. And consequently, the Pleasure of it must be as much Intellectual as that of the other is. To all which it may be added in the last place, That Music formally consisting in Proportion, and Proportion pleasing only as understood, the Pleasure of it must needs be Intellectual, as resulting from Thought and Understanding, as all other Intellectual Pleasures do. . . ."[95]

We shall not consider this argument in detail here, but only pause to admire the nicety of "Nor is it proper to say that we *hear* Musick," and to observe that this argument, in slightly different versions, still remains in circulation.

Of more importance at this point is a comparison of a musical poem of the same writer's with one of Strode's, quoted above. Norris' piece hews rather strictly to the doctrines of his own philosophical position, rather than indulging in a gossipy recapitulation of scraps of lore, like Strode. But Norris' poem represents Augustan exposition, rather than Metaphysical organization, as a norm, with the result that some of the metaphors in the argument take on the aspect of ineptly overdone Metaphysical conceits (the end of the first strophe is notable in this regard). In general, the tone of "On a Musician, supposed to be mad with Musick" is almost Cowleyan:

I.

Poor dull mistake of low Mortality,
To call that Madness, which is Ecstasy.
　　'Tis no disorder of the Brain,
His Soul is only set t'an higher strain.
Out-soar he does the Sphere of Common Sense,
　　　Rais'd to Diviner Excellence;
But when at Highest pitch, his Soul out-flies,
Not Reason's Bounds, but those of vulgar Eyes.

II.

So when the *Mystick Sybil's* Sacred Breast
Was with *Divine Infusions* possest,

[95] John Norris, *A Collection of Miscellanies* (1678), fourth edition (London, 1706), pp. 367-368.

'Twas *Rage* and *Madness* thought to be,
Which was all *Oracle* and *Mystery*.
And so the Soul that's shortly to *Commence*
A Spirit *free* from dregs of Sense,
Is thought to *rave*, when She discourses high,
And *breathes* the *lofty Strains* of *Immortality*.

III.

Musick, thou *Generous Ferment* of the Soul,
Thou universal Cement of the *whole*;
    Thou *Spring* of Passion, that dost inspire
Religious Ardours, and *Poetick Fire*,
Who'd think that *Madness* should b'ascrib'd to thee,
    That *mighty Discord* to thy Harmony?
But 'twas *such ignorance* that call'd the Gift Divine
Of *Various Tongues*, *Rage*, and th'*Effects of Wine*.

IV.

But thou, *Seraphick* Soul, do thou advance
In thy sweet *Ecstasy*, thy *pleasing* Trance:
    Let thy brisk Passions mount still higher.
Till they join to the *Element* of *Fire*.
Soar higher yet, till thou shalt calmly hear
    The Musick of a well-tun'd Sphere:
Then on the *lumpish Mass* look down, and thou
        shalt know
The *Madness* of the *World*, for groveling still
        below.[96]

The Augustan tone has not completely triumphed, here,
over the unassimilated images and turns of diction and allusions of earlier styles; but the tone is didactic and "proper"
enough to allow "A Spirit *free* from dregs of Sense" to seem
far-fetched and almost too easy. Neither Strode's little poem,
nor this considerably more ambitious effort, deals with

[96] *Ibid.*, pp. 22-23.

"solemn music"; but in the first case, the interests of a poetic style itself, and, in Norris', the demands of his Neoplatonist psychology, both result in a treatment of some of the material of *musica humana*. But Norris was, historically speaking, a kind of sport, and the fact of his poem can be taken as no evidence for the continuation of a tradition.[97]

We have observed, earlier in this chapter, that puritan writers were by and large uninterested in *musica speculativa*. The fact remains, however, that two poets strongly committed to the Commonwealth both used speculative musical material at considerable length. Milton's use of musical imagery and allusion, of course, is both more profound and more broad than Andrew Marvell's somewhat rare instances of them. But in each case, there is a very considerable poem to be dealt with. Marvell's "Musicks Empire," while not primarily devoted to religious music, is particularly interesting as a prophetic allegorization, and *encomium*, of the role of the Commonwealth in the cosmos, as well as in the body politic. Milton's "At a Solemn Music," on the other hand, recapitulates so many of the themes that we have been examining in this and previous chapters, that it had best be considered after Marvell's.

Marvell's Commonwealth and "The Empire of the Ear"

Occurrences of *musica speculativa* in the poetry of Andrew Marvell are relatively sparse. With the exception of *"Musicks Empire,"* Marvell's musical references are confined to conventional uses that have been observed heretofore. In two of the satires, for example, musical allusions are employed in the ridicule of particular faults and aspirations of the respective victims. In "Clarindon's House-Warming," popular

[97] In the more strictly Augustan devotional poem, the musical image becomes singularly static and uninventive. See, for example, John Austin's poem, published 1688, in *Restoration Verse*, ed. William Kerr (London, 1930), pp. 9-10.

objections to the costly town house of Charles II's Lord
Chancellor are used as an occasion for a general vilification
of Clarendon. After condemning the barrenness of Clarendon's daughter, wife of the future James II, Marvell harps
on the "vanity and folly" which Clarendon himself admitted
had characterized his own assumption of the prodigious construction costs.

> And wish'd that his Daughter had had as much grace
> To erect him a pyramid out of her Quarry.

> But then recollection how the harper *Amphyon*
> Made *Thebes* dance aloft while he fidled and sung.

> He thought (as an Instrument he was most free on)
> To build with the Jews-trump of his own tongue.[98]

(ll. 15-20)

"Jews-trump" or, more commonly, "jew's harp," was the
relatively simple twanging instrument still known to children
and rustics. In contrast to Amphion, builder of cities, Clarendon is depicted as having played on a rather opprobrious
substitute. But the real point here is that, as Dr. Percy Scholes
has pointed out,[99] the jew's harp was employed during the
later seventeenth century as a cheap gimcrack commodity for
barter with the American Indian. The "Jews-trump of his
own tongue," then, would refer to Clarendon's carelessness
about costs and to an implication that his money or his credit
was unsound.[100] In these lines, a musical reference is simply
part of an invidious mythological comparison, extremely
common in all satire, complicated by a further topical joke
that refers back to the original basis of the comparison as
between two builders.

A rather more simple piece of wit, but involving musical
lore to a greater degree, occurs in the satire "Fleckno, or an

---

[98] Andrew Marvell, *Poems and Letters*, ed. H. M. Margoliouth (Oxford,
1927), I, 137. Hereafter referred to as "Margoliouth."

[99] Scholes, *op.cit.*, pp. 23-24; see also pp. 381-384.

[100] Cf. Margoliouth's note on this line, I, 264.

English Priest of Rome." The poet, after having been bored
to distraction by his subject's monstrous verses, is subjected
to his music-making, when

> . . . the Tyrant, weary to persecute,
> Left off, and try'd t'allure me with his Lute.
>   Now as Instruments, to the same key
> Being tun'd by Art, if the one touched be
> The other opposite as soon replies,
> Mov'd by the Air and hidden Sympathies;
> So while he with his gouty Fingers crawles
> Over the Lute, his murmuring Belly calls,
> Whose hungry Guts to the same streightness twin'd
> In Echo to the trembling Strings repin'd.
>   I, that perceiv'd now what his Musick meant,
> Asked civilly if he had eat this Lent . . .[101]
>
> (ll. 35-46)

As the gut strings vibrate across the belly of the lute, so
rumble the entrails, in sympathetic vibration, of the unfortunate cleric who, for Dryden, "In Prose and Verse was own'd,
without disputes / Through all the realms of Non-sense,
absolute."

While Marvell may have been prompted by certain musical
and / or gastric habits of his target to pinion him in this fashion,
the passage is fairly typical of the tradition of Juvenalian,
or what Joseph Hall called "biting," satires. In its use of a
musical image to represent the feigning or aspirations of one
whose actuality is most unmusical, it is suggestive of Donne's
lines in his fourth "Satyre," ll. 77-78. The fawning sycophant
under attack answers the Poet's doubts as to the heuristic value
of supposed courtly virtues as "He, like to a high stretcht lute
string squeaked, O Sir, / 'Tis sweet to talk of Kings."

If these musical references are little more than accepted
satiric devices, a few examples of cosmological hyperbole
show rather nicely the course of this musical figure during

---

[101] Margoliouth, I, 84. Cf. Donne, "Satyre I," ll. 77-78.

the later seventeenth century. In his pastoral poems, Marvell conventionally employs the heavenly music as an image of perfection. In "A Dialogue Between Thyrsis and Dorinda," a pastoral seduction is conducted as an *Invitation au Voyage.* The promised "Elizium" where *"tout n'est qu'ordre et beauté"* stands to the Arcadian meadow upon which the dialogue occurs as that meadow stands to the world:

> Thyrsis. Oh, ther's neither hope nor fear
> Ther's no Wolf, no Fox, nor Bear.
> No need of Dog to fetch our stray,
> Our Lightfoot we may give away;
> No Oat-pipe's needfull, there thine Ears
> May feast with Musick of the Spheres.[102]
> (ll. 21-26)

This "Elizium" resounds to no rustic piping, and the rejection of the syrinx is a little like Polybius' angry denial of the pastoral myths that even in his own time had grown up about his native Arcadia. (It was an ethical realm, he insisted, echoing to no Panic flutes, but where "The children learn to cipher and to sing" in well-regulated academies.) In another poem, "Clorinda and Damon," the wild pastoral piping is itself transformed directly into the *harmonia mundi:*

Chorus

> *Of Pan the flowring Pastures sing,*
> *Caves eccho, and the Fountains ring.*
> *Sing then while he doth us inspire;*
> *For all the World is our* Pan's *Quire.*[103]

But traditional lore, wrenched from its banal use by a conceit, soon approaches mere overstatement. Thus, Marvell treats the appeal of the Sisters of Nun Appleton to the future Lady

[102] *Ibid.*, I, 19.
[103] *Ibid.*, I, 18. Cf. E. K.'s gloss on the May eclogue of *The Shepheardes Calender:* "Great Pan is Christ, the very God of all shepheards, which calleth himself the greate and good shepheard . . ."

Isabel Fairfax so as to employ this sort of figure, although
in the context of the poem he probably intends it as a sweet
but wanton wile, if not as a blasphemous one:

> Your voice, the sweetest of the Quire
> Shall draw Heav'n nearer, raise us higher.[104]
>   ("Upon Appleton House," ll.161-162)

A more elaborate version of such literally high-flown compliment occurs in "The Fair Singer":

> To make a final conquest of all me,
> Love did compose so sweet an Enemy,
> In whom both Beauties to my death agree,
> Joyning themselves in fatal Harmony;
> That while she with her Eyes my Heart doth bind,
> She with her voice might captivate my Mind.
>
> I could have fled from One but singly fair:
> My dis-intangled Soul it self might save,
> Breaking the curled trammels of her hair.
> But how should I avoid to be her Slave,
> Whose subtile Art invisibly can wreath
> My Fetters of the very Air I breath?
>
> It had been easie fighting in some plain,
> Where Victory might hand in equal choice,
> But all resistance against her is vain,
> Who has th'advantage both of Eyes and Voice,
> And all my Forces needs must be undone,
> She having gained both the Wind and Sun.[105]

This is very like a Cavalier lyric; we might call it a Metaphysical poem on an Augustan subject. The distinctions between eyes, physical beauty, and the sun, on the one hand,
and the voice, intellectual beauty, and the wind, on the other,
elegantly support the compliment which raises the lady to the

[104] Margoliouth, I, 64.   [105] *Ibid.*, I, 31.

order of the elements themselves. Without the consistent fabric of wit, the elevation would be an unsteady one.

Marvell's most elaborate use of a figure from traditional *musica speculativa* occurs toward the beginning of "The First Anniversary of the Government under O.C." This long musical conceit starts out with the observation that inadequate rulers "No more contribute to the state of Things, / Then wooden Heads unto the Viols strings," an image even more precise than the modern cliché of the figurehead upon the ship of state. Following this, a rather direct cosmological hyperbole leads into an elaborate comparison of Cromwell to Amphion, and a brilliant version of the old notion of the state as a musical concord:

> While indefatigable *Cromwell* hyes,
> And cuts his way still nearer to the Skyes,
> Learning a Musique in the Region clear,
> To tune this lower to that higher sphere.
> So when *Amphion* did the Lute command.
> Which the God gave him, with his gentle hand,
> The rougher Stones, unto his Measures hew'd,
> Dans'd up in order from the Qarreys rude;
> This took a Lower, that an Higher place,
> As he the Treble alter'd, or the Base:
> No Note he struck, but a new Story lay'd,
> And the great Work ascended while he play'd.
>
> The listning Structures he with Wonder ey'd,
> And still new Stopps to various Time apply'd:
> Now through the Strings a Martial rage he throws,
> And joyning streight the *Theban* Tow'r arose;
> Then as he strokes them with a Touch more sweet,
> The flocking Marbles in a Palace meet;
> But, for he most the graver Notes did try,
> Therefore the Temples rear'd their Columns high:
> Thus, ere he ceas'd, his sacred Lute creates
> Th'harmonious City of the seven Gates.

> Such was that wondrous Order and Consent,
> When *Cromwell* tun'd the ruling Instrument;
> While tedious Statesmen many years did hack,
> Framing a Liberty that still went back;
> Whose num'rous Gorge could swallow in an hour
> That Island, which the Sea cannot devour:
> Then our *Amphion* issues out and sings,
> And once he struck, and twice, the pow'rful Strings.[106]
>
> (ll. 45-74)

The "ruling Instrument" is the Instrument of Government of 1653 by means of which Cromwell established the Protectorate. Significantly, Marvell has clearly distinguished between the Instrument, or means, and the harmony of the state itself, or end. The heavenly figure in lines 47-48 is supported argumentatively by the reference, in the following couplet, to the traditional imitation of cosmic harmony in practical music. The actual creation of the state is allegorized in the story of Amphion's legendary founding of the city of Thebes in a marvellous way. The changes of pitch sounded upon the governing instrument control the corresponding architectural positions of the dancing masonry, and, by extension, create corresponding degrees in the order of nature. But following this (ll. 57-66), the already ordered structures again arrange themselves, this time with respect to differences of kind and use. These final arrangements, however, are effected not by the varying pitches of the music, but by the respective modes employed. As we have already seen, garbled notions of Greek modality, traditionally handed down, had become by the seventeenth century purely literary, esthetic concepts. Although no particular modes are mentioned by name in this passage, it is quite clear that Marvell's readers might have recognized in "a Martial rage" the Phrygian, in "a touch more sweet" the Hypolydian, and in "the graver Notes," the Dorian mode, their conventional affections being rousing, voluptuous,

[106] *Ibid.*, I, 104-105.

and stately, respectively. In running through various modes on his instrument, Cromwell-Amphion effects certain changes in the state of the world; I think that another myth can be seen to intrude itself here. Cromwell is being covertly invoked as Timotheus, the fictional musician of the court of Alexander the Great. A famous anecdote about him, retold by John Case in *The Praise of Music* and later employed by Dryden, tells how the fabulous performer, playing Phrygian and Dorian melodies in succession, first urges his monarch to the brink of war and then rapidly calms him again.

The stated comparison throughout this passage, however, treats Cromwell as Amphion, and all the precise elaboration can be seen as the kind of writing that would ordinarily be expected of Marvell, an intricate conceit employing knowledge, lore, and doctrine with the same immediacy as if they were the data of direct sensuous experience. And while the musical ideas here employed are of a completely conventional variety, Marvell's particular use of them in praise of Cromwell raises an interesting problem.

What looked to be a far-reaching critical controversy arose in the recent past over the nature of Marvell's political attitude toward Cromwell as expressed in the "Horatian Ode upon Cromwell's Return from Ireland." Cleanth Brooks, arguing from an ironic reading of the beginning phrase, "The forward Youth," and of

> So restless *Cromwell* could not cease
> In the inglorious Arts of Peace,
> But through adventurous War
> Urged his Active Star,[107]
>
> (ll. 9-12)

maintained that the received view that Marvell was unambiguously praising Cromwell would simply not do.[108] He

---

[107] *Ibid.*, I, 87.

[108] Cleanth Brooks, "Literary Criticism," in *English Institute Essays, 1946* (New York, 1947), pp. 127-158.

went on to insist that these and other ironies demanded a reading which would account for what he calls the "tension" in the poem's language by referring, in some way, to attitudes. Douglas Bush replied[109] that he could see no irony at all in the poem, that the praise intended was direct and bold. In describing Marvell as a "17th century liberal,"[110] Professor Bush seemed to imply that the poet's strong Republican feelings, as evidenced by his loyal and undissenting political service, could easily encompass the actions of a revolutionary leader whom an orthodox royalist would indict with the crime of Brutus. It might be added that while Marvell was willing to imply such a comparison himself ("And *Caesar's* head at last / Did through his Laurels blast"), his use of it in connection with a description of praiseworthy audacity might bespeak an interpretation vastly different from that of a royalist.

It was perhaps unfortunate that the whole controversy died out[111] before any enlightening discussion had occurred of two central problems: namely, the question of how indeed Marvell's attitude toward Cromwell might be determined from his poetry, and the more general question of the relationship of intentions to both poetic and ordinary languages of praise and blame.[112] As far as we are concerned, however, Marvell's treatment of Cromwell need present no crucial problem. We may perceive Marvell's fairly general literary program of describing the Commonwealth in orthodox cosmological and pastoral images, and of invoking its leader as a kind of emperor. And we may, as a consequence, deal with any particular rhetorical difficulty as an irony engendered by two conventionally antithetical modes of discourse, rather

[109] Douglas Bush, "Marvell's 'Horatian Ode,'" *Sewanee Review*, LX (1952), pp. 363-376.

[110] *Ibid.*, p. 376.

[111] Brooks retorted in *Sewanee Review*, LXI (1953), pp. 129-135.

[112] Indeed, the discussion soon drifted into one of critical theory, and the role of historicism as against that of the "ontological criticism" practiced by Brooks. It ended up as little more than a defense of each position; no fruitful conclusions were reached about the "Horatian Ode."

than as an irony in the more usual sense, resulting from a conflict of attitude and formal expression. Marvell's pastoral name for England is *Eliza,* and it was the cosmology, at the center of which that earlier reign considered itself, that provided the raw material for so many of his metaphors. If Cromwell's regicide could prove a mortal sin to a royalist, a parliamentarian could retort that

> 'Tis madness to resist or blame
> The force of angry Heavens flame.[113]
> ("Horatian Ode," ll. 25-26)

In Marvell's poetic universe, Cromwell's triumph vaulted over those of his actions that in an earlier Tudor "Elizium" might have been branded as infamies. Cromwell killed a king who "nothing common did or mean" at the scene of his death, and served as the leader of a state who, unlike the king he had replaced, could not perpetuate his leadership through natural inheritance. Similarly, Man, in "The Mower Against Gardens," develops the arts of horticulture and formal gardening and "in the Cherry" does "Nature vex, / To procreate without a sex," at once adulterating and giving order to the "wild and fragrant Innocence" of a pastoral scene. In both cases, however, the ordering by an Intelligence of what was once free and unruly is observed in passing to be *contra naturam.* But our observation must move, along with Marvell's, one step further past these ironies. For Man, the gardener, and Cromwell, the ruler, both govern model universes in which, if innocence is no longer possible, knowledge and the ordering power of imagination are in some sense necessary.

The point is simply that to understand Marvell's political ideology we must try to disentangle such quasi-paradoxes as arise in nearly all the poems (save perhaps for the later satires) by treating them as knots in the thread of the argument in which each occurs, rather than as clusters of conflicting attitudes. And we must realize that the kind of

[113] *Ibid.,* I, 88.

responsibility that Marvell maintained toward his government and toward his constituency in Hull shared his sincerity and even, perhaps, his belief with his commitments to his style. I have raised this point not only in connection with the musical passage in the "First Anniversary" poem, but because of its relevance to the earlier "Musicks Empire." The possible invocation of Cromwell in the final stanza of this apparently simple piece of *laus musicae* might otherwise easily be misinterpreted on the grounds that the poem's subject provides an uncongenial environment for such an allusion.[114] The entire poem had best be quoted:

MUSICKS EMPIRE

I.

First was the World as one great Cymbal made,
Where Jarring Windes to infant Nature plaid.
All Musick was a solitary sound,
To hollow rocks and murm'ring Fountains bound.

II.

Jubal first made the wilder notes agree;
And *Jubal* tuned Musicks *Jubilee*:
He call'd the *Ecchoes* from their sullen Cell,
And built the Organs City where they dwell.

[114] It has been traditional to read "a gentler Conqueror" as Marvell's patron, Fairfax; see Margoliouth's note, I, 226, for example. M. C. Bradbrook and M. G. Lloyd Thomas in *Andrew Marvell* (Cambridge, 1940), pp. 76-77, 81, also make this identification, assigning the poem to the years 1651-1653, when Marvell was at Nunappleton. Also see *ibid.*, pp. 2-3. Percy Scholes, *op.cit.*, p. 153, suggests Cromwell, probably basing his judgment on his own researches into the latter's personal love of music (see Scholes, pp. 137-149). It will be clear that I agree with him for different reasons. As long as the provenance and precise date of the poem remain uncertain, the identifications seem equiprobable on the basis of outside evidence; on the basis of my reading below, Fairfax might still form a *figura* with Cromwell as a type of the secular political leader celebrated as music in the poem.

III.

Each sought a consort in that lovely place;
And Virgin Trebles wed the manly Base.
From whence the progeny of numbers new
Into harmonious Colonies withdrew.

IV.

Some to the Lute, some to the Viol went,
And others chose the Cornet eloquent.
These practicing the Wind, and those the Wire,
To sing Mens Triumphs, or in Heavens quire.

V.

Then Musick, the *Mosaique* of the Air,
Did of all these a solemn noise prepare:
With which She gain'd the Empire of the Ear,
Including all between the Earth and Sphear.

VI.

Victorious sounds! yet here your Homage do
Unto a gentler Conqueror than you;
Who though He flies the Musick of his praise,
Would with you Heavens Hallelujahs raise.[115]

The subject here is hardly a traditional praise of music through allusion to *harmonia mundi*; in the first place, music is dealt with throughout as having undergone a kind of historical evolution, parallelling the social history of mankind. In the second place, *musica instrumentalis* is considered historically prior to the celestial harmony, and the normal notion of practical music as the macrocosmic model of the universal music is certainly rearranged, if not actually reversed. Most important of all, however, is that the musical conceit is combined with a political one in a way vastly different from the more traditional treatment in "The First Anniversary of the

[115] Margoliouth, I, 47.

Government Under O.C." for example, where conventional musical metaphors and myths are revitalized only in the wit.

"Musicks Empire" commences with the random sounds of nature. A physical world "as one great Cymbal made" is the sounding instrument struck by its own disordering elements. The winds themselves are qualified with a standard epithet of discord ("jarring"), but there is no indication that the untamed babble, the "solitary sound" which exhausts the domain of the audible, is in any metaphysical sense inharmonious. "Infant" nature's wildness gives promise of a growth into orderly maturity.

At this point, we are still in possession of an argumentative schema admitting of various interpretive developments; from what we have come to see of the treatment of both practical and speculative music in the writing of the period we might expect the poem to take any one of a number of courses. An elaborate description of harmony as an ordering principle might follow, personified in Orpheus or Amphion, for example, or perhaps some moralized recounting of the fabled Pythagorean "invention" of the intervals. But in the second stanza, Marvell introduces Jubal, "the father of all those who handle the harp and organ,"[116] as his heroic initiator of practical music. It is with Jubal that the metaphorical growth of empire begins. The echoes of the original natural music ("natural" as is the sound of the wind in native forests as compared to the sounds played upon the wood of those same hewn trees, fashioned into lutes—an old figure) are treated, here as throughout the poem, as men. "Sullen" means merely "solitary" here, and we have the sense of two images working at once: men are called from their poor, lonely caves (we are tempted to continue the paraphrase with "solitary, poor, nasty, brutish and short," for this stage of the growth of empire is the very birth of society itself). On the other hand, there is the distinct implication, in "Cell," of a monastic isolation, and music is here figured as breaking down the walls

[116] Genesis 4:21.

[311]

of monasteries by summoning forth the inhabitants into a world of cities, into the realities of Protestantism and political economy. The organ is almost completely a secular instrument here.

In the "Organs City" the population of musical sounds is fruitful and multiplies. Starting with the pun on "consort" as sexual mate and instrumental ensemble, the images of stanzas II-IV depict the gradual overproduction of sounds in the city of towering pipes, resulting in a varied and overflowing music, filling the whole world in search of *Lebensraum*. The "Progeny of numbers new" is undoubtedly all the musical compositions ever invented, here related through a quasi-genetic descent to the primal natural noises. "Harmonious" names both the populations and the political condition of these colonies.

What looks to be a rather conventional catalogue of the instruments in the fourth stanza is turned upside down by the fact that it is the music that seeks out the several instruments. We may see how, in the context between Welsh and English musicians in Drayton's *Poly-Olbion*, various dispositions of different men were satisfied by their choice of instruments when they

> Strooke up at once and sung each to the Instrument;
> (Of sundry sorts that were, as the Musician likes)
> On which the practic'd hand with perfect'st fingring
>   strikes,
> Whereby their height of skill might liveliest be
>   exprest.
> The trembling Lute some touch, some straine the
>   Violl best . . .[117]
>
>   (*Poly-Olbion*, Song IV, ll. 352-356)

But in "Musicks Empire" the composed sounds themselves choose the instruments by means of which they will applaud the triumphs, the successful advancing marches of human

[117] Michael Drayton, *Works*, ed. J. W. Hebel (Oxford, 1933), IV, 78.

enterprise. The allusion to "Heavens quire" seems almost like a gratuitous tag here, so completely does the idea of mundane expansion dominate the poem.

In the penultimate stanza, the rigor of the conceit appears to relax somewhat. Music, now generally personified, is described as "the Mosaique of the Air." In this remarkable image, however, the multiplicity of the "harmonious Colonies" is recalled by reference to the variegated tesserae of a mosaic which can merge, from any distant viewpoint, into an overwhelming unified figure. It is with a concerted effort of all its diversities in a "solemn" (i.e. religious) noise, corresponding to the assembled mosaic figure, that Music accomplishes her final triumph, gaining "the Empire of the Ear, / Including all between the Earth and Sphear." In the sense of the earlier metaphors, music's heaven is the ultimate civil and territorial acquisition. But in another sense the general personification of Music in this stanza has rendered it as more abstract, and the "Empire of the Ear" is its empirically proper dwelling-place, a heaven of pure audibility.

The word "Mosaique" resonates even further, however. Marvell may or may not have been aware of the common etymological origin of "music" and "mosaic" in the Greek *mousa* ("muse"); perhaps the juxtaposition of the two words in the line was for him the same kind of mock-etymological punning that he had effected earlier in the poem between "Jubal" and "Jubilee." The concealed allusion to Moses he had also employed elsewhere. In the woods about Appleton House, the Poet, "easie Philosopher," divines in the birds and the vegetation all the works of Man:

> Out of these scatter'd *Sibyl's* leaves
> Strange *Prophecies* my Phancy weaves:
> And in one History consumes,
> Like *Mexique Paintings*, all the *Plumes*.
> What *Rome, Greece, Palestine*, ere said
> I in this light *Mosaick* read.

Thrice happy he who, not mistook,
Hath read in Natures mystick Book.[118]
("Upon Appleton House," ll. 577-584)

Both the ascription of prophecy to fancy and the Hebraic
notion of the historical role of *torah*, the Mosaic Law, point
to a pun here involving the reading of "light *Mosaick*" as
both an adjective-noun and noun-adjective qualification. The
notion of music as "the *Mosaique* of the Air," then, might
reverberate in a moral and religious dimension as well; it is
as a Biblical moral leader that music finally gains the higher
reaches of the universe.

In the final stanza, the metaphoric ground again shifts a
little as laudatory music attendant upon triumphal processions
is recalled. The "Victorious" sounds are at once the flourishes
of victory and the actual conquerors of the foregoing parts
of the poem. But even they must bend the knee before "a
gentler Conqueror," a nobler leader, perhaps the Lord Pro-
tector himself. So closely does the growth of music's empire
hew to a condensation of human history that it is tempting
to suggest that Marvell may have in some way felt the gap
between stanzas IV and V to have covered the period 1649-
1653, at the end of which time the Protectorate was established. In any case, Cromwell may be said to have brought to
"Elizium" the Mosaic leadership historically necessary, a
Puritan would undoubtedly have argued, for heaven's consent.

The superimposition of musical lore on a persuasively
designed historical frame results, in "Musicks Empire," in a
reversal of the usual mythological treatments of *laus musicae*.
Earth is filled with sound before Heaven is; the music of the
spheres, only obliquely invoked, appears first as a kind of
cosmic, triumphal applause. The two conceits on music and
human political development interweave so closely that the
first five stanzas might be said to address themselves to the
subject of "Empire's Music," rather than the other way

[118] Margoliouth, I, 77.

around. Marvell's historical construction of speculative music is in many ways unique. What Cowley cast into pedantic footnotes appended to a handful of lines of the *Davideis*, Marvell took as the *données* of a compact pseudo-narrative. "Musicks Empire" is, after all, modelled on treatments of the praise of music that we have already considered, but only in the sense that Elizabethan lyrics are, by and large, modelled on *songs*, that Metaphysical lyrics are modelled on *arguments*. The last stanza is an *envoi* to Cromwell, replacing a salute to the Muse; its place there, given the historical narrative that has led to it, is inevitable.

We will see later on how John Dryden employed a narrative exposition of musical history in the first of his two St. Cecilia's Day odes, and to what differing purposes from Marvell's such an exposition was put. At this point, however, we shall turn to another historical treatment of the power of music and its domain, embodied in a poem that complements "Musicks Empire" even as it surpasses it in scope.

Milton's Renewed Song

In studying some of the ways in which sixteenth- and seventeenth-century poets employed the transmitted lore of *musica speculativa*, we have occasionally drawn an implicit distinction between the operations of experience and knowledge in the treatment of music as a subject matter for poetry. In a sense, such a distinction is already drawn by the classical bifurcation of speculative and practical music; but we have seen how poetic traditions as well contributed to the separation of the experience of actual music, as one of life's varied phenomena, and the response to a philosophy of music. Occasionally, as in Crashaw's "Musicks Duell," both the musical thought and the poetic language are of such a nature as to make for a subtle blending of the two. We are able to think of the poem as treating of actual music, that is, because its ideology is close to our own, and because that notion of music as a sensual ravishment allows for the description of the contest in elaborate erotic imagery that nevertheless always keeps to details of actual musical practice. I have suggested earlier in this chapter that George Herbert's spiritual music might have had as much personal meaning, with respect to the association of actual music with both solitary contemplation and loving fraternity in his own life, as it had a very definite meaning with respect to intellectual history and poetic conventions. But, by and large, Renaissance poetry tends to separate speculative and practical music, combining them only in the fairly inflexible relationship of the *encomium musicae*, in which the former is introduced in order to praise the latter.

In any consideration of Milton, the split between what is learned by studying and what is known more immediately must always seem an artificial one. I mean by such a split not so much the "dissociation of thought and feeling" that has become so much of a cliché, since its introduction by T. S. Eliot a generation ago,[119] in the criticism of seventeenth-century poetry, as perhaps a distinction like that drawn even longer ago by Bertrand Russell between "knowledge by acquaintance" and "knowledge by description."[120] At any rate, Milton is thoroughly an intellectual poet (and if he is also so in our most current sense of the word, it must be added that he is certainly a type of the *engagé* intellectual: in Professor Tillyard's words, he "considered literature mainly as a species of action").[121] The corpus of his poetry is a speculative monolith; poetry was for him, among other things, an instrument for bringing to bear the thought of history, as well as some of the history of thought, upon the problems of a rich and turbulent present. And in his poetry we find knowledge, speculation, invested with the intensity of direct sensual experience.

It would be hard to say, then, whether speculative or prac-

---

[119] In his essay on "The Metaphysical Poets," 1921.
[120] See *The Problems of Philosophy* (London, 1952), pp. 46-59.
[121] E. M. W. Tillyard, *Milton* (London, 1951), p. 362.

tical music played a more fundamental role in the thoughts and commitments of even the young Milton. Much has been written of his musical background, training and interests.[122] Even more attention has been paid to the rich profusion of musical reference, both speculative and practical, in the body of his work.[123] From the oratorical exercise of his schooldays on "The Music of the Spheres" ("*De Sphaerarum Concentu*") through the many passages of practical and theoretical musical allusion in *Paradise Lost*, Milton's vast knowledge of both the secular music of his own day and of Classical and Christian musical doctrine is amply revealed. Critics of the past thirty-five years have demonstrated the extent of that revelation. Attention has been paid primarily to the more expository treatments of Christian musical doctrine in Milton's poetry, such as "On the Morning of Christs Nativity," ll. 93-140, "Arcades," ll. 61-78, and the many sections on the music of heaven in *Paradise Lost*. It is certainly true that the greater number of such treatments and references manifest the received Christian Humanist interest in the ethical implications of the heavenly music, in the notion that, since the Fall, human imperfection rather than thresholds of hearing or custom has rendered that music inaudible.

While Milton's use of music to mean "poetry" in pastoral contexts is almost a truism, it has not been pointed out that Milton was able to absorb as well some of the Baroque doctrines about the rhetorical nature of music. A passage like that in Book IV of *Paradise Lost*, ll. 674-688, in which we learn that the heavenly music is indeed audible in heaven,

[122] Sigmund Spaeth, *Milton's Knowledge of Music* (Princeton, 1913), pp. 12-56; see also Ernest Brennecke, Jr., *John Milton the Elder and his Music* (New York, 1938); Willa McClung Evans, *Henry Lawes* (New York, 1941), pp. 79-109.

[123] See Spaeth, *op.cit., passim*; Theodore Howard Banks, *Milton's Imagery* (New York, 1950), pp. 26-31; Tillyard, *Milton*, pp. 63-65, 374-379; James Hutton, "Some English Poems in Praise of Music," *English Miscellany*, II (1951), pp. 43-59; Gretchen Lee Finney, "A World of Instruments," pp. 111-116; Spitzer (Part II), pp. 335-340; Nan C. Carpenter, "The Place of Music in *L'Allegro* and *Il Penseroso*," *University of Toronto Quarterly*, XXII (1953), pp. 354-367.

"With Heav'nly touch of instrumental sounds / In full harmonic number join'd . . . ," is often commented on with reference to Milton's use of traditional musical lore, for example. But in the demonic games in Book II, the poetry-music-rhetoric nexus comes up in a rather new way. After the military and athletic contests among the fiends of Hell have been described, we are told that

> Others more mild,
> Retreated in a silent valley, sing
> With notes Angelical to many a Harp
> Thir own Heroic deeds and hapless fall
> By doom of Battle; and complain that Fate
> Free Virtue should enthrall to Force or Chance.
> Thir Song was partial, but the harmony
> (What could it less when Spirits immortal sing?)
> Suspended Hell, and took with ravishment
> The thronging audience. In discourse more sweet
> (For Eloquence the Soul, Song charms the Sense,)
> Others apart sat on a Hill retir'd,
> In thoughts more elevate, and reason'd high
> Of Providence, Foreknowledge, Will, and Fate,
> Fixt Fate, Free will, Foreknowledge absolute,
> And found no end, in wand'ring mazes lost.
>
> (II, 546-561)

No matter what the perverse import of the text of the devils' epic song, the melody itself, partaking of the potency of the heavenly music, remains strongly effective. The notions of word and note are separated here in Hell; it is the doctrine which has suffered in the fall of the rebel angels, rather than the purely musical power to charm and move. But Milton carefully stipulates that it is the soul itself that is affected by the "rational" powers of "Eloquence," while "Song charms the Sense" alone and cannot, no matter how attractive, actually operate upon the highest psychic faculties. The philosophical discussions that are next described, although graceless, vagrant quests for the self-knowledge to which the fiends can never attain, must be "discourse more sweet," harmonious, and well attuned. The distinction between "Eloquence" and "Song" is certainly a step toward the later seventeenth-century bifurcation of the functions of language and music. It will be noticed that the passage moves from the epic "music" (i.e. poetry) of the games in Hell, to the musical skill retained by the fallen angels, to a contrast between this music, or even poetry-music, and actual doctrine. That the fiends can sing the wrong words to the marvellous melodies of angelic music is just another oddity of their utterly paradoxical predicament.

Nowhere in Milton, perhaps, are the affective properties of music used in a more complicated metaphoric fabric than in *Comus*. Even the passage from *Paradise Lost* mentioned above is primarily *expository* in its use of *musica speculativa* or of changes rung upon it by the exigencies of the poem's philosophic scheme. But in *Comus* the intricate combination of actual and theoretical music resonates far beyond the conventional play of masquers' identities represented by the casting of Henry Lawes, the masque's composer, as the Attendant Spirit-Thyrsis-Pan-Orpheus figure. In the first place, the Lady's song (one of a sparse five in a long and extravagant entertainment), while serving as a primary instrument in the action of the masque itself, is self-referential in two senses: it addresses itself to its own resonating effects (its echoes, here personified as the nymph Echo herself, not only a favorite pastoral figure but a favorite metaphor for the relationship of actual human music to the heavenly harmony), on the one hand; and on the other, it covertly refers to the Lady herself and her own predicament ("the lovelorn Nightingale" is taken up by the disguised Attendant Spirit's comments, ll. 566-567: "And O poor hapless Nightingale thought I, / How sweet thou sings't, . . .").[124] In the second place, from

[124] It seems difficult to agree with John Edward Hardy, in his essay on *Comus* in Cleanth Brooks and John Edward Hardy, *Poems of Mr. John Milton* (New York, 1951), p. 200, that the "Sweet Echo" lyric "is little

the Lady's opening remarks on the "Riot and ill manag'd Merriment" of Comus' dance, and on the fact that it is her ear which must be her "best guide now" (ll. 170-177), to the final invocation of the "Spheary chime" (l. 1021) as the summit of a purely material world surmounted by the influences of Virtue, musical figures of several sorts are employed.

But it is primarily the Lady's song that generates most of these intricacies:

SONG

> *Sweet Echo, sweetest Nymph that liv'st unseen*
> *Within thy airy shell*
> *By slow* Meander's *margent green,*
> *And in the violet imbroider'd vale*
> *Where the love-lorn Nightingale*
> *Nightly to thee her sad Song mourneth well.*
> *Canst thou not tell me of a gentle Pair*
> *That likest thy* Narcissus *are?*
> *O if thou have*
> *Hid them in som flowry Cave,*
> *Tell me but where*
> *Sweet Queen of Parly, Daughter of the Sphear,*
> *So maist thou be translated to the skies,*
> *And give resounding grace to all Heav'ns Harmonies.*
>
>   (ll. 230-243)

This song is in some measure a hymn in praise of music itself. As actual melody, it is "inchanting ravishment" for Comus, "raptures that move the vocal air" (and here, if anywhere in

___

more than a song to herself." It is certainly much more than that, being addressed to Echo as a figure of music's virtues of fluid ubiquity, and intended as a kind of prayer for deliverance. It is with the Lady's charming singing that both Comus' and the Attendant Spirit's affections are engaged, and the former appears ironically only in answer to the import of her text, although the fact that the music had charmed him is not ironic in the least. John Arthos, in *On "A Mask Presented at Ludlow-Castle"* (Ann Arbor, 1954), pp. 75-77, has some relevant remarks on the song in question as incantation, almost of the nature of a charm. Such is certainly its role on the literal level of action.

the course of the poem, is the musical pun on "air" employed
to enrich the terms of Comus' expression of wonder); for
the Attendant Spirit, it

> Rose like a stream of rich distill'd Perfumes,
> And stole upon the Air, that even Silence
> Was took e're she was ware, and wish't she might
> Deny her nature, and be never more
> Still to be so displac't. I was all eare,
> And took in strains that might create a soul
> Under the ribs of Death, . . .[125]

(ll. 556-562)

If there is an ironic parallel between the reactions of Comus
and the Spirit, it results in good measure from the transcendent power of the Lady's song; both nature's monster and the
airy pastoral musician are ravished by its charms. In address-
ing itself to Echo, the Lady's prayer may have suggested to
the audience at Ludlow Castle the echo songs, which became
increasingly more frequent during the seventeenth century,
and in which the echoes' repetition, by another voice or by a
chorus, of an ultimate word, phrase, or even syllable, cast
an intensifying or ironic light on the line of text itself. In
these songs, the echo gives the lie to what produces it. There
is no such betrayal here, of course, just as there is employed
no such device; but the thwarted expectation of a candidly
malicious "Echo" may have had in itself some effect. "Sweet
Echo" is more than merely the fabled nymph. In personifying
some of the characteristics of music itself, she brings persuasive eloquence to mind. Although in the first six lines, she
is addressed solely as the pastoral nymph, the second section
of the song entreats some higher, or at least more general,
power.[126] If the Lady is praising Echo by calling her "Sweet

[125] Cf. Orsino's lines in *Twelfth Night*, I, i, 8-10: "O, it came ore my
eare, like the sweet sound / That breathes upon a banke of Violets; / Steal-
ing, and giving Odour. . . ."

[126] Lawes, in his original setting of the song, seems to have intended an
emphasis on such a division. The opening lines form a kind of introduction;

Queen of Parly," it is in the role of eloquent, rhetorical, and governing music that she is praising her; not only is she the queen of all speech because of her resemblance to a disembodied *idea* of speech sounds, but she reigns over all "parly" in the other sense of concordant, conferential discourse as well.

Some questions have been raised as to the Christian elevation of the pagan nymph in the final lines; J. E. Hardy, in particular, points to what he feels to be some difficulty in the mind of the Lady with respect to the confusion of things Christian and pagan.[127] If we turn to the variant manuscript readings of these two final lines, however, we may be able to see how a possible addition of Christian reference may have occurred to Milton at some time during his revisions. In the manuscript version which contains the five songs and their settings (B.M. add. ms. 11518), ll. 242-243 read as follows: "So maist thou be transplanted to the skyes / & hold a Counter point to all Heav'ns Harmonies."[128] Here it is simply the pagan music of the spheres to which the nymph, lifted into the heavens in perfectly familiar Ovidian fashion, will add her music. With the substitution of "translated," and the even more revealing one of "resounding grace,"[129] the meaning of "Heav'ns Harmonies" actually changes into a reference to Christian celestial music, the singing of the angels that was

but despite the rather freely quasi-recitative style of setting, there is clear musical repetition of the musical phrase of "Canst thou not tell me" at the words "So maist thou be." Lawes was undoubtedly suggesting some kind of conditional relationship, in his setting, between the promise of the final lines and the answering of the Lady's plea.

[127] *Op.cit.*, pp. 201-202. Hardy makes much of "translated" here, insisting (p. 201) on a sense closer to "metamorphosed" than to the obvious one of "assumption into Heaven having circumvented death"; in any case, this word is a later addition (see below), and seems to represent an actual layer of composition in the Christian synthesis that Milton later added. For a discussion of the possible implications of the complimentary "Daughter of the Sphear," see Hardy, p. 201 and Hutton, *op.cit.*, pp. 48-49.

[128] For all the variant and MS. readings of *Comus* and "At a Solemn Musick" discussed below, see *The Columbia Milton*, I, 421-425 and 502.

[129] Both the Bridgewater and Trinity MSS. substitute "resounding grace" for "counterpoint," as does the British Museum MS. But only the latter retains "transplanted."

troped into the Classical notion. "Grace," of course, retains its musical meaning of "ornament" or "embellishment," which "resounds" because it is still that of Echo; the Christian implications of "grace" are secondary, but extremely strong. They seem to suggest that Echo-affective music-rhetoric's powers are manifestations not of natural skill merely but of something higher; surely it is significant that the Lady herself demonstrates, in the course of her entreaty and her praise, these powers to a remarkable degree.

It has been traditional to regard these changes as representing Milton's desire to substitute "a less technical word or phrase, as if he himself saw the possible danger to his poetry from his learning."[130] That this will probably not do is evidenced by more than the fact that "grace" is, if anything, more "technical" in the language of seventeenth-century musical discourse than is "counterpoint"; as an account of what lay behind the changes, it gives no consideration to any movement toward compactness that might have been at work, or to any possible enrichment or development of the thought. It is true that after the 1629 "Ode on the Morning of Christs Nativity," Milton's diction moves away from the Metaphysical in the direction of the more discursive and expository. And while this may be said to involve a turning away from the more farfetched conceit, it in no way implies a loss of the use of the extended figure. The removal of a highly technical term could be taken only for a desire to do away with *misplaced* specificity, not with specificity itself. We shall see in a moment how important this notion is in trying to account for some of the changes in "At a Solemn Musick."

If the foregoing cursive observations on some of Milton's musical imagery have shown that it does more than expound

[130] Laura E. Lockwood, "Milton's Corrections to the Minor Poems," *Modern Language Notes*, XXV (1910), p. 203. C. S. Lewis, in "A Note on *Comus*," *Review of English Studies*, VIII (1932), pp. 171-172, remarks only that the original "Hould a Counterpointe" is more "unexpected" a reading, without specifying why (although it is very possible that he had in mind much of what has been observed here).

traditional or adapted doctrine, they have also intended to suggest that stylistic considerations are here, as elsewhere, of some significance in the determination of the ways in which such imagery is to be used. "At a Solemn Musick" is most usually treated as the supremest example of Milton's exposition of *musica speculativa*. In the following discussion, we shall attempt to read it in the context of seventeenth-century attitudes toward sacred music, and also as a meditative poem involving the musical imagery of psychic tonus.

"At a Solemn Musick" is certainly a meditation, but not having the set topic, such as death, required by Professor Martz's stricter use of the term: the circumstance provoking the meditation is, or purports to be, an occasional one. The poem's movement, consequently, by no means resembles the involved "symbolic action" of the more Metaphysically oriented poem of religious contemplation; nor does the imagery involve the use of emblematic devices, the whole poem occasionally bearing the *impresa-motto* relationship to its title (as seems often to be the case with Herbert). Instead, the contemplation moves from the consideration of a concrete, mundane event through a synthesized Classical-Christian account of the universal significance of that event, to a final supplication based on that account. That the whole argument of the poem, preceding that final prayer, is handled in a single, twenty-four line sentence, and that the purely technical problem of sustaining the syntactic intensity through mazes of dependent clauses and varied line-lengths is brilliantly solved in the poem has been remarked before.[181] That the text appearing in the 1645 edition of Milton's poems is the product of arduous rewriting is obvious from the changes in almost every line of the three successive drafts of the poem; but many of the fundamental effects of these changes upon the poem's final successful state seem to have been ignored. Considerations of those emendations generally lump the cancellations and substitutions here with those at the end of "Sweet Echo" in

[181] See, for example, Tillyard, *op.cit.*, pp. 63-65.

Comus. In the words of a frequently quoted critic, the corrections are "designed to avoid the technical musical terms which are in the original readings, and which, as technical, might be obscure to the general reader."[132] But let us turn here to the text itself:

> Blest pair of Sirens, pledges of Heav'ns joy,
> Sphear-born harmonious Sisters, Voice, and Vers,
> Wed your divine sounds, and mixt power employ
> Dead things with inbreath'd sense able to pierce,
> 5 And to our high-rais'd phantasie present,
> That undisturbed Song of pure concent,
> Ay sung before the saphire-colour'd throne
> To him that sits thereon
> With Saintly shout and solemn Jubily,
> 10 Where the bright Seraphim in burning row
> Their loud up-lifted Angel trumpets blow,
> And the Cherubick host in thousand quires
> Touch their immortal Harps of golden wires,
> With those just Spirits that wear victorious Palms,
> 15 Hymns devout and holy Psalms
> Singing everlastingly;
> That we on Earth with undiscording voice
> May rightly answer that melodious noise;
> As once we did, till disproportion'd sin
> 20 Jarr'd against natures chime, and with harsh din
> Broke the fair musick that all creatures made
> To their great Lord, whose love their motion sway'd
> In perfet Diapason, whilst they stood
> In first obedience, and their state of good.
> 25 O may we soon again renew that Song,
> And keep in tune with Heav'n, till God ere long

[132] John S. Diekhoff, "Critical Activity of the Poetic Mind: John Milton," *PMLA*, LV (1940), p. 749. Diekhoff agrees completely with the comment of Miss Lockwood, quoted above. See also his comments on the emendations in "At a Solemn Musick" in "The Text of *Comus*, 1634 to 1645," *PMLA*, LII (1937), pp. 709-710.

> To his celestial consort us unite,
> To live with him, and sing in endles morn of light.[133]

Starting almost at the very beginning, we may notice how, in the successive versions of line 3, there is a movement from abstraction to misplaced concrete musical imagery and then to a proper balance between the two: the first reading is ". . . vine power & joynt force employ"; the second, "Mixe yor choise chords & happiest sounds employ"; and the third and final version corrects the grotesquerie of the application to words of "strings" ("chords," as well as the reading "vertical harmonic clusters," the former being the more conventional, older meaning usually employed in musical imagery in the sixteenth and seventeenth centuries). The redundancy of "power" and "force" is also removed, but the identity of voice and verse, preserved long enough for them to be "wed" rather than merely blurred, is of considerable importance. The sisterhood of music and poetry is a theme that we have observed before, and whether we are to read "Sphear-born" in the second line as "carried upon the spheres" or, like the Lady's Echo, "Daughter of the Sphear," the purely pagan cosmological compliment can be seen to be a conventional one. But from the very beginning, the Christian theme of the intimation of the heavenly music as seen in actual earthly singing appears in "pledges of Heav'ns joy";[134] and it is obvious that the invocation of the union of music and poetry will be made to signify more than merely a dual compliment, as in Barnfield's sonnet to Spenser and Dowland, in which music and poetry are sister and brother. It is just this union of "Voice, and Vers," heralded at the beginning of the poem, which some studies tend to lose sight of.

Perhaps the most significant emendation for a study of the poem's strategy, however, might be said to consist in the

---

[133] Text of edition of 1673. The most important variant in the printed 1645 edition is the reading of "content" for "concent" in line 6.

[134] Brooks and Hardy, in their essay on "At a Solemn Musick," *op.cit.*, pp. 117-119, read "offspring" for "pledges."

removal, after line 4 in the second draft, of four lines that would have tended to hasten the conclusion of the poem, and somewhat to trivialize the import. After the reference to the penetrating power of the words-music, and before the mention of the hearer's state of mind, the two sister Sirens[135] continued to be addressed:

> and whilst yor equall raptures temper'd sweet
> in high misterious holie spousall meet
> snatch us from earth a while
> us of our selves & home bred woes beguile . . .

In the first place, these lines continue the personification of music and poetry and reinforce the metaphor of wedding with an almost erotic image, the "temper'd sweet" of tuning coming under an interpretation of some mystical, quasi-sexual aura. That Milton wanted to reserve the traditional figure of temperament and tuning for later expansion seems obvious, and that the later section will avoid the use even of the conventional "sweet" in favor of the more unusual "fair" (because of the former word's frequent erotic, or at least amorous, use) seems to suggest something of what might have contributed to these lines' unsuitability. But it was probably the premature supplication, not a prayer to God, but to the semi-deified Christian muses, which rang most false; and the "snatch us from earth," after some serious consideration and fussing ("holie" replaced by "happie"; "native" for "home-bred"), had to go because of the almost hyperbolic quality of the image, when contrasted with the more staid, but more deeply believed, prayer at the end, in which the wish is expressed only that the human hearer-meditators may some day be brought into tune with Heaven.

The final major emendation is also a deletion. Instead of lines 19-25 of the final version, the earlier drafts give:

[135] The Platonistic sirens who produce the actual sphere-sounds are invoked here, but their presence is reinforced by what would seem to be Milton's covert allusion to the many allegorizations of the other Sirens as forces of eloquence leading men not to their destruction, but toward God.

by leaving out those harsh chromatick (later variant:
 ill-sounding) jarres
of sin that all our music marres
& in our lives & in our song . . .

The tentative change from "chromatick" to "ill-sounding"
was quite possibly designed to avoid a mistakenly over-specific
reading, in which it might be assumed that Milton was arguing
against the virtue of a particular musical style, or against an
association of, say, secular music with such a style.[136] Here,
"& in our lives & in our song" clearly differentiates, I think,
mundane existence from the special life of religious contemplation and prayer, and Milton seems to be using "song" much
as Herbert might. But instead of merely qualifying "rightly"
in line 18, the final version of these lines includes a reference
to Original Sin, and to one of his own favorite themes of the
prelapsarian audibility of the celestial music. "As once we
did" introduces the historical dimension, and clearly outlines
the reference of the final prayer's "O may we soon."[137]

"That song" is referred to three times, all preceded by the
same demonstrative pronoun. The "pure concent" to which
the hearers' attentions are raised is surely, as has been pointed
out,[138] the celestial harmony, which, in Milton's synthesis of
Christian and pagan themes, is prefigured by the music of the
siren-spheres just as the latter is anticipated by actual earthly
music. "That undisturbed Song of pure concent" is also characterized by the "pure concent," the agreement, of its own
component elements, text and melody. Milton's meditation

[136] For "chromatick" as a stylistic designation, rather than a specific
reference to harmonic or melodic texture, see John Daniel's "Chromatick
Tunes" songs, discussed above, Chapter IV.

[137] On this see Hutton, op.cit., pp. 50-51. The comments of Leo Spitzer
on the emendations here, in op.cit., Part II, 337, are of most interest when
they outline a specifically linguistic point, such as his intriguing remark
that the deletion of earlier line 11: "loud symphonie of silver trumpets
blow" may have turned on Milton's desire to rid so "Hebrew" a poem of
so Greek a word as "symphonie," whether used in a Greek technical sense
of consonance, or in a more modern sense, synonymous with "consort."

[138] Particularly by Hutton, op.cit., p. 49.

on "solemn" music ("its music is 'solemn,'" says Leo Spitzer, "because it has the primordial and primeval aim of all Christian music: religious elation")[139] leads him almost at once to his underlying theme of the true, "rational," "eloquent" music of both Greek theory and of its adaptation in Humanist *musica speculativa*; the strength of the continually referred-to song as a perfect, functioning union of voice and verse carries over into the jar and din and discord of lines 17-24. The implication is that the ancient harmony of melody and text was broken by the act of disobedience that brought human history into lamented being, aside from the harmoniousness of the "perfet Diapason," the great octave into which all creatures were cast by the moving power of divine love. It is almost as if all created life were being figured forth as moving, singing spheres themselves: such, at any rate, is the force of "whose love their motion sway'd / In perfet Diapason." But what is finally important here is that the "fair musick that all creatures made / *To* their great Lord" (my italics) is the music of prayer, the solemn singing whose temporary reunification of the divorced music and poetry is itself moving the poet to contemplation in the poem. Prayer, since the Fall, must needs be a consciously contrived process, a work, in fact, of poetic art; it cannot be automatic and spontaneous as once it was before "disproportion'd sin / Jarr'd against natures chime." "That song" is perfect prayer, possible, in an imperfect world, only through the act of liturgical-poetical-musical devotion. The traditional lament of early Baroque musical esthetics, to the effect that the music of Classical Antiquity possessed the perfect unification of text and melody from which the corrupt modern bifurcation of musical and poetic concern was a long fall, seems to lurk behind all this as a secular counterpart of the Christian Fall. And considering Milton's Classical-Christian syntheses, one might not be too far afield in suggesting that the "celestial consort" from which all has fallen away might have involved for him the union

[139] *Op.cit.*, Part II, 336.

of text and music, of rational eloquence and the cosmological operation of Christian grace, all mingled in a composite image.

The "high-rais'd phantasie" of line 4 refers, as Professor Hutton has pointed out,[140] to the imaginative faculty of the soul that meditates, in Christian Neoplatonist thought, between the body and the intellect; but he seems to miss the traditional use of "high-rais'd" to describe the psychic tonus. Although the conventional metaphor of the tuned instrument is lacking here, the clear implication of the "raising" (in pitch, in altitude, in tension, in moral power) of the soul, or part of it, is not. The subject of the poem is certainly as much the public prayer of its title as it is the moralizing of the relationship between *musica mundana* and *musica humana*, occasioned by the hearing of some practical music. Unlike the contemplative, solitary poetic treatment of personal prayer, "At a Solemn Musick" starts out with the fact of a high musical service, moves from it to an account of its effects, as we noted above, returns to the Biblical imagery of its immediate context (and of the text of an actual anthem?), and finally moves into the prayer for salvation. But it moves through the consciousness of a particular poet, for whom the concerns of the responsibilities of the poetic role and the poetic gifts were to become monumental. The relationship of poetry to the devotion of the inner voice can be figured in the relationship between public and private prayer, in a way; and Milton's personal engagement in the poem may be seen to appear in connection with this kind of comparison. The task of the poet was in the early 1630's at Horton beginning, for Milton, to assume a course parallel to that of the Priest-Shepherd, or, as we might put it, to that of the sacred composer whose obligation it was properly to unite holy text and influential music. Thus, in a sense, "At a Solemn Musick" ranges its meditation over the condition of the listening poet as well.[141]

[140] *Op.cit.*, p. 49.
[141] Some of the notions in this paragraph are hinted at in an unpublished Columbia University master's essay by William A. Darkey, Jr., entitled

If the harmony of word and sound has been soured, the composer of liturgical music can provide short moments of sweetness during which the pure, perfect source of all sweetness itself may be, if not glimpsed actually, then promised for an eventual eternity. So may the poet, by employing his skill in unison with proper intention, approach the perfection of inspired eloquence of the Psalmist himself.

For that Psalmist, music was the epitome of holy intercourse. We have seen how, during the middle of the seventeenth century in England, that epitomization received either qualification or change of emphasis in its treatment by poets. Milton's combination of the praise of music generally, in the fashion of the previous century, with the figurative equivalence of song and prayer of the contemplative tradition, the whole finally turned to a consideration of public prayer and public utterance (it is not so much the jarring of disproportioned *musica humana* that is bemoaned, but of customs and practices), represents to some extent a synthesis of these conventions. In "At a Solemn Musick" Milton seems almost to be consecrating his life and his art to a purpose figured forth as a liturgical one. Like most of its young author's subsequent productions in the next few years, it is an ambitious poem. And like them, its success seems all the more enhanced by its forward qualities.

"Milton's 'At a Solemn Musick'; a Commentary" (1949), to which I am indebted for the stress it puts on the continued importance of the initial invocation throughout the poem, a point missed by many commentators. See, for example, the insistence of Clay Hunt, in *Donne's Poetry: Essays in Literary Analysis* (New Haven, 1954), p. 133, that "the harmony of the soul which Milton contemplates is primarily an emotional harmony," a point which seems somehow either trivial, or misleading in its simplistic interpretation of what Milton might have meant by *musica humana*.

CHAPTER VI · THE SKY UNTUNED: THE TRIVIALIZATION OF UNIVERSAL HARMONY

The Music of Easy Praise

"*S*HE THAT with poetry is won / Is but a desk to write upon.*"* So argues the Widow in Samuel Butler's *Hudibras* in resisting the suit of her pedantic Knight as she visits him in prison. She goes on to catalogue the outrages to which the innocent recipients of versified compliment must submit, and shortly objects to the fact that

> The sun and moon, by her bright eyes
> Eclips'd and darken'd in the skies;
> Are but black patches that she wears,
> Cut into suns, and moons, and stars,
> By which astrologers, as well
> As those in heav'n above, can tell
> What strange events they do foreshow,
> Unto her under-world below.
> Her voice, the music of the spheres,
> So loud, it deafens mortal ears;
> As wise philosophers have thought,
> And that's the cause we hear it not.[1]
> > (*Hudibras*, Pt. ii, Canto i, 609-620)

While the opening lines of this passage satirize what might have been the target of many lampooning sonnets of the 1590's, the references to the music of the spheres seem to be aiming somewhere else. Indeed, it would not be amiss to assume that a particular conventional use of the notion of cosmic harmony had reached, by the time of the Restoration,

---

[1] Samuel Butler, *Hudibras* (Part ii pub. 1664), ed. T. R. Nash (London, 1847), Canto i, 202.

a general currency. Butler's closing joke is a simple, though clever one; it involves a literal reading of "loud" for "great" as descriptive of the sound that the spheres were supposed to have made as they spun about the central earth, rendering their harmonies too "great" for the narrow mortal compass of human hearing.

We have seen how such lore was preserved throughout the seventeenth century, either as doctrine for such *outré* synthesizers of knowledge as Robert Fludd, or as part of what was actually a rudimentary History of Ideas for interests as diverse as those of Milton or of committed Rationalists whose intent was to refute and emend. We have also observed the use of such scraps of *musica speculativa* in the English poetry of the era that I hope I may now refer to as "Baroque" without undue cavil, and how, by means of the elaborate technical resources of seventeenth-century English poetic diction, traditional ideas about the nature of music were put to varied purposes. The representation and celebration of the passions, the defense of the affective power of poetry itself, the involutions of pietistic religious meditation, and the swelling and compressed intellectual structures of Milton and Marvell respectively—all of these found, in a body of encyclopedic information that was becoming rapidly discredited as empirically untrue, a conventional subject matter, ready for poetic transformation. The literal fact of the music of the spheres had never held a formal place in Christian doctrine. During the course of the century it lost its own hold on secular natural belief. It is not surprising, consequently, to observe the persistent growth of a use of the notion of the heavenly harmony that would not depend upon such a belief in either its physical or metaphysical reality.

This use occurs in the more or less epigrammatic language of praise and compliment. Usually addressed to a lady, framed in honor of her accomplishments in the genteel and graceful arts of singing or playing, many poems employing figures of the music of the spheres, sacred and lofty choirs, musical angels, etc., are to be found wherever the qualities of Cavalier diction are to be seen, wherever the roots of an Augustan tradition may lie, and wherever the dominant ironies of Metaphysical wit make a well-turned compliment, politely employing a received metaphor, too obvious and trivial for serious consideration. Borderline cases, here as elsewhere, are naturally of interest. Here is Carew's "Song: Celia Singing," for example:

> Harke how my *Celia*, with the choyce
> Musique of her hand and voyce
> Stills the loude wind; and makes the wilde
> Incensed Bore, and Panther milde!
> Marke how those statues like men move,
> Whilst men with wonder statues prove!
> This stiffe rock bends to worship her,
> That Idoll turns Idolater.
>   Now see how all the new inspir'd
> Images, with love are fir'd!
> Harke how the tender Marble grones,
> And all the late transformed stones,
> Court the faire nymph with many a teare,
> Which she (more stony then they were)
> Beholds with unrelenting mind;
> Whilst they amaz'd to see combin'd
> Such matchlesse beautie, with disdaine,
> Are all turn'd into stones againe.[2]

In this simple little piece, the lady's singing and playing permit her to be identified with Orpheus; the anecdote of the stones responding to the Greek hero's art provides the center of the wit. The wry note of Celia's stoniness is almost inevitable, given the governing conceit, but it seems hardly to matter whether her coldness is being rebuked or admired. It is for the couplet about the statues in the first stanza and for the final twist of the image of petrifaction that the whole poem seems

[2] Thomas Carew, *Poems*, ed. Rhodes Dunlap (Oxford, 1949), p. 38.

to exist at all. It is little more than an expanded epigram, after all, as can be seen by comparison with Shirley's treatment of stony disdain, framed squarely as a rebuke:

Upon his Mistress Dancing

I stood and saw my mistress dance,
    Silent, and with so fixt an eye,
Some might suppose me in a trance,
    But being asked, why?
By one that knew I was in love,
    I could not but impart
My wonder, to behold her move
    So nimbly with a marble heart.[3]

In epigrammatic writing generally it is the success of a final, carefully prepared effect toward which the wit may be said to move; in this respect, what we would want to call Metaphysical wit covers a different kind of terrain, exploring the potentialities of the images and figures it has already produced. This is another way of saying that no single trope or figure, no one rhetorical unit of any kind in a unified, conceited portion of Metaphysical argument seems to be as necessary to some final effect as the clinching point of an epigram. In the period of gradual assumption by lyric verse of the Augustan virtues of "neatness, sincerity, and aptness of thought," it was the strategy of the epigram that came to prevail. The closure of portions of a poetic line of thought into discrete propositions resulted as much from the stopped couplets and syntactical symmetries of the tradition of Jonson, Herrick, the Cavaliers, and Waller as from a narrowing of subject matter toward the boundaries of the complimentary and the occasional. But it is in the complimentary expanded epigram, the occasional song, the amatory exhortation, and the commendatory ode, those proto-Augustan forms *par excellence*, that stock allusions and comparisons come to flower

---

[3] From *Poems, & c.* (1646), in James Shirley, *Poems*, ed. R. L. Armstrong (New York, 1941), p. 5.

almost as they do in the lower reaches and declining days of sonneteering.[4]

To trace the gradual course of standardization of the poetic treatment of the music of the spheres, one might well start out with the rather bald appearance of the device of musical praise in Herrick. Musical allusions in general abound in the *Hesperides*; more particularly several epigrams of the type of "Upon a Gentlewoman with a sweet Voice" may be cited here:

> So long you did not sing, or touch your Lute,
> We knew 'twas Flesh and Blood, that there sate mute.
> But when your Playing, and your Voice came in,
> 'Twas no more you then, but a *Cherubin*.[5]

Another, written upon Julia's voice, is even more direct:

> Let but thy voice engender with the string,
> And Angels will be borne, while thou dost sing.[6]

A peculiar property of this sort of praise is that it seems no more or less extravagant when extended toward some object for whom the cosmological extravagances are less hyperbolic. Here is "A Canticle to *Apollo*," for example:

> 1. Play *Phebus* on thy Lute:
>   And we will all sit mute:
>   By listning to thy Lire,
>   That sets all eares on fire.
>
> 2. Harke, harke, the God do's play!
>   And as he leads the way
>   Through heaven, the very Spheres,
>   As men, turne all to eares.[7]

And here is music itself, personified as a particular lady:

---

[4] See T. K. Whipple, *Martial and the English Epigram from Wyatt to Ben Jonson* (Berkeley, 1925), pp. 281-285.

[5] Robert Herrick, *Complete Poems*, ed. L. C. Martin (Oxford, 1956), p. 95.

[6] *Ibid.*, p. 102.   [7] *Ibid.*, p. 151.

To Musick. A Song.

Musick, thou *Queen of Heaven*, Care-charming-spel,
    That strik'st a stilnesse into hell:
Thou that tam'st *Tygers*, and fierce storms (that rise)
    With thy soule-melting Lullabies:
Fall down, down, down, from those thy chiming spheres,
To charme our soules, as thou enchant'st our eares.[8]

Two more little poems "Upon *Julia's* Voice" employ the
"soule-melting" image but with a subsequent transformation
that render a cosmological allusion unnecessary:

So smooth, so sweet, so silv'ry is thy voice,
As, could they hear, the Damn'd would make no noise,
But listen to thee, (walking in thy chamber)
Melting melodious words, to Lutes of amber.[9]

and again:

When I thy singing next shall heare,
Ile wish I might turne all to eare,
To drink in Notes, and Numbers; such
As blessed soules cann't heare too much:

Then melted down, there let me lye
Entranc'd and lost confusedly:
And by thy Musique strucken mute,
Die, and be turn'd into a Lute.[10]

The whole interest of both sonneteers and of later writers
employing a Neoplatonist soul-instrument correspondence for
devotional purposes would have been in representing the
specific mechanics of the metamorphosis that is merely stated
here. But Herrick's use of all the musical paraphernalia, the
instruments, the Orphean myths, and the celestial singing
itself, is perhaps more than anything else directed toward
augmenting the repertory of integral objects and events pro-
grammatically listed in "The Argument of his Book." His

[8] *Ibid.*, p. 103.   [9] *Ibid.*, p. 22.   [10] *Ibid.*

Muses' "country wit" and "meaner Minstralsie" he invoked not only in a tone of conventional pastoral irony, but with respect to his concentration on the particular and the immediate. But fragments of Classic myth and bits of musical lore come under the same gaze as the *"Blossomes, Birds,* and *Bowers,"* his Julia's every part, his Devonshire May-poles. In agreeing with Professor Douglas Bush about this "neo-pagan" element in Herrick's writing,[11] we should be hard put to it to list the characteristics of this gaze under either heading of "subject" or "style" alone.

Nor should this be considered a difficulty. We have seen thus far how music in general, both speculative and practical, fares very differently, as a subject matter for poetry, under the observation or control of different styles. During the middle of the seventeenth century, the growth of "the progeny of Numbers new" of the "tribe of Ben," the gradual reception of Augustan modes, tended to enforce a separation of musical lore from musical practice. They continue to be associated only in that references to the former become standard encomiastic epithets applied to occasions of the latter. To see myths of speculative music given any considerable treatment outside this complimentary domain is quite rare.

An interesting such case, however, is that of a poem by Ben Jonson himself. "The Musicall Strife" from his *Underwoods* (1640) is set "In a Pastorall Dialogue," thus permitting the "musicall" content of the argument between the two pastoral antagonists to escape reference to a world of actuality. At the heart of the debate itself is a point of love, but it is carried on in terms of two conceptions of speculative music, the celestial and the affective. It is significant that they are made somehow antithetical:

SHEE.

Come with our Voyces, let us warre,
    And challenge all the Spheares,

[11] See Douglas Bush, *English Literature in the Earlier Seventeenth Century* (Oxford, 1945), pp. 112-116.

Till each of us be made a Starre,
    And all the world turne Eares.

HEE.

At such a Call, what beast or fowle,
    Of reason emptie is?
What Tree or stone doth want a soule?
    What man but must lose his?

SHEE.

Mixe then your Notes, that we may prove
    To stay the running floods;
To make the Mountaine Quarries move;
    And call the walking woods?

HEE.

What need of mee? doe you but sing
    Sleepe, and the Grave will wake,
No tunes are sweet, now words have sting,
    But what those lips doe make.

SHEE.

They say the Angells marke each Deed,
    And exercise below,
And out of inward pleasure feed
    On what they viewing know.

HEE.

O sing not you then, lest the best
    Of Angels should be driven
To fall againe; at such a feast,
    Mistaking earth for heaven.

SHEE.

Nay, rather both our soules be strayn'd
    To meet their high desire;
So they in state of Grace retain'd
    May wish us of their Quire.[12]

[12] Ben Jonson, *Works*, ed. C. H. Herford and Percy and Evelyn Simpson (Oxford, 1925-1952), VIII, 143-144.

[339]

Throughout this poem the lady's wish is to merge with her swain in an act of idealized love, while his is to admire. In musical terms, these conflicting desires are figured forth in her injunction to her lover to join her in concerted singing and in his insistence on the Orphean power of her voice. In the first stanza, the lady's invitation to war is not meant to refer to an internecine combat between the two; but the "Call" in the second stanza means her voice, not the singing of both of them. He insists on this in the fourth stanza and, in the sixth, counters her preceding celestial reference with a move that might be said to sum up the whole tradition of trivialization of the *musica mundana* with which we have been concerned thus far. For the young man, the affective power of music subdues the cosmological order: the lady's singing attracts angels as easily as dumb beasts or stones. Such was the power of Dryden's Saint Cecilia, when, drawn by the power of music personified,

> An angel heard
> And straight appear'd,
> Mistaking earth for heaven.

Whether or not Dryden actually appropriated Jonson's line is unimportant here. What remains significant is the generality that such an argument was to attain. In the enclosed pastoral world of Jonson's lyric, it is the lady's Humanist doctrine of elevation of the soul through an imitation of the universal music which is given the last word. In the poetry of Jonson's successors, however, it is the view of the young man which prevails.

Robert Heath in his *Clarastella* (1650), for example, celebrates his lady's singing in just such a way. Heath seems to have been sufficiently anti-Copernican to celebrate Clarastella's dancing as follows:

> As when with stedfast eyes we view the Sun,
> We know it goes though see no motion;

So undiscern'd she mov'd, that we
Perceiv'd she stirr'd, but did not see.[13]

But in discoursing on her singing, he seems unconvinced of
the ultimate, transcendent power of the "harmonious spheres,"
treating it in the first stanza with other stock images. It is
only in the second, where the lady's visual beauty is equated
to that of her voice, that a refinement is introduced in which
she herself, conquering both senses, reaches angelic perfection:

Ye that in love delight
Approach this sacred Quire and feast your ears!
Whilst the sweetest *Syren* sings,
Whose musick equals the harmonious spheres,
And perhaps richer pleasure brings!
The dying Swan or *Philomel*
O' th' wood not warbles half so well;
Observe the cadence where each dying sound,
Creates new Echoes to a fifth rebound.

Here's musick to the sight.
She looks and sings with such Majestick grace,
That when I *Clarastella* hear,
She more a woman seems, her voice and face
Taking at once both eye and eare,
That which of these two senses may
Be most refresht, is hard to say.
To glorifie her after death, She'll ne'er
Need Change; She's Angel now, and Heav'n is here.[14]

The lady's name itself would seem to indicate that she is
already part of the heavenly orders; she is certainly closer in
this to a Petrarchan ideal heroine than to Herrick's homely
Julia, and it is obvious that any attempt to universalize or
epitomize her virtues would convey no new information
about her. To say of Clarastella that her "musick equals the

[13] In *The Oxford Book of Seventeenth Century Verse*, ed. Sir Herbert
Grierson and G. Bullough (Oxford, 1934), p. 718.
[14] *Ibid.*, p. 718.

harmonious spheres" is almost to assert what modern philosophers call an analytic proposition in which, as Kant defined it,[15] the meaning of the predicate is already contained in that of the subject. One might propose an analogue here in the domain of poetics, certainly within the sub-class of epigrams, where a certain degree of novelty always seems requisite. Jonson himself, in his *Conversations with Drummond of Hawthornden* (1619), remarked that "A Great many Epigrams were ill, because they expressed jn the end, what sould have been understood, by what was said."[16] An interesting problem might be posed, in this connection, with all of these commendatory poems on a particular lady's musical virtues: are they to be considered as mechanical in form and in treatment of the subject as, say, any dedicatory sonnet prefixed to a song collection and proclaiming the composer to be the latest avatar of Orpheus? Are they little more than exercise-pieces in a form which made hyperbolic citations of musical lore mandatory? Or are they to be judged within the range of Jonson's criterion for epigrams, and understood as having been so judged by their authors and their contemporaries?

I am not sure that there is any great difference between saying that the latter case is true, and that one can indeed find occasional good poems in among the "ill" ones, and saying that the content of these poems is completely governed by the avowed subject, but that occasionally we can find individual pieces that somehow rise above the convention, while purporting to represent it and no more. Such a poem, I think, is Lovelace's "Gratiana Dauncing and Singing" from his *Lucasta* (1649):

I.

SEE! with what constant Motion
Even, and glorious, as the Sunne,

[15] See *Prolegomena to Any Future Metaphysics*, with an introduction by Lewis W. Beck (New York, 1951), pp. 14-19.
[16] Ben Jonson, *Works*, I, 143.

Gratiana steeres that Noble Frame,
Soft as her breast, sweet as her voyce
That gave each winding Law and poyze,
   And swifter then the wings of Fame.

II.

She beat the happy Pavement
By such a Starre made Firmament,
   Which now no more the Roofe envies;
But swells up high with *Atlas* ev'n,
Bearing the brighter, nobler Heav'n,
   And in her, all the Dieties.

III.

Each step trod out a Lovers thought
And the Ambitious hopes he brought,
   Chain'd to her brave feet with such arts,
Such sweet command, and gentle awe,
As when she ceas'd, we sighing saw
   The floore lay pav'd with broken hearts.

IV.

So did she move; so did she sing
Like the Harmonious spheres that bring
   Unto their Rounds their musick's ayd;
Which she performed such a way,
As all th' inamour'd world will say
   The *Graces* daunced, and *Apollo* play'd.[17]

It is Gratiana's dancing, primarily, which affords room for invention in the second and third stanzas, with their conceit of pavement, heaven, roof and floor. At the end of the third stanza, the turn of wit is really completed, and the addition of the final strophe serves only to handle, rather anticlimactically, the praise of the lady's singing. But even the heavenly

[17] Richard Lovelace, *Poems*, ed. L. H. Wilkinson (Oxford, 1930), p. 25.

spheres, like the strings plucked by Crashaw's lutenist, are described as dancing to their own song; they are dancers primarily, and their singing is subordinated to their graceful movement. So, too, with Gratiana herself, whose very name suggests the Graces to whom she is likened at the end of the poem, and whose singing remains peripheral to the domain of the principal conceit. In general, it may be remarked of the concluding three lines that they express "what should have been understood by what was said" initially, that they possess the appearance, if not the function, of a tag.

In a sonnet in William Habington's *Castara* (1634) the introduction of the music of the spheres plays only a role in the larger action of the wit. Here the praise stays slightly more in bounds, perhaps because it is being directed specifically toward the lady's accomplished *pianissimo*.

To *Castara*, Softly
Singing to her Selfe

Sing forth sweete Cherubin (for we have choice
Of reasons in thy beauty and the voyce,
To name thee so, and scarce appeare prophane)
Sing forth, that while the orbs celestiall straine
To eccho thy sweete note, our humane eares
May then receive the Musicke of the Spheares.
But yet take heede, lest if the Swans of Thames,
That adde harmonious pleasure to the streames,
Oth' sudden heare thy well-divided breath,
Should listen, and in silence welcome death:
And ravisht Nightingales, striving too high
To reach thee, in the emulation dye.
  And thus there will be left no bird to sing
  Farewell to th' Waters, welcome to the Spring.[18]

Although she is called "sweete Cherubin" at the outset, what follows is in no way really redundant: the exquisite softness

[18] Text from edition of 1640, ed. Edward Arber (London, 1870), p. 21.

of her music enables us to hear the celestial music (and implicitly to be transported to a better world); because the spheres themselves, to outdo her in delicate quietness, can only overtax themselves with an unusually loud performance that finally, by reason of the increased dynamic, becomes audible to mortal ears. The remainder of the poem can add little to this in the way of praise, and thus turns to *caveat*, in which the standard musical birds, swan and nightingale, are employed. Without the boundless resources of the cosmic instrument, they can only perish, having been bested; the swan dies in an extraordinary silence, the nightingale in the true fashion of Strada's much-imitated bird.

In studying the development of these stock hyper-Orphean and ultra-celestial figures of praise, however, we must distinguish at least two cases in which apparently similar devices are put to rather different purposes. Another nightingale, apostrophized in sonnet xxiii of Drummond of Hawthornden's *Flowres of Sion*, becomes more the subject of devotion, and covertly linked to Christ and the Saul-healing David:

> What soule can be so sicke, which by thy Songs
> (Attir'd in sweetnesse) sweetly is not driven
> Quite to forget Earths turmoiles, spights and wrongs,
> And lift a reverend Eye and Thought to Heaven?
>   Sweet Artlesse Songstarre, thou my Mind dost raise
>   To Ayres of Spheares, yes, and to Angells Layes.[19]

Here the bird is an ecclesiastical rather than a civil musician. The question put in the final quatrain quoted above superficially resembles traditional appeals to the universality of music in its cosmic role (Lorenzo's famous speech in *The Merchant of Venice* v, i, for example: ". . . naught so stockish, hard and full of rage / But music for the time doth change his nature"). Actually, the question points to the uplifting effects, not of the celestial concert, but of the healing melodies

[19] William Drummond of Hawthornden, *Poetical Works*, ed. L. E. Kastner (Manchester, 1913), II, 31.

of the religious bird. The pun, in the couplet, on *songster-song-star* reinforces the figure of raising the mind to thoughts of heaven by associating the singer with the celestial orb itself. It is almost as if we were pointing out the difference between two different encomiastic uses of the word "heavenly." The first kind is figurative and, even if the word itself is taken to refer only to the phenomenon of sky, broadly hyperbolic; while the second use depends upon a specific religious, if not actually theological, meaning for "heaven" and what it concerns and entails.

In Praise of the Actual Musician

A variant of this case may be seen in another sonnet by Drummond of Hawthornden, which verges on the convention of invocation of the instrument as Muse that has been previously traced:

My Lute, bee as thou wast when thou didst grow
With thy greene Mother in some shadie Grove,
When immelodious *Windes* but made thee moue,
And *Birds* on thee their Ramage did bestow.
Sith that deare Voyce which did thy Sounds approue,
Which vs'd in such harmonious Straines to flow,
Is reft from Earth *to tune those Spheares aboue*,
What art thou but a Harbenger of Woe?
Thy pleasing notes, be pleasing notes no more,
But orphane Wailings to the fainting Eare,
Each Stoppe a Sigh, each Sound drawes forth a Teare,
Bee therefore silent as in Woods before,
   Or if that any Hand to touch thee daigne,
   Like widow'd Turtle, still her Losse complaine.[20]

Here the lady who sometime sang to the lute's voice joins

[20] *Ibid.*, I, 60. See also "A Lovers Heaven" (same edition, I, 100), where ". . . Make mee think yee are Heaven" is quite deliberately applied to the transcendent powers of the lover's imagination (cf. "The lunatic, the lover and the poet / Are of imagination all compact," Shakespeare, *A Midsummer-Night's Dream*, v, i, 7-8).

the heavenly concert by reason of her death; *"to tune those Spheares aboue"* is a figure expressing primarily the passing of her virtuous (and, to the poet, dear) life, and bearing only a secondary relevance to her musicianship.

There must also be distinguished here, I think, the case of the complimentary epigram addressed to an actual musician. Such poems range from the baldly commercial puff of the epistle or sonnet dedicatory prefaced to a songbook,[21] to the successful personal statement of Milton's sonnet to Henry Lawes; the convention in which they are cast goes back to the Greek Anthology, at least. But the operation of the compliment is always a different one from that of the developing cliché under consideration here. In the first place, it is actually the skill of the composer or performer that is being praised, however elaborately or undeservedly, rather than the beloved lady's power to charm the poet who is, usually, already passionately devoted to her. In the second place, there may be a bond of class, or craft, or faction between the author and the subject of his praise that may, in extreme cases, allow the praise to redound upon the original payer of the compliment. Erwin Panofsky has shown most convincingly how Jan Van Eyck, in adding the name "Tymotheos" to his inscription, "Leal Souvenir," on a portrait of the Burgundian composer Gilles Binchois, manages to elevate himself by association: the Burgundian court would become likened to that of Alexander and Van Eyck himself, of course, would be Apelles.[22] A strong connection between a musician and the maker of his poetic monument continued to be made by the almost automatic reference, overt or implicit, to Orpheus, who always

[21] See, for example, the prefatory poems to Thomas Ravenscroft's *A Briefe Discourse* (1614), reprinted with commentary by M. C. Boyd in *Elizabethan Music and Musical Criticism* (Philadelphia, 1940), pp. 304-307. Also, the volumes of *The English Madrigal School*, ed. Edmund H. Fellowes (Oxford, 1913-1924) for commendatory poems therein.

[22] Erwin Panofsky, "Who is Van Eyck's 'Tymotheos'?" *Journal of the Warburg and Courtauld Institutes*, XII (1949), pp. 80ff. Also see the same author's *Early Netherlandish Painting* (Cambridge, Mass., 1954), I, 196-197.

remains in Renaissance literature the musician as poet, as opposed to Amphion's role of musician as builder, as the Sirens' as seductresses, Terpander's as revolutionary, etc.

It is easy to see how the cosmic cliché finds its way into the dedicatory or commendatory poem in much the same manner as the Orphean reference: often a very gentle twist of novelty barely saves the allusion from becoming almost completely mechanical. Often the dedicatory verses to a musician's volume have been written by some fellow musician, of course, and the tone of the compliment becomes strongly interested, if not actually professionalist. The early seventeenth-century lutenist and instrumental composer, Antony Holborne, contributed a dedicatory sonnet to Morley's *Plaine and Easie Introduction* (1597) in which he concludes his praises with an overt acknowledgment of the commercial advantages to the professional music teacher that might eventually arise under the influence of what is, occasionally, actual advertising. (Philomathes, the pupil of the dialogue who is hungry for musical instruction, reports that at a banquet he was shamed by being unable to sing his part from a madrigal book: "Yea, some whispered to others, demaunding how I was brought up.")[23] But here, as elsewhere, it is the stock reference to Orpheus that is employed:

> Like Orpheus sitting on high Thracian hill,
>   That beasts and mountains to his ditties drew,
> So doth he draw with his sweet music's skill
>   Men to attention of his science true.
> Wherein it seems that Orpheus he exceeds,
>   For he wild beasts, this, men with pleasure feeds.[24]

Even the most ambitious poets were unable, under similar circumstances, to do more than deepen the groove of the convention. Thus Phineas Fletcher, writing in praise of John

[23] Thomas Morley, *A Plaine and Easie Introduction to Practicall Musicke* (1597), p. 1.

[24] Text from Morley, *op.cit.*, ed. R. A. Harman (New York, 1953), p. 4.

Tomkins,[25] insisted that whether said gentleman were composing secular or sacred music,

> The ravish't soul, with thy sweet songs consenting,
> Scorning the earth, in Heav'nly extasie
>   Transcends the starres, and with the angels train
>   Those courts survaies; and now come back again,
> Finds yet another heav'n in thy delightfull strain.[26]

Here the "ravish't soul," although transported heavenward, finds that the earthly and practical music of Tomkins' songs and anthems fulfills far more of the promises of heavenly joys that they bring to the hearer than does the "actuality" of heaven. With the addition of the proper moral, one feels, this could easily form a strong argument in the puritan case against elaborate music in the liturgy, a case which never for a moment denied the power of sound, but only the possibility of that power's being put to any beneficial effects whatsoever.

Only occasionally will a masterful turn of wit justify the almost obligatory extravagances of the commendatory poem; but even then the wit will not be of the Metaphysical sort that we have come to associate with the expression of complex states of attitude and feeling in the poet. It is rather a wit of embroidery. We might compare two bits of commendatory writing of Lovelace in this respect. Concluding his commendatory verses prefixed to Eldred Revett's *Poems* of 1657, Lovelace invokes his subject's heaven, his "proper Christalline; / Whence that Mole-hill *Parnassus* thou dost view," and finally apostrophizes:

> There move translated youth! inroll'd i'th' Quire,
> That only doth with holy lays inspire;
> To whom his burning Coach *Eliah* sent,
> And th' royal Prophet-priest his Harp hath lent,

---

[25] John Tomkins (1586-1638), from 1614 organist of St. Paul's.
[26] From *Poeticall Miscellanies* (1633), in *Poetical Works of Giles and Phineas Fletcher*, ed. F. S. Boas (Cambridge, 1904), II, 234.

Which thou dost tune in consort, unto those
Clap Wings for ever at each hallow'd close;
Whilst we now weak and fainting in our praise,
Sick, Eccho ore thy *Halleuiahs*.[27]

Except for the angelic applause at each musical cadence and
the physiological symptoms of the effectiveness of the music-
poetry being praised, there is little in the way of ingenuity
here; the image of tuning the harp (David's harp instead of
the more usual Apollonian lyre, probably because of the
"Moral and Divine" nature of the poetry) in consort with
the heavenly music, is the stock one. But the use of musical
conceits, both conventional and more inventive in nature, can be
seen in another commendatory poem, *"To my Noble Kinsman
T. S. Esq; On his Lyrick Poems composed by Mr. J. G."*[28]

1.

What means this stately Tablature,
  The Ballance of thy streins?
Which seems, in stead of sifting pure,
  T'extend and rack thy veins;
Thy *Odes* first their own Harmony did break,
For singing troth is but in tune to speak.

2.

Nor thus thy golden Feet and Wings,
  May it be thought false Melody
T'ascend to heav'n by silver strings,
  This is *Urania's* Heraldry:
Thy royal Poem now we may extol,
And truly *Luna* Blazon'd upon *Sol*.

[27] "To my Dear Friend Mr. *E. R.* On his Poems Moral and Divine." In
Lovelace, *Poems* (*ed.cit.*), p. 186.
[28] "T. S." is Thomas Stanley; the poem is prefixed to John Gamble's
Ayres and Dialogues (1656).

3.

As when *Amphion* first did call
   Each listning stone from's Den;
And with the Lute did form his Wall,
   But with his words the men;
So in your twisted Numbers now, you thus,
Not only stocks perswade, but ravish us.

4.

Thus do your Ayrs Eccho o're
   The Notes and *Anthems* of the *Sphœres*,
And their whole Consort back restore,
   As if Earth too would blesse Heav'ns Ears:
But yet the Spoaks by which they scal'd so high,
Gamble hath wisely laid of *Ut Re Mi*.[29]

Here a distinction between words and music is in keeping
with the nature of the dedication of the title; but it is handled
excellently in the first and third stanzas, while the second
and fourth (perhaps schematically distinguished by the addition of an extra foot in the "b" rhyming lines) specifically
commend the music to which the poems are set. The conceit of
a scaling ladder which enables the celebrated songs to sur-
mount the walls of heaven is drawn into the musical imagery
by the pun on "scale," as is the first syllable of the composer's
name made to resonate against the *Gamut* of the musical
compass. In separating the poet-musician role of Amphion,
the poem sets up the distinction invoked in the opening
question: "What is this musical notation doing to the body
and soul of your text, O poet?" and the compliment is able
to utilize the strategy of answering this question in order to
avoid banality. The cosmological cliché seems to have been
recognized as such, at least when employed in commendatory
poems, at the time that this piece was written. Lovelace's

[29] Lovelace, *op.cit.*, pp. 186-187.

younger brother Dudley contributed a poem to Gamble's songbook that commenced as follows:

To my much honored Cozen
Mr. *Stanley*, Upon his Poems set
by Mr. *John Gamble*.

I.

Enough, Enough, of Orbs and Spheres,
  Reach me a Trumpet or a Drum,
To *sound* sharp *Synnets* in your Ears,
  And *Beat* a Deep *Encomium*.

II.

I know not th' *Eight Intelligence*;
  Those that do understand it, Pray
Let them step thither, and from thence
  Speak what they all do Sing or Say:

III.

Nor what your *Diapasons* are,
  Your *Sympathies* and *Symphonies*;
To me they seem as distant farre
  As whence they take their Infant rise

IV.

But I've a gratefull Heart can ring
  A *peale* of *Ordnance* to your praise,
And *Volleys* of *small Plaudits* bring
  To Clowd or Crown about your Baies. . . .[30]

This is obviously a case of the traditional blustered disclaimer to any eloquence of the professional soldier; but in dismissing the eight intelligences that guide the singing spheres it seems to be rejecting the complimentary convention along with the

[30] *Ibid.*, pp. 324-325. "T'ascend to heav'n by silver strings"; cf. Morley, *Plaine and Easie Introduction* (1597), p. 179.

obsolete doctrine. But of course the remaining stanzas are relentless in draining the military conceit of its juice.

A curious, late blending of the commendatory poem and the idealized, complimentary epigram may be noticed, incidentally, in William Congreve's "irregular ode" on the professional singer and lutenist Arabella Hunt. Praised by Dr. Johnson as its author's best exercise in the genre, Congreve's ode, published in his *Poems Upon Several Occasions* (1710), is far more extravagantly passionate than most commendatory poems. This is perhaps because its subject is a woman. The end of the first strophe asks that the poet be allowed a musical ecstasy, but instead of the usual ravishment, the demand for a Baroque *Liebestod* is phrased in the equally conventional pun: "For I would hear her Voice, and try / If it be possible to die."[31] In the fourth strophe, that voice is finally heard:

> But hark! the heav'nly Sphere turns round,
>   And silence now is drown'd
>   In Extasie of Sound.
> How on a sudden the still *Air* is charm'd,
> As if all Harmony were just alarm'd!
>   And ev'ry soul with Transport fill'd,
>   Alternately is thaw'd and chill'd.
>   See how the Heav'nly Choir
>   Come flocking, to admire,
>   And with what Speed and Care,
> Descending *Angels* cull the thinnest *Air*!
> Haste then, come all th'Immortal Throng,
>   And listen to her Song;
> Leave your lov'd Mansions, in the Sky,
> And hither, quickly hither fly;
> Your Loss of Heav'n, nor shall you need to fear,
>   While she Sings, 'tis Heav'n here.

(ll. 52-68)

[31] William Congreve, *The Mourning Bride, Poems, and Miscellanies*, ed. Bonamy Dobrée (Oxford, 1928), pp. 222-224.

Only at the very end of the ode is the wish of the poet-listener finally fulfilled, when he is

> . . . wrapt in sweet Forgetfulness:
> Of all, of all, but of the present Happiness:
>   Wishing for ever in that State to lye,
>   For ever to be dying so, yet never die.

These cases in which a professional musician rather than a real or imaginary female amateur is being praised, or in which the heavenly music is made to stand metaphorically for the fact of the Christian heaven, must be separated from the main stream of the trivialization of the conceit. But it must also be remembered that, in both main stream and tributary, other considerations of diction and prosody draw the divergent practices deep into larger currents of style.[32] Thus the rather precious, minor metaphysical talent of a poet like Thomas Randolph turns, as we might expect, to employing the Orphean and cosmological musical figures in gentle little reversals of cliché that scarcely deserve the name, as it is used by contemporary literary analysts, of paradox. "The Song of Discord" from his *Poems* of 1638 concludes:

> Where neither voice nor tunes agree;
> This is discords harmonie.
> Thus had Orpheus learn'd to play,
> The following trees had run away.[33]

[32] In the case of the commendatory poem, for example, the extravagant figures of the examples discussed above may be compared with the more measured praise of Waller's verses prefixed to Henry Lawes' *Ayres and Dialogues* (1653):

> So in your airs our numbers dressed,
> Make a shrill sally from the breast
> Of nymphs, who, singing what we penned,
> Our passions to themselves commend;
> While love, victorious with thy art
> Governs at once their voice and heart.

In Edmund Waller, *Poems*, ed. G. Thorn-Drury (London, 1893), p. 19.
[33] Thomas Randolph, *Poems*, ed. G. Thorn-Drury (London, 1929), p. 87.

In "A Song," exhorting "Musick, thou Queene of soules" to arise and play and thus cause all the trees and rocks to move ("Musick" herself becomes Orpheus here), she is asked to interfere suddenly in the dance: "Then in the midst of all their Jolly traine, / Strike a sad note; and fix 'em Trees againe."[34] Perhaps the most extreme example of this sort of mild perversity occurs in "Upon a Very Deformed Gentle-woman, but of a Voice Incomparably Sweet," in which the elements of "sweet Lesbia's" unfortunate aspect are cata-logued rather archly in a musical conceit:

> Her Virginall teeth false time did keep,
> Her wrinkled forehead went too deep.
> Lower than *Gammut* sunke her eyes,
> 'Bove *Ela* though her nose did rise . . .[35]
>
> (ll. 17-20)

But although this encompassing of the scale is hardly appro-priate to the human features, it leads Randolph immediately to his little joke: "I'le trust Musitians now that tell / Best musique doth in discords dwell," alluding at once to his lady's redeeming gift, and to the basic tenet of the contrapuntal musical style that the entire fabric of musical composition is spun out of the resolution of dissonance into consonance. But what seems to be the central image in the poem functions peculiarly to dissolve what remains elsewhere in its eighty lines as an utter ambivalence toward the lady and the question whether her musical gift does in fact compensate adequately for her looks. Only here does the poet's strong feeling that it does so compensate come through; and only here does the heavenly hyperbole enter the poem in its perfectly conven-tional form:

[34] *Ibid.*, p. 87. This is reminiscent of the Carew poem quoted above.

[35] *Ibid.*, pp. 115-117. "Gammut" and "Ela" here are, in the Guidonian hexachord nomenclature, the old names for "low G and high e," the upper and lower bounds of the absolute scale (hence, later, "gamut").

> So I have seene a lute ore worne,
> Old and rotten, patcht and torne,
> So ravish with a sound, and bring
> A close so sweet to every string,
> As would strike wonder in our eares,
> And work an envy in the Spheares.

(ll. 33-38)

On the other hand, styles that move more toward a consummated Augustan diction seem to provide more of a narrative logic for the introduction of the notion of heavenly music, rather than relying heavily on a turn of wit, as in both the strictly Metaphysical and Jonsonian traditions. Waller himself, for example, in a poem of precisely the type under consideration, utilizes for his praise of the lady's singing only the commonplace of the ravished soul; his introduction of the heavenly music in the second stanza is more apt than if it had been made to operate merely to compliment the singing:

> While I listen to thy voice,
> Chloris! I feel my life decay;
> That powerful noise
> Calls my flitting soul away.
> Oh! suppress that magic sound
> Which destroys without a wound.
>
> Peace, Chloris! peace! or singing die,
> That together you and I
> To heaven may go;
> For all we know
> Of what the blessed do above,
> Is, that they sing, and that they love.[36]

If any wit is in operation here at all, it contrives to associate the blessed dead with the lovely living by means of ". . . that they sing, and that they love"; the implication is that love

---

[36] Waller, *ed. cit.*, p. 127. The poem was first published in 1645. Cf. "Of My Lady Isabella, Playing on the Lute," in *Poetical Works*, ed. Robert Bell (London, 1854), p. 118.

is as important (and perhaps, as powerful) as music, and it is the love toward which all has been tending. At any rate, an implicit equation is being urged between heavenly love and celestial music, on the one hand, and between earthly passion and the lady's music, on the other.

Habington, writing of his Castara in the preceding decade, incidentally, allows a harmony of love, rather than of music, to transport him figuratively to heavenly realms. But, true to the convention, the heaven is one of the here and now, of the actuality in which the lady dwells, and is loved.

The harmony of Love

Amphion, O thou holy shade!
  Bring Orpheus up with thee:
That wonder may you both invade,
  Hearing Love's harmony.
You who are soule, not rudely made
  Up, with Materiall eares,
And fit to reach the musique of these spheares.

Harke! when Castara's orbs doe move
  By my first moving eyes,
How great the Symphony of Love,
  But 'tis the destinies
Will not so farre my prayer approve,
  To bring you hither, here
Lest you meete heaven, for Elizium there . . .[37]

As opposed to the direct expository progress of Waller's argument, in which the possibility of being ravished to death leads to a consideration of the heaven in which the elected dead both sing and love, the conceit of the music of the spheres is employed in more of a Metaphysical argument. Eyes gazing into each other with love become the heavenly orbs, imparting motion to each other in some para-mechanical

[37] William Habington, Castara, ed. Edward Arber (London, 1870), p. 92.

fashion, the poet being here likened to the *primum mobile*. Heaven and earth are metaphorically commingled in that typically Metaphysical way, wherein the first term seems to be equated with the second as a result merely of being predicated of it. Although overly terse and elliptical in both its diction and its logic, this little poem seems on its way toward contributing to the gradual minimization of the cosmological significance of the music of the spheres.

Undone Angels: Outdone Orpheus

Examples of the complimentary poem in its received form occur extremely frequently during the decades immediately surrounding the Restoration, and common to almost all of them is the suggestion that heaven, whether populated by pagan Olympians or by Christian angels, defers openly to the skill and charm of the subject of the compliment. So, for example, William Strode in *Parnassus Biceps* (1656):

On a Gentlewoman that Sung and Play'd Upon a Lute

Be silent you still musique of the Sphears,
And every sense make haste to be all ears,
And give devout attention to her aires,
To which the Gods doe listen as to prayers
Of pious votaries; the which to heare
Tumult would be attentive, and would swear
To keep lesse noise at Nile, if there she sing,
Or with a happy touch grace but the string.
Among so many auditors, such throngs
Of Gods and men that presse to hear her songs,
O let me have an unespied room,
And die with such an anthem ore my tomb.[38]

[38] William Strode, *Poetical Works*, ed. Bertram Dobell (London, 1907), p. 39. The almost surrealistic second line is reminiscent of the same author's

In another poem in the same collection, Strode makes an inventory of the charms of "Heavens Best Image, His Faire and Vertuous Mistresse," and concludes with the observation that "Her voice" is "the sphear's best musick, & those twins / Her armes, a precious paire of Cherubs wings."[39]

In the same miscellany, two poems doubtfully ascribed to Strode also exemplify the convention. In the first of these, the poet descants "Upon a Gentlewoman's Entertainment of Him," and allows the music to provide the imagery with which to invoke the food:

> Whether, sweet Mistress, I should most
> Commend your music or your cost:
> Your well-spread table, or the choise
> Banquet of your hand and voyce,
> There's none will doubt: for can there be
> 'Twixt earth and heaven analogy?
> Or shall a trencher or dish stand
> In competition with your hand?
> Your hand that turns all men to ear,
> Your hand whose every joints a sphere:
> For certainly he that shall see
> The swiftnesse of your harmony,
> Will streightwayes in amazement prove
> The spheares to you but slowly move;
> And in that thought confess that thus
> The Heavens are come down to us. . . .[40]

"Song" (*op.cit.*, p. 1), which begins:
> When Orpheus sweetly did complayne
> Upon his lute with heavy strayne
> How his Eurydice was slayne,
>> The trees to heare
>> Obtayn'd an eare
> And after left it off againe.

See above, IV, 181-182.

[39] *Ibid.*, p. 127. Dobell attributes this to Strode, although there seems to be some question as to its authenticity.

[40] *Ibid.*, p. 131.

After some more of this, the food that his hostess had served the poet becomes the *panis angelicus*, "Those singing dainties of the air."[41] Here, in what is so much an occasional poem that it appears to be a mere *Albumblatt*, the automatic character of the complimentary device is quite obvious, I think. It might even be suggested, on the basis of this and other examples, that the widespread use of the heavenly music in verse of this sort may have been influenced in some part by the obvious series of rhymes: *ear, hear, sphere*.

Another poem of doubtful authorship figures forth the embarrassment of the angels in a most insistent manner:

On Alma's Voyce

What magick art
Compells my soul to fly away,
    And leave desart
My poor composed trunk of clay?
Strange violence! thus pleasingly to teare
The soul forth of the body by the eare.

    When Alma sings
The pretty chanters of the skie
    Doe droop their wings
As in disgrace they meant to die,
Because their tunes which were before so rare
Compar'd to hers doe but distract the air.

    Each sensitive
In emulation proudly stands,
    Striving to thrive
Under the bliss of her commands,
Whose charming voyce doth bears & tigers tame,
And teach the sphears new melodies to frame.

    The Angells all
(Astonisht at her heavenly air)
    Would sudden fall

41 *Ibid.*, p. 132.

> From cold amazement to dispaire,
> But that by nimble theft they all conspire
> To steal her hence for to enrich their quire.[42]

We will see later on in this chapter how, in his 1687 *Song for St. Cecilia's Day*, Dryden combined just such a conceit as that of the angel being charmed out of his accustomed round in heaven, with a traditional story of an angel's appearing when an actual, historical saint was praying. There are, of course, echoes of the Orphean accomplishment here as well, and, in the notion of drawing forth the soul from the body through the ear, reference to one of the more Pythagorean notions of the preceding age's musical theory.[43]

Samuel Pordage's *Poems on Several Occasions* (1660) contains "To Lucia Playing on Her Lute," in which this last figure is used with less assurance, although the poem steers free of the usual cosmological conceit.

> When last I heard your nimble fingers play
> Upon your lute, nothing so sweet as they
> Seemed: all my soul fled ravished to my ear
> That sweetly animating sound to hear.
> My ravished heart with play kept equal time,
> Fell down with you, with you did Ela climb,
> Grew sad or lighter, with the tunes you played,
> And with your lute a perfect measure made:
> If all so much as I, your music love,
> The whole world would at your devotion move;
> And at your speaking lute's surpassing charms
> Embrace a lasting peace and fling by arms.[44]

Despite considerable awkwardness in the first four lines, and despite an almost overwhelming banality, this piece moves

---

[42] *Ibid.*, p. 132.
[43] Cf. Benedick in Shakespeare's *Much Ado*, II, iii, 60ff. "Now divine air! Now is his soul ravished! Is it not strange that sheep's guts should hale souls out of men's bodies?" Also, *Twelfth Night*, II, iii.
[44] Text from Norman Ault, ed., *Seventeenth Century Lyrics* (London, 1928), p. 318.

into the relative ease of its final lines with much the same movement that we found in Waller. Its final couplet anticipates the complimentary tone of the very end of the century, when all extravagance comes under the control of a propriety of sentiment as well as of diction. Matthew Prior, for example, might be said to represent the culmination of this more properly Augustan line in his verses *To the Countess of Exeter, Playing on the Lute*, probably written before the end of the century, the lady in question having died in 1703.[45] After a certain amount of historical allusion, both musical and literary, the compliment moves into the received form:

> When to your native Heaven you shall repair,
> And with your presence crown the blessings there,
> Your lute may wind its strings but little higher,
> To tune their notes to that immortal quire.
> Your art is perfect here; your numbers do,
> More than our books, make the rude atheist know,
> That there's a Heaven, by what he hears below.[46]
>
> (ll. 29-35)

Here, with deftness and politeness, the rudeness of real hyperbole is avoided ("may wind its strings *but little higher*"), and it is almost as if a kind of metaphorical plausibility were being made the measure of the sincerity, rather than merely of the propriety, of the compliment.[47] Even the descending angel loses all the Baroque flourish of his fall from the heights, wrenched therefrom, in other poems, by the power of sound:

> As in some piece, while Luke his skill exprest,
> A cunning angel came, and drew the rest:

[45] See Matthew Prior, *Poetical Works*, ed. J. Mitford (Riverside Edition, Boston, n.d.), I, 27n.

[46] *Ibid.*, p. 29.

[47] As, for example, Pope, in *An Essay on Criticism*, II, 384-393. But see Dryden in *Essays*, ed. W. P. Ker (Oxford, 1926), I, 14-15. For a fuller discussion of this and other matters discussed below, see George Williamson, "The Pattern of Neo-Classical Wit," *Modern Philology*, XXXIII (1935-1936), pp. 55-81, especially pp. 67-81.

So, when you play, some godhead does impart
Harmonious aid, divinity helps art;
Some cherub finishes what you begun,
And to a miracle improves a tune. . . .[48]

(ll. 36-41)

But this surely represents a convention in which matters of
diction and tone exercise a firm control over image and allusion, and really serves to mark a boundary of the tradition of
praise of a fair singer that is under consideration here. In
another sense, however, the purely literary dependence of
Prior's poem upon the convention is a very strong one: there
is even less likelihood of his ever having actually encountered
the Countess playing a lute than there might have been in
the case of a poet writing before the close of the first decade
of the Restoration. Both as a professional and amateur instrument, the lute in England was undergoing a considerable
decline in use during the later years of the seventeenth century.[49] The arch-lutes, such as theorbos and *chitarroni*, were
still occasionally, although rarely, employed in the *continuo*
in ensemble music, occasional virtuoso performances are to be

[48] Prior, *op.cit.*, p. 29.
[49] On this question, see Thurston Dart, *The Interpretation of Music*
(London, 1954), pp. 112-113; Manfred Bukofzer, *Music in the Baroque
Era* (New York, 1947), pp. 164-169. Despite the attempts of Thomas Mace
in his rather chatty *Musicks Monument* (1676) to revive what was obviously
a flagging interest in the instrument, it soon perished both there and in
France. Mace inquires of his favorite instrument, "What is the cause, my
Dear-Renowned Lute, / Thou art of late so *Silent* and so Mute? / Thou
seldom now in *Publick* dost appear" (p. 33). Roger North, in *The Musicall
Grammarian*, ed. Hilda Andrews (Oxford, 1925), p. 21, remarks (of the
reign of Charles I and before) that "It was the mode for Gallants & ladys
to learne on the lute, wch produced that manner of 2 strained Lessons, w^ch
now are rarely affected. . . . But to shew that in this time they had their
Bizzarrie Ben. Johnson In one of his masques, mentions a consort of 12
lutes. therefore no age is to claime the monopoly of the stravaganzarias."
See also Dr. Burney's remarks, at the end of the eighteenth century, about
"the lute, without which no concert could subsist, was soon after so totally
banished" in *A General History of Music* (1789), ed. F. Mercer (New
York, 1957), II, 333. Also John Evelyn, in his entry for January 10, 1684,
mentions the music "that Mrs. Bridgeman made us on the guitar with such
extraordinary skill and dexterity." In John Evelyn, *Diary*, ed. Austin
Dobson (London, 1906), III, 120.

noted. But the guitar was beginning, in both France and England, to take precedence over the lute as an amateur accompanying instrument early in the eighteenth century. A poem addressed to a lady playing on a lute would tend to be more of a literary concoction pure and simple, and less of an occasional piece in the strictest sense, than it would have been previously.

It might perhaps be instructive to consider the analogy of this in portraiture; there we should want to distinguish between two situations in which, in the seventeenth century, for example, we might see depicted a lady with a lute and/or other instruments. The representation would tend to be either that of genre or that of allegory. The lady, that is, might be posed with the instrument and painted as an allegory of music, or as the Muse (see for example La Hire's *Euterpe* in the Metropolitan Museum in New York). On the other hand, portraits of men or women holding, tuning, or playing lutes by such Dutch painters as TerBorch, Hals, or even Vermeer seem to represent the subject playing as he or she was wont to do, or else playing a role in a formal subject, such as *The Music Lesson*, of which there are many examples.[50] It is interesting to note that there are bound to be cases in which the art or even the literary historian must remain unsure as to whether, in terms of Erwin Panofsky's famous distinction, his discussion of the instrument is *iconological* or *iconographical*: whether its actuality or its symbolic reference constitutes its role as subject matter.[51] We have seen how, throughout the Renaissance, a contemporary lute can stand for Biblical or minstrel harp, Apollonian lyre, or almost any other string, and it seems obvious that any verbal or graphic representation of

[50] See, for example, Georg Kinsky, *A History of Music in Pictures* (New York, 1951), pp. 96, 97, 131, 136, 137, 143, 145, 146, 147, for a few more accessible relevant examples. The equivalent in the domain of the visual arts for the commendatory poem to the professional musician can also be distinguished during this period.

[51] See his *Studies in Iconology: Humanistic Themes in the Art of the Renaissance* (New York, 1939), pp. 3-31.

that instrument must be approached with some caution. If the
lute is to be taken as a lyre, is its holder to be taken as Orpheus? Or is the lady in the long satin dress, tuning a meticu-
lously rendered theorbo-lute of the middle of the seventeenth
century, representative of a homely scene? Or, on the other
hand, is she merely a premature version of the eighteenth-
century bourgeoise, posing for a portrait with an instrument
which she could not play, but which might lend her an air
of accomplishment?[52] The famous portrait at Penshurst of
Lady Mary Wroth prominently displaying an imported
chitarrone is a case in point. From the dress, the portrait
would appear to have been painted *circa* 1610, and the instrument may very well have been one of the very first archlutes
seen in England. On the other hand, knowing the platonizing
and allegorizing tendencies of the whole Pembroke circle,
one might want to look for some other interpretation of the
portrait, and particularly of the prominence given to the
instrument.

To a certain extent, I feel, the same problems arise in connection with the commendatory and complimentary epigrams
under consideration here.[53] In the first place, there is the
question of the relative authenticity of the occasional character
of these poems, the question whether the lady whose ravishing voice is being praised so extravagantly has ever sung for
the poet at all. In the case of the utterly imaginary lady, of
course, there seems to be no problem, and the praise of Laura's
singing and playing can be taken as a kind of conventionally

[52] One suspects this in the case of some of TerBorch's women, who all
hold an identical instrument, a "theorboe-lute" of the common type that
consisted of an older shell often renecked and with an added, extended
peg-box to carry extra bass strings. It seems to have been a studio property.
Also see Walter L. Woodfill, *Musicians in English Society* (Princeton,
1953), p. 229: "Authentic information on how and when ladies and gentlemen entertained themselves by performing music is quite rare . . . the
possession of instruments and music is at most a suggestion of intention,
sometimes only of service to fashion, and never by itself a sure sign of
intensive musical activity."

[53] See Mario Praz, *Studies in Seventeenth Century Imagery* (London,
1939), I, 9-45.

set piece. But the poetic convention seems to stand equally for these imaginary conceits and for actual, occasional epigrams, and I think that we must conclude that the conventional figure of the heavenly charmer comes to dominate the practice in whatever separate genres we might want to distinguish. But in any case, historical information about musical practice during the age in which the convention flourishes can only serve to reinforce the conclusion, derived from the texts themselves, that the conceit of the sky untuned and outdone by the transcendent sweetness of the subject's musicianship had become, by the time of the Restoration, a purely literary commonplace.

Thus, even under the pressure of a growing Augustan demand for decorum, the cosmic figure remains sufficiently resilient to be useful. Sometimes, only shards of it appear, as in Thomas Flatman's "Celadon on Delia Singing" from his *Poems and Songs* of 1674. The poet hears singing and becomes convinced that it is Delia's voice he hears ". . . for nothing less could move / My tuneless heart, than something from above." He continues:

> I hate all earthly harmony:
> Hark, hark, ye Nymphs, and Satyrs all around!
> Hark, how the baffled Echo faints; see how she dies,
> Look how the wingèd choir all gasping lies
>   At the melodious sound;
>   See, while she sings
>   How they droop and hang their wings!
>   Angelic Delia, sing no more,
> Thy song's too great for mortal ear;
> Thy charming notes we can no longer bear: . . .[54]

This heaven of angels and pagan spirits, all mingled higgledy-piggledy, is outdone, in typical fashion, by Delia's voice. Yet in the notion that her song is "too great for mortal ear," we may detect a relic of the old doctrine of the music of the spheres that we observed, earlier in this chapter, being mocked

[54] *The Caroline Poets*, ed. G. Saintsbury (Oxford, 1921), III, 352.

by Samuel Butler. At the very end of the poem, Flatman carefully removes the necessity for any "willing suspension of disbelief" on the part of either reader or Delia, by carefully framing the whole poem in a pastoral monologue: "His passion thus poor Celadon betray'd / When first he saw, when first he heard the lovely Maid." But even though framed in a quasi-dramatic fashion, there can be no possible debate about the non-doctrinal character of the *musica speculativa* in these epigrams. It is not that a dramatic or truly disengaged use of such notions as the heavenly music is drawing deliberately upon doctrines of musical speculation in any of these cases. We might distinguish uses of this engagement of the element of belief from those instances in dramatic literature that resemble more closely our epigrammatic tradition, perhaps, by comparing sets of examples like Olivia's lines to Viola in *Twelfth Night*, III, I, 7-11:

> O by your leave I pray you.
> I bade you never speake againe of him;
> But would you undertake another suite
> I had rather heare you, to solicit that,
> Then Musicke from the spheares,[55]

and the conclusion to the Attendant Spirit's final Epilogue in Milton's *Comus*:

> Mortals that would follow me,
> Love vertue, she alone is free,
> She can teach ye how to clime
> Higher than the Spheary chime;
> Or if Vertue feeble were,
> Heav'n itself would stoop to her.[56]

$$\text{(ll. 1017-1022)}$$

In the first case, Olivia's mere hyperbole is reinforced by

[55] Text from Variorum Edition, ed. G. Furness (Philadelphia, 1901), p. 191.
[56] Text from *The Columbia Milton* (New York, 1931), I, i, 123.

the fact that she is entreating the disguised Viola to "sing" another song than the Duke's, a song that would, it is implied, transport her to a higher heaven than any conventional empyrean. But hyperbole it nevertheless remains, albeit a hyperbole that is more expressive than merely rhetorical, given the almost operatic tone of the scene in which it occurs. But the lines from *Comus* demanded of a seventeenth-century audience, and reader, much more of a commitment to the understanding of how such lore was to be interpreted in the light of practical knowledge, than do those from *Twelfth Night*. There are the *données* both of the convention of the masque and its supernaturalism, and of Christian humanist doctrine to support such allusions; and *musica speculativa* throughout the masque has already been sufficiently allegorized so that the Attendant Spirit's closing lines need not suddenly emerge into the harsh light of either misplaced literalness or unseemly flippancy. They describe a more real fictive apotheosis than do any examples of the trivialized figure.[57]

Representative of a rather rudimentary "dramatic" framing that, like the examples from Flatman and Shakespeare, demand in no way any hierarchy of senses in which the allusion is to be taken, is a lovely "Dialogue" by Lovelace from the *Lucasta. Posthume Poems (1659-60)*. Dialogues for two voices, with perhaps a chorus, are extremely common in both manuscript and printed songbooks of the Caroline period; their popularity may in some measure stem from the influence of masques. In Lovelace's "Lute and Voice," the two parts indulge in mutual admiration. With the exception of the fact that the images and references concerning the stringed instru-

---

[57] See John Arthos, *On "A Mask Presented at Ludlow-Castle"* (University of Michigan, Contributions in Modern Philology, 1954), pp. 24-26, 50; also, Rosemond Tuve, *Images and Themes in Five Poems by Milton* (Cambridge, Mass., 1957), pp. 143-144, for a consideration of Comus' ironic perversion of this in his "We that are of purer fire / Imitate the Starry Quire" (ll. 111-112). Also see Cleanth Brooks and John Edward Hardy, *Poems of Mr. John Milton* (New York, 1951), pp. 230-234, for Mr. Hardy's discussion of these lines and of the notion of "heavenly" here.

ment and the vocal one are carefully distributed between the parts, the whole dialogue falls squarely into the tradition of the musical epigram.

L. Sing *Laura*, sing, whilst silent are the Sphears,
And all the eyes of Heaven are turn'd to Ears.

V. Touch thy dead Wood, and make each living tree,
Unchain its feet, take arms, and follow thee.

Chorus.

L. Sing. *V.* Touch. O Touch, *L.* O Sing,
Both. It is the Souls, Souls, Sole offering.

V. Touch the Divinity of the Chords, and make
Each Heart string tremble, and each Sinew shake.

L. Whilst with your Voyce you Rarifie the Air,
None but an host of Angels hover here.

Chorus. Sing, Touch, &c.

V. Touch thy soft Lute, and in each gentle thread,
The *Lyon* and the *Panther* Captive lead.

L. Sing, and in Heav'n Inthrone deposed Love,
Whilst Angels dance and Fiends in order move.

Double Chorus.

What sacred Charm may this then be
In Harmonie,
That thus can make the Angels wild,
The Devils mild,
And teach low Hell to Heav'n to swell,
And the High Heav'n to stoop to Hell.[58]

The abashed spheres, the wooden instrument giving life to the forests from which it was made, the lowering of Heaven, the ordering of malignant and chaotic spirits are all conventional in the extreme. Lovelace's personal almost virtuoso

[58] Lovelace, Poems, *ed.cit.*, p. 160.

elegance shows up only in the way in which he weaves the commonplaces into the scheme of his wit of antithesis. The image in the second line seems to work more effectively than does Strode's ". . . every sense make haste to be all ears"[59] because the opposition of eyes and ears is immediately parallelled by one of arms and feet in the following line. There is also considerable invention in the couplet about the animals, where the strings become leashes, and in the preceding line, where "tremble" and "shake" refer to the names of ornaments in lute-playing of the seventeenth century as well as to physiological phenomena. But in any event, despite the form of the musical dialogue toward which the specific groupings and antitheses contribute, the essential strain of the complimentary poem is clearly recognizable.

Given the history of wit and diction in seventeenth-century English poetry, the fate of the image of the music of the spheres compared unfavorably to a particular singer's performance seems quite understandable. An avoidance of cliché is possible only when the device is enlivened, as in the case of Lovelace, Carew, or Herrick, or even rendered grotesque by Randolph, with the wit of *discordia concors* so highly disapproved of by Dr. Johnson.[60] The latter's judgment of Waller, incidentally, who he felt "added something to our elegance of diction, and something to our propriety of thought"[61] includes at one point a statement that suggests impatience with the cliché in question. He remarks, in connection with Waller's shorter poems, that

> Some applications may be thought too remote
> and unconsequential, as in the verses on the
> *Lady Dancing*:
> The sun in figures such as these
> Joys with the moon to play:

[59] See above, n. 38.
[60] See the famous passage from his life of Cowley in Samuel Johnson, *Lives of the English Poets* (Everyman Edition), I, 11.
[61] *Ibid.*, p. 176.

> To the sweet strains they advance,
> Which do result from their own spheres;
>   As this nymph's dance
> Moves with the numbers which she hears.[62]

While this is considerably less remote than the more terse and condensed conceits we have hitherto examined, it seems all the more "unconsequential" for being the more literally plausible, the "as" of simile dividing carefully what might otherwise mingle in the canonical form of the cosmic hyperbole.

An example of real banality in the treatment of the device, coming at what we might almost set as a point of decline of its use as compliment, is one from the poet and emblem writer Philip Ayres, from his *Lyric Poems* (1687). The beginning of "The Musical Conqueress" leads to an almost abrupt interjection of the heavenly music, unprepared and unqualified by any pattern of imagery:

> Led by kind stars one ev'ning to the grove,
> I spied my Cynthia in the Walk of Love;
> Her heav'nly voice did soon salute my ears,
> I heard, methought, the Music of the Spheres . . .[63]

And here the trivialization seems complete.[64] The fate of the

[62] *Ibid.*, p. 170.
[63] *The Caroline Poets*, II, 340.
[64] It seems hardly necessary to quote entire other poems employing this sort of allusion, empty of the slightest turn of phrase and bare of any embroidery. They are numerous throughout the 1660's: see, for example "Upon a Rare Voice" in Owen Felltham's *Lusoria* (1661), or the anonymous poem reprinted by Norman Ault in *Seventeenth Century Lyrics*, p. 422, beginning "When thou dost dance the spheres do play, / By night stars' torches, sun by day," etc. Also see William Kerr, ed., *Restoration Verse* (London, 1930), for the following examples: William Congreve, "On Mrs. Arabella Hunt, Singing," pp. 327-329; a poem of Thomas Fletcher (number 369, p. 318); Anne Killigrew's "On the Soft and Gentle Motions of Eudora," p. 264; also, p. 280. Also, in Nicholas Hookes' *Amanda* (1653), "To *Amanda*, over-hearing her sing" and "On *Amanda* praying" are almost identical in their use of the cliché. "To *Amanda*, on her picture drawn with a Lute in her hand" is of interest in connection with the problem mentioned in note 50, above. Also see *Seventeenth Century*

reference to the music of the cosmos, as to the perfect Orphean manipulation of behavior, thus seems sealed: it can at best serve as a pretty turn of speech.

A tradition of the use of these images for purposes of a purely mechanical grace is not long in developing. One of the *Sociable Letters* (1664) of the prolifically literary Duchess of Newcastle, a collection that resembles complete letter writers of a later century more than it does the garrulous and informed epistolary collections of James Howell, for example, contains what is unmistakably a model encomium. "On her Singing"[65] provides not only a sample of polite compliment of a professional singer, but a graceful disclaimer of any real ability on the part of the genteel amateur authoring the praise. It is addressed to "Sweet Madam Eleonora Duarti,"[66] and commences with a little anecdote in which the occasion for the praise and for the avowed modesty is framed:

Songs and Lyrics, ed. John P. Cutts (Columbia, Mo., 1959), pp. 88, 138, 205, 303, 314, 432-434, for relevant examples from song-texts of the period. Also, *The Plays and Poems of William Cartwright*, ed. G. Blakemore Evans (Madison, 1951), pp. 461-462, 565-566.

[65] Margaret (Cavendish), Duchess of Newcastle, *The Life of the First Duke of Newcastle and Other Writings*, ed. Ernest Rhys (Everyman Edition), pp. 287-288.

[66] An apparently fictional singer, undoubtedly modelled on the Italian singer Leonora Baroni, one of the most famous singers of the century. She was addressed three times in complimentary Latin epigram by Milton (*"Ad Leonoram Romae Canentem," "Ad Eandem," "Ad Eandem"*), perhaps written for a volume of poems in tribute to her entitled, *Applausi Poetici alle Gloria della Signora Leonora Baroni* and published in 1639; unfortunately, no copy has survived, for it might shed some more light on the problem of the extent of the cosmological convention in other languages. Milton's verses avoid all clichés, even, in one poem, substituting the torn-apart Pentheus for an Orpheus figure (also rent asunder by Bacchantes). The hyperboles and, for the orthodox, blasphemies that usually prevail Milton also avoids, although doctrine is turned into compliment, at the end of the first poem, with a lovely and delicate hedging: *"Quod, si cuncta quidem Deus est, per cunctaque fusus, / In te una loquitur, caetera mutus habet."* Signora Baroni was sufficiently well-known and widely celebrated, in any case, to allow the Duchess of Newcastle to address a *model* letter to a singer named *Leonora* with a sister named Caterina (although the other sister appears to be fictional: the real Leonora was often accompanied by her mother). See Dr. Burney's *General History of Music, ed.cit.*, II, 531. Also, Sigmund Spaeth, *Milton's Knowledge of Music* (Princeton, 1913), pp. 129-131.

". . . The last week your sister Katherine and your sister Frances were to visit me, and so well pleased I was with their neighbourly, and friendly visit, as their good company put me into frolick humour, and for a pastime I sung to them some pieces of old ballads; whereupon they desired me to sing one of the songs My Lord made, your brother set, and you were pleased to sing. I told them first, I could not sing any of these songs; but if I could, I prayed them pardon me, for neither my voice, nor my skill, was not proper, nor fit for them, and neither having skill nor voice, if I should offer to sing any of them, I should so much disadvantage My Lord's poetical wit, and your brother's musical composition, as the fancy would be obscured in the one, and the art in the other; nay, instead of musick, I should make discord, and instead of wit, sing nonsense, knowing not how to humour the words nor relish the notes. Whereas your harmonious voice gives their works both grace and pleasure, and invites and draws the soul from all other parts of the body, with all the loving and amorous passions, to sit in the hollow cavern of the ear, as in a vaulted room, wherein it listens with delight, and is ravished with admiration; wherefore their works and your voice are only fit for the notice of souls, and not to be sung to dull, unlistening ears. Whereas my voice and these songs, would be as disagreeing as your voice and old ballads, for the vulgar and plainer a voice is, the better it is for an old ballad; for a sweet voice with quavers, and trilloes, and the like, would be as improper for an old ballad, as golden laces on a thrum suit of cloth, diamond buckles on clouted or cobbled shoes, or a feather on a monk's hood. Neither should old ballads be sung so much in tune as a tone, which tone is betwixt speaking and singing; for the sound is more than plain speaking, and less than clear singing, and the rumming or humming of a wheel should be the musick to that tone, for the humming is the noise the wheel makes in the turning round, which is not like the musick of the spheres."

Here it is only the doctrine of the affections on which the

Duchess of Newcastle can twist her epistolary embroidery. She allows the "musick of the spheres" to stand merely for the other term in a comparison of extremes; it seems divested, even as a metaphor, of the feeling that accompanies the picturing of the soul "in a vaulted room," "ravished with admiration." The Duchess' refusal to sing may no doubt be laid to decorum and respect for the difficulty of singing recitative, rather than to the courtly anti-professionalism of preceding generations. But, at all events, the heavenly harmony functions for her as a neat, final fillip to suggest that her correspondent's voice is perfection itself, and the fact that "the noise the wheel makes in the turning round" can be treated as its pole of unworthiness indicates the degree to which even the conceited actuality of the image had vanished during the previous fifty years. To anyone who gave much thought at all to what sort of sound it was that Cicero's Scipio heard in his dream, the "rumming or humming of a wheel" could not help but present itself. But the celestial music has become for the model letter writer a dead metaphor.

If the changing poetic conventions of the seventeenth century helped to lay the ghost of that metaphor, however, some changes in musical practice during the same period helped to finish off its fellows. The complimentary epigram to the lady "Singing and Playing" praises the voice in terms of the heavenly music; but a lute, even in the latter part of the century, retains its typical Renaissance role as part of the Lute-Harp-Lyre *figura*. It is susceptible to association with all the assorted scraps of musical lore about strings and stringed instruments, and to elaboration in imagery like that of Lovelace in the "Dialogue" examined above. But the lute, as we have already remarked, was passing out of use during the later seventeenth century, and the next hundred years were to see the rise of the touch-responsive keyboard instrument, the pianoforte, as the amateur instrument *par excellence*. Already in Germany, during the 1650's, the clavichord's success as the delicate, private, contemplative boudoir instrument was being assured.[67] But in any case, it was the keyboard, rather than the lute, which, henceforth, one would expect to hear a lady playing, and singing to.

Richard Steele's *The Lying Lover* (first produced at the end of 1703) contains a song that, although perhaps not the first of its kind in English, is certainly representative of a fashion to come.[68]

To Celia's Spinet

Thou soft Machine that do'st her Hand obey,
Tell her my Grief in thy harmonious Lay.

To shun my Moan to thee she'll fly,
To her Touch be sure reply,
And, if she removes it, die.

Know thy Bliss, with Rapture shake,
Tremble o'er all thy numerous Make;
Speak in melting Sounds my Tears,
Speak my Joys, my Hopes, my Fears.

Thus force her when from me she'd fly,
By her own hand, like me, to die.[69]

Here the keyboard is no Orphean or even Apollonian attribute, but merely an instrument (in the general sense), an *engine* for the expression of feelings of the most rarefied kind ("my Joys, my Hopes, my Fears"). It is the mere fact of Celia's touch itself, not her transcendent skill, her amorous art of fingering, that associates the lover with the instrument ("To her Touch be sure reply. / And, if she removes it, die"). This is merely a love-song, wherein the music-making has all the signs of being a homely occupation, like fancy-work, a

[67] See Arthur Loesser, *Men, Women and Pianos* (New York, 1954), pp. 4-23, 57-63, 195-215 for an authoritative and lively account of this phase of the cultural history of keyboard instruments.

[68] Loesser, *op.cit.*, pp. 60-63, prints several examples of German poems of a similar type.

[69] Richard Steele, *Occasional Verse*, ed. Rae Blanchard (Oxford, 1952), p. 21.

female "accomplishment."[70] The poem, in romanticizing the relationship between the beloved and her occupation, has more affinities, perhaps, with such Elizabethan sonnets as Shakespeare's No. 128: "How oft when thou my musike musike playst," than with the epigrammatic convention of the intervening century.

About that convention, it should be remarked in conclusion that the form of the complimentary epigram in praise of a lady singing did not always entail the cosmological figure. On the other hand, it is the exceptional poem indeed that manages to avoid it, either through a turn of wit on some other bit of musical lore, or, in a rare case, through a highly individual style and its particular use of abstraction. To illustrate the first of these cases, we might cite in passing a "Song. *Celia singing*" of Carew, where it is the old theme that treats of how, in Yeats' words, "Love comes in at the eye." The parallel in Yeats' poem is that of wine entering at the mouth; here, it is that of music entering at the ear:

> You that thinke Love can convey,
>> No other way,
> But through the eyes, into the heart,
>> His fatall dart:
> Close up those casements, and but heare
>> This Syren sing;
>> And on the wing
> Of her sweet voyce, it shall appeare
> That Love can enter at the eare:
>> Then unvaile your eyes, behold
>> The curious mould
> Where that voyce dwels, and as we know,
>> When the Cocks crow,
>> We freely may
>> Gaze on the day;
> So may you, when the Musique's done
> Awake and see the rising Sun.[71]

[70] See Loesser, *op.cit.*, pp. 267-283.   [71] Carew, *Poems, ed.cit.*, p. 239.

Similarly, Drummond of Hawthornden plays upon the blindness of the mole and the proverbial deafness of the asp in his twenty-fourth of a set of madrigals, "To *Thaumantia* Singing":

> Is it not too much
> Thou late didst to mee prove
> A *Basiliske* of Love?
> And didst my Wits bewitch:
> Unlesse (to cause more Harme)
> Made Syrene too thou with thy Voyce mee charme?
> Ah! though thou so my *Reason* didst controule,
> That to thy Lookes I could not prove a *Mole*:
> Yet doe mee not that Wrong,
> As not to let mee turne *Aspe* to thy Song.[72]

And if the conventional allusion to the Sirens occurs here, it is in order to be balanced by the figure of the basilisk; it is almost the point of the poem that "Thaumantia" is possessed of the magic of both eye and ear, while the compliment merely proceeds to organize the parallel charms in a fairly obvious way. But the fact remains that, in both of these poems, an almost Metaphysical epigram has been turned without the assistance of the image of heavenly harmony. When, on the other hand, a poem's texture of image and concrete allusion is sufficiently rarefied, an encomium of singing can make its leap into ascribed perfection without benefit of the rungs of wit and traditional reference. The platonism of Herbert of Cherbury seeks, in "To a Lady who did sing excellently," more to give an account of the power of the lady's voice to charm, in the most abstract terms, than to present its bearer with any customary garlands. From its very beginning, it employs wit primarily to bend some Metaphysical common-places to a particular use:

[72] Drummond, *Poetical Works*, I, 109.

1.

When our rude & unfashion'd words, that long
    A being in their elements enjoy'd,
        Sensless and void,
Come at last to be formed by thy tongue,
    And from thy breath receive that life and place,
        And perfect grace,
That now thy power diffus'd through all their parts
        Are able to remove
All the obstructions of the hardest hearts,
    And teach the most unwilling how to love;

2.

When they again, exalted by thy voice,
    Tun'd by thy soul, dismiss'd into the air,
        To us repair,
A living, moving and harmonious noise,
    Able to give the love they do create
        A second state,
And charm not only all his griefs away,
        And his defects restore,
But make him perfect, who, the Poets say,
    Made all was ever yet made heretofore;

3.

When again all these rare perfections meet,
    Composed in the circle of thy face,
        As in their place,
So to make up of all one perfect sweet,
    Who is not then so ravish'd with delight
        Ev'n of thy sight,
That he can be assur'd his sense is true,
        Or that he die, or live,
Or that he do enjoy himself, or you,
    Or only the delights, which you did give?[73]

[73] Lord Herbert of Cherbury, *Poems*, ed. G. C. Moore Smith (Oxford, 1923), pp. 44-45.

Traditional doctrines of the soul as tuning, or scale, of the rational character of linguistic sounds seen as depending on the presence of soul to give them form (both of these are to be found in Aristotle, as we have seen)[74] are here marshalled to support a tenuous argument. But it is almost in its tenuousness, as well as in the kind of paradox entailed by the final question, that this poem seems complimentary at all. It is certainly closer to Donne than to Carew, in the sense that it employs an abstract, intellectual conceit (that of the lady's singing giving a rational form to the prior "substance" of "rude & unfashion'd" language). But despite its date (1618), the poem seems far from either of these in its avoidance of the concrete, the quotidian, as sources of the vehicles of its metaphors. In treating the way in which the formed sounds (always the subject of the poem's long single sentence) make perfect the love who "Made all was ever yet made heretofore," the poet makes the created "second state" stand to the first as does hearing to sight. In this, he may be covertly appealing to the same traditional notion about love that is used by Carew. But it remains completely implicit.

Music, Words, Opera and the Distrust of Speculative Music

Such poems as these that escape the use of the prefabricated figure of *musica coelestis*, however, remain exceedingly rare during the seventeenth century. We have seen how changing literary conventions tended to standardize the parts of that figure, and how Augustan propriety carried it over the brink of banality. Its status as legitimate doctrine had, of course, by the middle of the century become completely discredited. Arguments pro and con church music, various secular musical styles and practices, even the most general theoretical treatises, both formal and informal, based their authority for the value

---

[74] See *De Anima*, 407^b-408^a, 420^b-421^a.

of music upon its power to affect human behavior, and upon its particular virtue of being able appropriately to embellish significant utterance.[75] The later seventeenth century generally followed the opening remarks of Descartes' *Compendium Musices* (translated into English in 1653) when discussing the ultimate nature of music. In the version of Roger North, from his manuscript *Musical Recollections* covering all the seventeenth-century music in England, we find that "Therefore in order to find a criterium of Good musick wee must (as I sayd) look into nature it Self, and ye truth of things. Musick hath 2 ends, first to pleas the sence, & that is done by the pure Dulcor of Harmony, which is found cheifly in ye elder musick, of wch much hath bin sayd, & more is to come, & secondly to move ye affections or excite passion. And that is done by measures of time joyned with the former."[76]

The all-embracing, encyclopedic treatments of music, including as much lore and myth as actuality, such as the treatises of Mersenne and Athanasius Kircher, were rapidly giving way to more specialized studies of various aspects of musical practice.[77] A sharp division between the professional and amateur musician, only abetted by the flourishing of opera as a dominant genre, helped to drive a breach between the technical study, on the one hand, and the critical memoir, on the other. Musical criticism as such, often written in connection with literary, particularly theatrical, interests, also tended toward the more general esthetic bases of such eighteenth-century

[75] Dean Tolle Mace, *English Musical Thought in the Seventeenth Century: A Study of an Art in Decline*, unpubl. diss. (Columbia, 1952), covers this very thoroughly. Mace leans toward the view that the tenet of seventeenth-century aesthetic theory holding that language stands to music as learning to pleasure was responsible for the demise of English music; he also seems to hold Hobbes and Descartes to blame for many evils. See Frank Kermode's brilliant and long-needed discussion of this modish view in "Dissociation of Sensibility," *Kenyon Review*, XIX (1957), pp. 169-194.

[76] Roger North, *The Musicall Grammarian*, pp. 14-15. North's ascription of these two ends to the "causes" of harmony and rhythm is unorthodox.

[77] But see Roger North's remarks about the program for his MS. in Martin C. Burton, "Mr. Prencourt and Roger North on Teaching Music," *Musical Quarterly*, XLIV (1958), pp. 38-39.

studies as Charles Avison's *Essay on Musical Expression* (1752), or John Brown's *A Dissertation on the Union and Power, the Progressions, Separations and Corruptions of Poetry and Music* (1763). With the exception of the lingering interests of mathematicians, among whom certain Pythagorean mystiques flourished well into the eighteenth century,[78] the old *musica speculativa* had largely given way to legitimate acoustical studies based on the joint development of classical physics and mathematical analysis, and to more or less professional discussions of stylistic elements, such as the treatises on keyboard ornamentation of the eighteenth century. It would eventually come about that, no matter what the views of a particular writer concerning the relative merits of ancient or modern learning, the inherited rag-bag of musical lore (and especially the myth of the music of the spheres) would prove for him little more than a white elephant. In the third book of *Gulliver's Travels*, Swift's Laputans, those perverted philosopher-kings who have so little contact with the proverbial ground of reality save for coercing its inhabitants, are much given to Pythagoreanism. Not only do regular polygons and musical instruments serve them for icons and fetiches, but they are made to enact a gross parody of the harmony of the heavens, in which Gulliver serves as an unwilling Er or Scipio: "On the second Morning, about Eleven o'Clock, the King himself in Person, attended by his Nobility, Courtiers, and Officers, having prepared all their Musical Instruments,

---

[78] Consider, for example, the belief, of as great a mathematician as Euler, that the smaller the ratio governing the generation of an interval (as on the monochord), the *more pleasurable*, of necessity, the sound produced by sounding the interval as a chord. See Leonhard Euler, "Conjecture sur la Raison de quelques dissonances généralement reçues dans la musique" (1764), in *Opere Omnia* (Leipzig and Berlin, 1926), series III, vol. I, pp. 508-515. See also T. Salmon, "The Theory of Music reduced to Arithmetical and Geometrical Progressions," *Philosophical Transactions of the Royal Society*, 1705, 24, 2072; vol. IV, i, 469-474. Marjorie Nicolson, in *Science and Imagination* (Ithaca, 1956), pp. 120-123, discusses other such nostalgic backward glances at Pythagoreanism, notably the bewailing of S. Salvetti (in *Phil. Trans.*, 1698), of the fact that explanations of music's power had turned away from older, organic explanations based on universal harmony, and toward the superficial doctrine of the affections.

played on them for three Hours without Intermission; so that I was quite stunned with the Noise; neither could I possibly guess the Meaning, till my Tutor informed me. He said, that the People of the Island had their Ears adapted to hear the Musick of the Spheres, which always played at certain periods; and the Court was now prepared to bear their Part in whatever Instrument they most excelled."[79]

This is not the same Swift, perhaps, whose distaste for the fashionable Italian opera of his day led him to pillory the texts and rudely imitative settings of recitative and aria, with the musical assistance of the Rev. John Echlin, in "A Cantata" (1746).[80] The Italian opera, "an exotic and irrational entertainment," as Dr. Johnson called it, "which has always been combatted and always has prevailed,"[81] was becoming a considerable bone of critical contention at the turn of the eighteenth century, and musical polemic began to turn on nationalistic, as well as rationalistic grounds. What Swift, Addison, and Steele seemed quite agreed upon was that, whether sung in Italian or translated into English, the opera of Handel and others, modeled on Italianate lines, had dealt a death-blow to linguistically significant theater. According to Addison, in *The Spectator*, 18 (March 21, 1711), "the Poetasters and Fidlers of the town" had "laid down an established Rule, which is received as such to this Day, *That nothing is capable of being well set to Musick, that is not Nonsense.*"[82] Steele, in 1720, proposed a "Lyric for Italian Music,"

[79] Jonathan Swift, *Gulliver's Travels* (1726), ed. Herbert Davis (Oxford, 1941), pp. 147-149. Miss Nicolson, *op.cit.* (preceding note), p. 121, seems to feel that Swift's satire in Book III, Chapter II of *Gulliver* is directed primarily against some of the Royal Society musico-mathematical studies, rather than, as seems more likely, against the whole mystique of Pythagoreanism in all its forms, and the more universal follies which, he felt, made for its retention.

[80] Jonathan Swift, *Poems*, ed. Harold Williams (Oxford, 1937), III, 955-961.

[81] Samuel Johnson, "Life of John Hughes," in *Lives of the English Poets*, II, 320.

[82] Joseph Addison, Richard Steele, et al., *The Spectator* (Everyman Edition), I, 68.

which he claimed would give "no manner of disturbance to the head":[83]

I.

So notwithstanding heretofore
Strait forward by and by
Now everlastingly therefore
Too low and eke too high.

II.

Then for almost and also why
Not thus when less so near
Oh! for hereafter quite so nigh
But greatly ever here.[84]

And Addison goes on to make his charge a more general one:

"If the *Italians* have a Genius for Musick above the English, the *English* have a Genius for other performances of a much higher Nature, and capable of giving the Mind a much nobler Entertainment. . . . Musick is certainly a very agreeable Entertainment, if it would take the entire Possession of our Ears, if it would make us incapable of hearing Sense, if it would exclude Arts that have a much greater Tendency to the Refinement of Human Nature; I must confess I would allow it no better Quarter than *Plato* has done, who banishes it out of his Commonwealth.

"At present, our Notions of Musick are so very uncertain, that we do not know what it is we like; only, in general, we are transported with any thing that is not *English*: So it be of foreign Growth, let it be *Italian, French,* or *High-Dutch,* it is the same thing. In short, our *English Musick* is quite rooted out, and nothing yet planted in its stead."[85]

---

[83] Richard Steele, *Occasional Verse,* p. 98.

[84] *Ibid.,* p. 59.

[85] *The Spectator,* 18, *ed.cit.,* I, 71. Plato certainly does not banish all music from his model state (see *Republic* III). But Addison's arguments are in some ways much closer to Plato's attacks against certain "barbarous" keys, and against the textless music of the *aulos,* than were many more

The Italian opera controversy really flared up with the production of Handel's *Rinaldo* in 1711, but the complaint that English music had been "rooted out" had become an increasingly frequent one since the last decades of the seventeenth century. While native English traditions such as that of the viol consort and the "fancys" or fantasias written for it flourished throughout the Jacobean and early Caroline periods, and during the Commonwealth as well,[86] the Restoration was from the very beginning characterized by foreign musical tastes. So Roger North writes of Charles II: "He had lived some considerable time abroad, where the french musick was in request, wch consisted of an entry (perhaps) and then Brawles, as they were called, that is motive aires and Dances; And it was & is yet a mode among ye Monseurs, allwais to act ye musick, wch habit the King had got and never in his life could endure any that he could not act by keeping the time, wch made the common andante or els the step tripla ye onely musicall styles at court in his time. And after ye manner of france, he set up a band of 24 violins to play at his dinners, wch disbanded all the old English musick at once."[87] By this last remark, North undoubtedly meant to refer to the viol-music, but he, like other writers, seemed to allow this one musical genre to stand for a whole tradition of practice.

Protests against the development of an English opera, the history of which bracketed very nicely the period between

---

self-consciously Neoclassical doctrines than this rather pragmatic one. Also, cf. Jeremy Collier, in *A Short View of the Immorality and Profaneness of the English Stage* (1698), p. 278.

[86] See Manfred Bukofzer, *Music in the Baroque Era*, p. 192.

[87] Roger North, *The Musicall Grammarian*, p. 27. Also see his remark, p. 21, about how "the whole current of musick is turned into the Italian channel." Cf. also the same author's *Memoirs of Musick*, ed. Edward F. Rimbault (London, 1846), pp. 103-104: "King Charles the Second . . . had an utter detestation of Fancys . . . he could not bear any musick to which he could not keep time, and that he constantly did, to all that was presented to him; and for the most part heard it standing." North seems to have regarded this royal habit as emblematic of the musical manners of the Restoration.

the Restoration and the end of the century, followed a similar line. Although the recitative of the early Italian Baroque had found its way into the music of the masque early in the century, little or no concern was voiced as to its un-Englishness. Towards the end of the Commonwealth, the production of D'Avenant's *The Siege of Rhodes* (1657) heralded the brief hour of a musico-dramatic genre that made public in the theaters what had remained semi-private in castle revels.[88] The moment of perfection that barely redeemed that hour was Purcell's *Dido and Aeneas* (1689?). But as early as 1663, D'Avenant, in *A Play-House to be Let* (an attempt, in its earlier form, to string together a number of masque-like scenes already written and set to music) felt called upon to defend his adaptations of Italian *recitativo*. His character, the Musician, insists that

> Recitative music is not compos'd
> Of matter so familiar as may serve
> For every low occasion of discourse.
> In tragedy, the language of the stage
> Is rais'd above the common dialect,
> Our passions rising with the height of verse;
> And vocal music adds new wings to all
> The flights of poetry.[89]

The argument presented here is interesting if only for the fact that it reverses some of the basic tenets of the early-

[88] For the background of Restoration opera and its role in English music, see Bukofzer, *op.cit.*, pp. 180-190; Ernest Walker, *A History of Music in England* (third edition, rev. and ed. J. A. Westrup, Oxford, 1952), pp. 217-220. The best comprehensive survey of the subject is in Edward J. Dent, *Foundations of English Opera* (Cambridge, 1928). For the Handelian controversy see Bukofzer, pp. 324-332; Walker, pp. 220-242. The following articles might also be consulted: J. A. Westrup, "The Nature of Recitative," *Proceedings of the British Academy 1956* (London, 1956), pp. 27-43; John Harley, "Music and Musicians in Restoration London," *Musical Quarterly*, XL (1954), pp. 509-520; and Hugh Arthur Scott, "London's Earliest Public Concerts," *Musical Quarterly*, XXII (1936), pp. 446-457.

[89] William D'Avenant, *Works*, ed. J. Maidmont and W. H. Logan (London, 1872-4), IV, 23.

Baroque inventors of that recitative, the Florentine Camerata, who held that while it was the obligation of a dramatic musical setting not to obscure the text in polyphonic intricacies, it was nevertheless the virtue and the obligation of such a setting to heighten its expressive qualities, to retouch it, thus to enhance the power of the words to elicit passion in an audience. What D'Avenant is saying is that music is almost as expressive as verse is; it is not fanciful to think that he was appealing to what he supposed was some fundamental prejudice in his audience. Such a prejudice would have made Tragedy the truly sublime form; thus Thomas Rymer, in *A Short View of Tragedy* (1692): "The Grecians were for Love and Musick as mad as any Monsieur of 'em all; yet their Musick kept within bounds; attempted no metamorphosis to turn the *Drama* to an *Opera*. Nor did their Love come whining on the stage to effeminate the Majesty of their Tragedy. . . ."[90] Opera, even while serving, in the earlier seventeenth century, to crystallize the basic theses and practices of what was to become Baroque music in general, was becoming the focal point for much of the musical esthetics of Neoclassic England.

One of the effects of the combined changes in musical and in general speculative practices during the century was completely to discredit, as we have seen, the older, encyclopedic approaches to *musica speculativa*. Even that most susceptible of lore-mongers, the self-taught musical amateur with encyclopedic longings, tends, toward the end of the seventeenth century, to become chastened. During March and April of 1668, for example, Samuel Pepys was displaying a lively interest in musical theory. On March 29, John Bannister the composer came to visit him and, he records, "we sang, and Banister played on the theorbo, and afterwards Banister played on his flageolet, and I had a very good discourse with him about musique, so confirming some of my new notions about musique that it puts me upon a resolution to go and make a scheme and

[90] Thomas Rymer, *Critical Works*, ed. Curt A. Zimansky (New Haven, 1956), p. 117.

theory of musique not yet ever made in the world."[91] On
April 3 following, he mentions that he went to "Duck Lane,
to look out for Marsanne, in French, a man that has wrote
well of musique, but it is not to be had, but I have given
order for its being sent over, and I did here buy Des Cartes
his little treatise of musique. . . ."[92] Two days before, he had
heard Hooke and Lord Brouncker[93] give "an account of the
reason of concords and discords in musique, which they say
is from the quality of vibrations; but I am not satisfied in it,
but will at my leisure think of it more, and see how far that
do go to explain it."[94] On April 8 he purchased a recorder in
an attempt to learn to play an instrument by ear, disapproved
of the fingering system and resolved to invent another one.[95]
But after this there are no more entries on the subject of
Pepys' reforms in the subject of musical theory, and we may
suppose that reasonableness led him away from what he soon
realized was the domain either of the composer or of the
mathematician.

There were, indeed, a few recalcitrant general theorizers of
the older persuasion. Thomas Mace's *Musick's Monument,
or a remembrancer of the best Practicall Musick, both Divine
and Civil, that has ever been known to have been in the World*
(1676) has already been mentioned in connection with the
decline of lute playing. By and large Mace, a clerk at Trinity
College, Cambridge, keeps admirably to his subject, and his
treatise is extremely useful to musicologists because of its
extensive treatment of the whole question of lute ornamentation. But he allows himself to partake of numerological and
quasi-mathematical mystique, notably in his section entitled,
"Musicks Mystical and Contemplative Part."[96] He announces,

[91] Samuel Pepys, *Diary*, ed. H. B. Wheately (Random House edition,
New York, n.d.), II, 838.

[92] *Ibid.*, II, 844.

[93] The English translator of Descartes' *Compendium Musices*. See E. D.
Mackernesse, "A Speculative Dilettante," *Music and Letters*, XXXIV (1953),
pp. 236-252.

[94] Pepys, *Diary*, II, 843.   [95] *Ibid.*, II, 849.

[96] Thomas Mace, *op.cit.*, pp. 264-268.

for example, that there are three mysteries in music: "The 1st is, concerning the Two Differing or Contra-Qualities in whole *Nature*, viz. The *Good* or the *Evil*; *Love* and *Hatred*; *Joy* and *Sorrow*. . . ."[97] The second, he continues, is that of the Trinity, represented in the concord of the triad; the third is the mystery of the octave, in which Mace celebrates the trivial result that successive halvings of a string segment will produce an infinite series of octaves. Mace concludes the section with the following verses:

Great GOD

Mysterious Center of all Mysterie
　　All Things *Originate* Themselves *in Thee*;
And in Their *Revolution* wholly tend
　　To *Thee*, Their *Octave, their Most Happy End.*
　　All Things (what e're) in Nature are Thus Rounded,
　　Thus *Mystically limited* and *Bounded.*
　　Some *Harmonize* in *Diapasons* Deep,
　　Others again more *Lofty Circles Keep.*
　　But *Thou*, the *Moving Cause* in every thing;
　　The Mystick Life, from whence All Life doth Spring . . .

which he concludes with the hope that his nearing death will complete his own circle of perfection:

　　A *Unison* (at First) I was in *Thee*:
　　An *Octave* (now at last) *I hope shall be,*
　　To *Round Thy Praises in Eternity*
　　On th' *Unconceiv'd Harmonious Mystery.*[98]

The poem is surmounted with a diagram of an infinite spiral. Mace's closeness to the currents of Cambridge Platonism (Cudworth and More are listed prominently, along with many other Cambridge figures of the period, as subscribers to *Musick's Monument*)[99] seems to have been accompanied with

[97] *Ibid.*, p. 265.
[98] *Ibid.*, p. 269. Cf. a similar symbolic treatment in a much earlier lute treatise, Thomas Robinson's *Schoole of Musick* (1603).
[99] *Ibid.*, sig. Cl^r.

a dislike of the modish psychology of the affections. This dislike, in any event, operated, in conjunction with his rather antiquarian position with respect to his subject itself, to lead him to the celebration of the older *musica speculativa*.

But, generally speaking, the notion of heavenly harmony remained a purely literary rather than a truly speculative commonplace. Aside from its use in the complimentary and commendatory poems that we have examined above, the lore of both *musica mundana* and of the Baroque rhetorical music were employed in formal commendations of music, not treated as literary set pieces as in earlier *encomia musicae*, but written primarily to be set to music and sung, usually in a more or less elaborate cantata, with *soli* and choruses; in short, the corpus of traditional musical doctrine began to come under the jurisdiction of Addison's rule to the effect that what is sung is too silly to be said, at least as far as both occasional and discursive poetry was concerned. The formal praise of music had become, by the 1680's, a subject more fit for singing about than for seriously discussing. An epigram of Samuel Butler's represents very nicely the last stage in that declining tradition, the older form of musical praise in verse. Butler cannot help tying up the clichés with what, although ambiguously so, seems in the long run to be a raised eyebrow:

Musique

Musique is Bewty to the Eare
That Charms the Soules of all that Heare;
Attracts Devotion, with its Aire, and Words;
To string its Beads upon its Charming Cords . . .
Can sew Devotion to an Aire
And set a Saraband t'a Prayer.[100]

It is primarily in the form of the musical ode, then, that the figure of the celestial harmony passes into the eighteenth century. The use of that figure was revivified particularly in

---

[100] Samuel Butler, *Satires and Miscellaneous Poetry and Prose*, ed. René Lamar (Cambridge, 1928), p. 453.

the odes written over several decades for the musical St. Cecilia's Day celebrations in London, of which Dryden's two contributions remain the really impressive poems. In examining them, as well as the other musical odes that helped to establish the convention in which Dryden was working, we shall see how the schematic, almost programmatic structure of those odes allowed for a last gasp of renewed interest in the literary use of the universal harmony for concrete imagery, and how the problems of musical and encomiastic exposition could spark that interest which the changes in seventeenth-century rhetoric and poetic diction had caused to flag.

The Songs for St. Cecilia's Day

The St. Cecilia's Day celebrations for which Dryden's "Ode" and "Alexander's Feast" were both commissioned seem to have originated on the Continent in the latter part of the sixteenth century.[101] It was not until 1683, however, that annual "Musick Feasts" began to be held in London on the twenty-second of November by a group of musical professionals and amateurs calling themselves "The Musical Society." These occasions, which occurred more or less regularly until the middle of the next century, may have included a specially composed anthem for a musical service and a sermon in defense of music in churches.[102] Their high point, however, was a formal offering in praise of music, embodied in an ode,

---

[101] See William Henry Husk, *An Account of the Musical Celebrations on St. Cecilia's Day* (London, 1857), pp. 1-9.

[102] *Ibid.*, p. 12. The defense was probably of instrumental music, arguments against which were often quite subtle. Also, old, anti-Catholic objections to church music were still being raised, particularly after 1688. As late as 1725, Swift could some out against the St. Cecilia's Day Odes themselves with dire warnings:

> To act such an opera once in a year
> So offensive to ev'ry true Protestant ear,
> With trumpets, and fiddles, and organs,
>   and singing,
> Will sure the pretender and Popery
>   bring in . . .

Swift, *Poems, ed.cit.*, II, 521-522.

whose text and vocal and instrumental setting by a poet and a composer of repute were commissioned in advance.

The festivities must have had a fraternal quality which, while not as limited and parochial as that of the Catch-Societies, would appear to have emanated from a group of celebrating, self-congratulating connoisseurs. The text of "A Song, Sung at a Musick Feast" set by Pelham Humphrey some time before 1674, was probably intoned on some smaller, less official occasion. It has the light-hearted tone of a catch or a later glee:

> How well doth this Harmonious Meeting prove
> A Feast of Musick is a Feast of Love,
> Where Kindness is our Tune, and we in parts
> Do but sing forth the consorts of our hearts.
> For friendship is nothing but concord of votes,
> And music is made by a friendship of notes.[103]

From the tone of this solo, the chorus for three voices which follows hardly seems to have been a necessary injunction:

> Come then to the God of our Art let us quaff
> For he once a year is reputed to laugh.

The stock metaphor of musico-social concord is trivialized here utterly, and the "Feast of Love" is hardly a communion with the immutable order of the universe.

For the odes written for St. Cecilia's Day, however, a mood of reverent jubilation, rather than one of mere *camaraderie*, seems to have been requisite. These were nevertheless public poems. The decidedly introspective exuberance of Edward Benlowes' reflections on a musical evening might be cited to illustrate another extreme which the St. Cecilia's Day poems sought to avoid. Probably written during the 1660's or 1670's, "A Poetic Descant Upon a Private Music-Meeting" opens casually enough:

[103] Husk, *op.cit.*, p. 10.

> Muse! Rise and plume thy feet, and let's converse
> This morn together: let's rehearse
> Last evening's sweets; and run one heat in full-speed verse.
>
> Prank not thyself in metaphors; but pound
> Thy ranging tropes, that they may sound
> Nothing but what our paradise did then surround.
>
> (1-6)[104]

Benlowes' muse betrays him shortly thereafter, though. After a description of the ladies present in somewhat extravagant, abstract terms, a Pythagorean conjunction of male and female numbers is implied at the appearance of the musicians themselves:

> But, whist! The masculine sweet planets met,
> Their instruments in tune have set,
> And now begin to ransack Music's cabinet.[105]
>
> (19-21)

The various instrumentalists are then described as the various heavenly bodies, after which

> Last Mercury with ravishing strains fell on,
> Whose violin seemed the chymic-stone
> For every melting touch was pure projection.
>
> Chair'd midst the spheres of Music's Heaven, I hear,
> I gaze; charm'd all to eye and ear;
> Both which, with objects too intense even martyred were.
>
> Th'excess of fairs, distill'd through sweets, did woo
> My wav'ring soul, maz'd what to do,
> Or to quit eyes for ears, or ears for eyes forgo.

[104] *The Caroline Poets*, I, 482-3.

[105] This sudden intrusion of naturalistic explicitness seems quite gratuitous here, reminiscent of John Cleveland at his worst. This whole poem, incidentally, is in the meter of Benlowes' *Theophila*, about which one tends to agree with Saintsbury that it is one of the most awkward of stanza forms possible.

Giddy i' th' change which sex to crown with praise;
　　Time swore he never was with lays
More sweetly spent; nor Beauty ever beam'd such rays.

　'Twixt these extremes mine eyes and ears did stray,
　　And sure it was no time to pray;
The Deities themselves then being all at play.

　The full-throng'd room its ruin quite defies:
　　Nor fairs, nor airs are pond'rous; skies
Do scorn to shrink, though pil'd with stars and harmonies.

　Form, Beauty, Sweetness all did here conspire,
　　Combin'd in one Celestial Quire,
To charm the enthusiastic soul with enthean fire . . .

　　　　　　　　　　　　　　　　(49-69)

The rather forced ingenuity with which the two sexes are
associated with two senses represents the soggy lees of Metaphysical technique. It sorts ill here with the programmatic
promises of homeliness of diction in the first two stanzas.
Benlowes' piece is an essay, in a slightly more complex guise
than usual, into the convention examined earlier in this chapter; it differs from the normal musical compliment only in
that the range of the praise is so expanded as to include the
room as a whole. The universe into which that room is urged,
metaphorically, to merge is a polite one, and one feels that
it is a kind of formal *galanterie* alone that demands the
presence and equal status of the feminine counterpart of music,
visual beauty. The unconvincing unification of "fairs" and
"airs" in "one Celestial Quire" leads to a final apostrophe:

　Music! thy med'cines can our griefs allay
　　And re-inspire our lumpish clay:
Muse! Thou transcend'st; Thou without instruments can
　　　play.　　　　　　　　　　　　(73-75)

This particular Muse would seem undeserving of such praise,
were it not for the fact that the commendation of music itself,

[393]

in the two lines immediately preceding, is so mechanical. Benlowes' attitudes toward formal musical doctrine, as well as those of his age, prevented him from merely versifying the clichés relating *musica mundana* to actual performance. Unlike Marvell's, his wit was inadequate to the task of figuratively encompassing earth and heaven within the frame of human and cosmic music, and it was too ambitious to content itself with a smaller, well-turned but frankly hyperbolic observation of the type of Lovelace's "To Gratiana Singing and Dancing," for example.

A prototype of the musical ode may be found (as is so often the case with seventeenth-century poetic forms) in the works of Ben Jonson. "An Ode, or Song, by all the Muses. In Celebration of her Majesties birth-day" (1630) is a strophic poem which assigns a stanza to each of the Muses in turn. Those of Thalia and Euterpe are of interest here in that they combine the instrumental references with the encomiastic hyperbole in a way that anticipates the later St. Cecilia's Day Odes and, specifically, those of Dryden:

> 3. Thal. Yet, let our Trumpets sound;
> And cleave both ayre and ground,
> With beating of our Drums:
> Let every Lyre be strung,
> Harpe, Lute, Theorbo sprung,
> With touch of daintie thum's!
> 4. Evt. That when the Quire is full,
> The Harmony may pull
> The Angels from their Spheares:
> And each intelligence
> May wish it selfe a sense,
> Whilst it the Dittie heares.[106]

These two stanzas, as we shall presently see, might be said to represent a canonical form that the musical ode was eventually to assume.

[106] Jonson, *Works*, VIII, 239.

The earliest of the extant St. Cecilia's Day Odes are by no
means overly ambitious. Two odes written for the initial
celebration in 1683 and set by Henry Purcell are shorter by
far than the later ones, and in their opening invocations make
no extravagant claims to universality of subject. One of these,
written by one Christopher Fishburn, openly addresses the
assemblage itself:

> Welcome to the pleasures that delight
> Of ev'ry sense the grateful appetite!
> Hail, great assembly of Apollo's race!
> Hail to this happy place,
> This musical assembly, that seems to be
> The ark of universal harmony![107]

"Seems" in the penultimate line weakens the tone considerably, and narrows the range and the potency of any further
images of *harmonia mundi*. The remaining twenty-five lines
are primarily occupied with the joys that music can inspire.
Passing acknowledgment is made to

> Beauty, thou source of love,
> And Virtue, thou innocent fire,
> Made by the Powers above
> To temper the heat of desire; . . .

Only at the end is St. Cecilia mentioned at all. In another,
anonymous ode, her name never appears. This poem begins
with an injunction to the assembled instruments and voices
to sound: "For this is sacred Music's holiday"; it ends ana-
pestically on a note of good-hearted but undignified self-
congratulation:

> Apollo's delighted with what we have done,
> And clapping his hands, cries, "Iô, go on";
> With a smile he does all our endeavours approve,
> And vows he ne'er heard such a concert above.[108]

[107] Husk, *op.cit.*, p. 143.   [108] *Ibid.*, p. 145.

At the beginning of the ode, it is made clear that the god of music himself is expected to appear "Not to the eye, but to the ravish'd ear." Then follows a quatrain of tetrameters, quoting Apollo's command that "ev'ry gen'rous heart / In the chorus bear a part." The observation that, in response to this, "each pliant string / Prepares itself, and as an offering, / The tribute of some gentle sound does bring" leads to the conclusion with its reports of Apollo's delight. The metrical range of this simple piece is rather narrow; the odes that followed tended more and more to employ the elaborate resources of the Augustan "Pindaric" ode form. However, they shared its structure in that they remained narrative in the most primitive sense, their general order remaining roughly as follows: first came an exhortation to begin the music-making, then a description of the various instruments and observations of their respective powers to move the affections. These grew into separate strophes, each with a different metrical scheme. Appended to these was usually some exposition of the general value of harmony, often with a citation of the *harmonia mundi*. The final section of the odes returned to a hortatory diction, with some reference to St. Cecilia as the patroness of music, and a closing celebration of the heavenly singing.

To examine the odes for the next few annual celebrations is to see the growing elaboration of this basic theme. The 1684 poem, set by John Blow, was written by Dryden's friend John Oldham; that of the following year was by that Saint of Dullness, Nahum Tate. Both of these odes are longer than the earliest ones, and both reach into larger repositories of lore and doctrine for their observations on *musica speculativa*. Oldham, for example, remarks that

> When we are thus wound up to extacy,
> Methinks we mount, methinks we tow'r,
> And seem to antedate our future bliss on high.[109]

[109] *Ibid.*, p. 146.

This is a kind of specifically Christian allusion rare in any of the odes, with the exception of the mention of St. Cecilia herself. Nahum Tate's piece starts out with a flurry of instrumental reference; more usually, these were developed at length within the course of the ode.

> Tune the viol, touch the lute,
> Wake the harp, inspire the flute . . .[110]

One cannot be sure here whether actual musicians are being enjoined to play, or whether some more abstract entity is being called up to infuse the instruments with song. At any rate, despite this apparent hurry to include most of what was becoming a traditional catalogue of instruments to be mentioned on such occasions, Tate finds the time later on to make a strange observation:

> In vain do wit and sense combine,
> Without this art to make our numbers shine;
> Words are the body: Music is the soul.[111]

An older treatment of the metaphysics of music based an platonistic sources, such as Ficino's, for example, would have tended to reverse such an assertion on the grounds that words contribute an *ethos* to sounds, placing them in the relation of rational soul to body. Neoclassic thought might better tolerate such an image. "Musick and poetry have ever been acknowledged Sisters, which walking hand in hand, support each other: As poetry is the harmony of words, so musick is that of notes: and as poetry is a rise above prose and oratory, so is Musick the exaltation of poetry. Both of them may excell apart, but sure they are most excellent when they are joind, because nothing is then wanting to either of their perfections: for thus they appeare, like wit and beauty in the same person."[112] So wrote Dryden, in a dedication to an edition of the

110 *Ibid.*, p. 147.
111 *Ibid.*, p. 148.
112 Text printed in Roswell G. Ham, "Dryden's Dedication for *The Music of The Prophetesse* 1691," *PMLA*, L (1935), pp. 1065-1075.

music for Purcell's *The Prophetesse* in 1691. Tate's rather crude figure could thus, perhaps, be defended with reference to a notion that music animates a text and exalts it by giving life to its rhetorical power over the passions. What is most to the point here, though, is the arbitrary character of that figure in its argumentative context in the ode, where it cannot help but function as a shabbily supported, though perhaps "exalted" lyric gnome.

Tate's ode was bedecked with pastoral images of lambkins and frolicking kids, all protected by the beneficent power of St. Cecilia. It is not quite clear at exactly what point in history that Roman martyr became the patron saint of music. The legend that an angel, attracted by her beautiful musicianship, came down from heaven to visit her, seems to have been current before the fifteenth century.[113] It is this story which Dryden was to employ in both his odes. Before Dryden, the patroness of music tended to receive only passing mention, along with the various muses and the musical heroes of Antiquity. It was only in 1699, after the fame of Dryden's "Alexander's Feast" had become fairly secure, that Addison, in an ode set by Daniel Purcell, attempted any elaborate treatment of St. Cecilia. At the end of the celebrations of the several qualities of violins, flute, organ and trumpet, Echo too performs her part, who could surpass these others,

> And in a low expiring strain
> Play all the concert o'er again.

> Such were the tuneful notes that hung
> On bright Cecilia's charming tongue:
> Notes that sacred heats inspir'd
> And with religious ardour fired:
> The love sick youth, that long supprest

[113] See S. Baring-Gould, *The Lives of the Saints* (Edinburgh, 1914), XIV, 503-505. A fourteenth-century MS. of the *madrigali* of Francesco Landini contains a picture of St. Cecilia, with an organ as her attribute, weeping over the debased state of music. See Leonard Ellinwood, "Francesco Landini and his Music," *Musical Quarterly*, XXII (1936), p. 194.

His smother'd passion in his breast,
No sooner heard the warbling dame
    But by the secret influence turn'd,
He felt a new diviner flame
    And with devotion burn'd,
With ravish'd soul and looks amaz'd
Upon her beauteous face he gaz'd,
    Nor made his amorous complaint:
In vain her eyes his heart had charm'd,
Her heavenly voice his eyes disarm'd,
    And chang'd the lover to a Saint.[114]

Here it is the main story of St. Cecilia's martyrdom that Addison employs for musical purposes. The "love sick youth" was her pagan suitor Valerianus, persuaded by her beauty and virtuous example to abjure his desires for her and to accept, along with his brother, conversion to Christianity. The power of St. Cecilia's persuasion is figured forth in terms of musical virtuosity, and the two stories of her evangelical and angel-charming successes are blended into one. This could be only logical in an age when music itself was valued most highly as an instrument of persuasiveness rather than as a concrete fact representing universal abstract order.

The handling of music's patron saint was only one of the many problems facing the authors of the St. Cecilia odes, however. If we examine the poems produced by Shadwell, Congreve, Nicholas Brady, D'Urfey, Theophilus Parsons, Christopher Smart, and Pope himself, we can see the conventional shape of the St. Cecilia ode maintaining itself, on the one hand, through such crude devices as simple tag lines either passed down quite deliberately or else successively "rediscovered" by subsequent authors. Dryden's line (in the "Song for St. Cecilia's Day"), "What Passion cannot MUSICK raise and quell!" is obviously some version of Tate's "What charms can Musick not impart . . ." of three years earlier. On the

[114] Husk, pp. 185-186.

other hand, we can see the later odes, especially those of the eighteenth century, reacting to critical pressures that were being clearly formalized by writers on poetry and music during the 1730's and 1740's. It came to be expected of odes to be set to music in general, were they sacred poems, cantata texts, occasional pieces, or the St. Cecilia songs themselves, that they be historical or narrative, rather than merely mythological; that they be smooth metrically and "lyric" in style, infused with a degree of passion, yet preserving simplicity; and that they utilize sentiment rather than imagery, on the grounds that composers were far too apt to paint *words* like "high" and "low" rather than *ideas*, as should have been proper. It is fairly clear that many of these criteria arose in some measure from the almost universal approval that "Alexander's Feast" continued to accumulate throughout the eighteenth century.[115]

Our primary interest in all the St. Cecilia odes, however, remains confined to an understanding of a convention of formal and public *laus musicae* in which Dryden worked on two separate occasions, ten years apart, and which may be presumed to have solidified even during that interval. And although "Alexander's Feast" may be rightly judged, as indeed it has always been, superior to the earlier "Song for St. Cecilia's Day," the latter must remain of considerable interest to us as an example of Dryden's ability to hew extremely close to a convention while yet securing his finished work from the abyss of anonymity. It is only through a consideration of the varied problems that he faced in the composition of the first ode, and through a knowledge of the stylistic and ideological variables that governed the ideal model to which his poem must needs have conformed, that the elegance of his resulting effort may appear. Aside from some of the overall structural considerations which we have observed

[115] See Robert Manson Myers, "Neo-Classical Criticism of the Ode for Music," *PMLA*, LXII (1947), pp. 399-421, for an excellent treatment of the matters discussed in this paragraph.

already, there remain such questions as the suitability of the text to the musical setting it was to receive, the concurrences of major climaxes in the setting, the formal Pindaric verse structure and the argued praise of music as well.

In examining Dryden's two St. Cecilia odes we shall watch for his avoidance of the clichés of speculative music employed, barely changed, by his precursors; but even more, for the ways in which, operating within the limits of what was becoming a canonical form, he managed to stamp the two odes with an impress of his own. And we shall see how, in very different ways, the "Song for St. Cecilia's Day" and "Alexander's Feast" contrive to overflow the boundaries of their openly occasional purpose, and to represent with unequalled success the attitudes toward music of the community that commissioned and praised them.

Dryden's First Ode: The Cantata
of Musical Genesis

Any critical reading of John Dryden's 1687 St. Cecilia's Day ode would do well to keep in mind both the literary convention of the musical ode in praise of music and the general fate of the poetic applications of *musica speculativa* after the Restoration. In general, one would want to conclude with Dr. Johnson that, although the first of the two odes seems "lost in the splendour of the second," it nevertheless contains "passages which would have dignified any other poet."[116] But its particular success can perhaps be measured only against the resounding failure of Neoclassic poetry to versify musical doctrine in any but the most pedestrian fashion, on the one hand, and, on the other, against the relatively flabby way in which Dryden's predecessors had adapted the celebration of singing to the singing of that celebration, as it were, to the exigencies of a good cantata text.

On the first of these questions, we might turn for a moment

[116] *Lives of the English Poets*, II, 244.

to a prior case of Dryden's treatment of a theme of speculative music. Taken out of context, the opening of the third stanza of his great ode "To the Pious Memory of the Accomplisht Young Lady Mrs. Anne Killigrew, Excellent in the Two Sister-Arts of Poesie and Painting" (1686) might be thought to resemble some of the complimentary epigrams treated previously in this chapter:

> May we presume to say, that at thy *Birth*,
> New joy was sprung in HEAV'N as well as here on *Earth?*
> For sure the Milder Planets did combine
> On thy *Auspicious* Horoscope to shine,
> And ev'n the most malicious were in Trine.
> Thy *Brother-Angels* at thy *Birth*
>   Strung each his Lyre, and tun'd it high,
>   That all the People of the Skie
> Might know a Poetess was born on Earth.
>   And then if ever, Mortal Ears
>   Had heard the Musick of the Spheres! . . .[117]

                            (ll. 39-49)

But this superficial resemblance pales into insignificance before the poem's splendid elaboration of the theme of the angelic, the strict correspondence of poetry and music throughout, and the final commendation of earthly art itself toward which the whole elegiac structure moves. The "Musick of the Spheres" is no mere mechanical, intruded gesture of praise here, but has been prepared for in the first stanza's closing supplication:

> Hear then a Mortal Muse thy praise rehearse
>   In no ignoble Verse;
> But such as thy own voice did practise here,
> When thy first Fruits of Poesie were given,
> To make thyself a welcome Inmate there;
>   While yet a young Probationer,
>   And Candidate of Heav'n.

                            (ll. 16-22)

[117] Text from the second edition of 1693. Unless otherwise noted, I have used the texts of the poems in the edition of John Sargeaunt (Oxford, 1945).

The traditional relationship between *musica instrumentalis*, practical music at its most specific, and the *musica mundana* of celestial generality, is here applied to Anne Killigrew's life of art ("practise" seems to have the weight of both meanings here). The whole poem employs angels, earth, heaven, the traditional angelic activity of singing, etc., in substitution, in a way, for the conventions of pastoral elegy; and if the conceit of the "heavenly quire" is deemed overly conventional, it is because of its conventionality that it can be employed in such a way as it is here. Professor Tillyard has raised the issue of sincerity with respect to just this point about the angelic singing, but he sees quite rightly, I think, how if "there is no piety in his (Dryden's) references to heavenly music, yet through them he demonstrates how sincerely he prizes the practice of the arts on this earth."[118] The point is that Dryden is able to make use of such references precisely because they are unbelieved, and precisely because music can function consistently as a surrogate for both painting and poetry, with none of the engagement of questions of belief that are occasioned by praising an actual singer by equating her music with that of the Universe.

Dryden is, of course, also capable, in his verses "On the Death of Mr. Purcell" (written one year before his "Alexander's Feast"), of employing the music of the spheres in a fairly traditional, complimentary way. The lines were set to music by Dr. John Blow ("Master to the famous Mr. H. Purcell" as his tomb in Westminster Abbey rightfully attests), and it is interesting to note that, at the end of the first stanza, Dryden was preparing some of his techniques for the "Alexander's Feast." We shall see shortly how the elaborate repetitions of phrase in the latter were contrived to meet the exigencies of the kind of setting that the text would receive; the line "And list'ning and silent, and silent and list'ning, and list'ning and silent obey" (l. 9) prefigures this sort of repetition in a way in which nothing in the first ode

118 E. M. W. Tillyard, *Five Poems* (London, 1948), p. 52.

does. The conventionalities of perfect musicianship enter at the middle of the second stanza, and although they are rather nicely tied to an Orphean conceit which operates through the comparison of Hell and Earth, rather than of Earth and Heaven, the old device of the practical musician outdoing the heavenly choir is unmistakably at work here:

> We beg not Hell our *Orpheus* to restore;
> > Had He been there,
> > Their Sovereigns fear
> Had sent Him back before.
> The pow'r of Harmony too well they knew;
> He long e'er this had Tun'd their jarring Sphere,
> > And left no Hell below.

3.

> The Heav'nly Quire, who heard his Notes from high,
> Let down the Scale of Musick from the Sky:
> > They handed him along,
> And all the way He taught, and all the way they Sung . . .

There is undoubtedly an increment of dramatic power produced by the use of the Underworld motif, and tuning "their jarring Sphere" has more literary plausibility, in a sense, than the customary silencing of the sweet, heavenly one would have. The image at the beginning of the final stanza suggests what Professor Tillyard characterizes as "the outrageous assertion that Anne Killigrew will lead the poetic throng to heaven."[119] But the notion that the quasi-deified Purcell will ascend to heaven along a ladder of perfection that is so named as to suggest at once the musical gamut (in the Greek sense, the *harmonia*) and the *gradus ad Parnassum* of diligent practice and devoted effort, is extremely effective and moving.

The problems that Dryden faced in the composition of the 1687 "Song for St. Cecilia's Day" were virtually the same as those faced by Oldham and the other writers of the texts who

[119] *Ibid.*, p. 52.

had preceded him. But other impulses were at work in his case. There was his marvellous gift of exposition, particularly of summarizing, that triumphed in the dismissive conclusion of "The Secular Masque" (1700), wherein Diana, Mars and Venus, representing the three Stuart Courts, are appropriately and schematically rebuked:

> All, all of a piece throughout:
>> Thy Chase had a Beast in View;
> Thy Wars brought nothing about;
>> Thy Lovers were all untrue.
> 'Tis well an Old Age is out,
>> And time to begin a New.

And there was that happy faculty of Dryden's which took so well to the irregular versification of the so-called "Pindarick ode," that faculty invoked by Mark Van Doren in his observation that Dryden "was constitutionally adapted to a form of exalted utterance which progressed by the alternate accumulation and discharge of metrical energy."[120] In the first ode, these two talents combine to produce an admirable celebration of the power of music.

The ode falls into three main sections, commencing with an introductory narrative of the role played by music, treated as abstract Harmony at the beginning, in the Creation (ll. 1-15). A second section, comprising the next five strophes (ll. 16-47), poses the question "What Passion cannot MUSICK raise and quell?" (l. 16); and after a celebration of some original performance by Jubal upon "the chorded Shell," the original *testudo* or tortoise-shell thought to have been the first lyre, successive strophes go on to celebrate the particular affective and passion-eliciting qualities of trumpet, drum, flute, lute, violin, and organ. The last section (final strophe and added "Grand Chorus") introduces St. Cecilia, in comparison with whom Orpheus comes off unfavorably, and pro-

[120] Mark Van Doren, *John Dryden, A Study of his Poetry*, third ed. (New York, 1946), p. 189.

ceeds to complete the cycle whose commencement is invoked in the opening lines. Music, this time treated as the sounds of the ultimate trumpet, blown by the archangel to announce the end of that second of eternity containing all of human history, is seen as playing an equally effective role in the Destruction as it played in the Creation.

From the very beginning of the piece, the exposition is activated by a kind of narrative excitement:

> From Harmony, from heav'nly Harmony
> This universal Frame began;
> When Nature underneath a heap
> Of jarring Atomes lay,
> And cou'd not heave her Head,
> The tuneful Voice was heard from high,
> Arise, ye more than dead.
> Then cold and hot and moist and dry
> In order to their Stations leap,
> And MUSICK'S pow'r obey. . . .
> (ll. 1-10)

What jars here is not "disproportion'd sin," as in "At a Solemn Musick," but rather the atoms of chaos, which associate themselves with their proper elemental status "in order to their Stations" under the organizing influence of Harmony. While this seems only barely reminiscent of Marvell's recounting of music's creation of a world along specifically political lines, it suggests much more his treatment of Cromwell as Amphion in "The First Anniversary of the Government under O. C.," where the creative, wall-building music accomplishes its ends by ordering what had been chaotic previously.[121] The conclusion of the opening strophe turns a connective "from" into a "to," and changes the meaning of "Harmony" slightly; what is meant now is a melody, an interval, or more probably

[121] See above, Chapter v, pp. 304-305. Van Doren (*op.cit.*, p. 202) holds that stanza II of the "Song for St. Cecilia's Day" may have been influenced by "Musicks Empire."

a chord, instead of the abstract sense of harmony as order in the original and repeated lines:

> From Harmony, from heavenly Harmony
> This universal Frame began:
> From Harmony to Harmony
> Through all the Compass of the Notes it ran,
> The Diapason closing full in Man.
>
> (ll. 11-15)

The octave, that is, the perfect consonance (next to the unison, of course), is the proper "close" (or, in modern terminology, "cadence") for the actual musical composition of Creation, moving along, as Dryden probably meant specifically, over a thoroughbass, "From Harmony to Harmony." Man is that octave cadence, and his shaping crowned the whole act of Creation, and was followed only by the silences of the first Sabbath.

The central portion of the ode, employing separate sections for the celebration of the virtues of each instrument, holds more to the pattern of some of the earlier cantata-texts. Obbligatos on the appropriate instruments would seem to have been the order of the day (although Handel's setting, first performed in 1739, makes much more elaborate use of these than Draghi's original one appears to have done). Dryden does not seem to have kept in mind, in composing his text, that clear distinctions would be drawn, in the setting, between passages of recitative, aria, duet, chorus, etc.; his "Grand Chorus" is the only indication of a textual division that was obviously planned to correspond to a musical one.[122] The vivid metrical variation in strophe 3 ("The TRUMPETS loud Clangor / Excites us to Arms," etc.) is much more effective (with its abrupt switch out of its quasi-dactylic scheme, into "The double double double beat / Of the thund'ring

---

[122] Ernest H. Brennecke, Jr., in "Dryden's Odes and Draghi's Music," *PMLA*, XLIX (1934), pp. 1-36, deals admirably with just these questions of setting in the case of both Odes.

DRUM," and back again) on paper, than when set; although any late Baroque musical setting would set up rhythms of its own to correspond to the effects that Dryden's verse achieved. The second stanza does have the enrichment of the delicate second reference to the "Shell"-lyre:

> Less than a God they thought there could not dwell
> Within the hollow of that Shell,
> That spoke so sweetly, and so well . . .
>
> (ll. 21-23)

where the overtones of the roaring sea-shell seem implicit, somehow, beneath the conventional epithet.

But it is the concluding strophes, along with the first, that are of most interest here. The last one before the chorus compliments St. Cecilia in some of the same terms in which countless "Fair Singers" during the preceding fifty years had been complimented:

> Orpheus cou'd lead the savage race,
> And trees unrooted left their Place,
>   Sequacious of the Lyre;
> But bright Cecilia rais'd the Wonder High'r:
> When to her Organ vocal Breath was given,
> An Angel heard, and straight appear'd
>   Mistaking Earth for Heav'n.
>
> (ll. 48-54)

Dryden has here combined the two elements of the St. Cecilia legend into his little dramatic climax: the angel that the historical saint's *praying* summoned is here treated as having appeared at the sound of the organ, her visible attribute. One cannot be sure whether Dryden was consciously suggesting that it was the "music," the affective beauty of her prayer, which "drew an Angel down," or whether this is merely a rather effective bit of wit. Dryden may also very well have appropriated Ben Jonson's line from "The Musical Strife,"[123]

[123] Geoffrey Walton in *Metaphysical to Augustan* (London, 1955),

but there is certainly sufficient tradition for the figure in the complimentary convention to have allowed him to come upon it himself, quite naturally.

The final chorus, which together with the opening brackets the whole ode, is of a more original stuff:

Grand CHORUS

> *As from the Pow'r of Sacred Lays*
> *The Spheres began to move,*
> *And sung the great Creator's Praise*
> *To all the bless'd above;*
> *So, when the last and dreadful Hour*
> *This crumbling Pageant shall devour,*
> *The TRUMPET shall be heard on high,*
> *The dead shall live, the living die,*
> *And MUSICK shall untune the Sky.*

(ll. 55-63)

Just as the trumpet of Gabriel and of the Koran's Israfel is completely separate from the purely martial trumpet celebrated earlier in the ode, the music that untunes the sky must be referred back to the opening lines: it is only as the dissolvent counterpart of the original ordering that we can make more than the most extravagant sense of the final line. Dr. Johnson wished that "the antithesis of *music untuning* had found some other place";[124] and he evidently found the penultimate line so "awful in itself" that he could not bring himself precisely to designate it. But I think that the music untuning the sky is more than merely a figure representing the transcendence of music, even across the dissolution of the universe. "This crumbling Pageant" is the cosmos, of course; but Professor Van Doren may be hinting at something else, in his remark that Dryden's "finale is the blare of a trumpet,

---

p. 126, points out, *re* this possible borrowing, that "Jonson already has a declamatory note suggestive of the Restoration." Also see above, pp. 339-340.

[124] *Lives*, II, 245. It may, of course, have been merely the voraciousness of the "hour" in eating a "crumbling Pageant" that bothered him.

and his last glimpse is of painted scenery crashing down on a darkened stage."[125] The conclusion of the ode seems quite close to some of the conventions of the masque at this point. We have observed the self-congratulatory tone and import of some of the earlier St. Cecilia's Day odes. Here, the "Pageant" is the musical meeting itself, in much the same way as, in a masque, the allegorical texture of plot, dramaturgy, and theater come to equate the world of the masque's imagery with the parochial, but momentarily universal, world of the court in which it is presented.[126] The London music meetings had none of the masque conventions, of course, such as the identity of the masquers, the closing measures in which spectacle and audience unite, etc. But the marvellous finale quality of the chorus here is considerably enhanced by the fact that the whole cantata, starting up with the literal tuning of strings, should end with an "untuning"; by the fact that the text draws upon the conventional notion of psychic *tonus*[127] (although rather for praise, than for *prayer*, here) in a kind of reversal, implying that, now that the praise of music has been completed, the souls of the singers and hearers will "untune," or "slacken," as have the strings of the actual instruments.

But whatever the force of the ultimate line, it cannot be denied that it is the first and last sections of the ode that are truly distinguished. They are devoted to the eternal subsistence of music, seen as both abstract *harmonia mundi* and final trump; but like the outraged angels and humbled spheres of the epigrams, that "music," a sophisticatedly wrought construction from the stock of *musica speculativa*, is employed in praise of a practical music that is *mundane* rather than *mundana*, worldly rather than universal. The second member of this pair has become merely a term with which to exalt the other.

[125] *John Dryden*, p. 203.
[126] See Rosemond Tuve, *Images and Themes in Five Poems by Milton*, pp. 113-121.
[127] See above, Chapter V, pp. 266-299.

"Alexander's Feast": The Drama
of Musical Power

If the "opening" and "finale" of the first St. Cecilia's Day ode give evidence of a sense on Dryden's part of a kind of musical programmatic dramaturgy, however, it is to the "Alexander's Feast; Or, the Power of Musique" of ten years later that we must turn for the fulfillment of that promise. Questions ranging from that of overall theme to those of more minute details of arrangement of line and repetition of word, raised by the musical setting of the first ode, were settled quite definitively in the execution of the second one. Draghi's setting of the closing line, for example, actually involved the singing of "And Musick shall untune the sky, untune, untune, and Musick shall, and Musick shall. . . ," etc.[128] Then there was the problem of adapting the vigorous and flexible strophic structure to the exigencies of the setting's alternation of chorus, solo, duet, etc., and the final crucial matter of theme, and of a move from the expository to the dramatic. As a solution of all these problems, "Alexander's Feast" must be considered as a true libretto, rather than merely as another in the series of commendatory odes.[129] It is almost proverbial now how Dryden found the prospect of writing another ode "troublesome, & no way beneficiall,"[130] and how its actual composition was accompanied with great concern and some nervousness.[131] The original setting by Jeremiah Clarke (?1673-1707) was never published and no trace of it remains, so that we cannot know precisely the degree to which Dryden's efforts were successful in the case of some of the more technical matters

[128] Quoted by Brennecke, *op.cit.*, p. 29.

[129] *Ibid.*, pp. 34-35.

[130] See his letter of September 3, 1697, in *Letters*, ed. Charles E. Ward (Durham, N.C., 1942), p. 93.

[131] *John Dryden*, p. 204. Also see his letter to Tonson (in Ward's collection, pp. 96-97) about correcting his erroneous MS. substitution of *Lais* for *Thais*, *passim*. One cannot, of course, determine whether the former or the latter appeared as Alexander's distinguished camp-follower on his Persian campaign. Also Dr. Johnson in his "Life of Dryden," *op.cit.*, p. 255.

which he faced as librettist. But the authority with which the ode celebrates its epoch's dominant myth of music is unimpeachable, and its brilliance as a poetic text completely apart from its musical setting has always been dazzling.

His search for a subject could not have taken him far. His dramatic libretto called for one of the old stories of affective music: Orpheus, Arion (rather than the more strictly political Amphion), the Sirens, and Ulysses. Less likely candidates were the stories of the musical martyrs of one sort or another: Orpheus' dismemberment, Herakles' murder of his teacher Linus with the man's own lyre, the punishment of Terpander for adding an extra string to the lyre, the ridicule of the historical Timotheus of Miletus for his innovations along similar lines, Marsyas and his unfortunate espousal of the hateful *aulos*, Midas and his grossly ridiculed lack of taste. All of these must have seemed either overly grotesque or patently ridiculous. Even the story of St. Cecilia herself was too bare of canonical and familiar musical incident. The *philomelamachia* ending in death was not only unsuitable because of its tragic conclusion, but because such a subject would seem better adapted to a chamber dialogue than to the expansion of a cantata.[132] But another Timotheus, a purely fictional Alexandrian *aulos*-player who became confused with the historical composer of *nomoi* mentioned above,[133] had served from the very beginning as part of the Orpheus-figure, as a Baroque poet-musician-rhetorician-hero. Writers in English for the hundred years previous had used as an instance of the power of music the story of how Alexander the Great, in the version of John Case from *The Praise of Musicke* (1586), "sitting at a banquet amongst his friends, was nevertheles by the excelent skil of Timotheus a famous musician so inflamed with the fury of *Modus Orthius*, or as some say of *Dorius*, that he called for his spear & target as if he would presently

---

[132] J. S. Bach's "*Der Streit zwischen Phoebus und Pan*" (1731?), while a full cantata, may have been satiric in intent.

[133] See Erwin Panofsky (*op.cit.*, note 22 above) for a discussion of the history of this confusion, with relevant sources cited.

have addressed himself to war." But immediately thereafter, Case remarks, "the same Timotheus seeing Alexander thus incensed, only with the changing of a note, pacified this moode of his, & as it were with a more mild sound mollified & asswaged his former violence."[134] Aside from the fact that Case has his "modes" mixed up here (Dorian, as well as Phrygian, might be considered a "warlike" mode, but *"Modus Orthius"* is a purely rhythmic term having nothing to do with melody), his account remains pretty much the standard one in English. It has been observed how Cowley, Burton, Playford, and Jeremy Collier, among others, all have versions, of differing degrees of detail, of the Timotheus story;[135] as a probable source, Collier's recounting of the story has its date of appearance (1697) and the liveliness of the scene it sketches on its side: "One time, when *Alexander* was at Dinner, this man play'd him a *Phrygian* Air: The Prince immediately rises, snatches up his Lance, and puts himself in a Posture of Fighting. And the Retreat was no sooner Sounded by the Change of the Harmony, but his Arms were Grounded, and his Fire extinct, and he sat down as orderly as if he had come from one of *Aristotle's Lectures*. I warrant you *Demosthenes* would have been Flourishing about such a Business a long Hour, and may not have done it neither, But *Timotheus* had a nearer Cut to the Soul: He could Neck a Passion at a Stroke, and lay

---

[134] Text quoted in M. C. Boyd, *Elizabethan Music and Musical Criticism*, p. 30. Boyd (App. c, pp. 292-300) prints many relevant extracts from Case's book.

[135] See *John Dryden*, pp. 204-206. James Kinsley, "Dryden and the *Encomium Musicae*," *Review of English Studies*, New Series, IV (1953), p. 265, lists and quotes many of these versions. Mr. Kinsley's article is otherwise, I am afraid, rather misleading in its attempt to connect "Alexander's Feast" with the Renaissance tradition of the praise of music that was first outlined so well by Prof. James Hutton ("Some English Poems in Praise of Music," *English Miscellany*, II [1951], 1-59). But Mr. Kinsley seems utterly to ignore the genre of the poem, its relationship to musical lore as doctine and as mere decorative imagery, etc. etc. His expansion of the earlier tradition of the *encomium musicae* so as to include the ode, without any further needed qualification seems at worst, *simpliste*, at best, Procrustean.

it Asleep."[136] Here, as throughout this essay, incidentally, Collier seems to have been motivated by common sense as much as by his traditional modal *ethos*. "By altering the *Notes*, and the *Time*," he carefully remarks, he could sweeten a hearer's "Humour at a trice."[137] Any late seventeenth-century audience would comprehend such a notion that made no appeal to what had become the purely literary schemata of the music of Antiquity.

But however it came to him, the story of Timotheus was Dryden's program, as the ultimately persuasive powers of music were his theme. The ode's unity keeps to the story, and it is only in the seventh strophe that St. Cecilia is allowed to appear in a cadential, climactic way. As far as the overall structure of the ode is concerned, Dryden has not only repeated the closing lines of each strophe as a chorus, but he had so arranged each stanza that the truncated section, brilliant and summary in itself, would be no mere caudal appendage, but bound to the rest by rhyme or metrical phrase. The end of the third strophe, for example, starts out with the announcement of the arrival of Bacchus:

> Now give the Hautboys breath; He comes,
> > He comes.
> > *Bacchus* ever Fair and Young
> > > Drinking Joys did first ordain;
> > *Bacchus* Blessings are a Treasure;
> > Drinking is the Soldiers Pleasure;
> > > Rich the Treasure;
> > > Sweet the Pleasure;
> > Sweet is Pleasure after Pain.

> > > > > (ll. 53-60)

The last five lines are repeated as a chorus, and the repetitions and echoing of short phrases attest here, as elsewhere throughout the poem, to Dryden's concern for the safety of his text

---

[136] Jeremy Collier, "Of Musick," in *Essays on Several Moral Subjects* (second ed., 1698), II, 22.
[137] *Ibid.*, II, 22.

during the process of setting. But the overall scheme allows the various stanzas to contain, each within itself, a separate episode; a feeling appropriate to the action of each episode is exemplified throughout each strophe, and particularly in the chorus. Thus, in the first one, the scene is laid, and Alexander, "the lovely *Thais*" and "his valiant Peers" are shown feasting after the victory over Xerxes: "Their Brows with Roses and with Myrtles bound. / (So should Desert in Arms be Crown'd:)" (ll. 7-8). The atmosphere is one of love following victory, the myrtle of Venus and the sensual rose, it is pointed out, are the proper guerdon of warlike prowess.[138] Alexander and Thais, "In Flow'r of Youth and Beauty's Pride," are invoked in the chorus:

> *Happy, happy, happy Pair!*
> *None but the Brave,*
> *None but the Brave,*
> *None but the Brave deserves the Fair.*
>
> (ll. 16-19)

And here is the first of many cases of that brilliant shift from iambic to trochaic measures to the catalectic dactyls such as those of "*None but the Brave,*" etc., which marks in particular the prosodical artistry of the whole poem.

The next section introduces "Timotheus plac'd on high / Amid the tuneful Quire," surely not complimented in these lines (although the cliché of praise seems to be in evidence here), but rather depicted as in the high choir-loft or musicians' gallery, under "the Vaulted Roofs" of a sumptuous palace. In contrast to this, however, his playing is elaborately praised, as we are told how he

---

[138] James Kinsley, *op.cit.*, p. 266, points out a possibly relevant passage in Dryden's translation of Plutarch's life of Alexander, in which the burning of the palace is described as having been done by a garlanded Alexander. But I think that the implication about the relationship between heroic love and war is the principal point about this line.

> With flying Fingers touch'd the Lyre:
> The trembling Notes ascend the Sky,
> And Heav'nly Joys inspire.
> (ll. 22-24)

And while "Heav'nly Joys" commends rather more than describes, the remainder of the second section is devoted to the treatment of the theme of the empyrean. The muse governing this stanza, and Timotheus' first song, is Clio:

> The Song began from *Jove*;
> Who left his blissful Seats above,
> (Such is the Pow'r of mighty Love.)
> A Dragon's fiery Form bely'd the God:
> Sublime on Radiant Spires He rode,
> When He to fair *Olympia* press'd:
> And while He sought her snowy Breast:
> Then, round her slender Waist he curl'd,
> And stamp'd an Image of himself, a Sov'raign of the World.
> (ll. 25-33)

But the muse has become the patroness of fiction, rather than of history. The story, recorded in Plutarch, of how Alexander's mother Olympias claimed to have been impregnated by some divine dragon, was one which Dryden had elsewhere condemned in no uncertain terms: "Ye Princes, rais'd by Poets to the Gods, / And Alexander'd up in lying Odes, / Believe not ev'ry flatt'ring Knave's report. . . ,"[139] he warns the readers of his rewriting of Chaucer's *Nun's Priest's Tale*. But here the fiction is identified with the magic of the music, and is praised at the end when we are told that Timotheus "rais'd a Mortal to the Skies," almost as if the greatest triumph of his musicianship had been the creation of the noble fiction of

---

[139] "The Cock and the Fox," from *Fables* (1700), ll. 659-661. Kinsley, *op.cit.*, p. 266, calls attention to this, as well as to other material from Plutarch that Dryden seems to have employed, in one way or another, in filling out the scene of the poem.

Alexander's divine paternity. But it is as a God that Alexander is acclaimed by the crowd at the end of the strophe:

> A present Deity, they shout around:
> A present Deity, the vaulted Roofs rebound.
> > With ravish'd Ears
> > The Monarch hears,
> > Assumes the God,
> > Affects to nod,
> And seems to shake the Spheres.
>
> (ll. 35-41)

If the Spheres are disturbed as a result of Timotheus' transcendent musicianship, it is only through the almost rabble-rousing effects of his music and his fictions that create a din, on the one hand, and half-convince all that the Monarch "Assumes the God," on the other. Only here, in the entire poem, is the heavenly apparatus in evidence. The myth of music throughout is the affective one in terms of which music activates feeling through the medium of sense, and from this point on, Timotheus' playing is to move by persuasion, rather than to affect through "lying."

The third stanza celebrates Bacchus, starting out with the report of what subject it was that "the sweet Musician" actually sang, and then moving almost imperceptibly into the invocation, itself, of Bacchus: "Now give the Hautboys breath; He comes, He comes," etc. We are not told here, as we are in the fifth section, which *harmonia* it actually was that Timotheus played; we may presume that it was the Ionian, which, with the Lydian that in section five becomes the erotic mode, was designated by Plato as one of the "soft or drinking harmonies."[140] Dryden has carefully allowed only wind instruments to occur in this section. The fourth section recounts Alexander's hallucinatory, perhaps drunken (but whether on wine, or music, or both is left deliberately vague) revelry ("Fought all his Battails o'er again; / And thrice He routed

[140] *Republic*, 398-399.

all his Foes, and thrice he slew the slain"). But then, we are told,

> The Master saw the Madness rise,
> His glowing Cheeks, his ardent Eyes;
> And while He Heav'n and Earth defy'd,
> Chang'd his Hand, and check'd his Pride.
> He chose a Mournful Muse,
> Soft pity to infuse . . .
>
> (ll. 69-74)

This would have been a Mixolydian mode that Timotheus employed to chasten his King's exuberance by using it to accompany the reminder of the death of Darius, which had, according to Plutarch, moved Alexander deeply. His song of Darius, "Fallen, fallen, fallen, fallen, / Fallen from his high Estate," causes tears to come to the eyes of Alexander. But in the next strophe, we are told that the Musician sang in "*Lydian* measures" (l. 97), to soothe the king and turn him to amorous feelings. (It is interesting that Dryden should have called the Lydian melodic mode a metrical one, but the additional meanings of "dance" and "means," as well as the rhyme with "Pleasures" operate to enforce the equivalence, rather than the identity, of the two.)

> War, he sung, is Toil and Trouble;
> Honour but an empty Bubble.
> Never ending, still beginning,
> Fighting still, and still destroying,
> If the World be worth thy Winning,
> Think, O think, it worth Enjoying.
> Lovely *Thais* sits beside thee,
> Take the Good the Gods provide thee.
> The Many rend the Skies, with loud applause;
> So Love was Crown'd, but Musique won the Cause . . .
>
> (ll. 99-108)

Here again, the strophe moves into Timotheus' song itself. This time, it is as much moral argument as pure emotional

exhortation; it is a little like a Cavalier lyric about Love and
Arms inserted into the ode at this point. The theme of Mars
and Venus, at any rate, served to introduce the whole scene,
and the sixth strophe, the concluding one of the Timotheus
story, ends itself with a comparison of Thais to the greatest
heroine of war fought all for love. After the king had sunk
in sleep upon the breast of his courtesan, Timotheus struck
"the Golden Lyre" again, this time, we should guess, with
Phrygian strains. Certainly the prosody of this stanza is the
most varied and elaborate. "Revenge, revenge" is the musician's text, and a full complement of Furies, Snakes, ". . . a
ghastly Band, / Each a Torch in his Hand!" conjured up in
the minds of all by the ecstatic mode, incite the king to wreak
that revenge upon the very palace in which he has been
revelling:

> Behold how they toss their Torches on high,
>   How they point to the *Persian* Abodes,
> And glitt'ring Temples of their Hostile Gods.
> The Princes applaud with a furious Joy;
> And the King seized a Flambeau with Zeal to destroy;
>   *Thais* led the Way,
>   To light him to his Prey,
> And, like another *Hellen*, fir'd another *Troy*.
>   (ll. 142-150)

It is Love, then, which concludes the story, as it opened it.
In the final strophe, we are given the climactic mention of
Timotheus:

>   Thus long ago,
>   'Ere heaving Bellows learn'd to blow,
>   While Organs yet were mute,
>   *Timotheus*, to his breathing Flute
>   And sounding Lyre,
> Cou'd swell the Soul to rage, or kindle soft Desire . . .
>   (ll. 155-160)

[419]

The flute and lyre mentioned together may, of course, stem from the traditional confusion of the two Timotheus figures, the historical lyricist and the fictional *auletes*; but it also harks back to the opening theme of Love consummating the warrior's victory, with perhaps an overtone of Horace's second epode with its ". . . *bibam,* /*sonante mixtum tibiis carmen lyra,* / *hac Dorium, illis barbarum?*" wherein the battle of Actium was to be celebrated with mingled musics of a gravely victorious and a frenziedly celebratory nature.

But Timotheus is, finally, outdone, in a sudden intrusion of St. Cecilia that, on the surface, seems rather unconvincing. She is complimented as having "Enlarg'd the former narrow Bounds, / And added Length to solemn Sounds," that is, as combining the virtues of classical measures and of the benefits of the music of Christian worship. It cannot be for this only that Dryden demands,

> Let old Timotheus yield the Prize,
>   Or both divide the Crown:
> He raised a mortal to the Skies;
>   She drew an Angel down.
>
> (ll. 167-170)

Dr. Johnson remarked that this "conclusion is vicious; the music of Timotheus, which *raised a mortal to the skies,* had only a metaphorical power; that of Cecilia, which *drew an angel down,* had a real effect: the crown therefore could not reasonably be divided."[141] To debate this conclusion might not necessarily entail an excursion into ontology to show that for Dryden the power was metaphorical in both cases, but such a debate should be avoided in any event. The final appearance of St. Cecilia as a peculiar sort of *deus ex machina* must be understood as operating within the convention of the St. Cecilia's Day music meetings, with which Dryden was of course familiar. She triumphs over Timotheus (or only meets his accomplishment; Dryden is significantly non-committal)

---

[141] "Life of Dryden," in *Lives,* II, 255.

only through the antithesis of the final conceit, but the intention of this seems quite clear. The reference to her attraction of the angel is casually tossed off, as if to indicate that this story was an accepted part of what was almost a liturgy of these music meetings. The close of the ode is a conventional one, a ritual in itself, and the final piece of wit serves to tie the whole ode and its subject into its proper occasional function. But, in another sense, it is indeed St. Cecilia who has been unthroned.

For all of "Alexander's Feast" has gone to praise not only the power and glory of earthly, affective music, but it has gone to praise poetry as well. It is Timotheus the mythmaker, the forger of fictions, who is commended at the beginning of the poem and at the end; and throughout its course the ode seems to depend upon almost bootlegged poetic references, such as the "Measures" of line 97, and the argument about War and Love in the lines following. It is at any rate the "goddess PERSUASION," who, as Shaftesbury put it, "must have been in a manner the mother of poetry, rhetoric, music, and other kindred arts,"[142] that triumphs at the conclusion of the celebration of music.

Both as a libretto and as a poem, "Alexander's Feast" commends the power of that goddess. The brilliant musical dramaturgy of the cantata text gives way, on reading, to the marvellous metrical effects, which not only serve themselves to excite, calm, chasten, etc., but to imitate in some way the actual musical setting that they would receive, and in which they would be immolated. The poem is a "musical ode" in many of the senses suggested by that compound: an ode set to, about, purporting to resemble, and even substituting for music. More than that, it implicitly stipulates for its own age and for successive ones as well what music is, and how it should be considered. It is to be *made* rather than, as in the first ode, to be expounded like doctrine, even if that doctrine puts down

[142] Third Earl of Shaftesbury, *Characteristics* (1711), ed. J. M. Robertson (New York, 1900), I, 154.

all the cosmological orthodoxies about the music of universe. In a very real sense, the 1687 ode contains a program for the later one, just as it sums up so succinctly not the history of music in the lives of Western men, but the history of what those men have thought and felt and imagined that very music to be. Music itself, practical music, the music of opera and public concert, the music of the highly-trained, status-seeking professional, is the hero (or, in its variousness, a hero-heroine) of "A Song for St. Cecilia's Day." It has un-tuned the sky in the sense that it has already rendered the notion of heavenly music, whether as an actuality or in any one of the many, active metaphorical versions which we have studied above, as trivial as it rendered silent the singing spheres. The untuned sky is the abandoned monochord of *musica speculativa*, and "Alexander's Feast" is no mere strand of *exemplum* from that ancient instrument, but a brilliant performance whose only lesson is its own worth.

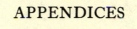

APPENDICES

APPENDIX A

(See pp. 60-61)

An Old English Song[1]

Un-comly in cloystre. i coure ful of care
I loke as a lurdeyn. and listne til my lare,
The song of the cesolfa. dos me syken sare,
And sitte stotiand on a song. a moneth and mare.
I ga gowlende a-bowte. al so dos a *goke*,
Mani is the sorwful song. it sigge upon mi bok;
I am holde so harde. un-nethes dar i loke,
Al the mirthe of this mold. for God i for-soke.
I gowle au mi *grayel*. and rore als a roke,
Litel wiste i ther-of. qwan i ther-to toke:
Summe notes arn shorte. and somme a song roke,
Somme kroken a-*weyward*. als a fleshoke.
Qwan i kan mi lesson. mi meyster wil i gon,
That heres me mi *rendre*. e wenes i have wel don:
Qwat hast thu don, dawn Water. sin saterdai at non?
Thu holdest nowt a note. by God! in riht ton.
Wayme, leve Water. thu werkes al til shame,
Thu stomblest and stikes fast. as thu were lame;
Thu tones nowt the note. ilke be his name,
Thu bitist a-sonder bequarre. for bemol i the blame.
Wey the, leve Water. thu werkes al to wondre,
Als an old cawdrun bigynnest to *clondre*,
Thu tuchest nowt the notes. thu bites hem on sonder:
Hold up for shame. thu letes hem al under.
Thanne is Water so wo. that wol ner wil he blede,
Andwendis him til William. and bit him wil to spede.
'Got it wot!' seys William. 'ther-of hadd i nede:
Now wot i qwou *judicare*. was set in the crede.
Me is wo so is the be. that belles in the *walmes*;

---

[1] From MS. Arundel. 292. f. 71v, printed in *Reliquae Antiquae*, ed.
Thomas Wright and J. O. Halliwell (London, 1845), I, 291-293.

I donke upon David. til mi tonge talmes;
I ne *rendrede* nowt. sithen men beren palmes:
Is is also mikel sorwe. in song so is in salmes?
Ya, bi God! thu reddis. and so it is wel werre.
I solfe and singge after. and is me nevere the nerre;
I horle at the notes. and heve hem al of *herre*:
Alle that me heres. wenes that i erre;
Of bemol and of bequarre. of bothe i was wol bare.
Qwan i wente out of .this word. and liste til mi lare,
Of effauz and elami. ne soud y nevere are;
I fayle faste in the fa. it files al my fare.
ʒet ther ben other notes. sol and ut and la,
And that froward file. that men clepis fa;
Often he dos me liken ille. and werkes me ful wa,
Miʒt i him nevere hitten. in ton for to ta.
ʒet ther is a *streiuant*. wit to longe tailes,
Ther-fore has ure mayster. ofte horled mi kayles;
Ful litel thu kennes. qwat sorwe me ayles,
It is but childes game. that thu witz David dayles.
Qwan ilke note til other lepes. and makes hem a-sawt,
That we calles a *moyson*. in gesolrent en hawt;
Il hayl were thu boren. if thu make defawt,
Thanne sais oure mayster. "que wos ren ne vawt."

APPENDIX B

(See pp. 96-99)

The prouerbis In the garet at the New lodge in the parke
of lekingfelde.[1]

1. When the philosophers putagoras and tuball
   From the pure sympill hammer and steth s(v)bstanciall
   The celestiall soundes of musyk first made and dyd
      expres
   They fot them not from curiosite nor grete riches.

2. Oute of the trewe plaine songe the(y) Judgyde the
      melody
   Curius conueyinge hydithe muche armanye
   Therfore of the playne nottis to sette a sure grounde
   Makithe a modulacion of moste parfyte sounde.
   In curiosite oftyme trowthe slippith by
   And in the playne trew nottis all the swetenes dothe lye.

3. A song myssowndithe yf the prickynge be not right
   So marryd is the melody for lac of fore syght
   The sownde of a trew songe makithe trew concorde
   But subtill prickynge mystymythe and causith grete
      discorde.

4. A naturall breste is goode with sowndes of moderacion
   A glorifiede beste is to curyus withe notis of alteracion
   But he that syngithe a trewe songe mesurithe in the
      meane.
   And he that rechithe to hye a trebill his tewnis is not
      clene.

[1] From Royal MS. 18. D. II, printed in J. C. Flügel, "*Kleinere Mitteilungen aus Handschriften*," *Anglia*, XIV (1891-1892), pp. 477-480. Also in
The Antiquarian Repertory, ed. Francis Grose, revised ed. (London, 1807-
1809), IV, 405-409; and in *Musicall Proverbs*, ed. Philip Wilson (Oxford,
1924).

5. Perfyte vowellynge of a songe to the eere is delectable
   He that quadribilithe to hy his voice is variable.
   But he is no goode Judge whiche disalowith the songe.
   When the ere of parcialite Judgithe it to wronge.

6. He that settithe a songe and makithe it new
   If his warbellis be more curyus than trew
   Or his songe be songe greate faute shall be fownde.
   In the dyuers proporciones of the mystvnyde sownde.

7. A breste to audible mowntithe to affexion
   He that mesurithe in the meane causithe more deuocion
   And he that caryethe more crochettis than his cunnynge
      can prove
   Makithe more discorde of doblenes then melody of loue.

8. He that hathe a brym brest and littill inspexion
      withe all
   Ought to be advisede twyse of his notis musicall
   For he whiche hathe a voice exaltynge to hy
   Fo(r) lac of goode knowledge marrithe much melody.

9. He that lyst to sett a goode trew songe
   May not make his breuys to short nor his largs to longe.
   He that triethe his tewnes tretabilly upon a trew
      grownde
   If connynge be smale the trouthe may make a plesan(t)e
      sounde.

10. The harpe is an instrumente of swete melodye.
    Rude intelligens of the sounde conceyuethe no armonye.
    But whoso in that instrumente hathe no speculacion.
    What restithe withyn the sownde borde hathe but smale
       probacion.

11. He that fyngerithe well the keyes of the clavicordis
       makithe a goode songe
    For in the meane is the melodye withe a rest longe.

[428]

If the tewnys be not plesant to hym that hathe no skyll.
Yet no lac to the Claricorde for he doith his goode will.

12. He that is a perfyte musicion
Perceyvithe the lute tewnes and the goode proporcion
In myddest of the body the stryngis sowndith best.
For stoppide in the freytis they abyde the pynnes wrest.

13. Many a swete refreet the musycion dothe synge.
Which is litill conceyvide of light herynge.
For whos sownde is applyede allway to discorde
Can never deserne the tewnes of a trew monacorde.

14. How may a mysmovede tymer Judge a trew instrument.
For in tunabill tewnys he hathe non experyment.
And he that hath an ere oblyvius and febill stomake
    of affexion
The tewnys of tuball sholde not prayse to Judge wher
    of he lackes discrecion.

15. A slac strynge in a virgynall soundithe not aright.
It dothe abyde no wrastinge it is so louse and light.
The sounde borde crasede forsith the instrumente.
Throw mysgouernaunce to make notis whiche was not
    his intent.

16. He that couytithe in clarisymballis to make goode
    concordaunce
Ought to fynger the keyes withe discrete temporaunce.
To myche wynd(in)ge of the pipis is not the best.
Whiche may cause them to sypher wher armoney shulde
    rest.

17. Immoderate wyndes in a clarion causithe it for to rage.
Soft wynde and moderate makithe the sounde to asswage.
Therfore he whiche in that instrument wolde haue swete
    modulacion
Bustius wyndes must leue and use moderacion.

18. A shawme makithe a swete sounde for he tunyth basse.
    It mountith not to hy but kepithe rule and space.
    Yet yf it be blowne withe to a vehemēt wynde
    It makithe it to mysgouerne oute of his kynde.

19. The swete orgayne pipis comfortith a stedfast mynde
    Wronge handlynge of the stoppis may cause þem sypher
        frō þer kynde.
    But he that playethe of pipes wher so grete nowmber is
    Must handill the keyes all lyke þt by misgouernance
        þey sounde amysse.

20. The recorder of his kynde the meane dothe desyre
    Manyfolde fyngerynge and stoppes bryngithe hȳ from
        his tunes clere.
    Who so lyst to handill an instrument so goode
    Must se in his many fyngerynge þt he kepe tyme step
        and moode.

21. A parfyte modulatour makithe his songe trew
    He mesurithe in the meane withe proporcion dew.
    But whose penne is to swift in prickinge of a songe
    He markithe so his mynnyms fro þe square þt it shall
        sownde wronge.

22. All theys musicalles well handilled and orderde in ther
        kynde
    Gevithe soundes of swetnes to euery goode mynde.
    Yet (*racionalis lingua expellit instrumentis*) all
    Wel tymede and tewnede for it is a master of all.

23. Musyke hathe her coloures of dyuersites
    Blake voyde, blakefull alteraciones of curiosite
    But the white is more comely and to clennes dothe
        accorde
    For purenes in the margent makithe a trew monacorde.

24. Blake color moste comely in armys the syluer shene
    Of virginall purenes whiche is farrest seane

In musyke makithe melody soundynge from all blame
Of the whiche shynythe the clere voce of a pure name
The margent syluer and the notis sabill
Shulde move us to remembrāce of the Joyes
    Intermynabill.

25. The notis pretendynge sabillis of sownde moste melodyus
Must make a meane in our musyke that we be not
    oblyvius
But to remembre thende of oure Fynall cantare.
When for right we shall haue right and payne for
    sinistre iudicare.

26. If thou a musicion a Judge shalbe
Pric nott thy notis in the lyne of peruersite
For that shall cause thy notis to haue a wronge sounde
And as thou makist thy sounde so to the it will rebounde.

27. As in the alteraciones thou mayst pric curiously
So may trouthe try the in thy noumbre made peruersly
For yf the sounde lene not to a good proporcion
Thow maist be Judged by a crochet of wronge notynge
    in thy presumpcion.

28. If thou pric a songe make no obliteracione
But se thy margent be clene withoute contamynacion
For yf thy notis be pricked wt to muche alteracion
It shall cause thy dytty lac of melody his goode operacion.

29. And yf thy melody be marrede and the swete sownde
By thy pervers prickinge whiche concordes dothe
    confounde
For peruersite of thy prickinge and myssoundynge of
    thy songe
And for thy sophysticall solphynge ite maladicti take it
    for thy wronge.

30. Musike is a science and one of the seuyn
Withe swete sowndes to prays the plasmator of heuyn

They that of protervite will not tewne well
Ve. Ve. Ve. theyre songe shalbe in hell.

31. He that lystithe his notis to tune welle and tyme
Muste measure in melpomene one of the musys IX
If he meddyll withe megera infernall is the sounde
Ibi erit fletus malange to confounde.

32. The modulacion of musyke is swete and celestiall
In the speris of the planettis makynge sownde armonicall
If we moder oure musyke as the trew tune is
In heuyn we shall synge *Osanna in excelsis*.

APPENDIX C

(See p. 99)

A parable betwene enformacon and musike.[1]

The Examples	Musike in his melody requirith true sounde(s) who settith a songe shulde geve hym to armony who kepith treue his tunys may not passe his soūdes his alteraciōs and prolaciōs must be prikked trewly. ffor musike is treue the mynstralles makith maistry The harper carieth nothinge but rewarde for his songe merely soundith his mouth when his tonge goth all wrōge.
the harpe	A harpe geuyth sounde as it is sett The harper may wrest it vntunablie If he play wronge good tunys he doth lett or be myssetunynge the vere trew armony A harpe wele plaide on showith swete melody A harper with is wrest may tune the harpe wronge Myssetunynge of an Instrumēt shall hurt a true sōge.
a songe	A song that is true and full of swetnes May be euyll song and tunyd amysse The songe of hymself yet neuer the les Ys true and tunable and syng it as it is them blame not the song but marke well this he that hath spite at another mannys songe will do what he can to haue it songe wronge.
A clarry-corde	The clarrycord hath a evynly kynde As the wyre is wrested hye and lowe So it tunythe to the players mynde

[1] From Royal MS. 18. D. II, printed in J. C. Flügel, "*Kleinere Mitteilungen aus Handschriften,*" *Anglia*, XIV (1891-1892), pp. 466-472.

ffor as it is wrested soo must it needys show
As by this reason ye may wele know
Any Instrument mystunyd shall hurt a true songe
yet blame not the clarrycord the wrester doth
    wronge.

A trum-   A trompet blowen hye w^t to harde a blast
pett   Shall cause him to varry from the tunable kynde
But he that bloweth to hard must swage at the last
And fayne to fall lower w^t a temperat wynde
And then the trompet the true tune shall fynde
ffor an Instrumēt ouerwynded is tunyd wronge
Blame non but the blower on hum it ys longe.

Trew   Who plaith on the harpe he shuld playe trew
councell   Who singeth a songe let his vo(i)ce be tunable
Who wrestith the clarricorde mystunynge eschew
Who bloweth a trompet let his wynde be
    mesurable
ffor Instrument^{es} in theym self be ferme and stable
And of trouth wold trouth to eu^{er}y mannys songe
Tune theym then truly for in them is no wronge.

Colours   In musike I haue lernyd iiij colours as this
of   blak full blaake wide and in likewyse reede
musyke   By thes colours many subtill alteracions ther is
that will begīle one thow in cunnyng he be wele
    spedde
W^t a prike of Jndicōn from a body that is dede
He shall try soo his nombre w^t swetnes of his song
That therer shalbe pleased and yet he all wronge.

The prac-   I pore man vnable of this science to skill
tiser   save a little practise I haue be experience
I meane but trouth and of good will
To remember the doers that useth suche offence
Not one sole but generally in sentence

Bycause I can skill of a litle songe
To try the true corde to be knowen fro the
    wronge.

Trouthe   Yet trouth was drowned he not sanke
But still didde fleete aboue the water
Enformacōn hade plaied hym such a pranke
That wᵗ power the pore had lost his mat
Bycause that trouthe beganne to clatyr
Enformacōn hath taught hym to solfe hys songe
Paciēce parforche content you wᵗ wronge.

truthe   I assaide thes tunes me t(h)owght them not swete
The concordis were nothynge musicall
I callyd mastres of musike cunnynge and discrete
And the first pʳⁱnciple whos name was tuball
Buido boice John de muris vitriaco and them all
I prayd them of helpe of this combrous songe
priked wᵗ force and lettred wᵗ wronge.

true   Thei saide I was hors I myght not synge
answere   Me voice is to pore it is not audible
Enformacōn is so curious in his chauntynge
That to bere the true playne songe it is not possible
His proporciōs be so hard wᵗ so high(t) a quatrible
And the playn songe in the margyn so exa(l)tely
    bounde
That the true tunys of tuball cannot haue the
    right sounde

trouthe   Wele quod trouthe yet onys I trust verely
To haue my voice and synge agayne
And to flet out trouthe and clarify it truly
And ete sugoʳ Candy a daye or twayne
And then to the deske to synge true and playn
Enformacōn shall not alway entune hys songe
My partᵉˢ shalbe true when his countrevers shalbe
    wrōge.

Enfor- Enformacōn hym enbolded of the monacorde
macōn   ffrom consount^{es} to concordys he mused his maistry
       I assaide the musike bothe knyght and lorde
       But none wold speke the sounde borde was to hye
       Then kept I the playn keyes that marred all my
           melody
       Enformacōn drave a crochet that past all my
           songe
       With *proporciō parforche* dreven on to longe.

dialoge Sufferance came in to syng a parte
       Go to quod trouth I pray yow begynne
       may soft quod he the gise of my arte
       ys to rest a longe rest or I set in
       nay be longe restynge ye shall nothing wynne
       ffor enformacōn is so crafty and so hye in his songe
       That if ye fall to restynge in faith it wilbe wronge.

Trouthe Enformacōn will teche a doctor hys game
       ffrom superacute to the doble diapason
       I assaide to acute and when I came
       Enformacōn was mete for a doble dyatesseron
       he songe be a pothorne that hath two kyndes in one
       With mony subtill semytunys most mete for his
           songe
       Pacience parforche content you w^t wronge.

Trouthe I kepe be rounde and he be square
       The one is be mole and the other be quarre
       yf I myght make tryall as I couthe and dare
       I shuld shew why thes jj kyndes do varry
       but god knowith all (/) so doth not kyng harry
       ffor if he didde then chaunge shulde this mi songe
       pitie for patience and conscience for wronge.

BIBLIOGRAPHY

I. PRIMARY SOURCES

Addison, Joseph, Richard Steele, et al. *The Spectator*. Everyman Edition, 4 vols. London. 1930.

Alciati, D. A. *Emblemata*. Lyons, 1551.

Anglo-Saxon and Old English Vocabularies, ed. R. P. Wulcker and Thomas Wright, second edition. London, 1884.

Apel, Willi, and Archibald T. Davison. *Historical Anthology of Music*, rev. ed. Cambridge, Mass., 1949.

Arbeau, Thoinot. *Orchesographie*. Langres, 1589.

Aristotle. *On the Heavens*, tr. W. K. C. Guthrie. Loeb Edition. London, 1939.

Aristotle. *Problems*, tr. W. S. Hett. Loeb Edition. 2 vols., London, 1953.

Ascham, Roger. *English Works*, ed. W. A. Wright. Cambridge, 1904.

Ascham, Roger. *Toxophilus*, ed. Edward Arber. London, 1868.

St. Augustine. *Confessions*, tr. E. B. Pusey. Everyman Edition. London, 1907.

Bacon, Francis. *The Advancement of Learning*, ed. William A. Wright, fifth edition. Oxford, 1926.

Bacon, Francis. *Philosophical Works*, ed. J. M. Robertson. London, 1905.

Ban, Jan Albert. *Dissertatio Epistolica De Musica Natura*. Leyden, 1637.

Barclay, Alexander, tr. *The Ship of Fools*, ed. T. H. Jamieson, 2 vols., London, 1874.

Batman, Stephen. *Batman Upon Bartholome*. London, 1582.

Beaumont, Joseph. *Minor Poems*, ed. Eloise Robinson. London, 1914.

Beowulf, ed. F. Klaeber, third edition. New York, 1950.

Blome, Richard. *The Gentleman's Recreations*, second edition. London, 1710.

Bodin, Jean. *The Six Bookes of a Commonweale*, tr. Richard Knolles. London, 1606.

Boehme, Jacob. *The Way to Christ*, tr. John Joseph Stoudt. New York, 1947.

Boethius. *De Consolatione Philosophiae*, ed. H. F. Stewart. Loeb Edition. London, 1946.

Boethius. *De Consolatione Philosophiae*, trans. John Walton, ed. Mark Science. London, 1927.

Boria, Juan de. *Emblemata Moralia*. Berlin, 1697.

Browne, Thomas. *Religio Medici*, intr. C. H. Herford. Everyman Edition, London, 1906.

Bunyan, John. *A Book for Boys and Girls: or Country Rhimes for Children*. London, 1686.

Bunyan, John. *Whole Works*, ed. George Offor. 3 vols., London, 1862.

Burmeister, Joachim. *Musica Poetica: Definitibus et Divisionibus breviter delineata. . . .* Rostock, 1606.

Burton, Robert. *The Anatomy of Melancholy*, ed. Floyd Dell and Paul Jordan-Smith. New York, 1951.

Butler, Charls. *The Principles of Musik*. London, 1636.

Butler, Samuel. *Hudibras*, ed. T. R. Nash. 2 vols., London, 1847.

Butler, Samuel. *Satires and Miscellaneous Poetry and Prose*, ed. René Lamar. Cambridge, 1928.

Byrd, William. *Psalmes, Sonets and Songs of Sadness and Pietie*. London, 1588.

Campion, Thomas. *Works*, ed. Percival Vivian. Oxford, 1909.

Carew, Thomas, *Poems*, ed. Rhodes Dunlap. Oxford, 1949.

Cartwright, William. *Plays and Poems*, ed. G. Blakemore Evans. Madison, 1951.

Case, John. *Apologia musices cum vocalis quam instrumentalis et mixtae*. London, 1588.

Case, John. *The Praise of Musicke*. London, 1586.

Castiglione, Baldassare. *The Courtier* (1528), tr. Thomas Hoby (1561). Everyman Edition. London, 1948.

Cavendish, Margaret, Duchess of Newcastle. *The Life of the First Duke of Newcastle and Other Writings*, ed. Ernest Rhys. Everyman Edition. London, 1915.

Caxton's Book of Curtesye, ed. F. J. Furnivall. EETSES 3. London, 1868.

Caxton's Mirrour of the World, ed. Oliver H. Prior. EETSES 110. London, 1913.

Chaucer, Geoffrey. *Works*, ed. F. N. Robinson, second edition. Cambridge, 1957.

Chief Pre-Shakespearean Dramas, ed. J. Q. Adams. Cambridge, Mass., 1924.

Child, F. J. *English and Scottish Popular Ballads*. London, 1892.

Cicero. *De Re Republica*, tr. C. W. Keyes. Loeb Edition. London, 1928.

Collier, Jeremy. *Essays upon Severall Moral Subjects*, second edition. 2 vols., London, 1697.

Collier, Jeremy. *A Short View of the Immorality and Profaneness of the English Stage*. London, 1698.

Congreve, William. *The Mourning Bride, Poems and Miscellanies*, ed. Bonamy Dobree. Oxford, 1928.

Cooper, Antony Ashley, 1st Earl of Shaftesbury. *Characteristics*, ed. J. M. Robertson. 2 vols., New York, 1900.

Coryate, Thomas. *Coryats Crudities Hastily Gobled up in Five Moneths Travells*. London, 1611.

The Court of Sapience, ed. Robert Spindler. Leipzig, 1927.

Cowley, Abraham. *Poems*, ed. A. R. Waller. Cambridge, 1905.

Crashaw, Richard. *Complete Works*, ed. A. B. Grosart. London, 1872-1873.

Crashaw, Richard. *Works*, ed. L. C. Martin. Oxford, 1927.

Cudworth, Ralph. *The Intellectual System of the Universe*, ed. Thomas Birch. 2 vols., Andover, 1837.

Daniel, Samuel. *Poems and a Defense of Ryme*, ed. A. C. Sprague. Cambridge, Mass., 1930.

The Daunce of Death (Ellesmere MS.), ed. Florence Warren. London, 1931.

D'Avenant, William. *Dramatic Works*, ed. J. Maidment and W. H. Logan. 5 vols., Edinburgh, 1872-1874.

Davies of Hereford, John. *Complete Works*, ed. A. B. Grosart. London, 1878.

Davies, Sir John. *Complete Poems*, ed. A. B. Grosart. 2 vols., London, 1876.

De Lauze, F. *Apologie de la Danse*, tr. and intro. Joan Wildeblood. London, 1952.

Descartes, René. *Oeuvres*, ed. Charles Adam and Paul Tannery. Paris, 1902.

Donne, John. *The Divine Poems*, ed. Helen Gardner. Oxford, 1952.

Donne, John. *Poems*, ed. Sir Herbert Grierson. 2 vols., Oxford, 1912.

Donne, John. *Sermons*, ed. George R. Potter and Evelyn M. Simpson. 9 vols., Berkeley, 1953-.

Douglas, Gavin. *Poetical Works*, ed. John Small. 4 vols., Edinburgh and London, 1874.

Drayton, Michael. *Minor Poems*, ed. Cyril Brett. Oxford, 1907.

Drayton, Michael. *Works*, ed. J. W. Hebel. 5 vols., Oxford, 1931-1941.

Drummond of Hawthornden, William. *Poetical Works*, ed. L. E. Kastner. 2 vols., Manchester, 1913.

Dryden, John. *Essays*, ed. W. P. Ker. 2 vols., Oxford, 1926.

Dryden, John. *Fables*. London, 1700.

Dryden, John. *Letters*, ed. Charles F. Ward. Durham, N.C., 1942.

Dryden, John. *Poetical Works*, ed. John Sargeaunt. Oxford, 1945.

Earle, John. *Micro-Cosmographie*, ed. E. Arber. London, 1868.

Elegy and Iambus, with the Anacreonta, ed. J. M. Edmonds. Loeb Edition. London, 1931.

Elizabethan and Jacobean Pamphlets, ed. George Saintsbury. New York, 1892.

Elizabethan Sonnets, ed. Sidney Lee. 2 vols., London, 1904.

Elyot, Thomas. *The Boke Named the Gouernour*. Everyman Edition. London, 1907.

Emblems for the Improvement and Entertainment of Youth. London, 1769.

An English Garner, ed. Edward Arber. 8 vols., London, 1877-1890.

Euler, Leonhard. *Opere Omnia*. 29 vols., Leipzig and Berlin, 1911-1956.

Evelyn, John. *Diary*, ed. Austin Dobson. 3 vols., London, 1906.

The Exeter Book, Part II, ed. W. S. Mackie. EETS 194. London, 1934.

Fellowes, E. H., ed. *English Madrigal School*. 36 vols., London, 1913-1924.

Fellowes, E. H., ed. *English Madrigal Verse*. Oxford, 1929.

Fellowes, E. H. *The English Madrigal Composers*, second edition. Oxford, 1948.

Felltham, Owen. *Lusoria*. London, 1661.

Felltham, Owen. *Resolves*. London, 1840.

Fletcher, Giles and Phineas. *Poetical Works*, ed. F. S. Boas. 2 vols., Cambridge, 1904.

Fludd, Robert. *Utriusque Cosmi Maiori scilicet et minori Metaphysica, Physica, atque technica Historia*. Oppenheim, 1617.

Fraunce, Abraham. *The Arcadian Rhetorike*, ed. Ethel Seaton. Oxford, 1950.

Gascoigne, George. *The Glasse of Government and other Works*, ed. John W. Cunliffe. Cambridge, 1910.

Gascoigne, George. *The Posies*, ed. John W. Cunliffe. Cambridge, 1907.

Gaultier, Denis. *La Rhétorique des Dieux*, ed. André Tessier. Paris, 1932.

Giraldus Cambrensis. *Works*, ed. J. S. Brewer, G. F. Warner and J. F. Dimock. *Chronicles and Memorials of Great Britain and Ireland during the Middle Ages*, number 21. 8 vols., London, 1861-1891.

Goodman, Godfrey. *The Fall of Man*. London, 1616.

Googe, Barnaby. *Eglogs, Epytaphes, & Sonettes*, ed. Edward Arber. London, 1871.

Gosson, Stephen. *The Schools of Abuse*, ed. Edward Arber. Birmingham, 1868.

Gower, John. *Complete Works*, ed. G. C. Macaulay. 4 vols., Oxford, 1899-1902.

Grose, F. *Antiquarian Repertory*. 4 vols., London, 1808.

Guiney, Louise Imogen. *Recusant Poets*. 2 vols., New York, 1938.

Habington, William. *Castara*, ed. Edward Arber. London, 1870.

Hawes, Stephen. *The Pastime of Pleasure*, ed. William Edward Mead. EETS 173. London, 1928.

Heinrichen, J. D. *Der Generalbass in der Composition*. Dresden, 1728.

Henryson, Robert. *Poems and Fables*, ed. H. Harvey Wood. Edinburgh and London, 1933.

Herbert, Edward. *Poems*, ed. G. C. Moore Smith. Oxford, 1923.

Herbert, George. *Works*, ed. F. E. Hutchinson. Oxford, 1941.

Herrick, Robert. *Complete Poems*, ed. L. C. Martin. Oxford, 1956.

The Hieroglyphics of Horapollo, tr. George Boas. New York, 1950.

Higden, Ranulph. *Polychronicon Ranulphi Higden Monachi Cestrensis*, ed. Joseph R. Lumby. The Rolls Series, no. 41. London, Oxford, Cambridge, Edinburgh, and Dublin, 1871.

Hobbes, Thomas. "The Answer to the Preface to Gondibert." *English Works*, ed. Sir William Molesworth. 11 vols., London, 1839-1845.

Hooker, Richard. *Laws of Ecclesiastical Polity*, ed. R. Bayne. Everyman Edition. 2 vols., London, 1907.

Hookes, Nicholas. *Amanda*. Reprinted New York, 1927.

Johnson, Samuel. *Lives of the English Poets*. Everyman Edition, 2 vols., London, 1950.

Jonson, Ben. *Works*, ed. C. H. Herford and Percy and Evelyn Simpson. 11 vols., Oxford, 1925-1952.

Joyce, James. *Finnegans Wake*. New York, 1947.

Kelten, Joannes Michael van der. *Apelles Symbolicus*. Amsterdam, 1699.

Kepler, Johannes. *Harmonices Mundi*, tr. Charles Glenn Wallis. Great Books of the Western World. Chicago, 1952.

Labé, Louise. *Love Sonnets*, tr. Frederic Prokosh [sic]. New York, 1947.

Langland, William. *Piers the Plowman*, ed. W. W. Skeat, tenth edition. Oxford, 1900.

Le Brun, Charles. *Méthode pour apprendre à dessiner les passions proposée dans une confèrence sur l'expression générale et particulière*. Paris, 1698.

Leibniz, Gottfried Wilhelm. *Philosophical Papers and Letters*, tr. and ed. Leroy E. Loemken. 2 vols., Chicago, 1956.

Leibniz, Gottfried Wilhelm. *Philosophischen Schriften*, ed. C. J. Gerhardt. 7 vols., Berlin, 1880.

Locke, John. *Philosophical Works*, ed. James Augustus St. John. 2 vols., London, 1913.

Lovelace, Richard. *Poems*, ed. L. H. Wilkenson. Oxford, 1930.

Lydgate, John. *Pilgrimage of the Life of Man*, ed. F. J. Furnivall. 3 vols., EETSES 77, 83, and 92. London, 1899-1904.

Lydgate, John. *Reason and Sensuality*, ed. Ernest Sieper. 2 vols., EETSES 84 and 89. London, 1901 and 1903.

Mace, Thomas. *Musicks Monument*. Cambridge, 1676.

Macran, Henry S., ed. *The Harmonics of Aristoxenus*. Oxford, 1902.

Macrobius. *Commentary on the Dream of Scipio*, tr. W. H. Stahl. New York, 1952.

Marvell, Andrew. *Poems and Letters*, ed. H. M. Margoliouth. 2 vols., Oxford, 1927.

Meres, Francis. *Palladis Tamia*. London, 1598.

Mersenne, Marin. *Harmonie Universelle, Contenant la Théorie de la Musique*. Paris, 1636.

Mill, John Stuart. *Autobiography*. New York, 1924.

Milton, John. *Complete Poems and Major Prose*, ed. Merritt Y. Hughes. New York, 1957.

Milton, John. *Works*, ed. Frank Allen Patterson, et al. 20 vols., New York, 1931-1940.

The Mirrour of Maiestie, ed. Henry Green and James Croston. London, 1870.

Montaigne. *Essayes*, tr. John Florio. The Tudor Translations. London, 1908.

Monumenta Germanica Historica. Poetae Latini aevi Caroli, ed. E. Duemmler. 4 vols., Berlin, 1881-1923.

More, Thomas. *Utopia*, trans. Raphe Robynson, ed. J. Rawson Lumby. Cambridge, 1940.

Morley, Thomas. *A Plaine and Easie Introduction to Practicall Musicke*, ed. R. A. Harman. New York, 1953.

Mulcaster, Richard. *The First Part of the Elementarie*, ed. E. T. Campagnac. Oxford, 1925.

Nettl, Paul, ed. *The Book of Musical Documents*. New York, 1948.

Norris, John. *A Collection of Miscellanies*, fourth edition. London, 1706.

North, Roger. *Memoirs of Musick*, ed. Edward F. Rimbault. London, 1846.

North, Roger. *The Musicall Grammarian*, ed. Hilda Andrews. Oxford, 1925.

Old English Ballads 1553-1625, ed. Hyder Rollins. Cambridge, Mass., 1920.

The Old English Elene, Phoenix and Physiologus, ed. Albert S. Cook. New Haven, 1919.

Oracus, Henricus. *Viridarium Hieroglyphico-Morale*. Frankfort, 1619.

The Owl and the Nightingale, ed. J. W. H. Atkins. Cambridge, 1922.

The Oxford Book of Seventeenth Century Verse, ed. Sir Herbert Grierson and G. Bullough. Oxford, 1934.

Palingenius. *The Zodiacke of Life*, tr. Barnaby Googe. London, 1576.

The Paradise of Dainty Devices, ed. Hyder Rollins. Cambridge, Mass., 1927.

Parrish, Carl and John F. Ohl, ed. *Masterpieces of Music Before 1750*. New York, 1951.

Peacham, Henry. *The Compleat Gentleman*, second edition of 1634. Reprinted Oxford, 1906.

Peacham, Henry. *The Garden of Eloquence*. London, 1593.

Peacham, Henry. *Minerva Brittana*. London, 1612.

Pepys, Samuel. *Diary*, ed. H. B. Wheately. Random House edition, 2 vols., New York, no date.

Philo. *De Sacrificiis Abelis et Caini*, tr. F. H. Colson and G. H. Whitaker. Loeb Edition. London and Cambridge, Mass., 1949.

The Philosophical Transactions (From the year 1700 to the year 1720) Abridg'd and Dispos'd under General Heads. London, 1749.

Plotinus. *Enneads*, tr. Stephen MacKenna, rev. B. S. Page. London, 1956.

Plutarch. *Lives, Englished by Thomas North*. The Tudor Translations. 6 vols., London, 1895-1896.

A Poetical Rhapsody, ed. Hyder Rollins. Cambridge, Mass., 1931-1932.

Prior, Matthew. *Poetical Works*, ed. J. Mitford. Riverside Edition, 2 vols., Boston, no date.

A proper new Boke of the Armonye of Byrdes, ed. J. Payne Collier. The Percy Society Series, vol. VII. London, 1842.

Prynne, William. *Histrio-Mastix, the Players Scourge*. London, 1633.

Quarles, Francis. *Divine Fancies, Digested into Epigrammes, Meditations, and Observations*. London, 1641.

Quarles, Francis. *Emblems, Divine and Moral: Together with Hieroglyphicks of the Life of Man*. London, 1736.

Rastell, John. *The Nature of the Four Elements*, facsimile prepared by J. S. Farmer. Tudor Facsimile Texts. London, 1908.

Ravenscroft, Thomas. *A Briefe Discourse of the true (but neglected) use of Charact'ring the Degrees.* . . . London, 1614.

[Redford, John]. *The Moral Play of Wit and Science*, ed. J. O. Halliwell for the Shakespeare Society. London, 1848.

Reliquae Antiquae, ed. Thomas Wright and J. O. Halliwell. London, 1845.

Renatus Des-Cartes Excellent Compendium of Musick: With Necessary and Judicious Animadversions Thereupon. By a Person of Honour. London, 1653.

Restoration Verse, ed. William Kerr. London, 1930.

Robinson, Thomas. *Schoole of Music.* London, 1603.

Ronsard, Pierre de. *Oeuvres Complètes*, ed. Paul Laumonier. Paris, 1914-1919.

Rymer, Thomas. *Critical Works*, ed. Curt A. Zimansky. New Haven, 1956.

Saintsbury, G., ed. *The Caroline Poets.* Oxford, 1921.

Sandys, George. *Ovid's Metamorphoses Englished, Mythologiz'd and Represented in Figures.* London, 1632.

Seventeenth Century Lyrics, ed. Norman Ault. London, 1928.

Shakespeare, William. *Complete Works*, ed. G. W. Harrison. New York, 1952.

Shakespeare, William. *Sonnets*, ed. Hyder Rollins. Variorum Edition. 2 vols., Philadelphia, 1944.

Shirley, James. *Poems*, ed. R. L. Armstrong. New York, 1941.

Sidney, Sir Philip. *Complete Works*, ed. Albert Feuillerat. Cambridge, 1912-1926.

Sir Orfeo, ed. J. A. Bliss. Oxford, 1954.

Skelton, John. *Poetical Works*, "principally according to the edition of" Alexander Dyce. 3 vols., Boston, 1856.

Smith, G. G., ed. *Elizabethan Critical Essays.* Oxford, 1904.

Spenser, Edmund. *Complete Works*, ed. R. E. Neil Dodge. Cambridge, Mass., 1908.

Steele, Richard. *Occasional Verse*, ed. Rae Blanchard. Oxford, 1952.

Stevens, Wallace. *Collected Poems.* New York, 1955.

Strode, William. *Poetical Works*, ed. Bertram Dobell. London, 1907.

Strunk, Oliver, ed. *Source Readings in Music History*. New York, 1950.

Swift, Jonathan. *Gulliver's Travels*, ed. Herbert Davis. Oxford, 1941.

Swift, Jonathan. *Poems*, ed. Harold Williams. Oxford, 1937.

Sylvester, Joshua. *Du Bartas His Divine Weekes and Workes*. London, 1641.

Taylor, Jeremy. *Whole Works*, ed. Reginald Heber and Alexander Taylor, rev. C. P. Eden. 10 vols., London, 1852-1861.

Traherne, Thomas. *Poetical Works*, ed. Gladys I. Wade, third edition. London, 1932.

Vaughan, Henry. *Works*, ed. L. C. Martin. 2 vols., Oxford, 1914.

Waller, Edmund. *Poems*, ed. G. Thorn-Drury. London, 1893.

Waller, Edmund. *Poetical Works*, ed. Robert Bell. London, 1854.

Walton, Izaak. *Lives*, ed. S. B. Carter. London, 1951.

Watson, Thomas. *Poems*, ed. Edward Arber. London, 1870.

Whitney, Geoffrey. *A Choice of Emblemes*. Leyden, 1586.

The whole Psalter translated into English Metre, which contayneth an hundred and fifty Psalmes. London, 1560.

Wood, Anthony à. *Athenae Oxoniensis*. 2 vols., Oxford, 1691-1692.

Wyatt, Sir Thomas. *Collected Poems*, ed. Kenneth Muir. London, 1949.

Wyclif, John. *English Works*, ed. F. D. Matthew. London, 1880.

II. SECONDARY SOURCES

A. BOOKS

Abrams, Meyer. *The Mirror and the Lamp*. New York, 1953.

Arthos, John. *On "A Mask Presented at Ludlow-Castle."* University of Michigan, Contributions in Modern Philology. Ann Arbor, 1954.

Bailey, Margaret Lewis. *Milton and Jakob Boehme, A Study of German Mysticism in Seventeenth-Century England*. New York, 1914.

Banks, Theodore Howard. *Milton's Imagery*. New York, 1950.

Baring-Gould, S. *The Lives of the Saints*, new and rev. ed. 16 vols., Edinburgh, 1914.

Bennett, H. S. *Chaucer and the Fifteenth Century*. Oxford, 1947.

Blom, Eric. *Music in England,* revised edition. London, 1947.

Boyd, Morison Comegys. *Elizabethan Music and Musical Criticism.* Philadelphia, 1940.

Bradbrook, M. C., and M. G. Lloyd Thomas. *Andrew Marvell.* Cambridge, 1940.

Brennecke, Ernest, Jr. *John Milton the Elder and his Music.* New York, 1938.

Brooks, Cleanth. *The Well-Wrought Urn.* New York, 1947.

Brooks, Cleanth, and John Edward Hardy. *Poems of Mr. John Milton.* New York, 1951.

Brumbaugh, Robert S. *Plato's Mathematical Imagination.* Bloomington, Indiana, 1954.

Bukofzer, Manfred. *Geschichte des Englischen Diskants und des Fauxbourdons nach den Theoretischen Quellen.* Strassburg, 1936.

Bukofzer, Manfred. *Music in the Baroque Era.* New York, 1947.

Bukofzer, Manfred. *Studies in Medieval and Renaissance Music.* New York, 1950.

Burney, Charles. *A General History of Music,* ed. F. Marcer. 2 vols., New York, 1957.

Burtt, E. A. *The Metaphysical Foundations of Modern Science.* New York, 1954.

Bush, Douglas. *English Literature in the Earlier Seventeenth Century.* Oxford, 1945.

Bush, Douglas. *Mythology and the Renaissance Tradition in English Poetry.* Minneapolis, 1932.

Buxton, John. *Sir Philip Sidney and the English Renaissance.* London, 1954.

Carpenter, Nan C. *Music in the Medieval and Renaissance Universities.* Norman, Oklahoma, 1958.

Carpenter, Nan C. *Rabelais and Music.* Chapel Hill, 1954.

Cassirer, Ernst. *The Platonic Renaissance in England,* tr. James P. Pettegrove. Austin, 1953.

Coate, Henry. *Palestrina.* New York, 1949.

Collingwood, R. G. *The Idea of Nature.* Oxford, 1945.

Cornford, Francis M. *Plato's Cosmology.* New York, 1952.

Coussemaker, E. de. *Oeuvres Théoriques de Jean Tinctoris.* Lille, 1875.

Cowling, G. H. *Music on the Shakespearian Stage.* Cambridge, 1913.

Cutts, John P. *Seventeenth Century Songs and Lyrics.* Columbia, Mo., 1959.

Darkey, William A., Jr. "Milton's 'At a Solemn Musick'; a Commentary." Unpublished Master's essay, Columbia, 1949.

Dart, Thurston. *The Interpretation of Music.* London, 1954.

Davis, R. B. *George Sandys, Poet Adventurer.* London, 1955.

Dent, Edward J. *Foundations of English Opera.* Cambridge, 1928.

Dolmetsch, Arnold. *The Interpretation of the Music of the XVIIth and XVIIIth Centuries.* London, no date.

Elson, Louis C. *Shakespeare in Music.* Boston, 1901.

Erlich, Victor. *Russian Formalism.* The Hague, 1955.

Essays in Honor of Albert Feuillerat, ed. Henri M. Peyre. New Haven, 1943.

Evans, Willa McClung. *Henry Lawes.* New York, 1941.

Fränger, Wilhelm. *The Millennium of Hieronymus Bosch,* tr. Eithne Wilkins and Ernst Kaiser. Chicago, 1951.

Freeman, Kathleen. *Ancilla to the Pre-Socratic Philosophers.* Oxford, 1952.

Freeman, Rosemary. *English Emblem Books.* London, 1948.

Galpin, Francis W. *Old English Instruments of Music,* second edition. London, 1911.

Gibbon, John Murray. *Melody and the Lyric from Chaucer to the Cavaliers.* London, 1930.

Gilbert, Katharine Everett, and Helmut Kuhn. *A History of Esthetics.* Bloomington, 1953.

Green, Henry. *Andrea Alciati and his Books of Emblems.* London, 1872.

Guthrie, W. K. C. *Orpheus and Greek Religion.* London, 1935.

Harrison, Frank Ll. *Music in Medieval Britain.* London, 1958.

Holt, Elizabeth Gilmore, ed. *A Documentary History of Art.* 2 vols., New York, 1958.

Hunt, Clay. *Donne's Poetry: Essays in Literary Analysis.* New Haven, 1954.

Husk, William Henry. *An Account of the Musical Celebrations on St. Cecilia's Day.* London, 1857.

Izard, Thomas C. *George Whetstone, Mid-Elizabethan Man of Letters*. New York, 1942.

John, Lisle Cecil, *The Elizabethan Sonnet Sequences: Studies in Conventional Conceits*. New York, 1938.

Kant, Immanuel. *Prolegomena to Any Future Metaphysics*, intr. Lewis W. Beck. New York, 1951.

Kerman, Joseph. *Opera as Drama*. New York, 1956.

Kinsky, Georg. *A History of Music in Pictures*. New York, 1951.

Knight, G. Wilson. *The Shakespearian Tempest*. Oxford, 1932.

Lanier, Sidney. *The Science of English Verse*, ed. Paull F. Baum. Baltimore, 1945.

Leichtentritt, Hugo. *Music, History, and Ideas*. Cambridge, 1954.

Lever, J. W. *The Elizabethan Love Sonnet*. London, 1956.

Lewis, C. S. *The Allegory of Love*. Oxford, 1938.

Lewis, C. S. *English Literature in the Sixteenth Century*. Oxford, 1954.

Life in Shakespeare's England, ed. J. Dover Wilson, third edition. London, 1944.

Loesser, Arthur. *Men, Women, and Pianos*. New York, 1954.

Mace, Dean Tolle. *English Musical Thought in the Seventeenth Century: A Study of an Art in Decline*. Unpublished dissertation, Columbia, 1952.

Mahood, M. M. *Poetry and Humanism*. New Haven, 1950.

Manifold, J. S. *The Music in English Drama*. London, 1956.

Marrou, H. I. *A History of Education in Antiquity*, tr. George Lamb. London, 1956.

Martz, Louis L. *The Poetry of Meditation*. New Haven, 1954.

McAllester, David P. *Enemy Way Music: A Study of Social and Esthetic Values as Seen in Navajo Music*. Papers of the Peabody Museum of American Archaeology and Ethnology, Harvard University, vol. XLI, no. 3. Cambridge, Mass., 1954.

Mellers, Wilfrid. *François Couperin and the French Classical Tradition*. New York, 1951.

Mellers, Wilfrid. *Music and Society*. New York, 1950.

Meyer, Leonard B. *Emotion and Meaning in Music*. Chicago, 1956.

Mourgues, Odette de. *Metaphysical, Baroque, and Précieux Poetry*. Oxford, 1953.

Music and Medicine, ed. Dorothy M. Schullian and Max Schoen. New York, 1948.

Musique et Poésie ou XVI⁴ Siècle. Colloques Internationaux du Centre National de la Recherche Scientifique, Sciences Humaines, v. Paris, 1954.

Naylor, Edward W. *Shakespeare and Music*, second edition. London, 1931.

Nettl, Bruno. *Music in Primitive Culture*. Cambridge, Mass., 1956.

Nicolson, Marjorie. *Science and Imagination*. Ithaca, 1956.

Noble, Richmond. *Shakespeare's Use of Song*. Oxford, 1923.

Owings, Marvin Alpheus. *The Arts in the Middle English Romances*. New York, 1957.

Panofsky, Erwin. *Albrecht Dürer*. 2 vols., Princeton, 1948.

Panofsky, Erwin. *Early Netherlandish Painting*. 2 vols., Cambridge, Mass., 1954.

Panofsky, Erwin. *Studies in Iconology: Humanistic Themes in the Art of the Renaissance*. New York, 1939.

Pattison, Bruce. *Music and Poetry of the English Renaissance*. London, 1948.

Pfatteicher, Carl F. *John Redford*. Kassel, 1934.

Pirro, André. *Descartes et la Musique*. Paris, 1907.

Portney, Julius. *The Philosopher and Music*. New York, 1954.

Praz, Mario. *Studies in Seventeenth Century Imagery*. 2 vols., London, 1939.

Praz, Mario. *The Flaming Heart*. New York, 1958.

Reese, Gustave. *Music in the Middle Ages*. New York, 1940.

Reese, Gustave. *Music in the Renaissance*. New York, 1954.

Richards, I. A. *The Principles of Literary Criticism*. New York, 1952.

Rose, H. J. *The Eclogues of Vergil*. Berkeley, 1942.

Ruhnke, Martin. *Joachim Burmeister*. Schriften des Landesinstitut für Musikforschung, Kiel, Band 5. Kassel and Basel, 1955.

Russell, Bertrand. *The Problems of Philosophy*. London, 1952.

Sachs, Curt. *The Commonwealth of Art*. New York, 1946.

Sachs, Curt. *Rhythm and Tempo: A Study in Music History*. New York, 1953.

Sachs, Curt. *The Rise of Music in the Ancient World*. New York, 1943.

Schlesinger, Kathleen. *The Greek Aulos*. London, 1939.

Scholes, Percy. *The Puritans and Music*. London, 1934.

Simson, Otto von. *The Gothic Cathedral*. New York, 1956.

Spaeth, Sigmund. *Milton's Knowledge of Music*. Princeton, 1913.

Summers, Joseph H. *George Herbert, His Religion and Art*. Cambridge, Mass., 1954.

Swain, Barbara. *Fools and Folly During the Middle Ages and the Renaissance*. New York, 1932.

Sypher, Wylie. *Four Stages of Renaissance Style*. New York, 1955.

Thorpe, Clarence DeWitt. *The Aesthetic Theory of Thomas Hobbes*. University of Michigan Publications, Language and Literature, Vol. XVIII. Ann Arbor, 1940.

Tillyard, E. M. W. *The English Epic and its Background*. New York, 1954.

Tillyard, E. M. W. *Five Poems*. London, 1948.

Tillyard, E. M. W. *Milton*. London, 1951.

Tillyard, E. M. W. *Sir Thomas Wyatt*, London, 1929.

Tuve, Rosemond. *Elizabethan and Metaphysical Imagery*. Chicago, 1947.

Tuve, Rosemond. *Images and Themes in Five Poems by Milton*. Cambridge, Mass., 1957.

Tuve, Rosemond. *A Reading of George Herbert*. London, 1952.

Van Doren, Mark. *John Dryden, A Study of his Poetry*, third edition. New York, 1946.

Waite, William G. *The Rhythm of Twelfth Century Polyphony*. New Haven, 1954.

Walker, Ernest. *A History of Music in England*, third edition rev. and ed. J. A. Westrup. Oxford, 1952.

Walton, Geoffrey. *Metaphysical to Augustan*, London, 1955.

Warren, Austin. *Richard Crashaw: A Study in Baroque Sensibility*. Baton Rouge, 1939.

Weber, Max. *Gesammelte Aufsätze zur Religionssoziologie*. 4 vols., Tübingen, 1947.

Weiss, Roberto. *Humanism in England during the Fifteenth Century*. Oxford, 1941.

Wellesz, Egon. *A History of Byzantine Music and Hymnography*. Oxford, 1949.

Whipple, T. K. *Martial and the English Epigram from Wyatt to Ben Jonson*. Berkeley, 1925.

Whorf, Benjamin Lee. *Language, Thought, and Reality*, ed. John B. Carroll. New York, 1956.

Willey, Basil. *The Seventeenth Century Background*. New York, 1950.

Wittkower, Rudolf. *Architectural Principles in the Age of Humanism*, second edition. London, 1952.

Woodfill, Walter L. *Musicians in English Society*. Princeton, 1953.

Worsthorne, Simon Towneley. *Venetian Opera in the Seventeenth Century*. Oxford, 1954.

Yates, Frances A. *The French Academies of the Sixteenth Century*. London, 1947.

Zandvoort, R. V. *Sidney's Arcadia: A Comparison between the Two Versions*. Amsterdam, 1929.

B. ARTICLES

Beechcroft, T. O. "Crashaw and the Baroque Style." *The Criterion*, XIII (1934), pp. 407-425.

Brennecke, Ernest H., Jr. "Dryden's Odes and Draghi's Music." *PMLA*, XLIX (1934), pp. 1-36.

Brennecke, Ernest H., Jr. "A Singing Man of Windsor." *Music and Letters*, XXXIII (1952), pp. 33-40.

Brooks, Cleanth. "Literary Criticism." *English Institute Essays*, 1946. New York, 1947.

Brown, Arthur. "Two Notes on John Redford." *Modern Language Review*, XLIII (1948), pp. 508-510.

Burton, Martin C. "Mr. Prencourt and Roger North on Teaching Music." *Musical Quarterly*, XVIV (1958), pp. 32-39.

Bush, Douglas. "Marvell's 'Horatian Ode.'" *Sewanee Review*, LX (1952), pp. 363-376.

Carpenter, Nan C. "The Place of Music in *L'Allegro* and *Il Penseroso*." *University of Toronto Quarterly*, XXII (1953), pp. 354-367.

Dart, Thurston. "Miss Mary Burwell's Instruction Book for the Lute." *The Galpin Society Journal*, XI (1958), pp. 3-62.

Diekhoff, John S. "Critical Activity of the Poetic Mind: John Milton." *PMLA*, LV (1940), pp. 748-772.

Diekhoff, John S. "The Text of *Comus*, 1634 to 1645." *PMLA*, LII (1937), pp. 705-727.

Duhamel, Albert. "The Function of Rhetoric as Effective Expression." *Journal of the History of Ideas*, x (1949), pp. 344-356.

Ellinwood, Leonard. "Francesco Landini and his Music." *Musical Quarterly*, XXII (1936), pp. 190-216.

Emerson, Oliver Farrar. "Originality in Old English Poetry." *Review of English Studies*, II (1926), pp. 18-31.

Finney, Gretchen L. "Ecstasy and Music in Seventeenth Century England." *Journal of the History of Ideas*, VIII (1947), pp. 153-186.

Finney, Gretchen L. "A World of Instruments." *ELH*, xx (1953), pp. 87-120.

Finney, Gretchen L. " 'Organical Musick' and Ecstasy." *Journal of the History of Ideas*, VIII (1947), pp. 273-292.

Flügel, Ewald. "Kleinere Mitteilungen aus Handschriften." *Anglia*, XIV (1891-1892), pp. 460-497.

Ham, Roswell C. "Dryden's Dedication for *The Music of The Prophetesse* 1691." *PMLA*, L (1935), pp. 1065-1075.

Handschin, J. "Die Musikanschauung des Johan Scotus Erigena." *Deutsche Viertesjahrsschrift fur Literaturwissenschaft und Geistesgeschichte*. V (1927), pp. 316-341.

Harley, John. "Music and Musicians in Restoration London." *Musical Quarterly*, XL (1954), pp. 509-520.

Heckscher, William S. "Renaissance Emblems." *Princeton University Library Chronicle*, XV (1954), pp. 1-63.

Hollander, John. "The Empire of the Ear." Unpublished master's essay, Columbia, 1952.

Hollander, John. " 'Moedes or Prolaciouns' in Chaucer's *Boece*." *Modern Language Notes*, LXXI (1956), pp. 397-399.

Hollander, John. "The Music of Poetry." *Journal of Aesthetics and Art Criticism*, XV (1956), pp. 234-238.

Hollander, John. "Organized Violence." *Kenyon Review*, XVIII (Winter 1956), pp. 145-150.

Hollander, John. "Twelfth Night and the Morality of Indulgence." *Sewanee Review*, LXVII (1959), pp. 220-238.

Hutton, James. "Some English Poems in Praise of Music." *English Miscellany*, II (1951), pp. 1-63.

Kermode, Frank. "Dissociation of Sensibility." *Kenyon Review*, XIX (1957), pp. 169-194.

Kiefer, Christian. "Music and Marston's 'The Malcontent.'" *Studies in Philology*, LI (1954), pp. 163-171.

Kinsley, James. "Dryden and the Encomium Musicae." *Review of English Studies*, New Series, IV (1953), pp. 263-267.

Kristeller, Paul Oskar. "Music and Learning in the Early Italian Renaissance." *Journal of Renaissance and Baroque Music*, I (1946-1947), pp. 255-274.

Lewis, C. S. "A Note on *Comus*." *Review of English Studies*, VIII (1932), pp. 171-172.

Locke, Arthur W. "Descartes and Seventeenth Century Music." *Musical Quarterly*, XXI (1935), pp. 423-431.

Lockwood, Laura E. "Milton's Corrections to the Minor Poems." *Modern Language Notes*, XXV (1910), pp. 201-205.

Long, John H. "Blame Not Wyatt's Lute." *Renaissance News*, VII (1956), pp. 127-130.

Lowinsky, Edward. "Music in the Culture of the Renaissance." *Journal of the History of Ideas*, XV (1954), pp. 509-553.

Mackernesse, E. D. "A Speculative Dilettante." *Music and Letters*, XXXIV (1953), pp. 236-252.

Meech, Sanford B. "Three Fifteenth-Century English Musical Treatises." *Speculum*, X (1935), pp. 236-252.

Meyer-Baer, Kathi. "Nicholas of Cusa on the Meaning of Music." *Journal of Aesthetics and Art Criticism*, V (1946-1947), pp. 301-308.

Myers, Robert Manson. "Neo-Classical Criticism of the Ode for Music." *PMLA*, LXII (1947), pp. 399-421.

Nakaseko, Kazu. "Symbolism in Ancient Chinese Music Theory." *Journal of Musical Theory*, I (1957), pp. 147-180.

Nelson, Lowry, Jr. "Góngora and Milton: Toward a Definition of the Baroque." *Comparative Literature*, VI (1954), pp. 53-63.

Nugent, E. M. "Sources of John Rastell's *The Nature of the Four Elements*." *PMLA*, LVII (1942), pp. 74-88.

Olson, Clair C. "Chaucer and the Music of the Fourteenth Century." *Speculum*, XVI (1941), pp. 64-91.

Panofsky, Erwin. "Galileo as a Critic of the Arts." *Isis*, XLVII (1956), pp. 3-15.

[454]

Panofsky, Erwin. "Who is Van Eyck's 'Tymotheos'?" *Journal of the Warburg and Courtauld Institutes*, XII (1949), pp. 80-90.

Pincherle, Marc. "Virtuosity." *Musical Quarterly*, XXXV (1949), pp. 226-243.

Pinkerton, Richard C. "Information Theory and Melody." *Scientific American*, 194 (February, 1956), pp. 77-86.

Pirotta, Nino. "Temperaments and Tendencies in the Florentine Camerata." *Musical Quarterly*, XL (1954), pp. 169-189.

Rogerson, Brewster. "The Art of Painting the Passions." *Journal of the History of Ideas*, XIV (1953), pp. 68-94.

Ross, Thomas W. "Five Fifteenth Century 'Emblem' Verses from Brit. Mus. Addit. MS. 37-49." *Speculum*, XXXII (1957), pp. 274-282.

Salmon, T. "The Theory of Music reduced to Arithmetical and Geometrical Progressions." *Philosophical Transactions of the Royal Society*, 1705, 24, 2072; vol. IV, pp. i, 469-474.

Schueller, Herbert M. "The Use and Decorum of Music as Described in British Literature, 1700-1780." *Journal of the History of Ideas*, XIII (1952), pp. 73-93.

Scott, Hugh Arthur. "London's Earliest Public Concerts." *Musical Quarterly*, XXII (1936), pp. 446-457.

Spitzer, Leo. "Classical and Christian Ideas of World Harmony." *Traditio*, II (1944), pp. 409-464; III (1945), pp. 307-364.

Springer, George P. "Language and Music: Some Parallels and Divergencies." *For Roman Jakobson: Essays on the Occasion of his Sixtieth Birthday*, ed. Morris Halle et al. The Hague, 1956.

Sternfeld, F. W. "Music in the Schools of the Reformation." *Musica Disciplina*, II (1948), pp. 99-122.

Stevens, John E. "Rounds and Canons from an Early Tudor Songbook." *Music and Letters*, XXXII (1951), pp. 29-37.

Stevenson, Robert. "Thomas Morley's 'Plaine and Easie' Introduction to the Modes." *Musica Disciplina*, VI (1952), pp. 177-184.

Van, Guillaume de. "La Pédagogie musicale à la fin du moyen âge." *Musica Disciplina*, II (1948), pp. 75-97.

Walker, D. P. "The Aims of Baïf's Académie de Poésie et de Musique." *Journal of Renaissance and Baroque Music*, I (1946-1947), pp. 91-100.

Walker, D. P. "Ficino's *Spiritus* and Music." *Annales Musicologiques*, I (1953), pp. 131-150.

Walker, D. P. "The Influence of *Musique Mesurée de l'Antique* Particularly on the Airs de Cour of the Early Seventeenth Century." *Musica Disciplina*, II (1948), pp. 141-163.

Walker, D. P. "Musical Humanism in the Sixteenth and Early Seventeenth Centuries." *The Music Review*, II (1941), pp. 1-13, 111-121, 220-227, 288-308; III (1942), pp. 55-71.

Walker, D. P. "Orpheus the Theologian and Renaissance Platonists." *Journal of the Warburg and Courtauld Institutes*, XVI 1953), pp. 100-120.

Wallerstein, Ruth. *Studies in Seventeenth-Century Poetic*. Madison, 1950.

Ward, John. "The Dolfull Domps." *Journal of The American Musicological Society*, IV (1959), pp. 111-121.

Wellek, René. "The Concept of Baroque in Literary Scholarship." *Journal of Aesthetics and Art Criticism*, V (1947), pp. 77-109.

Werner, Eric, and Isaiah Sonne. "The Philosophy and Theory of Music in Judaeo-Arabic Literature." *Hebrew Union College Annual*, XVI (1941), pp. 251-319 and XVII (1942-1943), pp. 511-572.

Westrup, J. A. "The Nature of Recitative." *Proceedings of the British Academy 1956*, pp. 27-44. London, 1956.

Williamson, George. "The Pattern of Neo-Classical Wit." *Modern Philology*, XXXIII (1935-1936), pp. 55-81.

Wolf, Johannes. "Die Musiklehre des Johannes de Grocheo." *Sammelbände der Internationalen Musikgesellschaft*, I (1899), pp. 65-130.

INDEX

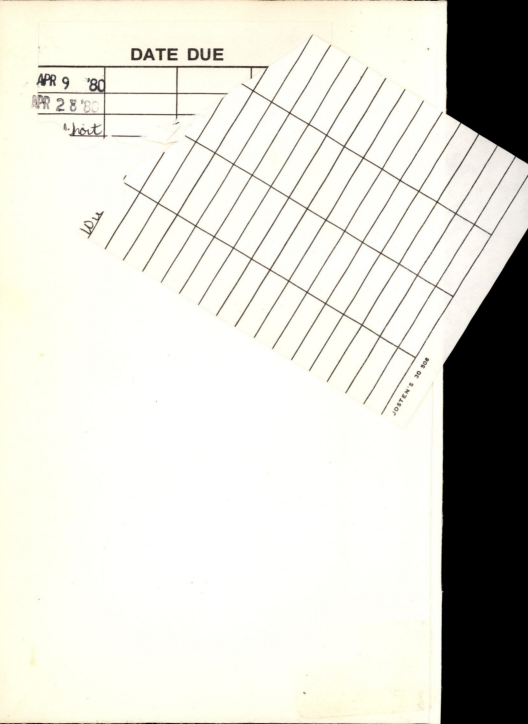

JOSTEN'S 30 508